No More Idols!

Crystal Y. Holt

authorHOUSE®

AuthorHouse™
1663 Liberty Drive
Bloomington, IN 47403
www.authorhouse.com
Phone: 1-800-839-8640

First published by AuthorHouse 1/17/2011

ISBN: 978-1-4520-9496-0 (sc)
ISBN: 978-1-4520-9497-7 (e)

Library of Congress Control Number: 2010916623

Printed in the United States of America

This book is printed on acid-free paper.

In 1996, as I looked through "My rose-colored glasses" at an image that appeared to reflect me I remember like it was yesterday, God spoke directly to me in a soft, gentle, audible and crystal clear voice and said "It is not my will!"

NO MORE IDOLS!

Written by Crystal Y. Holt

LITTLE CHILDREN, KEEP YOURSELVES FROM IDOLS. AMEN.
(1 JOHN 5:21).

*This word was quickened to my spirit in 1996, yet at that time I did not fully understand it. One might ask what exactly is an **IDOL** and how do you keep yourself from an **IDOL**? An **IDOL** is anything and everything you put before God! The rest is my story to tell ...*

Contents

My Purpose

"Even for this same purpose have I raised thee up, that I might shew my power in thee, and that my name might be declared throughout all the earth". (Romans 9:17).

As I matured in Christ over the years, I discovered the true meaning of my purpose. Purpose can be defined as: A goal of an action intentionally undertaken. What is my purpose? What did God place me on this earth to do? What is it going to take to catapult me into my God-given purpose? These are questions I often asked myself and God time and time again, initially not fully understanding it all for it would all be revealed unto me in His timing.

What I discovered and knew without a doubt while writing this book was that my sole purpose for living and writing this book was to give God glory. It was my heart's desire to share with the world His goodness and to tell the whole world how He alone kept me on my spiritual journey. God took me to and through a God-ordained process to reach my destiny. The only thing that was required of me to obtain it was total obedience to God. Throughout my journey, my disobedience to God cost me some things, in fact it cost me many things, and made what was supposed to be an 11-day journey take what seemed like 40 years as I wandered on and off the path that He had set before me to follow. Yet, because of His grace and His mercy, I did not miss the mark and most importantly I did not miss God.

I thank Him for His grace and His mercy as He never gave up on me and He never let go of my hand for He loved me and cared too much to allow me to abort the assignment He had placed within my womb. For He foreknew me and that I would be impregnated with His purpose and He alone knew the expected date of delivery. Although there is a lot written between the lines and pages of this book, I hope you take your time in reading it in order to obtain both wisdom and understanding. "Counsel in the heart of man is like deep water; but a man of understanding will draw it out". (Proverbs 20:5). I pray that every reader will be blessed by the reading of this book by not only the content of the story, but by the message given by God directly to the reader, that speaks much louder and even clearer than the story.

This book was not written to hurt anyone, curse anyone or bring anyone shame. Wise counsel once told me that the truth shall set you free. In writing this book, the truth set me free and it is my desire that you too can be free. As much as I wanted to cover a multitude of sins with the love of God within me, I had to be obedient and not sugarcoat the message and the truth of the message.

In total obedience to God, I had to plant the seeds that were given to me by Him to sow and nurture and water the same. Yet, God was the one who gave the increase and that increase was released through this book to His kingdom. God desires that no one be lost or left behind to perish by not knowing all the tricks and devices that the enemy uses to make those who lack godly wisdom and understanding fall prey.

God is a sovereign God that reigns on the throne. He sits high, yet He looks and reaches low and is well able to deliver His people out of every affliction. The glory belongs to Him for He alone is worthy of all the honor, all the glory and all the praise for my healing, my deliverance, my salvation and for the revelation of ***NO MORE IDOLS***.

In 2007 God Further Speaks

Turn ye not unto idols, nor make to yourselves molten gods: I am the LORD your God. (Leviticus 19:4).

Ye shall make you no idols nor graven image, neither rear you up a standing image, neither shall ye set up any image of stone in your land, to bow down unto it: for I am the LORD your God. (Leviticus 26:1).

And I will destroy your high places, and cut down your images, and cast your carcases upon the carcases of your idols, and my soul shall abhor you. (Leviticus 26:30).

The idols of the heathen are silver and gold, the work of men's hands. (Psalms 135:15).

For every one of the house of Israel, or of the stranger that sojourneth in Israel, which separateth himself from me, and setteth up his idols in his heart, and putteth the stumblingblock of his iniquity before his face, and cometh to a prophet to enquire of him concerning me; I the LORD will answer him by myself: (Ezekiel 14:7).

Acknowledgements

God has made it very clear from the beginning of time that we are to serve one and only one God. He is the true and living God, and we are to put no other gods before Him. He has given us ample examples in His word of what has happened to individuals in the past that chose to serve and worship **IDOLS**. He continues to give us examples in the present and future of what will happen if we continue to choose to worship **IDOLATRY** and **IDOLS**. All you have to do is look around you and you shall see it and hear it with your own spiritual and natural eyes and ears. He gives us specific instructions in His word that He is a jealous God and will not allow this type of behavior to continue, even if it takes Him and Him alone to stop us dead in our tracks!

Take heed there are consequences for not being obedient and not abiding by the Ten Commandments, the word of God and applying the principles of God therein. I spent most of my life trying to live right and abide by godly principles that I was taught at an early age and throughout adulthood. God loved me before I was even conceived in the womb and He predestined my life for His purpose and His glory, yet I never thought I would be pleasing in His sight because there were some things that I chose to handle on my own, some things that I did not want to let go of, and some things I felt I could not let go of, in order to allow God to do a great work in me.

These things that I held on to brought about curses in my life, opened the door to evil spirits, placed hindrances and roadblocks in my way, delayed my blessings and led me to a crippled, depressed, apathetic state. I was like the walking dead, physically, spiritually, emotionally, financially, socially maimed/lamed, broken/shattered into pieces. I was unstable/unbalanced, wanted/needed, desired/lacked at the same time. A double-minded state. All thought processes were blocked. I had no vision, no plan, no motivation or determination. Hope was failing and resources were few.

Although I wanted to blame someone or something, I took full responsibility for my present state. I knew the ungodly choices and decisions I made had led me to this place. A place that negatively enabled me, destroyed me, hurt me, robbed me, and brought about a lot of unnecessary suffering, grief and pain. I was in a place where most people would have given up and thrown in the towel. This state literally took the wind from beneath my wings. I was in a place that most people would have not survived and would have died in that very place.

Yet, the spirit within me soared and mounted up like eagles reaching higher to the wings of fate. Something on the inside of me would not allow me to die. Something on the inside of me spoke life into places and situations that had died. A little voice within me said "You shall not die, but live, and declare the works of the Lord", (Psalm 118:17). I now know it was the voice of God and Holy Spirit comforting me. Had it not been for the grace of God there is no doubt where I would be. Yet, through it all, God reserved a special place for me and that place was within His loving arms. He carried me through to get me to my God-given purpose and His plan for my life. I owe everything to Him.

Dedications

The LORD hath appeared of old unto me, saying, Yea, I have loved thee with an everlasting love: therefore with lovingkindness have I drawn thee. (Jeremiah 31:3).

This book is dedicated to God *First* and *Foremost.* Secondly, I thank God for everyone that He utilized to bless me and to help me through my spiritual journey. I want to dedicate this book to all of those individuals because they were instrumental in helping me to remain focused and bring this book into fruition. Sometimes I doubted myself but never God. In the beginning stages of writing this book, I was unable to grasp the full understanding of it all. As the years went on I became more aware that the book was not only to be written but to be lived out.

Thank you for your ongoing love, encouragement and support. It is because of your obedience to God that I was able to excel in this endeavor and many other endeavors beyond my imagination. I thank God for magnificently leading and guiding you to help me through the process. May God bless you richly. My continual prayer for you is that you always receive God's very best.

I must also be obedient in thanking all of my enemies and give them their rightful acknowledgement as well for God even had a purpose for my enemies in my life in that He used them as my footstool, just as He said in His word He would do. So, without further ado, this book is thirdly dedicated to my enemies because you are the true reason I did not give up when the going got tough. I needed to be strong for your very deliverance. I wanted and needed you to know the power and might of the God I serve. Everything you took me through made me stronger, every time you hurt me I ran to God and God renewed me daily. Every time you caused me pain, God comforted me so that I could comfort others and you. You were my enemy yet I loved you with an everlasting love, with the love of God, knowing that God was going to bless me just to bless you. Fully aware and knowing that the love of God I had for you was going to draw you closer to Him. You helped me write each and every chapter of this book, sentence by sentence, page by page, day by day, I stayed on task even for you.

Through the years and through the tears, everyone that God placed in my life and that God connected me with, know that you played a major part. You all were true keynote speakers in my life story. You strategically helped me obtain the starring role in heaven and on earth as God's Leading Lady C. No grammy is required. I just want to take this opportunity to thank you and send my love to each and every one of you.

Watchmen on Post

Thus saith the LORD, stand ye in the ways, and see, and ask for the old paths, where is the good way, and walk therein, and ye shall find rest for your souls. But they said, we will not walk therein. Also I set watchmen over you, saying, hearken to the sound of the trumpet. But they said, we will not hearken. Therefore hear, ye nations, and know, O congregation, what is among them. Hear, O earth: Behold, I will bring evil upon this people, even the fruit of their thoughts, because they have not hearkened unto my words, nor to my law, but rejected it. (Jeremiah 6:16-19).

I thank God for the watchmen on post that took their rightful place in my life and did not allow the enemy to abort the assignment that God deposited in me. Thank you to the midwives that stood by my side while I carried destiny in my womb. Thank you for the comfort you provided to me as a buffer so that I did not feel the full blow of the weapons and the fiery darts that the enemy launched for my demise. Thank you for standing with your feet flat on the ground and your face set like flint as you looked to the Lord for guidance and strength to console me during my pregnancy, labor and delivery of destiny. Thank you for remaining by my side and nurturing me through the entire process with the love that only God could have given you. It was a long time coming but we made it with God's help. I do not want any one of you to think that your good deeds went unnoticed because I would have surely became weary and fainted in well doing or worse. I would have died an untimely death had you stepped off of your post or even took your eye off your assignment for one second. You diligently watched and you prayed just as God had instructed you to do and I now live in Christ because of your obedience. You have shown me how to be a diligent, good and faithful servant even when it seemed like situations in my life did not warrant such. God is faithful! As I began to trust him totally, it was just as you had said. God began to show me that He had already made provision for everything that I needed along the journey and that provision included you. He already had a ram in the bush waiting on me. I love you all with the love of God.

Again, this book is dedicated first and foremost to God in that it is God-inspired. Although it is my ultimate heart's desire to bless others with this book, I have to give credit where credit is due. The sole credit belongs to God for He is the one who placed the desire in my heart to write. He is the one who gave me the gift of writing at an early age and as the gift began to stir up on the inside of me, he anointed and appointed me to write and to minister to His people through my writing. God has anointed my voice and skilled my hands for His purpose and His glory. By faith, I worked diligently and relentlessly on this assignment, with the favor of God and man. It is through my faith in God and the unfolding of this book that one of my biggest and greatest life's dreams, aspirations and endeavors has come true.

Secondly, I would like to acknowledge and thank my true earthly role models and spiritual leaders as well as my very best friends, Apostle Willie and Prophetess Kimberly Sims of New Life in Christ International Ministries. What stands out most to me at this time is our long history together that started as a divine connection and grew into a special friendship and then kinship, in good times and bad, happy and sad, through each passing season you were there for me and my family. Thank you for believing in me even when I did not believe in myself. You held me accountable at all times and even when I messed up repeatedly and made no progress, you loved me just the same. You simply corrected me and sent me back out into the kingdom to be about my Father's business. You continued to intercede in prayer for me and my family. You anointed us with oil and placed a covering of protection over our lives through the power of prayer. You blessed, anointed and appointed the house, the car, the job and the resources to cooperate with God's plan for our lives. You assigned angels to encamp around us to watch over us and protect us. You prayed that God would place a hedge of protection around us to keep us from harm's way. You taught me the value of God's word, faith and prayer and how to correctly utilize and apply Godly principles to obtain kingdom blessings. You taught and showed me that earthly blessings have little if any value at all. You did not compromise your godly standards and taught me to do the same. You taught me to honor and value myself and my relationship with God. You taught me the difference between religion and personal relationship with God. You encouraged me to walk in the spirit and not in the flesh at all times and in all situations. You prophesized, declared, decreed, ordained and confirmed that this book would be written and that it would be a bestseller and that God had deposited so much potential in me. When prophets from afar confirmed it, it was no surprise to me for you had already declared and decreed it to be so. You professed kingly blessings upon my life and confessed that through God's mighty power that I would bless nations and kingdom build. You constantly reassured me that I had so much purpose and so much to offer the kingdom of God. You encouraged me to embrace what God was building me up to be and encouraged me to grow into it even when the tangible was intangible. You told me to believe that I would do greater works in Him. I now know that all that I went through was not even about me, just as you had said, it was about God's plan for my life. All I had to do was just cooperate with His perfect plan for my life. I now know the worldly things that I sought were not for my good and the spiritual things that I sought were waiting on me to mature enough to receive them. I guess you can say they were on layaway in the spirit until God got them out and released them to me in the natural.

What I learned through the entire process is that everything belongs to God and all I have to do is seek Him first, His kingdom and His righteousness and all things would be added unto me. I now know that God will not withhold any good thing from me. I pray that this book goes out into the kingdom on assignment and does exactly what it was assigned to do. I know it will not come back void for it is rooted and grounded in the word of God. God declares in His word "So shall my word be that goeth forth out of my mouth; it shall not return unto me void, but it shall accomplish that which I please, and it shall prosper in the thing whereto I sent it" (Isaiah 55:11), and so it is with this book. You have always given me true prophecy and words from the Lord, yet you did not give me the next chapter. You knew I would live each chapter, chapter by chapter and once I lived it, you knew writing it would be no problem. From the bottom of my heart, thank you for everything.

I would like to thank my family. My beloved father Orlando Holt, Jr. and my beloved mother Hazel Holt, my darling children, from oldest to youngest, Marcus (26), Krishina (25) , Che'Andrea (21), De'Jonay (13), Jaqi' (12) and Kha'Leel (8) Holt, Ja'Mari (6) Tidwell and Christian (4) Holt-Tidwell, my precious grandchildren Kevin Foster, Jr. (5), De'Jae Collins (4), Kev'Andre Foster (2), De'Jon Poltniz (1) and Earrion Nesbit (7 months), my loving aunt Ora Branum a/k/a Dimple and my tenacious cousin Tyron Branum, who were more like my second mom and brother, my charming sister Cheryl Holt-Chatman, my handsome brothers Darren Humes, Derick Reynolds and Darryl Holt, and a host of other beautiful cousins, nieces and nephews. Blessings to all the Holt/Winfrey Family, the Marks/Branum Family, the Humes Family, the Tidwell Family, the Stuckey Family.

I would like to thank my spiritual family, Lady Ida Lee - my God-mom/friend and my children's God-grandmother, Lady Nikkia Daniels n/k/a (now known as) Mrs. Nikkia Holloway - my God-daughter/friend and my children's God-sister, God-ordained babysitter and Sunday school teacher, Rising Sun Baptist Church, the church I grew up in - Pastor John Gibson, the late First Lady Vicki Gibson and the present First Lady "GG", Word of Faith Christian Center - Bishop Leroy Davis and Pastor Helen Davis and the late Mother Rose Davis, City of Refuge - Pastor Tim and First Lady Sherry Criss, Gospel Experience, my present church home - Pastor Richard Hammond, Christian Family Center - Pastor Tony Pierce and Family, Prophet Sidney Jones - my very special friend/a true prophet of God, Bob Kaiser - Jubilee Ministries and all the members therein, Pastor Johnny and First Lady Gia Jones - Word of Faith Christian Center - Bloomington, Gail Wright, Cassandra Castenallos, and Joie Hightower-Thompson – my dear friends/sisters in Christ.

My online spiritual family, including but not limited to Apostle Cauline Thomas of End Time Army Ministry, my spiritual sisters and brothers in Christ of End Time Army Ministry. Special thanks to Apostle Carmichael of Power of Prayer Ministries International. Thank you Apostle Carmichael for your prayers and purchasing my very first prayer shawl. I absolutely love it. It is simply beautiful. When I placed it over my head I felt the anointing. A special thanks to all my sisters and brothers in Christ; namely, Elder Hammond of Power of Prayer Ministries International Prayerline, Prophetess Glenette Wilcher of Women With A Purpose Ministries, Annette Sanders of A Family That Prays Together, Melodie Williams of Women Empowering Women, Apostle Ranard Teach of University of the Prophets,

Prophet Adrienne Williams of School of the Prophets, Apostle Tina Edwards of Kingdom Women of Destiny International.

I would like to thank my professional mentors who taught me how to "handle business"; namely, Arthur Welch, John Stenson, Agbar Bryson, Robin Berry, Michelle Sanders, and too many more to name, but I thank you all in genuine sincerity.

I would like to also thank my online social network friends on myspace, facebook, ning and my colleagues, coworkers, supervisors, mentors and acquaintances, my kids' teachers/instructors, principals, coaches, everyone named and unnamed.

I would like to personally thank and bless everyone who has blessed my life in any kind of way, big or small, everyone who supported me along the way. I would even like to thank those of you who wanted to help and were not able to do so. You are all my heroes and sheroes. You were all very instrumental in my life, even more than words can express. You were more than the wind beneath my wings. For my genuine love for you and your genuine love for me helped me stay focused on my goal of writing this book.

It is because of all of you as a whole that I was able to by faith walk out my destiny. You see I always knew in my heart that this book would one day be written and published, yet I went through many, many, many trials and tribulations and sacrifices to bring it into fruition to bless the kingdom of God. Thank you for being there for me then, now and always. More than words can say I just want you all to know that I love you all with the love of God and want you to know that you have truly been a blessing to me.

Lastly, I would also like to thank my haters who I must say through it all became my motivators.

I hope you all as a whole enjoy reading this book. I hope you hold it near and dear to your heart knowing that it is just a small part of me. In this book, in my own special way, I am allowing you to come into my inner circle, where I am transparent, naked before God and man. I would ask that you while reading this book, you begin to appreciate the value of my open book story about my journey with God, as I humbly unroll the tablets of my heart and share a love story between me and my Lord, my King, my First Love, my Jehovah-Jireh. This book is a true, inspiring, courageous novel written and approved by God to bless each and every one of you.

Introduction:

"Life Is What You Make of It" (Author Unknown)

Looked at and touched the wrong way at an early age, spiritually uncovered at age 12 when my grandparents relocated to their retirement home, raped, robbed, mistreated and mishandled by individuals I thought I could trust ages 15 through 21, left feeling I was to blame, abused emotionally and physically from ages 12 through age 43. Became pregnant at age 17, graduated with my high school class in the Top 70s of my class, walking in my cap and gown with a big belly, proud but ashamed at age 18. Delivered my firstborn child who was born with multiple developmental anomalies, left for college five weeks later at my parents' prompting and request to advance my education and obtain a better life for myself and my family by becoming a first generation college graduate, instead of pursuing my own dreams and inspirations which included moving to New York to live with an aunt in order to pursue my personal dreams of becoming a fashion model, fashion designer or famous book writer or journalist.

Fall 1984, left my newborn baby in my mother's care, grieved my whole first semester in college due to separation anxiety and depression, successfully passed one out of six classes receiving five F's and one B in medical terminology, the only class that I was interested in because it helped me better understand my firstborn son's medical condition, returned home for the holidays to visit family and friends and returned back to school pregnant with my second child, same father, finished up the semester with a 2.5 overall grade point average and returned home again to deliver my second child, my first daughter, with hopes of returning to school at a later date, delivered my second child and worked multiple jobs to make ends meet, 1st and 2nd shift, 5 am to midnight, six to seven days a week. Limited resources and support. My maternal grandmother, who was currently living out her retirement years in Southern Illinois with my maternal grandfather, her beloved husband, intervened and asked to help out by keeping my precious baby girl temporarily while I finished my schooling. With my grandmother's assistance and God's help, I did just that. My grandmother was very, very, very careful in assuring me that she was only going to do this temporarily until I was able to properly care for my child and myself, for she knew the pain that I faced and endured not being able to properly care for my firstborn son.

Fall 1988, pregnant with my third child, I felt obligated to not return home without getting married. So, Spring 1989, wed THE MAN OF MY DREAMS and celebrated Mother's Day, graduation and my birthday simultaneously, a big celebration with again another big belly. Age 23, mixed feelings of happy, proud, but still ashamed. Ashamed that now I have three children to take care of and one not even in my care and still limited resources and help. Well, "give me lemons and I will make lemonade", so I tried to find my way in life as best I knew how. Upon graduating from college, I relocated to Chicago, Illinois and beat the pavements daily trying to find work to no avail. No doors would open in the Windy City so I returned to my hometown and successfully landed several temporary jobs with the hopes of gaining some work experience and possibly returning to Chicago at a later date. I could not obtain a full-time job at that time due to lack of experience. The college degrees alone still was not enough. Go figure! Well, that did not stop me. I never went a day without work. All bills were paid and ends were met. I was going to make it somehow, someway.

I obtained my first full-time job in 1990 at a local law firm. Life appeared to be grand as far as my career was concerned. My grandparents' health began to deteriorate, so they returned home to Central Illinois to be near family. Although I could not restore their health in my own strength, I did my best to give them back what they had given me and that was unconditional love. My grandparents raised me from a newborn through my preteen years and on into adulthood. They were my spiritual covering. My grandmother took me along to church with her every time the church doors opened. I had a praying grandmother who introduced me to God as a small child.

In September, 1995, Labor Day, God called my loving grandmother home. She was my rock on earth. God was my rock in heaven. Now with a troubled past, the loss of my maternal grandmother/my foundation/my rock, the loss of my fraternal grandmother, an uncle, a best friend and both grandfathers, combined with too many unhealthy relationships to count on both hands and both feet, twice divorced, eight children, five grandchildren, where do I turn?

I faced all of the above trials and tribulations, yet I did not lose faith. Through the years I began to spiral downward in the natural. Yet in the spirit, my faith soared and grew beyond measure. God was the only thing in my life that remained constant. I had very few friends and limited support. I began to isolate myself so that no one would know my troubles, my hurt, my pain, my sorrows, my fears, my grief, my struggles, my weaknesses. I only wanted everyone to see and know the person I strived to be, an independent woman who had everything going for herself and wanting for nothing. You know that song by Jamie Foxx, Ne-Yo & Fabolous "She got her own, an independent queen looking for her throne ...". Yeah, that was the image I was trying to attain. I tried to hide the real me. I was ashamed of the real me, the person who knew that she could do nothing and was nothing without God. For (John 15:5) states "I am the vine, ye are the branches: He that abideth in me, and I in him, the same bringeth forth much fruit: for without me ye can do nothing". This was a lesson I had yet to learn.

Chapter I

Rebirth

SPIRITUAL AUTOBIOGRAPHY OF CRYSTAL Y. HOLT
LOOKING BACK AND NARRARATING MY OWN STORY 1989-2007

In the words of God's Leading Lady C ...

Some of Crystal's Christian journey includes having her first child out of wedlock at 18 and her last child at 39 by marriage, yet still out of the will of God. From the beginning, she had dreams of becoming a fashion model, a fashion designer, a fashion boutique owner, a lawyer, a best seller author, a famous journalist. She willingly modified her dreams and aspirations to incorporate her family and their needs.

In 1989, Crystal obtained an AAS degree in Legal and Executive Secretary, Certificate in Stenography and then went on to obtain a BA degree in Social Justice in 1994 and a MA degree in Human Development Counseling in 2001, graduating with Honors at the Top of her Class with a GPA of 3.8. Crystal worked both part-time and full-time and went to school around her work schedule and her family's schedule. Crystal has been gainfully employed since age 9 when she was a paper girl and an Avon lady doing both simultaneously. During her college years, she relied on public and private assistance through the help of state, government and local community agencies and her family and friends to balance her workload.

In May, 2001, despite hopes of continuing her education to obtain a doctorate degree, she finished her college studies upon diagnosis of Type 1 insulin-dependent diabetes which took precedence over everything in her life. She now had a better understanding that her body was God's temple and that she would have to start taking better care of herself in order to continue taking care of others and attain all of her life aspirations. This was the first time in her life that she realized she was not indispensible and infallible and could not do everything as if she was Super Woman. Time went on and the clock just kept ticking.

In March, 2006, Crystal picked up her bed and began to walk. She began speaking life into areas in her life that had died. She began speaking life to herself, her family and her finances. She began to confess daily "I shall live and not die". As many people around the world viewed and admired her success, what she entitles "The Strong Man's House" (Matthew 12:29), she was glad to let everyone know that God was truly her foundation. She continues to tell the story for God's glory.

In May, 2006, right after the death of her spirit and drained soul due to divorce, she experienced a rebirth as she successfully planned and carried out her 40th Birthday Bash. Crystal in all of her 40 years had never even had a birthday party, nor any type of celebration that she did not plan herself or that she even enjoyed. It seemed as if every celebration that she planned turned out to be a disaster when it was all said and done. She would oftentimes just resort to buying herself a cake and candles, ice cream, birthday hat, money pin, birthday outfit, balloons and decorations and celebrate herself alone or with her children who always enjoyed every moment and every occasion. It really did not take much to make Crystal happy for the simple acts of kindness meant more to her than the grandest gestures. It was always more stressful for Crystal to try and get others to participate in her joyous occasions, but she continued to try her best to no avail.

Crystal knew in her heart, spirit and soul that this time would be different. She learned throughout life that if you keep doing the same thing, you will keep getting the same results. Crystal wanted something different out of life this time. She wanted and needed different results. She wanted to celebrate herself, her life, and her accomplishments. This was a special celebration, for she was definitely proud, thankful and grateful to make it 40 years by faith, so she decided to do something different.

She took a personal trip alone for her 40th Birthday Bash. It was a special birthday gift to herself, something that she had never done before, to the beautiful island of Montego Bay, Jamaica. It is there that God showed Crystal her true worth, the way others saw her for they treated her like royalty. It is there where God showed her another world outside of her own. It was there that God revealed to Crystal her heart's desire of ministering to the nations, to the Caribbean islands, one nation at a time, one island at a time, in this lifetime. Crystal said "The beginning of my journey felt like paradise, for it is truly a journey and I plan on writing about every experience. My book won't be complete until the end of my journey".

Crystal goes on to add that the beginning of her journey started with her visit to the islands of Aruba, Puerto Rico and now Jamaica. Crystal adds, "As I flew over the Caribbean by plane and looked down at the aqua blue waters and surrounding islands, I said a prayer to God, "Lord if it be thy will, allow me to just touch my feet on the ground on each Caribbean island before I die to minister to your people for your glory".

God listened as He comforted her heart, spirit, mind and soul. The sorrow of her past and yesterday was now just a vapor as she basked in the sun, simply relaxing on the beach. As she looked up at the deep blue skies and out towards the ocean waters listening to the soothing sound of the ocean waves, as she walked barefoot in the white sandy shores, as she admired the tropical flowers, trees and scenery surrounding her, the fresh air, the island music, the delicious food, the fun and entertainment, the people, the culture and things she had never saw before, from tropical animal life, sea life to plant life, it was truly amazing.

As she embraced the serenity and solitude that God had allowed her to experience, she looked out at the ocean as far as her natural and spiritual eyes could see. She listened closely to the ocean waves as they pushed to and away from the shore right in front of her and she lifted up her hands to the heavens and looked up to God and said "My eyes have seen all of Your beauty and my ears have heard all of Your beauty, my feet and hands have touched Your beauty. Marvelous are Your works. You are a Great Architect. Everything belongs to You. You created everything, all of this for my enjoyment to live life abundantly."

Crystal for 40 years had felt like she was imprisoned in her mind, body, soul in a familiar place that she called and knew as home; but a house is not a home, for home is where your heart is. Crystal was searching for that sacred place. God was now showing her something different as she was now alone with Him enjoying His paradise that He had prepared for her on earth. Crystal was now free in His presence, away from the cares of the world, zero distractions. She was free to be who He created her to be and Crystal knew this very moment her ministry. Her desire was that she wanted everyone to be free and experience what she not only envisioned in her heart and spirit for many years before it ever manifested, but she was now living out the vision. Crystal continued to praise, worship and thank the Lord for "The Rebirth".

Crystal says "Yes, it took all of this for me to see it, yet I thank the Lord for allowing me to live to see it". God's people near and far saw God's glory in Crystal, even when she did not see it. Satan thought He had blinded her and shut her mouth and left her for dead but God reached deep down into the murky clay and said I can use you for My glory and I am going to make you international. I am going to train and equip you to go out into the nations and teach and preach the gospel. I have saved you for such a time as this. God said "You are the light of the world. A city that is set on a hill cannot be hid". (Matthew 5:14-15). It was then and only then that Crystal found a reason to stop hiding and begin to live out her destiny in God, a new sense of appreciation for life, as she began to experience a life worth living in the Caribbean for it captured her heart.

God wanted Crystal to see that what she thought to be junk was actually a jewel and treasure to someone else. While she was feeling sorry for herself in the past, God allowed her to see the oppression of His people in the present. God placed her in a position that she could not turn her back to or close her eyes to it and act as if it did not exist, for it was right before her to see and experience. She did not have to see or hear about this from the media or a third party, for God allowed her to see if for herself. It was an eye opener. It touched her heart, deep down to her soul and spirit and she said to God "Yes, Lord, send me; I will make a difference in the lives of Your people. Yes, Lord, please send me."

Crystal tells the story about how "God's people on the islands of Aruba, Puerto Rico, Jamaica faced great oppression yet they were thankful and grateful to God for everything. It was as if I had finally connected with my brothers and sisters, God's children. I had a newfound hope. From this point forward I would never devalue a measly $1.00 bill, for any amount of money that I placed on the table for the waiter or waitress they received with a smile of gratitude. This gratitude made me even more willing to give. I realized at that moment that all my life I had given of myself and never really received anything in return, not even a simple smile of gratitude, yet God had blessed me so much over the years and I always knew without a doubt that you cannot beat God giving, for the more you give the more He will give to you. As I continued to give of myself, my time, my resources, God continued to bless me hundredfold, not always in monetary value but in what counted most to me and that is being able to bless the lives of others."

Crystal further stated "It was in the Caribbean islands that I received appreciation for who I am, for I was treated as royalty. I had been mistreated most of my life, but on the islands that felt like paradise on earth, I was treated with so much kindness and brotherly and sisterly love. I was never alone for the resort staff went above and beyond to ensure that every moment was enjoyable and memorable." You might say "They were just doing their job". I will then say to you "Well, I am going to start doing my job, because in 40 years in America, I have never experienced this."

Crystal says "I did not take anything for granted that I experienced in the Caribbean. Looking back over my life and all the time I was feeling sorry for myself was for no good reason. I was not living in oppressed conditions where the luxuries we take for granted were scarce, such as newly built single family homes, the finest home furnishings and decor, fancy cars and designer fashions, advanced technology of electronics, cell phones, computers, internet service, equal opportunity in pay, jobs, educational opportunities, affordable or available healthcare."

"No, my brothers and sisters that I met in the Caribbean islands thought it to be a blessing just to have food in their cupboards and quality utility service, which was not a guarantee. Some of the people I met and talked to did not have a washing machine and dryer and would have to wash their clothes in a wash tub or sink and hang their clothes on the line to dry. They did not have a microwave, regular mail delivery service, digital camera, and a car to get to and from work. Most of the people I met and talked to had to ride a bus to and from work and they had to work long, hard hours and bring their meals to work, as they were not allowed to eat or drink at the same five star all-inclusive hotel resort that I had the luxury of staying in. Most of them had to work two jobs with minimal sleep in order to make ends meet. During my stay, I shared everything I had with them, even my heart and my time. I was supposed to be celebrating my birthday but I was now celebrating life, their life, their dreams, and their aspirations."

"I learned so much during my stay in Jamaica. My brothers and sisters in Jamaica demonstrated to me that they were thankful and grateful and happy, even in their positions of servitude. They were thankful, grateful and happy to serve because they knew it meant the difference of having and not having food on the table and clothes on their back, shoes on their feet and a roof over their head. Everything was everything, "No Problem Mon", "Don't Worry Be Happy". I felt right at home as I listened to the reggae music and enjoyed the culture of the island. They did not have a college degree, an elite class or status in life, yet they believed and had faith and hope. They increased my faith and my hope. God set this all up for purpose. I knew from the time I departed from my home and got off the airplane and touched the ground and placed my bare feet in the white sand and looked up at the blue clear skies and looked out at the deep blue ocean that my life would never be the same and it wasn't". I guess (Matthew 13:57) is true when it says "A prophet is not without honor, save in his own country, and in his own house."

Crystal adds "It was in Jamaica that I discovered that my present vulnerable state was not my fate. I began to minister to everyone I met in Jamaica of how God was my source. They began to minister to me as they said to me "How do you stay so beautiful at the age of 40?" and I said to them "God". They agreed that it must be God, for they saw the light of Christ in my beauty. They continued to look at and admire my outward beauty but what they were really seeking and did not know was my inward beauty that was now overflowing onto them. I continued to minister to His people, letting my light shine before men. The love of Christ within me was now international. The love of Christ within me now reached as wide and as deep as the oceans and beyond borders, territories and horizons, beyond what the natural eye could see. In the spirit, I knew I was now connected to my new spiritual family for I had made contact through my prayers in the heavenlies.

Crystal further adds "It was in Jamaica that I began to tap into newfound power and strength within. I now view the first 40 years of my life as my wilderness experience. Looking forward, in my new life in Christ, I desire only to focus on what God has purposed in my heart to do. I plan to regain my focus on my God-given purpose and plan for my life. I now have to allow God to stir up the gifts that He had already deposited in me even before the beginning of time. I now have to give up some things and leave my past behind in order to launch into my promising future with God. I have to "forget about the former things, neither consider the things of old, for God is getting ready to do a new thing and when it springs forth, I will know it." (Isaiah 43:18-19). I have to "lay aside every weight, and the sin which doth so easily besets me, and run with patience the race that is set before me" (Hebrew 12:1)."

In the words of God's Leading Lady C ...

"Crystal Y. Holt, 42-year-old, twice divorced, single mother of eight beautiful children ranging in age from 2 through 24, five boys and three girls. Crystal was featured in the December, 2007 Special Edition Essence Magazine in an article entitled "How I Made It" written by Leslie Royal."

In the words of Leslie Royal, freelance writer for Essence Magazine ...

"On August 17, 2007, God blessed Crystal and her family with a newly built two story, 4 bedroom, 2.5 bath home. This was just a fraction of her true accomplishments, what she overcame to achieve her goal of home ownership. In the past, Crystal and her family were homeless on several occasions due to being entrapped and entangled in unhealthy relationships and not being a good steward of her God-given resources. With God's help and her faith and trust in God she overcame the pain of her past which included years of emotional and physical abuse, divorce and poverty to name a few. It was only after emerging from years in the valley of what seemed like death, having turned these crises into golden opportunities and realizing major victories. Struggling as a single mother meant juggling her quest for career success with the more immediate demands of survival. At present, she is currently employed full-time as a medical transcriptionist at a local hospital. Her employer allows her to work from home where she has the flexibility of spending more time with her children. She resides is her new home with her five small children." (Essence Magazine, 2007).

In the words of God's Leading Lady C ...

"December, 2007, Crystal and family made local publicity after a three page leading story "How I Made It" was featured in Essence Magazine. Crystal and family were also featured in the local Peoria Citizens Committee for Economic Opportunity (PCCEO) newsletter. Crystal was even asked to be featured on two local television broadcasts, but she chose to not pursue that avenue in that it would mean that she would be allowing the world to come into her home, her inner circle, her sacred place. Just a portion of the fat of the land that God had promised her in His word. In other words, her house was not in order ... yet. When I say house, I am not referring to a residential structure. I am referring to her life for Crystal was still growing into the process that God was taking her through. Yes, the story was not over even after she told the world 'how she made it'."

REFLECTIONS 2001-2008

Crystal continues to reflect further back on her life and the story continues to be told. By faith, from day one of her diagnosis of Type 1 diabetes in February, 2001, Crystal believed the word of God as she confessed with her mouth "But he was wounded for my transgressions, he was bruised for my iniquity: the chastisement of my peace was upon him; and with his stripes I am healed". (Isaiah 53:5). Yet, she allowed the doctors, whose hands she prayed over and claimed were anointed by God, to manage her ongoing care. She knew that as a part of her healing process she would need the help of others so she began to surround herself with positive people that could help her get to her next level in Christ as she continued to walk in her healing.

Crystal knows that she is a blessed and highly favored, virtuous woman of God that deserves God's very best and she shall not settle for less, so in 2008 this is her new stance. She and her children are members of Word of Faith Christian Center under the leadership of Bishop Leroy Davis.

CRYSTAL'S GREATEST LIFE ATTRIBUTES 1966-2007

Some of Crystal's greatest life attributes include being raised by her motherly grandmother who was a God-fearing, strong Christian woman and a stay-at-home hardworking wife who with God's help and the help of her hardworking, committed and dedicated Christian husband brought up three generations in the Lord. Crystal's natural parents were both present in her life, but they were working and her maternal grandmother and grandfather took over the responsibility of taking care of all the children in the family while their parents worked. The sole responsibility was on Crystal's maternal grandmother because her full-time job was seeking God and her ministry was raising up her children and her children's children in the Lord, everything else was just an overflow of the charity that first began at home and spread abroad.

Crystal credits a lot of her values, morals, ethics and beliefs to her maternal grandmother and grandfather who were her first role models and taught her the basic life skills that were necessary to live a successful life. Her grandmother first and foremost introduced her to Jesus. Her grandmother taught her to pray, to read the bible and showed her the way to salvation. Crystal gave her life to Christ at the age of 7. When Crystal was 12 years old, her grandfather retired and her grandparents relocated to a little town in Southern Illinois where her grandfather was born and Crystal was returned to her mother's care.

This was very traumatic time for Crystal because she knew that in her grandmother's absence that she would be spiritually uncovered. Even though at the age of 12 she did fully understand the definition of spiritually uncovered, she knew there was a major void. What Crystal did not know at that time, but later found out, is the power of prayer and that there was no distance in the spirit. Crystal had a praying grandmother who did not cease to pray for her and her family even in her absence.

Grandma prayed until the blood was no longer running in her veins and at that point God took over the prayer mantle and called her home because her purpose on this earth was done. Crystal was the only one present in the hospital room when her grandmother died. As she stroked her grandmother's fine gray hair ever so gently with her grandmother's comb, something she loved to do and something her grandmother loved for her to do on a regular basis, she miraculously "passed the torch" on to Crystal and she took her last breath. God arranged this divine appointment and for that Crystal is very thankful.

Crystal and her grandmother shared a lot in common, even the diagnosis of Type 1 insulin-dependent diabetes, with her grandmother living for God until the ripe age of 83. What they shared most in common is the belief that "For God we shall live and for God we shall die" (Roman 14:8). This "passing of the torch" experience can best be described as if God was saying directly to Crystal "You are the chosen one and no one else will do". So Crystal takes great pride and honor in knowing that she was chosen to continue in her grandmother's footsteps bringing up her family and generations to come in the Lord, "... and greater works than these shall she do ..." (John 14:12), knowing that the same spirit that carried her grandmother through 83 blessed years is going to carry her through as well. The bible says "For many are called, but few are chosen" (Matthew 22:14). Crystal now knows that everything that she has been through is for a reason and that reason is she is chosen and Crystal plans to walk boldly with the wisdom, understanding and confidence of God knowing and owning the power within.

Crystal is presently raising and bringing up eight children and three grandchildren in the Lord with God's help. She is proud of her three praise dancers, five psalmists and three steppers for the Lord. She knows that all of them have purpose and knows the power of her tongue when she constantly confesses over their life that "All of them are anointed and appointed, have callings on their lives and are blessed from the womb to the tomb". She confesses "Lo, children are an heritage of the Lord: and the fruit of the womb is his reward". (Psalm 127:3). Crystal knows that since God has blessed her with these children that He expects her to take care of what He has entrusted to her.

Crystal admits that at times in her flesh she does not always feel blessed and oftentimes feels overwhelmed, but she knows there is power in the word of God and she utilizes the word of God in every situation in her life. In the spirit, she knows that she is covered by the word of God and His precious blood, so in the natural she continues to just simply walk it out.

Part 1

The Beginning of a Well-Written, Beautiful Love Story Between God and God's Leading Lady C

When Crystal feels like she cannot handle it, she knows that God's word says (2 Corinthians 12:9) "My grace is sufficient for thee: for my strength is made perfect in weakness. Most gladly therefore will I rather glory in my infirmities, that the power of Christ may rest upon me".

When Crystal feels afraid, she knows God's word says (2 Timothy 1:7) "For God hath not given me the spirit of fear; but of power and of love, and of a sound mind".

When Crystal feels there is no peace, she knows that God's word says (Isaiah 26:3) "Thou wilt keep me in perfect peace, when my mind is stayed on thee: because I trust in thee".

When Crystal feels lack, she knows God's word says (Philippians 4:19) "But my God shall supply all my needs according to His riches in glory by Christ Jesus".

When Crystal feels her work is in vain, she knows God's word says (1 Corinthians 15:58) "Therefore, my beloved daughter, be ye stedfast, unmovable, always abounding in the work of the Lord, forasmuch as ye know that your labor is not in vain in the Lord".

When Crystal feels weary, she knows God's word says (Isaiah 40:31) "But they that wait upon the Lord shall renew their strength; they shall mount up with wings as eagles; they shall run, and not be weary; and they shall walk, and not faint".

When the fiery darts of the enemy hit her and Crystal feels like waving the white flag, she knows that God's word says (Isaiah 54:17) "No weapon that is formed against thee shall prosper; and every tongue that shall rise against thee in judgment thou shall condemn. This is the heritage of the servants of the Lord, and their righteousness is of me, saith the Lord".

God further reminds Crystal to suit up daily for battle and to fight (Ephesians 6:11) to "Put on the whole armor of God, that ye may be able to stand against the wiles of the devil". In addition, God's word says (Ephesians 6:13-18) "Wherefore take unto you the whole armor of God, that ye may be able to withstand in the evil day, and having done all, to stand. Stand therefore, having your loins girt about with truth, and having on the breastplate of righteousness; And your feet shod with the preparation, of the gospel of peace; Above all, taking the shield of faith, wherewith ye shall be able to quench all the fiery darts of the wicked. And take the helmet of salvation, and the sword of the Spirit, which is the word of God. Praying always with all prayer and supplication in the Spirit, and watching thereunto with all perseverance and supplication for all saints".

During her most trying times, she prays without cease and she patiently waits like a queen awaiting her King's prompt. As she remains in God's flow, she confidently makes affirmations that confirm that God has left her with many promises in His word to comfort her. She knows she is not forsaken.

SOME OF GOD'S PROMISES TO CRYSTAL

"He is the keeper of my soul" – The Lord shall preserve thee from all evil: he shall preserve thy soul. (Psalm 121:7).

"He will never leave or forsake me" – Be strong and of a good courage, fear not, nor be afraid of them: for the Lord thy God, he it is that doth go with thee; he will not fail thee, nor forsake thee. (Deuteronomy 31:6).

"My joy will be full" – I am the true vine, and my Father is the husbandman. Every branch in me that beareth not fruit he taketh away: and every branch that beareth fruit, he purgeth it, that it may bring forth more fruit. Now ye are clean through the word which I have spoken unto you. Abide in me, and I in you. As the branch cannot bear fruit of itself, except it abide in the vine; no more can ye, except ye abide in me. I am the vine, ye are the branches: He that abideth in me, and I in him, the same bringeth forth much fruit: for without me ye can do nothing. If a man abide not in me, he is cast forth as a branch, and is withered; and men gather them, and cast them into the fire, and they are burned. If ye abide in me, and my words abide in you, ye shall ask what ye will, and it shall be done unto you. Herein is my Father glorified, that ye bear much fruit; so shall ye be my disciples. As the Father hath loved me, so have I loved you: continue ye in my love. If ye keep my commandments, ye shall abide in my love; even as I have kept my Father's commandments, and abide in his love. These things have I spoken unto you, that my joy might remain in you, and that your joy might be full. (John 15:1-11).

"I shall reap an expected harvest in due season" - And let us not be weary in well doing: for in due season we shall reap, if we faint not. (Galatians 6:9).

Crystal knows without a doubt that she has come this far by faith and she knows that God is going to take her to newer and greater horizons as she continues to have great faith in God. At midnight, she may be sowing tears of sorrow, but she knows that joy cometh in the morning, where she will reap tears of joy. She knows God is going to turn her mourning into dancing, her midnight into daybreak. She awakes each day anew and views each dawning day as a gift from God. Each day she thanks God for another chance. She continues to confess with her mouth "This is the day that the Lord has made, I shall rejoice and be glad in it".

Crystal concludes with these final thoughts, "As long as the blood is running through my veins and God allows air to flow freely to and through my body, my life is purpose-driven and knowing that alone, I am all about my Father's business. Some might view me as a "diamond in the rough", yet, I see myself as God sees me. I am one of God's most sought out precious jewels, His handmaiden, His queen, one of God's "leading ladies" and that is why I call myself God's Leading Lady C. As I walk daily by faith as God's Leading Lady C, I know that what God has in store for me is a "designer original". I hold onto and cherish all of God's promises, especially (1 Corinthians 2:9) "Eye hath not seen, nor ear heard, neither have entered into the heart of man, the things which God hath prepared for them that love him" and Oh, how I love Jesus and Oh, how He loves me.

GOD GIVES CRYSTAL SPECIFIC INSTRUCTIONS TO FOLLOW FROM THIS DAY FORWARD: EXODUS CHAPTER 20 "AND GOD SPAKE ALL THESE WORDS, SAYING, I AM THE LORD THY GOD, WHICH HAVE BROUGHT THEE OUT OF THE LAND OF EGYPT, AND OF THE HOUSE OF BONDAGE …"

The Ten Commandments

1. Thou shalt have no other gods before me.
2. Thou shalt not make unto thee any graven image, or any likeness of any thing that is in heaven above, or that is in the earth beneath, or that is in the water under the earth: Thou shalt not bow down thyself to them, nor serve them: for I the LORD thy God am a jealous God, visiting the iniquity of the fathers upon the children unto the third and fourth generation of them that hate me; And showing mercy unto thousands of them that love me, and keep my commandments.
3. Thou shalt not take the name of the LORD thy God in vain; for the LORD will not hold him guiltless that taketh his name in vain.
4. Remember the sabbath day, to keep it holy. Six days shalt thou labor, and do all thy work: But the seventh day is the sabbath of the LORD thy God: in it thou shalt not do any work, thou, nor thy son, nor thy daughter, thy manservant, nor thy maidservant, nor thy cattle, nor thy stranger that is within thy gates: For in six days the LORD made heaven and earth, the sea, and all that in them is, and rested the seventh day: wherefore the LORD blessed the sabbath day, and hallowed it.
5. Honor thy father and thy mother: that thy days may be long upon the land which the LORD thy God giveth thee.
6. Thou shalt not kill.
7. Thou shalt not commit adultery.
8. Thou shalt not steal.
9. Thou shalt not bear false witness against thy neighbor.
10. Thou shalt not covet thy neighbor's house, thou shalt not covet thy neighbor's wife, nor his manservant, nor his maidservant, nor his ox, nor his ass, nor any thing that is thy neighbor's.

Their land also is full of idols; they worship the work of their own hands, that which their own fingers made: And the mean man boweth down, and the great man humbleth himself: therefore forgive them not. Enter into the rock, and hide thee in the dust, for fear of the LORD, and for the glory of His majesty. (Isaiah 2:8-10).

Come now, and let us reason together; saith the LORD: though your sins be as scarlet, they shall be white as snow; though they be red like crimson, they shall be as wool. If ye be willing and obedient, ye shall eat the good of the land: but if you refuse and rebel, ye shall be devoured with the sword: for the mouth of the LORD hath spoken it. (Isaiah 1:18-20).

And the idols he shall utterly abolish. (Isaiah 2:18).

Chapter II

Today

Today is December 28, 2007. I just got my new laptop. I am so excited so let's get to writing. This is my third attempt at writing this book in that I lost the original documents when my other two computers hard drives were destroyed. The devil is a liar. I am trying to setup internet options and to no avail. The kids are crazy and I am really beginning to stress. Where are the experts when you need them? I think I will call it a day. I am still trying, one call coming in, two calls and counting going out trying to make sense of it all. Babies crying, kids with attitudes, Lord when will this all end? I am sick and tired of burning a candle from both ends.

Someone once told me that in order to get out of this season I would have to embrace it. Well that person did not know what else to say because how can you embrace pain with no relief? How can you embrace pressure with no release? You simply cannot respond to someone in distress with mere words you must indeed be true to yourself and others and be less self-centered and self-absorbed and be willing to meet individuals where they are at and not be afraid of helping individuals meet their basic needs and you must be able to encourage them to have wants and desires just as the Lord himself designed them to have and be the vessels of honor He designed them to be.

Can a vessel of honor endure great distress with no rest? I think not! Even Jesus rested on the sabbath day. Well I say to you, in all sincerity, that "I am tired and exhausted and in dire need of rest". So instead of continuing to have a tantrum like a two-year-old child, I will take a timeout to open the Holy Bible and read what the word of God says regarding finding rest.

GOD SPEAKS TO GOD'S LEADING LADY C THROUGH HIS WORD

Come unto me, all ye that labor and are heavy laden, and I will give you rest. Take my yoke upon you, and learn of me: for I am meek and lowly in heart: and ye shall find rest unto your souls. For my yoke is easy, and my burden is light. (Matthew 11:28-30).

And on the seventh day God ended his work which he had made; and he rested on the seventh day from all his work which he had made. And God blessed the seventh day, and sanctified it: because that in it he rested from all his work which God created and made. (Genesis 2:2-3).

For ye are not as yet come to the rest and to the inheritance, which the Lord your God giveth you. (Deuteronomy 12:9)

But when ye go over Jordan, and dwell in the land which the Lord your God giveth you to inherit, and when he giveth you rest from all your enemies round about, so that ye dwell in safety; (Deuteronomy 12:10).

Therefore it shall be, when the Lord thy God hath given thee rest from all thine enemies round about, in the land which the Lord thy God giveth thee for an inheritance to possess it, that thou shalt blot out the remembrance of Amalek from under heaven; thou shalt not forget it. (Deuteronomy 25:19).

This reminds me of a story in which I went to church one Sunday morning tired and exhausted from the day before and tired and exhausted from waking up early to dress five small children and myself and arrive at morning worship by 9 am. I really did not feel like being churched. I needed a word from the Lord to help me, to give me strength, to renew me so that I could get through this day and a word that would take me through the week until the next Sunday. I needed spiritual food. I hungered for righteousness and needed to be filled. A motivational sermon on prosperity was not going to be enough today. A sermon on faith was not going to be enough today. I needed something I could apply to a real life situation that I was experiencing. I was having baby mama drama and "I was the baby mama". I was tired and wore out! I needed a word from the Lord. I needed the meat and not the milk. You see when a baby is small it drinks formula in the form of milk in a bottle but as the baby continues to grow and mature, that same baby needs meat for nourishment. Well I was at the point where milk was no longer nutritious. I wanted to hear more than "When praises go up, blessings come down".

So this particular Sunday, I arrived at church knowing in my heart, mind, body, soul and spirit that my attitude was "Where is the Beef?" For I had done exactly what the Proverbs 31 virtuous woman did, I had "riseth also while it is yet night, and giveth meat to her household, and a portion to her maidens ...". Following Proverbs Chapter 31 and the thirty-one verses therein and trying to make sure my household was taken care of by making preparations for each day and each season was not an easy task, to say the least, yet I persevered. Many Sundays I struggled just to get to church on time and enter into the presence and the house of the Lord where there is freedom and liberty.

Let me stop here and tell you that it was not the building that I was seeking; it was the presence of God. God is omnipresent so I could have stayed at home, but I wanted and needed to come into the house of God to fellowship with other believers for it says in (Proverbs 27:17) "Iron sharpeneth iron; so a man sharpeneth the countenance of his friend". This was not a time to play church with me. At this point in my life that would not do, because I knew that God was everpresent. I was not about no games when it came to Jesus. This was serious to me. If I wanted to hear just any sermon, I could turn on the radio, turn on the TV or even watch morning worship and service on the internet in the privacy of my own home. In my relationship with God I knew that God was only a prayer away. I had called on Him so much I had his direct line. I had Jesus on speed dial.

This particular Sunday morning, I pressed through the crowd like the woman in the bible with the issue of blood for 12 years who knew that if she could only touch the hem of Jesus' garment she could be healed of her infirmity, because in my spirit I knew I had a divine appointment. The bible says in (Luke 4:4) "That man shall not live by bread alone, but by every word of God". In addition, in (Matthew 4:4) "Man shall not live by bread alone, but by every word that proceedeth out of the mouth of God". I was ready for my word from the Lord.

On this particular day we had a visitor at the church, an old acquaintance of mine, a girl I used to work with. I never really established any deep, close and personal relationship with her, not because I did not want to, but at that time it seemed as if we were from two different worlds and that we shared very few things in common. Whether this is true or false, I did not know for sure at that time or present. As a matter of fact, I never questioned the reasons why at the time, but I just felt that at that time it was not the right time. We never really took the time to have lunch together and everything was basically friendly small talk. Sound familiar?

Nevertheless, many years were placed in between us and one day she appears at "my church". Not that it was literally "my church" or "my seat" or "my pastor" in that I am not "religious" nor did I pay for any of it, no pun intended. After service she remained outside the church, just waiting and standing alone and I walked up to her and greeted her with a hug and a friendly kiss and welcomed her to our church and encouraged her to come again for fellowship. She indicated that she enjoyed herself today and that she would try to visit again. She began to minister to me and I began to minister to her and we just simply talked about God's goodness and it appeared we both knew how to share that. I then began to tell her about some of my testimonies of what the Lord had done for me and she shared some of her testimonies of what the Lord had done for her as well. As God allowed me and her to share, she began to tell me about her journey with God.

Oh how wonderful it is to fellowship one with another. This is a major part of what God means by the word fellowship. It is not about just coming to church. It is about relationship and helping others see the God in you and making others want to come to church to get just a taste of His glory that is reflected in you. So many people have been hurt by people in the world and worse by people in the church because individuals do not understand this basic concept of Christian fellowship. Because of this worldly hurt combined with church hurt, some individuals choose to simply remain in their present state, or choose to simply stay at home and watch church on the TV or on the internet or listen to a sermon on the radio, via teleconference, or read an inspirational book or read the bible, or listen to gospel music to stay inspired. I say all of this because I want you to fully understand that it is not about you or me. We all need to take the time to bless others as the Lord leads. So then it clicked. God had set this all up.

God knew that she needed to be here at this exact time and that I needed to be here at this exact time. Just think if I had of chose to be "self-righteous" and stayed at home, I would have missed my divine appointment with Sheila. I shared with Sheila that I was so tired and weary and did not have any help, but God. Sheila answered without hesitation. "Well, God is all you need". You see, this statement from probably anybody else would have pissed me off, excuse my frankness, but when Sheila said it, it sounded different. My spirit received her spoken word and rested like never before. It was as if my spirit agreed with her spirit at that very moment.

You see, Sheila had a personal story in her belly that she needed to give birth to in that moment and it was birthed by her confessing to me, "God is all you need". You see Sheila like most of us have tried to travel life's journey accepting whatever we felt at the time would get us through, get us by, and get us to our self-designed destination. In so doing, we went out in our own strength and returned weary. Weary in what we thought was well-doing. If we only knew then what we know now, that God is all we need, we would have had fewer burdens to bear.

I then shared with Sheila that "I know that God is all I need but I am tired and need rest". She said without hesitation "You are getting rest, look around you". I did better than that, I looked at her like she was crazy and then I looked around me and all that I could see was five anointed children running laps around me, her and the cars, as we were in the church parking lot. She continued and said "You have your whole family here at church. I wish I could have done that when my children were young and maybe mine would not have ended up in the jail/prison system, in the child welfare system, in the juvenile system".

It was clear that she knew a different type of rest than what I was referring to, so I listened. She explained to me that there is a difference between physical rest and spiritual rest. Spiritual rest is when God allows you to rest in him, even when your circumstances do not warrant such. You can rest in him and know that everything is going to be alright and that by faith everything already is alright. Physical rest is when you get eight hours of uninterrupted sleep and you awake fully rested in the physical sense only. Sheila went further to say "Complete physical rest cannot happen unless you first have spiritual rest".

There was my revelation. That was the word from the Lord that I needed and it did not come from the pastor. That was a rhema word from God through his ordinary, common vessel, Sheila. Hallelujah! Don't let the devil trick you into thinking your life has to be perfect, your kids have to be perfect, your marriage has to be perfect, your house has to be perfect, you have to have this license, that degree, this IQ status, that financial status, male or female, young or old, God can use whoever and whomever He chooses to use, whenever and however He chooses to use them. All they have to do is be obedient to his instruction. Continue to confess and believe "The Lord will perfect that which concerneth me" (Psalm 138:8), and He will do just that.

I will not tell you Sheila's entire story but I hope she writes a book one day because it truly blessed me. Thank you Sister Sheila for sharing your story. You blessed me that day more than you know. That day I felt so weary in spirit but you helped me and allowed me to know and distinguish the difference between spiritual rest and physical rest. I did not fully understand the difference until then. God allowed you to bless me with a word in due season. So everyone within the sound of my voice take Sheila's advice and obtain spiritual rest while you have time for one day physical rest alone will not sustain you. God Bless Sheila and Family.

DECEMBER, 2007 – FEATURED IN THE SPECIAL EDITION ESSENCE MAGAZINE

The December, 2007 Special Edition Essence Magazine featured Prophetess Juanita Bynum-Weeks on the front page, where she shared her personal story of "I Have Come This Far by Faith". Prophetess Juanita Bynum is one of my favorite female evangelists. I felt honored to be in the same magazine and talking about the same faith and the same God that brought us through almost the same story. Prophetess Bynum ministered to me many days and nights through books, music, video recordings, cassette recordings, Christian broadcasts and conferences and gave me step by step techniques on how to come out of ungodly relationships ex. "No More Sheets" (Bynum, 1998) and how to be willing and obedient and have faith and live for God. I believed it all and I admired her so much and wanted to be able to bless others just like she blessed me. I wanted to minister to the world just like she ministered to me. I thought just because she was in the pulpit she was free from the worries and troubles that I was presently experiencing. Years later, God placed us in the same magazine talking about our trials and tribulations and how we got there and how He alone brought us both out. WOW, God is so awesome!

PERSONAL PRAYER

God thank you for all the opportunities that you have given me for destiny and purpose. I pray that you would give me a creative idea that will bring an expected harvest. Sow into my spirit the seeds of success that you wish. Sow into my spirit the gifts that you choose. Sow into my spirit a newness that can only come from you. Allow Your Holy Spirit to do a new thing in me. Equip me with everything I need to make a difference in this lifetime. Lord, I will be careful to "not withhold good from them to whom it is due, when it is in the power of thine hand to do it" (Proverbs 3:27). Knowing that whatsoever good thing any man doeth, the same shall he receive of the Lord, whether he be bond or free. (Ephesians 6:8). Amen!

MY LAND OF MILK & HONEY

My story was similar to Prophetess Bynum-Weeks yet different for God designed each and every one of us different with different callings and different life plans. We are all "designer originals" in God's eye. No one's story is quite the same, yet we are all created by the same creator, God. God gives us all different spiritual gifts, natural and spiritual skills, talents and expertise for our specific God-given purpose and His plan. He gives us different heart's desires for the same reasons. So we do not have to envy one another and compete for God's love and blessings because what He has for each and every one of us belongs solely to the rightful owner.

My story was entitled "How I Made It" written by freelance writer Leslie Royal. Who I must say did an excellent job in telling the story. Her article was a synopsis of the book to come. Leslie, thank you for being a blessing to me and my family. God truly utilized you for His glory. I know it was only God that allowed you to respond to a lead from my good friend Robin Berry, realtor for PCCEO who contacted you to inform you of my story of becoming a first time homeowner. It was like a dream come true to be in an internationally known top African-American magazine to share about God's goodness to all whom may read. That story not only blessed me, it blessed a lot of people, more than I could imagine and know. The story of three courageous women who made it; each individually sharing and giving credit where credit was due and the leading story was the one and only, God's Leading Lady C. Giving God all the glory and personally knowing "all praises are due to God and only the mistakes were mine".

As onlookers looked and often asked the questions how and why, I simply responded with God's help. Ultimately, it was neither me, nor my strength at all. In fact, I know that I never could have made it without God and I was at a point in my life that I was not ashamed to tell it. You see, without God it is so easy to get into situations that you find hard if not almost impossible to get out. I mastered getting myself into things that were not originally planned for my life. In fact being out of the will of God is at the opposite extreme on the continuum which I was at most of my life. I fully understand what "If it had not been for the grace of God, where would I be?" means.

Yes, there is nothing new under the sun and I discovered that before and even after reading the book of Ecclesiastes over and over again. I did not get the revelation of it until God quickened the full meaning and understanding into my spirit. That is why I am glad that God has no respect of persons, what He has done for others, He will do the same for me, vice versa (Romans 2:11). There is nothing too hard for him. He delivered sinners as well as saints out of the same wages of sin when He died on the cross for our sins. There is no condemnation and nothing will separate us from His love for us. So there is no need to try to cover our sins we need to run to Him when we mess up instead of running to the devil and becoming another one of His pons or imps.

We, meaning all of us, need to run to God instead of the lusts of the world, i.e. sex, gambling, alcohol, drugs, crime, shopping, and other addictions. We all need to run to God for the wages of sin is death. I know this first hand for I paid a major cost for my disobedience to God. So if we choose to live and not die, we should run to God.

In Jesus, there are rivers of flowing living waters where we can be cleansed of our sins and our thirst can be quenched so that we will never thirst again. The world cannot cleanse us or quench our thirst. Nothing else can fill the voids in our lives like God can. God alone is the only one who has the power to do so. No man, no woman, no job, no book, no computer, no addiction, nothing can fill the voids in our life, not wealth, power or fame, only God.

Can you think of any situation you quickly ran to and had to ultimately run from, thinking it would fill a void in your life, only to be left unfilled and depleted? Where do and did you run to be restored, renewed and rehabilitated? I ran to a lot of things, too many to name, but now I know only God could cleanse me and restore me to a state of being that actually made me complete, "Nothing Missing, Nothing Broken, Complete in Him".

God does not want us to be in despair. He wants our joy to be complete and full in Him. The devil wants to kill, conquer and destroy every aspect of your life. Run so far from him and his tactics that all you can see in front of you is destiny. I know I did on several occasions.

Do not bother looking back on your past mistakes, problems and situations. For the past is just what it is, past, passed, time spent. Go forward with God, with grace, despite your fear. Go forward with the courage that your life is in God's hand and that no one can take you out of His hand. Go forward knowing that whatever you commit to God, He will keep.

So I ask you right now, have you committed everything to God that you value or have you left some things prey to state or fate? Yes, there are a lot of things we just need to let go of for our good. We only need to hold on and commit to God everything we value most and want to keep, like our mind, body, soul and spirit, our family, our loved ones, our God-given gifts, talents, abilities, our heart's desires like our dreams and inspirations. Everything else that is weighing us down, we need to simply let go! If we are holding onto something that is not helping us get closer to our God-given destiny, then we need to Let Go! ex. a person, place, thing, situation, **IDOLS**, let go! That is what God means when He says "let us lay aside every weight, and the sin which doth so easily beset us, and let us run with patience the race that is set before us" (Hebrews 12:1).

If we can allow God's will and not our own to take precedence in our lives we are on our way to a victorious state. The opposite of state is fate. Beloved, think it not strange concerning the fiery trial which is to try you, as though some strange thing happened unto you. It is just satan once again up to his same ole tactics, But rejoice, inasmuch as ye are partakers of Christ's sufferings; that, when His glory shall be revealed, ye may be glad also with exceeding joy (1 Peter 4:13).

Yes, my heart hurts really, really, bad at times. Yes, my feelings are very, very low sometimes, but joy still remains deep down in the inside, love still remains deep down in the inside, everything that God has deposited in me still remains deep down in the inside. My joy is complete in Him. My assignment still remains. My name in the Book of Life still remains. The song in my heart still remains, "I still got joy, I still got joy, after all that I've been through I still got joy. I still got love, I still got love, after all that I've been through I still got love. I still got peace …", repeat chorus. Continue to sing praises unto God. Allow God to give you your own song, a new song in your heart and know that your joy is also made complete in Him.

Count it all joy. My brethren, count it all joy when ye fall into divers temptations; Knowing this, that the trying of your faith worketh patience. But let patience have her perfect work, that ye may be perfect and entire, wanting nothing (James 1:2-4). Everything that happened to you in your past, count it all joy.

We oftentimes grieve when we lose things but the bible tells us that "Every branch in me that beareth not fruit he taketh away: and every branch that beareth fruit, he purgeth it, that it may bring forth more fruit" (John 15:2). So everything in our life that is not producing fruit we need to allow God to take it away. We need to also allow God to prune the remaining branches to produce more fruit. The bible says in (Matthew 7:16) "Ye shall know them by their fruits". When you bear good fruit, people will know that you have the favor of God over your life.

When God prunes us and purges us we need not go back and try to pick up the branches. We need to just let go! When God delivers you out of ungodly relationships, we need to just let go! We should not want to hold on to **IDOLS** that make us look like we had not only a breakup but a breakdown. We should not look like orphans tossed to and fro or live like we are living on Barely Get Along Street when our Heavenly Father is the King of kings and Lord of lords. We should look like royalty and not impoverished children left astray. We should walk with a clear vision of where we are going and not like we are lost and have no hope. God wants us to return home to Him. Even the prodigal son returned home to his father after he came to his senses and you know he went out and came home a hot mess just like we did, but didn't his father meet him and greet him as if he was royalty? That is because he was royalty and so are we.

I took note that God does not bless no mess. I am too blessed to be stressed, too anointed to be disappointed, so let's just keep it moving. "To the left, to the left …. everything you own in the box to the left" or whatever song you come up with in your mind, let's just not live in the past. I am so glad I did not die in my past mess and that God saved a wretch like me for purpose and destiny. Let's live in the present and look forward to our future in God. Today is a new day, it is time to move on.

DAUGHTER'S GRADUATION

On January 13, 2008, my daughter Che'Andrea a/k/a (also known as) Che', graduated with her GED from a local high school alternative program at Tri-County Urban League. Those present included her father, mother, sister, grandfather, nephew and son and all supporting friends and school staff. We sat through all the videotapings, speeches and then we took the pictures and passed the cards and money and said the proper best wishes. Oh and yes, most importantly, the certificate/diploma of achievement.

After all the appropriate acknowledgments and thank you's, my daughter walks over to me, gives me her certificate/diploma of achievement and says "Mom, I want you to hold this and keep this and take care of it for me". The smile on my face turned to the biggest grin, from ear to ear, and the biggest surprised look. To me, she had given me her future to hold and to cherish. What an honor. Of course, I know the truth was that she just wanted me to keep up with her things like she did when she was young so that she would not lose it, but there is a slight possibility that she was just giving credit where credit was due. You see as a mother you find yourself sometimes living each day thinking you accomplish nothing when it comes to making a great difference in your children's lives and then one day your third born daughter, the one that you were ashamed to be pregnant with because you were an unwed mother, the one that was a scheduled/canceled abortion appointment, gives you her everything, all that she has worked for.

How can a simple 8 x 10 signed sheet of paper bring a mother the greatest joy at that very moment? I can only assume it was her special way of saying "Mom, thank you, everything you did made the difference and your work was not in vain". "I love you Che' and today I know that you love me". Yes, I gave her the typical congratulations card and a $100 dollar bill to show her I was proud of her hard work, but nothing meant more than her saying, without saying, "Mom hold on to what is important to me for I will not value it like you do". If only she could have given me her teenage years to hold and to treasure. I guess "bought sense" is the best kind to have for she too has a calling on her life that she can only obtain through her walk with God.

Mommy cannot bear her cross but mommy will hold on and treasure everything she gives me for safekeeping, just as our Heavenly Father does for each and everyone of us. Everything we commit and dedicate to Him, He has promised to keep. That is why I committed my children to him at a very young age and some even while they were in the womb, because I knew His hand could reach where mine could not reach and his eye could see when mine were blinded. I trusted that He knew what was best for them in all situations. For I knew that God loved me and everything concerning me and that His love for me and my children was even greater than a mother's love. God is truly amazing!

AND THEY SERVED THEIR IDOLS: WHICH WERE A SNARE UNTO THEM. PSALM 106:36

Chapter III

Dejavu

LOOKING BACK & SHARING MY STORY - 2002

Dejavu, it was **MY IDOL** again a/k/a lucifer, the adversary, the devil, the enemy, satan himself tempting me to fall short of God's grace. Throughout the book I will be referring to **MY IDOL** and his pons and imps by different names i.e. **MY IDOL**, the devil, lucifer, the adversary, the enemy, satan but they are one in the same. **MY IDOL** can also be described as "anything and everything I put before God". It can be a person, place, thing, a job, a loved one, a friend, a relationship, an addiction, etc.

January 12, 2002, I returned to a former state of oppression, like a dog returning to his own vomit. The bible says in (Proverbs 26:11) "As a dog returneth to his vomit, so a fool returneth to his folly". I returned to worry, despair, and an apathetic condition. I began to experience sleepless nights, making calls after calls to no avail, awaiting the doorbell ring, looking out the window, listening for the sound of the parking car and footsteps at the door.

Dejavu, I had definitely been here before, out of the will of God. In this chapter I lived the word of God in the story of The Woman at the Well and The Woman Caught in Adultery. The Modified G rated script reads as follows. I know you were probably thinking that I was getting ready to give you the juicy juicy gossip on how I committed fornication, which is sex outside of marriage, any type of sexual act including and not limited to and yes even the sexual toys and how I committed adultery, which is sex with a man or woman that is not your spouse and that I was actually worse than a prostitute, because I gave it away for free, without any payment or compensation in return. No, I am going to be Christ-like and give you the word of God on the whole matter just like God gave it to me, I am going to give it to you.

MY WOMAN AT THE WELL EXPERIENCE (JOHN 4:6-29)

Verse 6 – Now Jacob's well was there. Jesus therefore, being wearied with his journey, sat thus on the well: and it was about the sixth hour.

Verse 7 – There cometh a woman of Samaria to draw water: Jesus saith unto her; Give me to drink.

Verse 9 – Then saith the woman of Samaria unto him, How is it that thou, being a Jew, askest drink of me, which am a woman of Samaria? for the Jews have no dealings with the Samaritans.

Verse 10 – Jesus answered and said unto her, If thou knewest the gift of God, and who it is that saith to thee, Give me to drink; thou wouldest have asked of him, and he would have given thee living water:

Verse 11 – The woman saith unto him, Sir, thou hast nothing to draw with, and the well is deep: from whence then hast thou that living water?

Verse 13 – Jesus answered and said unto her; Whosoever drinketh of this water shall thirst again.

Verse 14 – But whosoever drinketh of the water that I shall give him shall never thirst; but the water that I shall give him shall be in him a well of water springing up into everlasting life.

Verse 15 – The woman saith unto him, Sir, give me this water, that I thirst not, neither come hither to draw.

Verse 16 – Jesus saith unto her, Go, call thy husband, and come hither;

Verse 17 – The woman answered and said, I have no husband. Jesus said unto her, Thou hast well said, I have no husband:

Verse 18 – For though hast had five husbands; and he whom thou now hast is not thy husband: in that saidst thou truly.

Verse 19 – The woman saith unto him, Sir, I perceive that though art a prophet.

Verse 25 – The woman saith unto him, I know that Messias cometh, which is called Christ: when he is come, he will tell us all things.

Verse 26 – Jesus saith unto her, I that speak unto thee am he.

Verse 28 – The woman then left her waterpot, and went her way into the city, and saith to the men,

Verse 29 – Come, see a man, which told me all things that ever I did: is not this the Christ?

MY WOMAN CAUGHT IN ADULTERY EXPERIENCE (JOHN 8:3-11)

Verse 3 – And the scribes and Pharisees brought unto him a woman taken in adultery; and when they had set her in the midst.

Verse 4 – They say unto him, Master, this woman was taken in adultery, in the very act.

Verse 5 – Now Moses in the law commanded us, that such should be stone: but what sayest though?

Verse 6 – This they said, tempting him, that they might have to accuse him. But Jesus stooped down, and with his finger wrote on the ground, as though he heard them not.

Verse 7 – So when they continued asking him, he lifted up himself, and said unto them, He that is without sin among you, let him first cast a stone at her.

Verse 10 – When Jesus lifted up himself, and saw none but the woman, he said unto her, Woman, where are those thine accusers? Hath no man condemned thee?

Verse 11 – She said, No man, Lord. And Jesus said unto her, Neither do I condemn thee: go, and sin no more.

LOVE COVERS A MULTITUDE OF SINS

I remember how I used to get so angry when someone hurt or offended me but God continued to work on building my godly character by reminding me to forgive and showing me how to forgive and helping me to continue loving those individuals with the love of God as He illustrated to me that they were just on assignment by satan, the one they serve. God continued to comfort me through His word and during those times when I wanted to hate those that hurt me, He continued to tell me to "Love …".

God taught me how to forgive and how to love. I loved God so much and I wanted to be so much like Him that I made it a point to do everything He was teaching me and He told me that the greatest gift I can give is that what He had given me and that is Love. He went further to tell me that it was already in me to give. Throughout the years, I had been looking for love in so many ways, forms and fashions and it was already in me. It was in me all along.

GOD CONTINUES TO SPEAK TO GOD'S LEADING LADY C

For we wrestle not against flesh and blood, but against principalities, against powers, against the rulers of the darkness of this world, against spiritual wickedness in high places. (Ephesians 6:12). The bible tells us in (Ephesians 6:13) "Wherefore take unto you the whole armor of God, that ye may be able to withstand in the evil day, and having done all, to stand".

Watch and pray, that ye enter not into temptation: the spirit indeed is willing, but the flesh is weak. (Matthew 26:41).

There hath no temptation taken you but as is common to man: but God is faithful, who will not suffer you to be tempted above that ye are able; but will with the temptation also make a way to escape, that ye may be able to bear it. (1 Corinthians 10:13).

Now unto him that is able to keep you from falling, and to present you faultless before the presence of his glory with exceeding joy. (Jude 1:24).

Why did I think the devil had changed? For the bible says in (Matthew 7:16-20) "Ye shall know them by their fruits. Do men gather grapes of thorns, or figs of thistles? Even so every good tree bringeth forth good fruit; but a corrupt tree bringeth forth evil fruit. A good tree cannot bring forth evil fruit, neither can a corrupt tree bring forth good fruit. Every tree that bringeth not forth good fruit is hewn down, and cast into the fire. Wherefore by their fruits ye shall know them."

Fooled Again! Well what the devil meant for evil, God meant for good. (Genesis 50:20). *Lord, I Get It! Time for a spiritual pep talk. "I was tricked for spiritual growth. God allowed me to go through this to strengthen me and build my Godly character. He won't put more on me than I can bear and He won't let me get in situations and stay in situations that are unbearable so what the devil is doing is really for my benefit. Yes, it does not feel right and it does not feel good but God still has the final say. When spirits do not agree, they cannot walk together. Isn't God a good God? He will not let any evil spirit or evil worker dwell among you. He will take any spirit not of God out of your path. He will put a hedge of protection around you. He will cover you with His precious blood. The enemy cannot penetrate the precious blood of Jesus. He cares that much about me that He would not allow me to continue in any ungodly relationship. He would not let me abort what He has impregnated me with. So tomorrow is a new day and I am renewed daily in Him for His grace is new each dawning day and His mercy endureth forever. All praises due to God".*

THEREFORE SAY UNTO THE HOUSE OF ISRAEL, THUS SAITH THE LORD GOD; REPENT, AND TURN YOURSELVES FROM YOUR IDOLS; AND TURN AWAY YOUR FACES FROM ALL YOUR ABOMINATIONS. EZEKIEL 14:6

Chapter IV

Prayer Room – Beyond the Veil

In the day of my trouble I will call upon thee: for though wilt answer me. (Psalm 86:7).

Lord, please hear my prayer and accept my plea with Your abounding love. Lord I am still on this journey for Your glory. Please continue to make me an instrument of Your perfect will. ~cyh~

And thou shalt love the Lord thy God with all thine heart, and with all thy soul, and with all thy might. (Deuteronomy 6:5).

Lord, I love you with all my heart, soul and might! ~cyh~

But I will sing of thy power; yea, I will sing aloud of thy mercy in the morning: for thou hast been my defense and refuge in the day of my trouble. (Psalm 59:16).

Lord, I trust you! ~cyh~

GOD ANSWERS GOD'S LEADING LADY C THROUGH HIS WORD

But I say unto you, Love your enemies, bless them that curse you, do good to them that hate you, and pray for them which despitefully use you, and persecute you; That ye may be the children of your Father which is in heaven: for he maketh his sun to rise on the evil and on the good, and sendeth rain on the just and on the unjust. (Matthew 5:44-45).

We are bound to thank God always for your brethren, as it is meet, because that your faith growth exceedingly, and the charity of every one of you all toward each other aboundeth. (2 Thessalonians 1:3).

Though I speak with the tongues of men and of angels, and have not charity, I am become as sounding brass, or a tinkling cymbal. And though I have the gift of prophecy, and understand all mysteries, and all knowledge; and though I have all faith, so that I could remove mountains, and have not charity, I am nothing. And though I bestow all my goods to feed the poor, and though I give my body to be burned, and have not charity, it profiteth me nothing. Charity suffereth long, and is kind; charity envieth not; charity vaunteth not itself, is not puffed up. Doth not behave itself unseemly, seeketh not her own, is not easily provoked, thinketh no evil; Rejoiceth not in iniquity, but rejoiceth in the truth; Beareth all things, believeth all things, hopeth all things, endureth all things. Charity never faileth. (1 Corinthians 13:1-8).

A new commandment I give unto you, That ye love one another; as I have loved you, that ye also love one another. By this shall all men know that ye are my disciples, if ye have love one to another. (John 13:34-35).

Beloved, if God so loved us, we ought also to love one another: No man hath seen God at any time. If we love one another, God dwelleth in us, and his love is perfected in us. Hereby know we that we dwell in him, and he in us, because he hath given us of his Spirit. (1 John 4:11-13).

SWEET COMMUNION

This morning I had a little talk with God and I informed him that I was not going to get out of bed until He paved the way for me and guess what, He did. Yes, today He made a way out of no way once again. God keeps proving to me that He is awesome! You have truly reached spiritual maturity when you know that you can do nothing without Him. I now know that I am the branch and He is the true vine. I now know that I am in right relationship with Him at this very moment because of this new found knowledge. **MY IDOL** is defeated once again. As long as I am connected to the vine I am destined to be successful in every situation, in due season, in His timing. I will go from victory to victory to victory in Him.

GOD SPEAKS TO GOD'S LEADING LADY C THROUGH HIS WORD

"Who shall separate me from the love of Christ? shall tribulation, or distress, or persecution, or famine, or nakedness, or peril, or sword? Nay, in all these things I am more than a conqueror through him that loved me". (Romans 8:35, 37).

Nothing will separate me from the Love of God, know way, no how, nothing, no one. God is my source, not man, not family, not friends, not job, not material things, etc. Knowing that no one, nothing, no how will I ever be separated from His love brings me so much hope. God loves me and that settles it. He is merciful and faithful. He is a restorer. He knows the tears I cry even before they fall, everything that touches me touches him. I am near and dear to His heart and He is near and dear to my heart. I will continue on the journey with the hope I have in Christ.

For I am persuaded, that neither death, nor life, nor angels, nor principalities, nor powers, nor things present, nor things to come, Nor height, nor depth, nor any other creature, shall be able to separate us from the love of God, which is in Christ Jesus our Lord. (Romans 8:38-39).

GOD'S LEADING LADY C SPEAKS TO GOD PRAYER FOR A HUSBAND

Lord when is my husband coming, I am tired of being alone. I am tired of having to be strong and doing everything on my own and making decisions on my own. Well I won't say I as in "I", because I know that You are with me and that You are my source, so I should be saying "We". Yet, when I get in a hurry for something to happen in my life and during those times that I don't want to bother You and I go out in my own strength thinking You have my back, I fail miserably. So I guess I need to keep in mind that "I am the head and not the tail" only through You and not without You. Nevertheless, Lord, I still long for a husband designed and sent specifically to me by You. I won't let You regret it and I will be careful to honor him and give him reverence just as I honor You and give You reverence. Thank You in advance Lord, Amen!

GOD SPEAKS TO GOD'S LEADING LADY C & ASKS "WHAT KIND OF HUSBAND?"

GOD'S LEADING LADY C RESPONDS WITH A VERY VERY VERY LONG LIST

Someone who is God-fearing, puts God First, me second, family third, everything else accordingly, someone who walks with me and not in front of me or behind me, someone who loves children, who is available to be a family man, faithful, loyal, someone who I will be the apple of His eye, someone who will love and cherish me, someone who loves himself as well as he loves others, someone who loves life, values life, lives life abundantly, someone full of the joy, peace and the love of Christ, someone who desires to please me, someone able to provide for me, someone secure in himself, someone who has a passion for others and a passion for Christ, someone who is a hard worker, positive thinker, wise steward, intelligent, charming, a romantic, someone good with his hands, someone pleasant to the eye and soothing to the mind, body, spirit and soul, a good listener, a motivator, an encourager, someone supportive, fun, loving, good sense of humor, someone giving with a very generous heart, someone with a beautiful mind and kind heart, someone with a gentle, humble spirit, someone who is strong, confident, powerful and courageous in the spirit and in the natural, someone with the wisdom and understanding of God, someone who seeks God early in the morning, prays without cease, believes in the power of prayer, praise, faith and the word of God, someone who walks in the spirit, someone who is a wise protector. Lord, to make a long list short, someone who loves You, someone just like You, Lord. Someone who has walked in the path of righteousness so long that they look and act just like you Lord. That is my heart's desire. I know God was saying, without saying, "You already have that in Me". God is a gentleman. He did not say one word. He remained quiet and just kept smiling. So I continued to seek God's face!

GOD FURTHER ANSWERS GOD'S LEADING LADY C THROUGH HIS WRITTEN AND AUDIBLE VOICE: I AM ALL THAT YOU NEED

PROVISION

But thou shalt remember the Lord thy God: for it is he that giveth thee power to get wealth, that he may establish his covenant which he sware unto thy fathers, as it is this day. (Deuteronomy 8:18).

STRENGTH

And he said unto me, My grace is sufficient for thee: for my strength is made perfect in weakness. Most gladly therefore will I rather glory in my infirmities, that the power of Christ may rest upon me. Therefore I take pleasure in infirmities, in reproaches, in necessities, in persecutions, in distresses for Christ's sake: for when I am weak, then am I strong. (2 Corinthians 12:9-10).

A LOVE LETTER FROM GOD TO GOD'S LEADING LADY C

My darling Crystal, "Your haters will be your motivators". You have the power to birth nations, your children and your children's children. You have the power to set the captives free by bringing them to Christ, glory shall come in your weakness, for I am strong when you are weak. Do not strive to be strong, strive to be humble and content in whatever state you are in, hold on to the power that I have given you because it is going to save this generation. Come forth, walk through the door that I have opened for you, it is time. Make yourself happy even when your circumstances do not warrant such, remember the joy of the Lord is your strength. There is no sorrow in Me, know that your joy is full in Me. Know who you are in Me. Don't keep looking or going back, keep moving forward in Me. Believe, receive, claim, own your destiny, it is yours. I have given it to you and no one can take that which I have given you out of your hands. You have come this far by faith and faith is going to take you higher and higher in Me. Great is Your Faith!

GOD CONTINUES TO MINISTER TO GOD'S LEADING LADY C

COURAGE

For God hath not given us the spirit of fear; but of power; and of love, and of a sound mind. (2 Timothy 1:7).

There is no fear in love; but perfect love casteth out fear: because fear hath torment. He that feareth is not made perfect in love. (1 John 4:18).

GOD'S LEADING LADY C PONDERS

Talks like this with God make me want to shout Hallelujah, for it is the highest praise!

All my life I was afraid of something, even knowing that God hath not given me the spirit of fear but the spirit of power, love and a sound mind. Yet, fear when utilized correctly can put you in position to act and reposition yourself, win or lose, ride or die attitude.

Throughout all my life experiences, I had to learn to trust God, even in fearful times. I may have been "shaking in my boots", but I had to continue to love and live through my fears and tears. I had to keep pressing and pushing and move past my fears. I had to press and push through the storms of life knowing that God is my refuge, my help, my protector, my provider. I had to keep my eye on the prize. I had to keep going forward walking hand in hand with God. I had to confess Psalm 23 over my life, "The Lord is my shepherd; I shall not want". I had to praise him with song, "Precious Lord take my hand, lead me on, let me stand, I am tired, I am weak, I am worn. Through the storm, through the night, lead me on to the light, take my hand precious Lord and lead me on".

GOD SPEAKS

God continued to speak and show me "When all you have is Me, you have something to be thankful and grateful for. I am really all you need! Any problem or situation you are facing, I am the answer, for the world today, above Me there is no other, for I am the way, the truth and the light".

God spoke "Cast all your care upon me; for I care for you". (1 Peter 5:7). God showed me how to not discuss my problems with someone not qualified to help me. God told me to bring it to Him in prayer, seek Him and then and only then will I get to know Him and His ways.

GOD'S LEADING LADY C RESPONDS TO GOD'S LOVE LETTER

Lord, I will call upon You in the midnight hour, in the midday, I will call You. I know You are the answer. I know You are waiting on me to call just so You can answer and come through for me once again. God, I am calling You right now, I am ringing Your number right now, Can You hear me? Can You help me? I know Your timing is perfect and I know that You will answer me in Your timing. I know that You are able to help me and that You will help. I know You are faithful and that You are a just God. I know that all power is in Your hand. Lord I need You and I cannot live without You. Lord, please hear my plea and honor my petition. God, You are worthy of all the honor, all the glory, and all the praise. You are an awesome, magnificent God. Lord, You are my everything. Thank You Lord for being my everything!

God then begins to comfort my soul and spirit. He assures me that "It is Time". *This is the moment that I have been waiting for, I lived for this moment. Lord as I take You by the hand, I feel safe and secure in You. I have the confidence and mind of Christ. You have anointed me from the top of my head to the bottom of my feet with Your holy oil. Your Holy Spirit flows to me and through me. I am guaranteed success through You. My life is blessed because You declared and decreed it to be so. You designed me for purpose, so I say yes to Your will and to Your way. I will come forth just as You have asked. I will walk through the door that You have opened for me to walk through. Lord, wherever You lead me, I will follow. Yes Lord!*

God, You are my everpresent help in the time of trouble. I am not alone for You are with me. I will stay connected to You, the true vine, as a branch. I will continue to abide in Your Word and delight myself in You knowing that You will give me the desires of my heart according to Your perfect will.

A TWO-WAY COMMUNICATION BETWEEN GOD AND LADY C

In any good relationship communication is key. As God and God's Leading Lady C become one in the spirit they begin to commune with each other and share everything as they draw closer and closer to each other there is no turning back now for God's Leading Lady C. God's Leading Lady C does not know the road she is about to travel but she is confident knowing that her King leads the way as they walk hand in hand on the journey.

THE ROAD TO REPENTANCE/DELIVERANCE

Do they not err that devise evil? but mercy and truth shall be to them that devise good. (Proverbs 14:22).

The Lord is not slack concerning his promise, as some men count slackness; but is longsuffering toward us, not willing that any should perish, but that all should come to repentance. (2 Peter 3:9).

Therefore I will judge you, O house of Israel, every one according to his ways, saith the Lord GOD. Repent, and turn yourselves from all your transgressions; so iniquity shall not be your ruin. (Ezekiel 18:30).

Then said I unto them, Cast ye away every man the abominations of his eyes, and defile not yourselves with the idols of Egypt: I am the Lord your God. (Ezekiel 20:7).

The Lord is my rock, and my fortress, and my deliverer; my God, my strength, in whom I will trust; my buckler, and the horn of my salvation, and my high tower. (Psalm 18:2).

MY PERSONAL PRAYER

Gracious Lord, I repent of every sin and ask for Your forgiveness. I come boldly to Your throne of grace today seeking Your face and not Your hand. I need You to do a great work in me Lord. Search my heart Lord, take anything out that is not of You. I know who I am, I am Your child. I am royalty for You are King of kings and Lord of lords. I need to know what it is You would have me to do as Your vessel of honor. I need to know my purpose. I need to know my calling. I surrender my will to Your perfect will and say yes to Your will and way. Lord teach me, lead me and guide me, hold my hand Lord as I aspire to be more like You daily. Strengthen me, motivate me, keep me in perfect peace as I walk and move forward in Your grace. Give me rivers of living water so that I will never thirst again. As I hunger for righteousness, fill me with Your daily bread. Lord, only You can fill every void. Lord, as I abide in You and Your word abides in me; allow me to do Your will. Allow me to perform that which You require of me. Equip me, supply every need according to Your riches in Glory. Father, as I am about Your business, I would ask that You take care of mine, everything concerning me. Bless me Lord so that I may be a blessing to others, to this generation and generations to come. Allow me to continue to come forth to be what You designed me to be for I was fearfully and wonderfully made by You for Your glory. You created me for purpose and I would ask that You reveal that purpose to me so that I may be pleasing in Your sight. Lord, I am Your servant, Your handmaiden. Show me Your way. Show me those things hidden and seen that You want me to see. Equip me with whatever I need to continue to be Your good and faithful servant, Your diligent disciple. Lord, give me my portion as You see fit. I ask these petitions by fervent prayer, believing by faith that You hear me and that You will answer. I am believing, naming, claiming and owning all Your promises in Your precious name. Lord, I thank You in advance for answering me. I will continue to follow as You lead me. I will continue walking in my God-given gifts, talents and abilities, singing praises unto You with a thankful and grateful heart and humble spirit, possessing all fruit of the Spirit given by You and You alone, knowing life is a gift and each day is a blessing from You, the giver of all good gifts. Lord, only You can complete me, heal and make me whole. Only You can save me and deliver me from the wages of sin and death and all my troubles. Only You can deliver me and set me free from bondage and strongholds. Only You can deliver me out of all my afflictions, trial and tribulations. Lord, if You choose not to take this cup from me, please send Your Holy Spirit to comfort me and teach me Your way as I continue on my journey as a soldier in the army for the Lord, in the mighty name of Jesus I pray and seal this prayer with Your precious blood, Amen.

GOD CONTINUES TO MINISTER TO GOD'S LEADING LADY C

GUIDANCE

For I know the thoughts that I think toward you, saith the LORD, thoughts of peace, and not of evil, to give you an expected end. (Jeremiah 29:11).

The steps of a good man are ordered by the LORD: and he delighteth in his way. Though he fall, he shall not be utterly cast down: for the LORD upholdeth him with his hand. (Psalm 37:23-24).

God is speaking through His word and saying, "I know how I feel about you; I know what plans I have for you. Your steps are ordered by me. I strategically planned and designed everything in your life to work out for your good. I did not plan/design your life for you to live any way you choose, because you do not know what is best for you, only I do".

GOD'S LEADING LADY C SPEAKS

Can you think of anything you chose to do on your own that did not turn out well? Well compare that to what God chose for you that you are currently experiencing and enjoying. Take a moment to look at those blessings in your life that did not bring sorrow and shame. If you cannot think of one good thing that God did for you then you need to do some soul searching and see what master you are serving.

The devil cannot give good gifts. He is the "father of all lies" and he is a deceiver that tricks you into believing what he has for you is good and not evil, like he did Eve in the Garden of Eden. He tricked Eve first and then Adam was tricked by Eve, who was only on assignment by the devil and look at the consequences.

When satan tries to come to you in the same way as he did Eve with the apple from the forbidden tree and say "This is good and not evil", you tell him this:

"Lucifer, you need to talk to my Heavenly Father. My Father which art in heaven has everything that I need and it is all in His hands, including my very life. I answer to no one but Him. Where He leads I will follow. If He says proceed, I will proceed and if He says stand, I will stand. I can only hear His voice and I can only be led by His hand. Excuse yourself satan, because I can only see my God-given destiny before me, everything else is a distraction, major deduction.

My Heavenly Father not only created this world. He created me and everything therein. How can you promise me anything when you do not own anything? How can you say I will give you this and I will give you that when you really don't even have a "pot to piss in" as my late grandmother would say? For my Heavenly Father owns everything and supplies my every need daily. I want for nothing. He is the Good Shepherd. I belong to Him! I am not tossed to and fro, I am His child. I am royalty!

I rebuke you satan in the mighty name of Jesus! Get behind me, you have nothing I need or want! To the left, to the left ... everything you own in the box to the left. Take your no good gifts and place them in the box to the left and GO, BABY BYE!

I have a divine appointment to get to. I have to put on my Sunday's Best. The King is waiting on His queen. That modeling career you tried to prevent from taking off. Well I am God's supermodel, one of His elite top models. I am on the runway as we speak, modeling the finest apparel for His glory, the whole armor of God daily. I am His leading lady. I am His "Trophy Woman". So, you can take back the gifts of low self-esteem, low self-worth and low self-confidence you gave me. "I found love under new management" and the rightful owner holds my key to the kingdom.

I have not forgotten how you traded me in like a used, broke down car, but My God tells me daily that I am brand new. I am shining like new money with the light of Christ deep down on the inside of me illuminating outward. I am His glamour girl. You can take back the poverty mentality you gave me because my father has given me the power to get wealth and I am going to go get my Abraham inheritance. You can take back the hurt, pain, and bitter feelings because my God, the true and living God, has renewed me and given me the peace and joy that the even the whole wide world cannot take away from me for the world did not give it to me. He has given me the peace that passeth all understanding. Satan you and your evil workers know nothing about this peace that I am talking about because you don't have a relationship with Him. The air that I breathe, the very breath within me, the blood in my veins are all gifts from Him and God is going to turn everything around in my favor for my good. My mind, body and soul belongs to Him, my life belongs to Him.

Yes satan, you thought you killed me and left me for dead, but I got up out of that grave you dug for me and now I have a new life in Christ, a second chance, a new beginning a new direction in Him. Let the past be the past because it was only part of the process. That chapter in my life is over! Yes, new level, new devil, but I have my Louis Vuitton luggage packed and I plan on moving forward with God. I plan on keeping my mind stayed on Him and He will unfold my future as it was originally planned, right before my eyes and your eyes.

Step by step, day by day, I will trust Him. My mom and dad cannot take credit, my friends cannot take credit, my loved ones cannot take credit. God utilized them in great and special ways, but the sole credit belongs to God. I had to go to God for myself and seek His face and not His hand. I had to go through to get to. Devil, after you had got done with me, I had to go to God just as I was, beat up, broke down, heartbroken and destitute, and He showed me who I am in Him. I had to listen to His voice only and go behind the veil and see things that are new and beyond my imagination in my relationship with Him and He elevated and exalted me from my low estate. There is no turning back from this point. I have tasted His Goodness and there is no turning back. All I can say is Thank You Lord!"

Chapter V

Friendship

A very special chapter in my life to always be treasured ...

A man that hath friends must show himself friendly: and there is a friend that sticketh closer than a brother. (Proverbs 18:24).

"What a friend I have in Jesus, all my sins and griefs to bear,
what a privilege to carry everything to God in prayer".

Throughout the most difficult years of my life, God stuck closer to me than any brother or sister. I can testify that He is a friend to the friendless. This is a special chapter in my life and probably one of the hardest chapters I will every have to write and indeed the longest chapter. I kept this chapter in my heart for many years not wanting to let go of even the pain, the disappointment, the hurt, the sorrow and the grief therein. I thought I needed to hold on to every memory, every moment. It was as if I did not want to remember nor did I want to forget. God saved me and delivered me and set me free from bondage so that I could release what was not meant for me to contain. God had to breath a new breath and new life into me. God held me by my hand and spoke to my spirit these words "Talitha cumi, which is, being interpreted, Damsel, I say unto Thee, arise. (Mark 5:41). I arose and I walked and by His grace and His mercy, I am alive and here today to tell the story.

There was a time in my life not too long ago, that I was isolated within the four walls that I placed myself in. A room where I found "solitude without peace and serenity". Whether it was lying in the bed or lying on the couch reflecting over my life, it was a place that I found comfort and that no one was welcome. This was all set up by the enemy. The enemy wanted to isolate me from individuals that truly loved and cared about me. The enemy had a plan.

Within these four walls, the enemy spoke things to me that were never written in the word of God and were not meant for me to hear, but I listened to every word from the enemy that was spoken and the words became seeds that I allowed to be sown into my mind and my heart and these seeds brought about an unexpected harvest. The enemy began to whisper in my ear and tell me that I was ugly, that I looked old like time spent and that I had been traded in like a used car. The enemy further said "If God loved you, then why do bad things happen to you? Like the loss of your loved ones and friends, relationships that you held near and dear to your heart have been lost and/or destroyed. People you loved dearly have walked out on you. You have no friends. You are alone. You have no help. Where is your help? You have prayed and you have prayed but you are still stuck in this place. Stuck in a rut. Why don't you just lay down and die? Why don't you just take your life, you can see that it is not worth living. What do you have to live for?"

I would often look in the mirror and see a person that my eyes could not bear to see. For many years I felt ugly on the outside but beautiful in the inside and could not understand. I would often stay inside and not go out because I was ashamed and I felt others could see right through me. I felt like a fake, a phony, a person pretending to be all together but knowing deep down inside that I was incomplete. I stayed in the bondage of these four walls way too long. During this time, I would read my bible often falling asleep with my head in the very pages and I would pray without cease, but somehow I would always go out in my own strength and return to the comfort of these same four walls. If I were to describe it properly, "I was imprisoned within my own home, bondage within my own body and mind".

I had thought about the words that the enemy placed in my mind over and over again throughout my life and I had planned two "perfect murders" that no one would be able to find out about or if they did it would be too late, but God's mercy said NO!

The first incident was when I was 24 years old. I was raising two beautiful little girls, ages 1 and 5, and the enemy a/k/a the devil, satan, lucifer, the adversary, **MY IDOL**, was whispering in my ear saying "You have nothing to live for you are not worthy to raise these two beautiful girls. They deserve so much better than you. You are irresponsible. Look at you".

My mother had just gave me a 10-day eviction notice from the landlord from whom we were renting the adjoining duplex home from. The landlord had asked her to personally serve me with the eviction notice. I had just gotten off a long, hard day's work and as my mom handed the eviction notice to me my head dropped as I began to walk slowly to my efficiency apartment with my girls by my side, my soul silently began to cry out to God. My mind was very disturbed. I fed my daughters dinner. I gave them a bubble bath and put on their pajamas. I turned on the TV so they could watch their favorite cartoons. I made sure they were comfortable and content. I then began to contemplate how I would find relief from the pain, misery and suffering that I currently faced. I knew **MY IDOL** had a point because the eviction notice pretty much summed it all up for me. My daughters would be better off without me. We had no where to go. We had been tossed to and fro too many times from friends, family, shelters, etc.

We had just moved into this apartment. I had just graduated from college and I was trying to get some experience under my belt and obtain permanent work and self-sufficiency and now this. My marriage was shaky to say the least, my firstborn son was not in my care and now I was responsible for two beautiful girls that I could not even provide for. So I continued to contemplate how I would take my life. I looked around the apartment and thought about different ways. I was a wimp so I thought what can I do that will be minimal pain. I knew I needed something that would do the job fast and that would not harm the children if they happened to get into it before help arrived. I would definitely have to finish everything off and leave nothing behind for them to get into. I thought long and hard. I did not want the girls to know what I was doing so I secretly plotted and staged my death.

MY IDOL gave me a perfect idea. He said "Remember that acid your mother gave you to unclog the toilet, if you drink that you will die quickly". I pulled back the curtain and looked out the window to my back stairs to see if the bottle of acid was still there. My mom had asked the previous day for me to return it and I placed the bottle of acid on the back steps so that she could retrieve it. My mother lived in the house below me. I made it a point not to leave any poisonous products in the house with my small children for safety reasons. My mother had yet to retrieve the acid from my back stairs, so it was a for sure thing that I had access to it.

I then went to kiss both of my beautiful daughters goodbye. I kissed them and hugged them with tears in my eyes for I had loved them so much and I knew that I did not want to leave them but the pain was so bad that I could no longer bear, so I felt this was best. They would be better off without me. My daughters welcomed the love and affection but they never took their eyes off of the TV for it was just a normal day to them.

I walked away from my daughters toward the door to retrieve the bottle of acid from the back stairs and take my life in the privacy of a locked bathroom. As I approached the door and opened the door and began to walk out onto the back porch, I looked down at the steps as I walked, teary-eyed but very focused on what I was about to do and as I continued to walk down the stairs, I stopped to look in front of me to retrieve the bottle of acid and … the bottle of acid was … no longer there.

ANY QUESTIONS?

My tears dried up instantly and joy filled my spirit as I walked back up the stairs and went back in the house and hugged my daughters so tight and kissed them on their foreheads and cheeks and me and my daughters watched TV together that night as a family until we fell fast into a deep, sweet and peaceful sleep.

That day I realized, without a doubt, that we were not alone in that randown efficiency apartment and that I indeed had something to live for, if only God and my two beautiful daughters, that was enough. I woke up the next day and I never looked back on that day the same. I knew that God's mercy said NO! So the question now was "Why did God's Mercy say NO?" Me and my daughters did eventually move from that place and from that point on, God never closed a door without opening another. God had so much more in store for us than that randown efficiency apartment. Life in God has no limits.

The second incident was when I was 34 years old, I was working full-time at a hospital as a medical transcriptionist, 2nd shift 5:00 p.m. to 1:30 p.m. and 3rd shift 10:00 p.m. to 6:30 a.m. I was simultaneously working on my graduate degree. Attending school full-time and taking night classes, at least three nights a week. I was studying and sleeping when I could and on top of all of that I had the responsibility of caring for my four children at home, ages 15 year old, 11 year old, 3 year old and 2 year old, plus the memory of not being able to care for my oldest son still haunted me. My oldest daughter was becoming very rebellious and going through her teenage years. I was tired and weary to say the least from my present life stressors, unhealthy relationships, no support system in place, the stress from my job, the stress from school in trying to not only attend college, but achieve and maintain good grades while simultaneously trying to be a successful career woman, the best mother and person possible under the circumstances. What hurt the most was my teenage daughter's rebellion. Some how I knew I was the cause of her rebellious behavior and the guilt from this really made me internalize it all.

I began to search in all the wrong places for the answer, when God was the answer. I began to seek help from doctors, counselors, the pastor, I leaned to friends, my boyfriend, my family and no one had the answers. I continuously cried out to God, read my bible and prayed as time permitted. The answer still did not come to me. I felt so alone in my sorrow. I was too tired to have a pity party and I knew that this was not the answer, but I felt like I was so alone in this place. Alone in these four walls again and I was so afraid of failure. I was trying so hard not to fail, but it seemed like everything I touched seemed to fail somehow, someway. I was getting minimal sleep because my hands were indeed full and I had so much on my plate.

MY IDOL began to talk to me and replay everything that was going on in my life, but he made what should have been a molehill in the spirit by faith through my spiritual eyes, look like a huge mountain in the flesh through my natural eyes. Now I knew that if I had the faith of a mustard seed I could move mountains, but I was so tired from trying to do everything in my own strength. Nobody understood how tired I was. Everyone keep cheering me on and pushing me forward, but no one saw or cared that I needed rest. I kept asking for help in so many different ways.

I kept telling every one I spoke to "I am so tired" and they would say "Well, let's just say they kept giving me more of what I did not need". They kept giving me more and more burdens, whether it was a phone call at 10:00 a.m. right after I had just fell fast asleep from a long night's work and or a call right after I had just placed my small children down for a nap and the call would awaken both me and my sleeping babies with the conversation consisting of only "I was just calling to see if I could stop by and visit with you". Sometimes I would just hang up the phone politely and other times well, no comment! Then I would get the calls right after I had placed the babies down for another nap and had fallen back to sleep and the conversation consisted of only "I am bored and so and so did this and so and so did that ...".

Then I would get the calls from the bill collectors, from the school, from the truant officers, from the legal/court system regarding my teenage child getting in trouble almost daily. I could not take the phone off the hook because as soon as I did that the whole world would fall apart or end and I would be the only one that did not get the phone call, the email or the memo, you know what I mean? My daughter's grades were failing, she basically stopped going to school. She started hanging out with the wrong crowds.

I had no where to turn, so I went to doctor after doctor and poured out my heart to them and they prescribed me depression and anxiety medication because they thought I was depressed and anxious. What a diagnosis. Imagine that! So I took the medicine and I was so high. It felt good to be legally high for free because my job's health insurance paid for the doctors' visits and the medicine, but guess what, four hours later, the problems were still there. So now what?

I went back to the follow-up appointment with the doctor and told him that I was high most of the time but the symptoms and the problems still existed. One doctor asked me "Do you notice a difference in coping with current life stressors while on the medicine?" I said "I mostly notice that I am high most of the time". He said "Have others noticed a difference, like your coworkers?" I said "I am not sure if my coworkers even notice a difference before or after the medication, but my teenage daughter notices a huge difference because I seem to be in agreement with everything she does". He then asked "Are you in any type of pain?", as he looked down at a form that he was now filling out. He further asked me to rate my pain on a scale of 0 to 10 with 0 meaning no pain and 10 meaning extensive pain. I wanted to say 10 for emotional pain, but I knew from the pain rating chart on the wall that he was referring to physical pain so I said "0". I was probably high as a kite then and not a reliable historian. He then increased the dose of my medications and told me to drink a glass of wine to relax me and calm me down, as needed. I thought to myself "Okay, now I will be a happy and calm drug addict and alcoholic with the same problems when I become sober". WOW!

My teenage daughter was estranged now. We basically had no relationship other than the times I would go to the streets looking for her any time of day and any time of night, even in dangerous areas where I knew it was not safe to go or be. My other smaller children were now fending for themselves because all my energy was now on saving my teenage daughter from the streets. My other children at home noticed that I was not my typical self because I was basically allowing them to do anything they wanted to do. If they said mom can I go to ... I would immediately say yes before they even finished the question or sentence. I was so high on the prescribed drugs. They started to act out by tearing up the house and making unnecessary messes and getting in trouble just to get some attention. Everything was "A, okay".

I was so high it did not even matter. They could have burnt the house down and I would have been like "Don't worry, be happy". Yeah, so you know now how bad off I was. Everything was happy, happy, happy on my "happy pills". Everything was "take a chill pill" on my anxiety drugs. I began to grieve internally and externally by my actions and behaviors. The grief was from the loss of self. I had no idea who I was anymore.

PRETTY LIKE GLORIA

My best friend Gloria was the only one I could trust during this time with everything I was currently facing. We became very, very close friends and we confided in each other. She had recently been diagnosed with lupus and I did not know anything about the illness but she began to share with me her illness, her life and her world.

I was very fond of Gloria and although she was younger than me, I looked up to her and I wanted to be just like her. There was nothing that I would not do for her. As I began to share my life and my world with Gloria, Gloria did what she does best, she took action. Gloria intervened and became not only my best friend and God-sister, but a God-mother and auntie to my children.

At the time, she was going to nursing school and I was so proud of her. It is funny how our relationship started. Gloria was a lot like me. She did not allow people to get close to her because she had been hurt so many times before and so we shared this bond. We trusted each other and could share our heart with each other. We appreciated each other and had an unwritten covenant that we would always be there for each other.

Gloria was the sister/friend that I never had. Someone just like me who understood me. She was a single mother of two kids and divorced. She was an excellent mother and spent quality time with her children and her children loved her and she loved them. I remember going over to her house and she would be watching TV and her children would be right at her side, stuck like glue and Gloria would hug and caress them. They were a team. Everyone worked together in their respective roles. They were so happy together and it showed. They were small children but they were very protective of their mother and she was very protective of them. I definitely wanted the same for my children. Gloria and I experienced some of the same day to day struggles. She knew firsthand about being in unhealthy relationships and recovering from the same.

Gloria had made a commitment with me to begin to put God *First* in her life. I don't want to take full credit for leading Gloria to Christ, but I do know that I once invited Gloria to church with me on one occasion and she came. As I continued to go to church with my family, she continued to go to church with her family. As we continued to fellowship with one another, we both grew closer and stronger as friends and closer and stronger as sisters in the Lord.

Gloria looked up to me because of my faith in God and because of my strength and determination and my endurance to win against all odds. She cherished the "real me", the "real me" that I was hiding from everyone else. The "real me" that was broken and shattered into pieces and that was trying with everything I had to put the pieces back together. I did not have to put on facades for Gloria. I could say to her "I am hurting, I am wounded, I am sad, I am afraid, I am alone, I am in pain" and she would listen and understand. She would do her best to be there for me and comfort me and I would do the same for her.

She was so beautiful to me, inside and out. I loved how she carried herself and would often ask for fashion tips and she would eagerly help by doing my hair, letting me borrow an outfit or even allowing me to keep something of hers that we both treasured. I still have a white knit dress that she let me borrow for an occasion. It looked much better on her but when I placed it on it was as if I not only wore her dress, I wore her spirit. She was known for her fur coats and fine apparel that she picked up at different second hand stores, thrift shops, bargain sales and specialty boutiques and shops. She was so giving. She would give gifts just because. I would try to convince her not to buy so much and to save her money, but she would not listen. She was determined to bless those that she cared about. She reminded me so much of me, giving, loving, loyal and thoughtful.

She kept going in and out of the hospital and I was always there by her side. I prayed over her. I loved her. We were going to win this. God would never take her from me because He knew she meant so much to me. He was going to heal her. She was going to be yet another miracle that took place in my life.

I remember one day visiting her in the hospital. I always had a way of making her smile and vice versa. We would laugh about life, the good, the bad and the ugly. We would laugh and cry together. This time during the visit it was different. I could not cheer her up. She was down in her spirits. She had to take her nursing exam soon and the deadline was quickly approaching and she did not have the money. Her graduation was right around the corner. As she lay in the hospital bed not looking up at me, but continuing to pour her heart out to me with tears in her eyes. I held her hand and I said with all sincerity "Have faith in God! He is going to work it all out for you and while you are having faith in God, let me help you. I will give you the money for your exam and I want you to take it and pass it and not worry anymore. I don't want you to worry about anything. You have enough to deal with trying to recover from your present illness".

She immediately sat up in her bed and looked up at me and the smile on her face was priceless. Her spirit was lifted that moment. She knew that I was a woman of my word. She knew I was not like the rest. She knew that I wished above all things for everyone I came in contact with to prosper and be in good health even as their soul prospereth, just like our Heavenly Father. She knew most importantly that I really meant this scripture for her for my ongoing love and kindness toward her and her family proved it.

A lot of people talk and they have no action, but I was just like Gloria, we both believed in action and believed that talk was cheap. That is why a lot of times in life I never opened my mouth to speak, but I would always be quick to act without speaking. This time was different, I had to open my mouth and act and BE THE VOICE TO SAY "YOU WILL WIN .... I AM GOING TO HELP YOU!" So Gloria thanked me from the bottom of her heart and said "I will pay you, I promise, as soon as I get my check I will repay you". I said to her "Don't worry about repaying me; God is going to repay me. You are going to repay me by passing the test. You need only to focus on passing the test." We hugged each other and we laughed and made jokes. I then had to leave to get back to work for I worked at the hospital she was presently an inpatient.

Later on Gloria passed that test with flying colors and she graduated from nursing school and was offered a full-time position as an RN at a local hospital even before graduation. I was so proud of her. I did not attend her graduation ceremony because I was within my four walls in a depressed state and did not have the strength to prepare myself and four kids for the occasion. I think Gloria may have been just a little disappointed, but not really because I stood by her side all the way. Actually, I think I was more disappointed in myself for not attending than she was disappointed in me.

Not too long after her graduation her mother became ill with cancer. Gloria confided in me during this time and I was there for her to lean on and I tried to comfort her by just being a listening ear. I truly understood her feelings for I had experienced the pain and sorrow of loved ones being ill and had even lost loved ones due to illnesses and other traumatic causes. I internalized her pain, her sorrow and her suffering and I attentively listened. I wanted to act, but this was a time to listen. This was not a time to laugh or to even make jokes. This was serious. We talked and we talked and we talked. I encouraged her in the Lord. We prayed. I then closed the conversation like I always do with "I love you" and she would always say "I love you too" in return and we would then hang up the phone. I was always uncomfortable saying I love you, especially to a female, but since the loss of my grandmother I said to myself that I would never leave someone's presence that I cared about without saying I love you, for the next second is not promised to us. So, we ended the conversation and I went fast to sleep.

I recall before ending the conversation that night I had briefly mentioned to Gloria something that concerned me, in that I valued her advice. I had been having symptoms that I was unsure about and I asked her advice as a nurse and she tried to assist me with what she thought might bring me some relief or even remedy the symptoms, then she followed by saying, "Hell, I don't know how can I help you when I am sick myself, I can't even help myself". We both just laughed out loud. So I kept my symptoms and she kept her illness and symptoms, but both of us knew that laughter was like medicine for the soul. Gloria felt better and I did too at the end of all of our conversations.

When I awoke in the morning I began to get ready for the day. The phone was ringing. It was an early morning call and I do not normally take morning calls because I am too pressed for time with all that I have to do. As I ran toward the phone, I was wondering who was on the other end of the receiver because I had to be at work at 8:30 a.m. and it was about 7:00 a.m. and I still had to get myself and the kids ready, drop them off at school and then get to work on time.

Well, it was Gloria and she never calls me this early so she had my full attention. She told me that she had been admitted to the hospital emergently. She then went on to discuss with me that her mother had been admitted to the same hospital on another floor and that the doctors said her mother's undetected cancer was now progressive and that she may only have six months to live. So now she was not only grieving her illness but her mother's illness and I too was grieving both. My heart dropped. I said "I am so sorry, is there anything I can do?" I was thinking to myself, "I can pray". She said "No" with a choked up voice. I said "I am on my way to the hospital, I will be right there". I dropped everything I was doing. I got the kids to school and I then headed straight to the hospital.

When I arrived at the hospital she was visiting with her sister and an aunt and she introduced me to them. I was so pleased to meet them because Gloria was like family to me, so they too were like family to me. I am never tardy for work or call in or miss work, but this was so serious to me. I told my supervisor with tears in my eyes and a broken voice that I would be in late today because I had a family emergency. My supervisor said "Okay" in a concerned response for she knew it was not the norm for me to call in. She knew I had a track record of being a reliable, loyal, dedicated and a hardworking employee. My supervisor at the time also had a friend who was presently suffering from lupus, so after I later explained the situation to her, she did not even think about writing me up for this incident and the fact that this was my first call in to date, she simply pardoned me. I was very thankful and grateful but at this time nothing mattered more to me than to make sure Gloria was going to be okay.

Gloria and I began to talk as I stood by her side and she introduced me to her aunt and sister with high spirits saying "This is my beautiful friend, isn't she beautiful?" I said "You are my beautiful friend, I wan't to be "Pretty Like Gloria". It was the norm for her to be lying in a hospital bed with her hair all done up, looking like a hot diva with blue eye shadow, red lipstick, top and bottom of her eyelids lined, long eyelashes, foundation and blush and I will never forget the black dotted on beauty mark above either side of her lip depending on her mood, fresh pedicure and manicure, with her high fashion outfit and heels snugged away in the hospital closet ready for her departure. She always looked like a glamour girl instead of a patient. She had the prettiest and brightest smile. Her smile could brighten a room. Her smile was contagious. I used to tease her and say "You are going to mess around and get you a doctor looking all cute up in here". She would just laugh and say "Uh Uh, they looking at you, they are more concerned about you than my condition". We would both just laugh endlessly.

I had made up a song for my baby daughter De'Jonay who was Gloria's God-daughter from birth and I would sing it to my daughter daily. My daughter was now 2 years old and she would smile from ear to ear every time I sang this song and Gloria would just laugh at the song. It was so corny. The words were "Pretty like Gloria, Pretty Like Gloria, Pretty like Gloria ……" Me and my daughter would sing it and the rest of my family would look at us like we were crazy. Gloria was everything I wanted to be, that is for sure.

My heart was right and I meant her well, always. We continued to talk and laugh about the song and we talked about De'Jonay and other things, nothing about herself or her illness or the grief she was presently facing because it was too difficult to bear. Nothing about me or my problems, we only focused on the happy things and good things in life that were important to us like friendship and family.

We then began to escape reality and began to live a fantasy in that moment thinking, dreaming and believing in a happy ending story. I had to get ready to leave her presence because I had to get to work and I really did not want to go because my spirit told me this time was different, but I did not know or I did not want to accept this truth so I continued to hold on for life to this moment and did not want it to ever end. She completed me in her own special way. She filled a void in my life that no one else but her could fill in that season. Her last words to me on this day were "You are too beautiful and you are too good for him". I listened attentively and I knew what she meant and I sensed the seriousness of her comment and I received it with full understanding, but I did not want her to worry about me. I wanted to do all the worrying for the both of us. I said to her jokingly, but serious "I know ..., but if I get rid of him, who else are we going to get to cut our grass?" We both laughed out loud with a big hearty laugh. The whole room was laughing, but they did not know what we were talking about, but we did. She then said jokingly, "You are right ... you are definitely right".

As we continued to laugh, I then said "I don't want to go but I have to leave to go to work, but if you need anything, I mean anything, I want you to call me, okay?" I repeated myself twice because I knew she was just like me not good about asking for help. I went on to say "I will be praying for you and your mother and I want you to know that I love you". She nodded her head as to say "Okay" with a smile and then said "I love you too". We gave each other a hug before parting, but this time the hug was different. It was the type of hug where you don't want to let go but you know you have to.

I went to work that day grieving over my best friend's present state and now her mother's state as well. I began to pray and intercede, but I really did not know what to pray or even what I prayed. I believe God had to have interceded. What I remember and my memory is not well during this time because it was so traumatic to me, but I remember that was the last time I talked to my best friend and that was the last time we laughed together, that was the last time I made her smile and that was the last time she made me smile. She had taken a turn for the worse after she was released home from the hospital that evening and had slipped into a coma.

I remember it was late at night when I got the news after several unanswered and unreturned phone calls to her home. I rushed to the hospital to the intensive care waiting room that was now full of family and friends, some of them I knew and some of them I didn't, but it was a waiting room of people that loved and cared for Gloria deeply. Everyone waited patiently to see her because only two to three people at a time were allowed a 10 minute visit. I was consumed by it all. I was numb. I was so sorrowful at that moment. Nothing else mattered at that time. I just wanted to see her and make sure she was okay. I don't even know if I prayed. I am sure I did because that is what I do when I do not know what else to do.

I do remember when I went in the room I almost did not recognize her because her hair was unkept and her eyes were rolled back in her head and she was in a coma and I touched her forehead and prayed over her with the prayer of faith. I held her hand, but her hand was limp and it was as if she was lifeless. I do remember praying and saying "Gloria give me a sign if you hear me" and she moved just like my firstborn son did in the incubator when they said he would never move his limbs and he kicked his legs right before my eyes and the doctors said it was only a reflex. Gloria moved and opened her eyes briefly and in my mind I thought, "maybe that was just a reflex", but in my heart I knew she knew I was there. I held back some of the tears because I could have fell apart that very moment, but instead I attempted to maintain a strong appearance on the outside and on the inside, I internalized everything.

At the end of my allowed 10 minute visit, I did not even ask God how or why, I just left out the room. Before I left out the room I held her hand and looked down at her and I hugged her and I said "I love you" and kissed her on her forehead and there was a long pause. As I began to walk away slowly toward the door and looking back at her and holding onto every second, this was the first time since I had known her that she did not say "I love you" back. I waited in the waiting room afterwards until it got really late and I knew I had to get home to my family who were waiting on me.

When I got home that night, I returned to the safety of my four walls and layed in my bed and I cried and I cried and I cried. I was mentally and physically drained from everything my past, my present and now with my best friend in a coma my future looked doom and gloom. I continued to cry hysterically.

I often think back from time to time on the words **MY IDOL** said to me that night "I am sick of you acting like this ... I have needs too ... you spend all your time and your attention on everybody else but me ... you and Gloria were not even that good of friends anyway ...".

My tears dried up instantly in that moment, but I knew the wounds and the scars from those very words would take God to heal. **MY IDOL** would often bring that incident back to my remembrance and I would often think "Was Gloria really not my friend?" Even after her visitation and the funeral, even after every special moment we spent together and that our families shared together, even after all the special gifts and the quality time we spent together as friends and sisters, the laughs together, the love we shared together, even after all the good times because there were no bad times, even after she made me pledge to be her friend by making me walk up and down three flights of stairs, during my first, second and third trimester of pregnancy, on a regular basis to see her and sometimes she would be at home and would not open the door because she did not want me to see her sick and in a depressed state.

I would not give up on her. I would just go home to call her and leave her a message on her answering machine that said "I was just checking on you to make sure everything is okay, I love you, call me when you can, bye". When she returned my call it was always the same we would pick right back up where we left off and I would climb up and down those three flights of stairs again and again just to sit on her couch and laugh and cry and laugh and cry. Sometimes she would come over my house, but usually I would go to hers. That was the norm. You mean to tell me one word from **MY IDOL** and I even question "Was she really my friend?" Unbelievable! This is evidence that the devil is truly a liar!

Back to the second incident, I had suffered the loss of both grandmothers, both grandfathers, an uncle and now my best friend, my teenage daughter was acting crazy, everyone I loved and cared about in different ways let me know that they were not getting my undivided attention and that they felt unloved and neglected, but not once did I say "What about me?". Not once did I say "Does anybody care about how I feel?" NO! I was silenced by the pain and I just kept quiet and I just kept giving and giving and giving and never receiving anything in return. I kept loving with the love of God even when I never really received love in return. The kids were now basically fending for themselves, my health was failing right before my eyes, but I did not care about myself. I only cared about others for I personally wanted to die. I began to stop taking care of myself and I started taking care of everyone and everything else instead.

MY MARTHA/MARY EXPERIENCE – GOD WAS CALLING ME TO SIT AT HIS FEET, BUT I WAS JUST TOO BUSY

The fights continued, the arguments continued, the babies kept coming, half of them I believe I conceived in a deep sleep because with each positive pregnancy result I was like "How did this happen?" I did not drink so I could not blame it on the alcohol so I had to blame it on the happy pills. I worked 70+ hours a week, I went to school full-time, I took care of every situation that came my way, but not my own situations. Then I did it! You might ask "Did what?" I successfully took care of everyone and everything but myself and I learned a very valuable lesson and that lesson is "You can't please and make everybody happy, no matter how hard you try!"

I started experiencing symptoms, some I questioned and some I ignored. One morning I woke up after a few hours of rest, maybe three hours divided. I had two small babies to care for who were depending on me and my other children were in school. I tried to perform as usual but this day was different. I didn't quite feel right. I felt lightheaded and dizzy, my heart was racing, my chest was pounding, and I was sweating all over. Lying down until I felt better was not an option, because I had to care for my babies. I kept trying to perform my day-to-day activities as usual but I couldn't. I began to pray. My symptoms were still there. I then called the ER and explained to them my symptoms hoping they would be able to give me a home remedy. They asked that I come to the ER to be seen. I was very reluctant because I did not want to take the babies to the ER but at this point I had no choice. So I prepared myself and my two babies for a trip to the ER. When I arrived at the ER and went through triage, I explained to the medical staff as best I could that I was having symptoms of chest palpitations, rapid heart beat, sweating, lightheadedness and dizziness. I had both babies on my hip at this point because they were both unable to walk well independently being born 11 months apart.

As I continued to explain my symptoms to the ER nurse and as he continued with the physical exam he looked at my physical appearance, my emotional state and the babies on both hips and he said very kindly "No wonder you are having chest pain, rapid heart beat, lightheadedness and dizziness, I would too if I had two babies on my hips. I would probably be having a stroke or a heart attack". We both laughed out loud, but we both knew it was not funny. After I had been seen by the ER physician, the ER nurse came back in the room and discussed my discharge information which included the following recommendations, reduce the stress in my life and follow up with my primary care physician. No one ever told me how to successfully reduce the stress in my life, but I was discharged home with my discharge papers in my hand and two babies on both hips.

I often think back from time to time on the words **MY IDOL** said to me that day "There is nothing even wrong with you ... you're this ... you're that ... and now you're ... (you fill in the blanks)". I was thinking to myself "Yeah, there is nothing wrong with me other than the fact that I am about to have a nervous breakdown that just went undiagnosed". All I knew was I had two small babies on my hips and it felt like I was having a stroke, heart attack, and an aneurysm all at the same time. My first guess was that I was having a panic attack but that would be unlikely in that I was on anxiety and depression medication, so I just went to the hospital to be evaluated just to be safe. How selfish of me to think about my well being, huh? What in the world?

MY IDOL used this incident and other incidents to make me feel like I was being selfish and only thinking of myself and trying to make others feel sorry for me "When nothing was even wrong with me". The truth is I knew that I was selfless at the very core of my heart. This incident not only hurt me deeply it haunted me over and over again. Although I knew this was another lie from **MY IDOL**, I remained silent because I did not have a voice. It seemed as if every time I would speak it was as if no one was listening. Absolutely no one was listening but God! I kept moving forward, fighting harder and stronger with whatever strength I had left, mainly fumes. I was a walking ticking time bomb.

The next day I went to my college internship in a hospital setting. I was a student counselor working with young teenage girls and young women diagnosed with eating disorders. I was required to complete a 1 year working (nonpaid) internship at an approved site in order to gain training/working experience as a counselor and complete my degree requirements. My clients really liked me and looked up to me, just as I had looked up to Gloria and I really cherished this. I tried to talk to them as not only a professional counselor in training, but also a layperson, who genuinely cared about their overall well-being.

I also had the opportunity to work with mental health patients at the hospital. I functioned very well in my capacity as a student counselor and was able to work well with diverse populations. I have never had a problem working with and/or relating to diverse populations and never viewed or judged or treated anyone different because of the color of their skin, race, age, gender, creed, religion, sexuality, class, status, appearance, etc. I loved everyone with the love of God.

My clients accepted me as someone who genuinely cared about them, regardless of my shortcomings and regardless of their shortcomings. As a student counselor, in an effort to establish rapport with my clients, I began to look more at the commonalities we shared than the differences. They did not see that I was depressed or that I had been wounded and hurt and that I faced some of the same day-to-day life stressors that they were currently experiencing and suppressing. What we shared in common was that we were all looking for an answer, the same answer. That answer was to be healed and made whole yet not embracing in totality the one who could heal us and make us whole.

As a vessel of God for His service, I began to not only counsel the ladies I worked with at the eating disorders inpatient setting, but also minister to these young women for God desires that we all be healed and made whole. I would minister to them and lead by example. I would eat with them. I would teach them that food is not bad if you eat the right foods and the right amount of food and that all food groups were good if you eat in moderation. I would tell that not to worry about their weight, but to be more concerned about maintaining a healthy body weight based on their body mass index and not based on their actual body size. I would eat different foods in front of them, even food I did not like to eat for it was hospital food and it did not always look or taste good. I would talk to them as I ate and I would say "See I am eating and I am okay and if you eat you will be okay". Little did I know that I was not okay and the food I was eating, I probably should not have been eating.

They had a fear of food. They felt food was the enemy and that it would make them gain weight. They too had a battle going on in their minds. The enemy was trying to defeat them in their mind just as he was trying to defeat me in my mind. They thought I was beautiful, even when I felt I was ugly. I had the same distorted image when I looked in the mirror as they had when they looked in the mirror and saw an out-of-proportion body image. Some of them would not even look in the mirror or get on a scale to be weighed because of fear of what they would see.

I saw them as beautiful and they saw me as beautiful. It was important to me to show them that they were beautiful and that it was important for them to be a healthy body weight in order to be healthy. I educated them on how to obtain and maintain optimal health and well-being by not only eating healthy foods, but by ongoing care and maintenance of their mind, body, soul and spirit through proper physical and spiritual food, exercise and rest. I wanted them to see that the very word "diet" contained a negative connotation in that it contained the three letters "die". I wanted to help them regain their focus on living instead of "die-t-ing". I encouraged them that in order to live, they would have to make some changes in their lifestyle. I even went further and told them what these changes were.

These individuals had suffered hurt, pain and sorrow from abuse and neglect and experienced physical, emotional, social, financial, job, spiritual, family stress and other stressors, just like I had. I was a healed helper in practice. I was growing into my ministry "Total Wellness in God". I was growing through the whole process. I absolutely loved helping people that were hurting and in need of assistance. My clients slowly began to trust me and began to eat in front of me and with me. I would counsel them, but they were really counseling me. I wanted to see them all succeed in life.

Since I had established a good rapport with them from the beginning, they began to trust me and open up to me more and more. We laughed together and they began to release their hurt and pain through tears and I retained mine and began to carry theirs. At that time in my life I felt I needed to be strong for everyone. "Never let them see you sweat", remember that commercial ad? I felt I had to be strong for everyone, because ... I had no specific reason, just because. I had to be strong for them on the outside, but on the inside I was literally dying. I wanted them to believe what I preached even though I did not even believe or practice in totality what I preached.

I worked Monday through Friday from 8:00 a.m. to 4:30 p.m. at my internship. I then went to my full-time job and worked 5:00 p.m. to 1:30 a.m. Going home for a few hours only to turn around and do the same thing in a few hours. This day and night was different. I began to have feelings of lightheadedness, blurred vision, the computer screen was blurry. I started to see three heads instead of one on each individual that passed in the hallway. I worked for a group of doctors at the hospital, so one doctor in particular came in my office and I said to him, "I see three of you" and he laughed out loud because I was known to be sarcastic and make people laugh, but this time I was serious. Out of all the doctors who worked in the department, he should have known something was wrong because he knew firsthand about the symptoms I was having. He was so focused that evening on his work that he was not aware that his intervention was needed at this time. I don't think I ever mentioned this incident to him later for I knew we both did not know the nature of my symptoms at that particular time.

Due to my strange behavior that night, my coworkers in the office began to wonder if everything was okay with me, including me. One of my coworkers, Jennifer, turned around and said "Are you okay?" and I never answered, but asked her "What are the symptoms of diabetes?" At that time I did not know why these words came out my mouth, how I was able to ask this specific question or even why I asked this question. Do you see God in this? Yes, I had a physician already at work. She then began to tell me the symptoms, but it was as if I somehow already knew what she was going to say before she spoke it. Her words were just confirmation. I knew the symptoms of diabetes in the natural from my grandmother's illness, but God was revealing to me now in the spirit. God had already told me beforehand to do an internet search on the symptoms that I had been questioning for months now. Remember months ago I confided in Gloria about the symptoms I had been having? Remember months ago I had went to the ER because I was having unexplained symptoms?

I thought to myself everything has to be okay because everything checked out okay at my last ER visit. All the lab work and tests came back normal. I was currently being treated by doctors, counselors. Everything had to be okay or someone would have told me different, right? Well, God had all along been telling me different, but I was just too busy to listen!

The symptoms were just as I had already known, but did not understand everything in full for it was given to me in part by God or maybe I was just receiving everything in part by God i.e. 25 pound unexplained weight loss, blurred vision, dizziness, frequent urination, sweating, irritability, mood swings, depression, anxiety, fatigue, etc. Remember the ER visit for unexplained chest palpitations and sweating with two kids on my hips with lightheadedness, racing heart, dizziness, sweating, mood swings, irritability, fatigue, etc. God was revealing to me these signs and symptoms then and now. He had been speaking all along and I did not take heed to His voice. I was too focused on everything and everyone else.

God was telling me to sit at His feet and He was going to take care of me and teach me how to take care of myself and my household, but I was just too busy trying to ... I just kept going full speed ahead to ... I don't know why I was too busy or where I was going. The bible says in (Matthew 7:13-14), "Enter ye in at the straight gate: for wide is the gate, and broad is the way, that leadeth to destruction, and many there be which go in by it: Because straight is the gate, and narrow is the way which leads to life, and there are few who find it". I do believe I took the road where the sign said "Destruction, turn right and keep straight, full speed ahead".

My coworker, Jennifer, was a Type 1 diabetic and she asked me if I wanted to check my blood glucose levels and I said "Yes". She showed me how to check my glucose levels with her Accu-Check blood glucose meter. The result came up on the screen. It said "SEEK MEDICAL ATTENTION NOW" Both of our eyeballs met and locked and we ran to the ER like grade school kids to seek help in fear of what this meant for she told me that she had never seen her blood glucose meter give this result. When we got to the emergency room I told triage staff what had just happened in the department and they rushed me into an exam room and they rechecked my levels and it said the same result on their Accu-Check blood glucose meter. They then drew my blood to obtain a more accurate blood glucose level through a complete blood workup that they sent to the lab for a stat result. The standard Accu-Check blood glucose meter will only measure glucose levels up to 500 and anything over 500 you will get the "SEEK MEDICAL ATTENTION NOW" alert.

The nurse then injected insulin subcutaneously in an effort to bring my glucose levels down to a normal level, "on a wing and a prayer". I was calm as ever as everyone else scurried about. My coworker was shaking and pale white in the face. I tried to comfort her for she looked like she had seen a ghost. The medical director of the ER came into my exam room and he knew me personally as I was the former ER secretary and he said to me "You are one lucky lady, you were at stroke levels". I just smiled because I knew I was blessed and not lucky. The ER doctor then went on to further explain to me my diagnosis of type 1 diabetes. It was as if I had tuned out everything he had said and stood on the word of God that said "By His stripes I am healed!"

I began to claim and profess "By His stripes I am healed". I then asked the doctor if he could quickly give me whatever medicine I needed to take now or a prescription to take with me and I would get it filled later because I had to get back to work in that I only had a 30 minute lunch break. He politely said "You don't understand you are getting ready to be admitted". I was looking at him like "You don't understand I have a 30 minute lunch break and I have already claimed the word of God that says "By His stripes I am healed!" I really liked and respected this doctor, but I was thinking to myself "What part don't you understand?" Now this got me nowhere. The supervisor of nursing had been contacted by phone to personally come to the ER to inform me that I could most certainly not go back to work. The supervisor of nursing was in charge of all the floors including the floor I worked on so I basically had to surrender my will of going back to work that night and comply.

I then placed a call home to inform my family. My children were so concerned about me and when I explained to my daughters, Krishina and Che' my condition they asked "What does this mean?" I told them that this means "Mommy has to start taking better care of herself". That was an understatement, ya think? My family really did not know what to do without me for I was in the hospital about three days. My middle daughter Che' blamed herself for my illness in that she thought her favorite candy bar Hershey's Cookies n Crème gave me the illness because she would always buy me one daily when she bought herself one. It was our little shared treat. I assured her that this was not the case. Nevertheless, Che' nor I never ate our favorite candy bar again. Me and Che' had a special bond that I will share later.

Sure enough, my family managed to survive while I was in the hospital for three days and I managed to survive three days without my family. During my hospital stay the staff took me through a crash course of Diabetes 101 self-care. I was not given the option of taking pills. I was placed directly on injections. I absolutely hate needles and I remember once telling my grandmother when I was very young that "If I ever get diabetes I would die because I cannot give up sweets and I could not give myself a shot with a needle" and she said to me ever so sweetly "Well baby, you will just have to die then". I remember those words, "Oh, too well". For now I know she was telling me the truth. Even though she was old and as young children you don't always think adults know much, yet indeed they know everything. Grandma knew the truth. She knew that if you don't give up sweets, meaning excessive intake of white sugar, starches, carbohydrates that can kill your pancreas, you run the risk of getting the diagnosis of diabetes and if you obtain the diagnosis of diabetes and don't take the insulin shots required to keep your glucose levels within normal limits, you will surely die. Grandma did not believe in sugarcoating the truth. I had to first practice giving injections on an orange and then myself.

I remember going to my first follow-up appointment after discharge from the hospital to see an endocrinologist specialist. I told the endocrinologist specialist that I was going to eat right, exercise and beat this and I asked him could I try the pills instead of the insulin injections. He said to me very kindly "Honey, I know you mean well but there are marathon athletes who are in the best of shape who are living with diabetes, but you sure can try to take the pills, you don't have anything to lose by trying". I tried the pills for one day and my glucose levels were at stroke levels again, so I surrendered my will again and agreed to continue on the insulin injections.

Shortly thereafter, my medical insurance no longer covered this particular endocrinologist specialist because he was no longer on the network provider list. This was unfortunate because I really liked this endocrinologist, he was the best in the region but unaffordable without medical coverage. I was referred to another endocrinologist specialist who on my first appointment told me frankly as I discussed with him optimistically that I believed somehow or someway I was going to be healed from my infirmity, he said "Diabetes is until death, for there is no cure". He then ordered a plethora of unwarranted lab tests to rule out cancer, thyroid disorders and every body and organ function test you can name, I mean a complete workup and some.

He then told me to take high blood pressure medicine to prevent high blood pressure, a baby aspirin to prevent stroke and heart attack. He then suggested I take cholesterol medication to lower my cholesterol and other medications to prevent kidney failure, thyroid dysfunction, and other organ failure, etc. I tried sample after sample of different medications and guess what, I only had one diagnosis of diabetes, what was all the rest about? I started experiencing side effects from the high blood pressure medication. I began to have blurred vision, lightheadedness and a feeling that I was going to blackout. I would bend over and when I would stand up, I would see what looked like twinkling stars before me.

I said to myself, "No way am I going to continue taking all of this medication and I am definitely not going back to him". I did go back to him one more time and my glucose levels were at coma levels in his office and I treated myself by injecting insulin to try to bring my levels within a normal range. I explained to the doctor with great detail my pre-meal glucose levels, what I ate, how much insulin I took and my post-meal glucose levels and how much insulin I took to correct the high levels and he said bluntly "If your levels are high you are not supposed to eat". I thought to myself, "Well, who knew, excuse me!"

He never said anything positive to me, it was always doom and gloom and more samples to try. I felt like a guinea pig. He was the complete opposite of my first endocrinologist specialist. I was very concerned and I immediately sought out his replacement and was very successful. I managed to find a very optimistic young, smart, qualified, nice, kind doctor with good bedside manners who assured me that he was competent and that he could manage my diabetes and ongoing care. Thank God!

Every time I went to see him I felt good about my managed care. He would always take the time to sit down and listen to my concerns and help me come up with ideas, suggestions, alternatives and resolutions that I not only understood, but that also fit my lifestyle and met the needs of my ongoing care. He included me in the process and decision making. When he praised me for optimal lab work results, he would always say "What have you been doing your lab work looks great?" and I would say "I have been praying without cease and taking care of myself". He would just smile and say "Keep up the good work". When my lab work did not look optimal, he would sincerely say "We need to do this and this in order to better manage your diabetes for we want you to be around a long time for not only yourself, but your family and your loved ones who depend on you". He would then look at me directly and await my response. I cannot say that I was the best patient because I tried to treat myself a lot on my own, but I would always listen to him and he listened to me. That is what I needed was a doctor who listened. I was growing into the process of taking care of myself properly. I was not there yet.

BACK TO LIFE AS USUAL

I cannot believe this. I have to give myself injections with a needle every time I eat or drink. I just told my clients that food was good and that it would not hurt you and now I am sick and cannot eat certain foods, especially the ones I like. WOW! I just preached on this and said that diet means "die-t" and now I am on a "permanent die-t". From this point forward, I never saw food the same way. Even though food was not the root of the problem, I placed the blame there. I had a new set of rules. I will never eat anything sweet or salty again. I won't eat anything greasy or saucy. I won't eat this or that or this or that. I won't do this or that. In my personal perspective, everything was now "black or white". WOW! How would I minister to and counsel my clients and tell them that food was okay now?

My illness was a gradual process that became progressive when I ignored the early warning signs and symptoms that God and my body were giving me time and time again. My standing rule was that I was just too busy to get sick! I could not get sick for who would take care of everyone and everything if I didn't? In the past, there were times I would be driving around town with a car full of kids and I would have blurred vision and could not even see in front of me. God would tell me to go to the ER. Instead I knew I had the kids and did not want to take them to the ER so I would attempt to treat the symptoms myself.

One time I pulled over into the parking lot of Walgreens drugstore on my way home from running errands with the kids and I had my middle daughter Che', who was always my "dedicated nurse on duty" even as a small child, go in the store and buy some orange juice because I felt like I had to pass out and I felt if I drank some juice it would give me a second wind, some energy and I would feel better for I was so tired. This tiredness went untreated and undiagnosed for months or maybe years, because I was the typical "overstressed, overworked mother that was not getting enough rest". No one suspected the red flag, possible diabetes.

Well anyone who knows anything about diabetes knows that orange juice was not the correct choice in this particular case because orange juice raises your blood sugar levels instead of lowering it. For example if you had a 500 glucose level and you drink orange juice you would probably have a 1000 glucose level which correlates into being at stroke levels, in a coma or dead. Well, I drank the orange juice and drove home with my children in the car. When I got home I got the kids fed and situated comfortably and I laid down to rest because I was so tired. I was treating myself or let's be honest and say God was my physician even then. Even in my disobedience, He was keeping me.

Untreated diabetes and high glucose levels cause you to feel tired, fatigued and weary. No wonder I was experiencing these symptoms. In addition, the recent ER and doctor visits, lab work and tests in which I had chest palpitations, unexplained sweating, frequent urination, irritability, mood swings, etc., all signs of untreated diabetes. I was also having severe, chronic constipation. It is a known researched and well-studied fact that a lot of illnesses and diseases are brought on when the body is not able to detoxify itself properly. The body can detoxify itself naturally by eating the right foods and having regular bowel movements and/or by fasting to cleanse the body of all toxins. The body can also detoxify itself by sustaining from toxic foods and drinks. You may also eat certain foods, use natural herbs and stimulants or more stronger medicines and regimens to help regulate your digestive system.

From my personal experience, I now know that chronic constipation is often an early sign of diabetes that often goes undetected. My colon system had basically shut down and I had to take very strong laxatives and stimulants to even get rid of the waste/toxins in my body. No one had ever told me that if you don't get rid of toxins in your body that it could lead to illnesses such as cancer, infection, organ failure or worse, death. I would not have a bowel movement for weeks, if not more, for it felt like months, when normal bowel movements are to take place daily.

I had recently went to the ER on several occasions with severe, chronic abdominal pain. The colonoscopy, the KUB, and all diagnostic exams all came back normal except for the finding of chronic constipation which meant "take more drugs", "take more tests", a revolving cycle and then when nothing else works "we will do surgery" instead of treating the root of the problem. I am being sarcastic, but this is REAL TALK. This is a good example of the woman with the issue of blood for 12 years. How she went and spent all of her money going to different physicians to help stop her hemorrhaging and then she simply touched the hem of Jesus' garment and was made whole instantly.

Just think I only went to the doctor for stress, symptoms of sorrow and a broken hurt and spirit and they gave me drugs for depression and anxiety and told me to drink wine to relax. I must have been the perfect picture of health because no doctor ordered the necessary lab tests to diagnose and treat diabetes. Well, I was just one happy, calm and blessed child of God on those depression and anxiety drugs with untreated diabetes. I never drank the wine, but I should have. I should have drunk a whole lot of wine, because now I can't drink it because it has sugar in it! So thank God for being my physician and my healer, for saving me and keeping me even then.

THE TURNING POINT

I am really trying to get to the second incident, promise. The second incident was brought on by a phone call. Now you do recall everything I mentioned above that I just came out of, right? Well believe me I left out so much and I cannot give it all to you because I am sure we are on the same page by now and this book is not to bring shame to anyone, but to only bring glory to God. I am not like the Enquirer. This is not a gossip column or gossip magazine. This is my life and I can only speak the truth about my life for purpose, that purpose being to bring glory to God.

Okay, I cannot hold my peace any longer; the next incident was the icing on the cake. I was a survivor as evidenced by all that I just went through and came out of and all that I was currently going through and believing and trusting God that I was going to come out of and the fact that I was still living and breathing and in my somewhat right frame of mind all added up to one thing, I was a survivor. I was "knee deep in diapers", I was living through my daughter's teenage rebellious years, I was trying to raise my children, I had very few friends in this state, if any at all, mostly because I voluntarily removed myself from the real world to dwell within the comfort of my four walls of solitude a/k/a solitary confinement within my mind, body and home. Everyone had their own problems and issues to deal with; I did not want to burden anyone, not even God. I was alone at home in my room, the four walls once again. I was once again reflecting over my life.

YOU ARE A HOT MESS

MY IDOL began to lay it out clearly to me. I don't recall the exact words but to sum it all up he said, "YOU ARE A HOT MESS!"

Now when I say this phrase to people, I mean it as a compliment because this is something my mom used to always say and we would laugh about this very phrase. It really said it all, but it was a compliment when we used it. When **MY IDOL** said it, it meant something totally different to me. I began to reflect and think, I am so tired, I am so weary, my life is a hot mess, and my house is a hot mess. I couldn't remember the last time I cleaned the dishes, vacuumed or swept the floor, washed clothes, cooked, dusted or polished the wooden furniture or cleaned the glass or stainless steel fixtures, mopped or waxed the floor, etc. My teenage daughter is still not home with me and now I have another daughter who has also found her home in the streets and I don't even have the strength to chase her like I did my oldest daughter. I don't even have the strength to pray. My bible has dust on it now. I had lost all the bookmarks.

As I laid there in my bed of despair, I looked at the pile of clean and dirty clothes mixed together in my room that looked like a huge mountain and I looked at it and remembered when that huge mountain was small and I even kind of vaguely remembered when it was not even there at all, and I remembered saying to myself "I will do it tomorrow, I will get to that later ..., later ...., later ..." and now it was definitely later. I had totally lost myself in my job, school, and in everything and everyone that I put before God only to find myself empty and depleted at the end of the day and now I have the diagnosis of type 1 insulin-dependent diabetes. Yes, that does sounds like a hot mess.

Oh, and to top that all off **MY IDOL** is cheating on me! Was it the first time? Probably not, but I was probably stronger then, probably. Oh, and it gets better it's a white girl. Now I know I said earlier in the book that I do not discriminate, but the point I must make here is that I was looking sideways at all black females when I should have been looking sideways at all the colors in the rainbow. Yes, I admit, I was out of order on that one, but it is time for REAL TALK now. Have a seat. This one is for free! My thinking was out of order! My life was out of order! My house was out of order! No man or woman should have to look at anybody sideways to keep each other faithful. When a man and woman come together as husband and wife, they become one flesh; the husband is supposed to love his wife like Christ loved the church and gave himself for it. The wife is to submit herself unto her husband as unto the Lord and reverence her husband. (Go read the book of Ephesians Chapter 5) ... but ..."When you are not married and not one flesh, then you need to just sit it down before GOD shuts it down!"

I often think back from time to time on the words **MY IDOL** said to me "You never cook, you never clean, your this, your that and now your ... (you fill in the blanks) ... tell me something, why is it that everybody else can do this and that and you can't do nothing, you keep using your diabetes as an excuse. I know a lot of people who have diabetes and they live a good life, look at you ... (sigh of disgust)." Those words and actions were so powerful that they should have killed me dead and took the last breath out of me, but I continued to seek God's face daily. I held on to His unchanging hand and would not let go. I kept the faith.

I was lying in my bed alone in a still quiet room one day. God said "Get up and walk!" This time there was no doubt in my mind that He meant it. It was a stern voice that roared and resonated throughout my whole entire body. So I got up out of the bed and I came out of the four walls and I tried ... I tried .... I mean I really tried to perform at an acceptable level of functioning. I tried to make dinner, tacos. It was not just any kind of tacos. My family loved my "famous tacos". Everyone loved my "famous tacos". I got the recipe from my dad and mom. It was passed on through the family. It was fried flour tortillas, seasoned beef, pinto beans, shredded cheddar cheese, taco sauce and salad mix, tomatoes and whatever else you wanted to add. I believe they are called Quesadillas now but I called them my "famous tacos". I could never make enough of them and everyone loved them, even **MY IDOL** who does not even like tacos loved them.

So as I was cooking for the ones I loved, the phone rings, I said "Hello …". The caller said "YOU NEED TO TELL **YOUR IDOL** TO KEEP HIS D@#K IN HIS PANTS". Now, Holy Woman of God does not use language like this, I am just trying to demonstrate to you how I received it (and it was not @# in the middle). Do you need me to spell it out for you, repeat it, rewind, fast forward, pause, playback, double back? I could have dropped the phone, but somehow it stayed close to my ear. I don't know who was holding the receiver. I did not stop cooking my "famous tacos", but suddenly at seven months pregnant, cooking over a hot stove, enough food for probably only me to eat according to my eyeballs for it looked and smelled so good, well not now because I had suddenly lost my appetite.

The caller went on to explain to me the last two years of my life and it is a good thing she did because she had a total different version than I did. You see the last two years of my life was just a blur to me because due to the stress I was under I was living a fantasy that "Everything is perfect … happy, happy, happy …". She even knew the night I was diagnosed in the hospital with diabetes and she knew the time, the place, the setting and the circumstances better than me. She even knew the one night out of five years on my job that I showed up 15 minutes late to work due to the train delaying the normal regular schedule of the car leaving her house and then going en route to my house to pick me up and take me to work. WOW! was that really worth ruining my perfect attendance, no call-ins, no tardiness record at work? Geez. She even knew that I was a "lazy, trifling, and good for nothing …WH@#E … (and it was not @# in the middle) who sat on the coach or laid in the bed all day and did nothing". WOW!

All this time I thought **MY IDOL** was hard at work, working long, late hours trying to take care of his family. The least I could do for **MY IDOL** is keep everything else together, like my appearance, the kids, a clean house, a clean car, cook a nice nutritious breakfast, lunch and dinner and three snacks, and set the perfect atmosphere so when he arrived home from a hard day of work he would be ever so comfortable. You know the perfect picture of a happy family like in the movies, on TV, in magazines and photo frames like you see everyday in "Crystal in Wonderland". You know, when he gets off of a long, hard day of work and he walks in the house and you are looking your very best and you have prepared dinner by candlelight and turn on the song by Destiny's Child "Let Me Cater To You". You know, pull out his favorite slippers, run his bathwater and bring his towel and favorite robe and stroke his ego like a good woman would, should, could". Well, that was not the case, I was a HOT MESS!

I was totally numb to everything around me yet I was attuned to all that was being said on the phone. Oh wait, I do remember one thing **MY IDOL** was now "nervously cleaning the house". He sure could keep a clean house. I mean a real, real, real, real, real, real, real clean house. Maybe he was always nervously cleaning the house and I am just now noticing it. Ladies, if your man is fixated on keeping a real, real, real, real, real, real, real clean house and he is nervously cleaning the house all the time. I say it is time to invest in a GPS tracking system. You know they have tracking devices for cell phones too. "Let Me Upgrade U"!

Back to the story at hand. At this point, I continued to listen to the caller, but I just could not act. I could only listen. At the end of the call, I said "Thank you for having the courage to tell me and I am not mad at you. I am not upset with you and I honestly thank you". At that time, I did not realize how God had put the very words in my mouth to speak and they came out so perfectly. It was a miracle in action for real! I remained silent. I served dinner. I prepared for work. I arrived at work. I did my job. Then it hit me all at once. I became so angry. I picked up the office phone to make a phone call.

The girl that told me about the secret affair had also given me the secret cell phone number that I knew nothing about, so I called it and sure enough it was **MY IDOL's** voice. "Yes, this is @#$%^@#$%@!#$%^&*@#$%^ please leave a message and I will get back with you". I left a message, in a very weak, shaky and strained voice, and the message said "I cannot believe you did me like this. I want you to leave right now and I never want you to contact me again, goodbye". I know way to nice of a message but I was Christ-like.

You already know what I wanted to do in my flesh had I not been saved, sanctified, justified and filled with the Holy Ghost. Looking back in the flesh right now, I am ready to warm up the minivan, take out my earrings, roll up my sleeves, put some Vaseline on my face and ... Ooh Wee, let me get back in the spirit, thank you Jesus for saving and keeping me and while I am at it I thank you for even saving and keeping **MY IDOL** from that butt kickin he so deserved. Ooh wee, thank you Jesus for backspace, autocorrect and spell check on the keyboard. Hallelujah!

When the call was returned to me about 10 minutes later on my job this was the response "Well, you knew we were having problems ...". I calmly said "Yes, I knew we were having problems but I did not know that unfaithfulness was one of them – CLICK". I hung up the phone. I went and sat back at my desk and I looked directly at my computer monitor and placed my fingers on the home row keys and I held back some of the tears and I cried out to God once again. I was so distraught at that moment, but I kept it together and finished my shift at work.

From that time forward I kept taking my happy pills, I remained under a doctor's care, I went to church when I could, I read the bible when I could and prayed when I could. I loved and cared for my children and others when I could, but basically I was crippled with depression. The girl called my house once again to tell me that she had been fired from her job because her secret affair with her coworker was out. Her coworker who just so happened to be **MY IDOL**. I guess they had a little, tiny disagreement on the job and she was let go. If only they could have never agreed to begin with.

I welcomed her call and I began to minister to her about placing her faith in God and not man. I let her know that we were in the same position having to turn to God and having to have faith in God that He would deliver us out of even this situation. Both of us were experiencing a loss, hurt, pain, and suffering. Even though in the flesh I wanted to hate her and **MY IDOL**, in the spirit God was allowing me to minister to **MY IDOL's** mistress and **MY IDOL** for they too were His children being used as another one of the devil's pons/imps. In fact, **MY IDOL'S** mistress was now in worse shape than me for she was now unemployed. She now no longer had the luxury of having an affair. She now had two or three children to take care of on her own.

Let this be a valuable lesson to everyone that God does not keep an ungodly relationship. It will fall apart and unravel right before your eyes. If you are presently shacking up with someone i.e. meaning dating someone and living together and acting like you are married, playing house with someone that ain't your husband or wife for real, know without a doubt that it won't be a Happily Ever After ending. If you continue to be disobedient to God, the above will be your portion, or worse. God has no respect of person. As the word of God applies to me and my life and my life situations and circumstances, so it applies to you and yours.

Although God gave me the strength to minister to **MY IDOL's** mistress and **MY IDOL**, in that my heart's desire is to help all those who are lost, wounded and hurting, I could not in my own strength even open up an envelope to take out a bill and pay it. I could not keep a clean house, cooking turned into anything that made it to the table, grocery shopping was not even natural anymore. It was as if I forgot everything that once came so natural to me. I could not even comb whatever hair I had left. My wig was on sideways. I did not leave the house other than to go to work. My life consisted of work and to the gas station so that I would have gas to get to work and sometimes the grocery store so that we would have food in the refrigerator and cabinets to eat, the bare minimum but basically I had shut down and allowed **MY IDOL** to control my life and my happiness, everything surrounding me and everything concerning me. I no longer had the will to live so I just held on to the strength I had left to possibly exist.

I really hit rock bottom and could not keep myself together. I would lay on the coach or bed indefinitely just thinking, just praying, just watching, just waiting, just hoping, just believing, just trusting, just holding on for dear life. No TV, no radio, no books, no visitors, no outings, no recreational or educational activities, just solitary confinement within my mind, body and home and of course **MY IDOL** was my live entertainment. This was the beginning of me realizing that God was carrying me and keeping me all along. Yet, I was still trying to hold on to my life, wanting to handle things on my own. Even when I knew I couldn't handle it, I was still trying. I was really really ... really ... really trying to handle things on my own.

I was home alone, within the four walls and **MY IDOL** continued to replay my life to me only in **MY IDOL's** version of reality. A thought came to mind, "a perfect murder" to relieve me of all my misery and pain. I was an insulin-dependent diabetic, probably brought on by all the stress I was under. All I would have to do is inject an abundance of insulin and I would die immediately, a peaceful death. I had nothing to live for, isn't it apparent? Everyone that I loved had turned their face and their back on my despair. The phone wasn't ringing other than the **MY IDOL's** mistress. The doorbell was not ringing. It seemed as if no one was there for me. I was all alone once again. Again! I began to talk to the only friend I had left. Yes, I began to talk to Jesus.

"God I am sorry for disappointing you. I really tried to do what was right. I really know that you are against suicide, but if you cannot take my life and take me out of this misery, you leave me with no other choice. I know that you say that you won't put more on me than I can bear, but Lord I think you trust me too much. You were wrong this time. This was the last straw. I know a lot of times people attempt suicide to get attention and never carry it out, but this time I have come up with the perfect murder and no one will even know because they will just assume it is natural causes and the bottom line is I won't have to feel this pain."

So I get my insulin pen together and the needles and I am crying thinking about what I am about to do knowing that it is irreversible. Knowing this is not the end that God had designed or planned for life, but I guess He must have thought I was stronger, but I am not. I am not strong enough to bear all of this. Then I thought about my kids, knowing that when my kids get home from school they will be looking for me and I won't be here. I never even got the chance to say goodbye and hug them and kiss them and tell them that I love them and I did love them. I just was not strong enough.

So I prepare to take my life with tears running down my face to the point I almost could not even see, in my room within the four walls that I was all too familiar with, all alone. To my surprise, the door to the bedroom opens wide and it is … THE LOVE OF MY LIFE! THE LOVE OF MY LIFE walked in the bedroom door and without saying a word he grabbed me and he held me tightly and he did not let me go and he then said, "I am so sorry and I love you and I never want to lose you …". I continued to cry hysterically and said "nobody loves me or cares for me … I can't take it anymore … I can't do this … I want to die …". He interrupted me and said "I love you, the kids love you … and … and … and …". I interrupted him and said "I don't have anything to live for, everything has fallen apart because of me, what do I have to live for, name one thing?" He said "You have a lot to live for, live for me, live for the kids, we love you …". I don't remember all he said because I was slain in the spirit … the insulin pen dropped to the floor.

ANY QUESTIONS?

I never shared this with anyone until now, for it was too painful to share at that time. I don't even think THE LOVE OF MY LIFE knew that God was using him even then. My best friend, Prophetess Kimberly (also know as Kim), would constantly minister to me and speak a word from the Lord and say "Crystal, God is saying you need to make some decisions". Prophets from afar would prophecy to me and speak a word from the Lord saying "You need to forgive and make some decisions ...". I very well knew what they meant. I would pray to God continuously to help me for I wanted to be obedient but I just … I just couldn't.

My loved ones would ask why I stayed in an unhealthy relationship with **MY IDOL** and why I remained loyal to **MY IDOL.** I even often wondered why I applied the principle of God "Love covers a multitude of sins..." to justify my reasons for not letting go and walking away from that relationship. I kept telling myself that the adversary was using **MY IDOL** over and over again for my demise, yet God continued to turn it around for my good, but that was only a small portion of it. I really felt obligated to stay with **MY IDOL** for **MY IDOL** had saved my life from this incident and God used **MY IDOL** later on several occasions to save my life. **MY IDOL** caused me heartache after heartache, after heartache, enough to kill me, but **MY IDOL** also continued to be my hero by saving my life with God's help. So it was a balancing act.

The worldview is to look at the disadvantages and the advantages and if the advantages outweigh the disadvantages remain in the relationship. God's view is "Thy kingdom come. Thy will be done in earth, as it is in heaven ...". To make a long story short, I loved **MY IDOL** and I was not ready to make a decision. What I later found out in my disobedience to God is not making a decision is a decision!

MY PLANNED WEDDING CEREMONY

There is a huge difference between planning a wedding ceremony versus preparing for and carrying out a marriage.

I remember a time years later when me and THE LOVE OF MY LIFE were married, even after God on my wedding day said directly to me "It is not my will!" Even after I cried on my wedding day when I ran into a good friend of mine and brother in Christ, Ed, who gave me a word from the Lord four hours before my wedding ceremony. I loved THE LOVE OF MY LIFE and I could not imagine life without him. I kept convincing myself that God would not have allowed THE LOVE OF MY LIFE to save my life if it were not meant for us to be together. God was just going to have to understand. God would surely bless the mess I was getting ready to get myself into. I continued to think to myself, if we married then God would honor the marriage and we would live happily ever after just like in the fairy tales.

I was going to plan the perfect wedding ceremony, the perfect marriage, the perfect life, all on my own. Oh, and yes God, you can bless it after I get done with the planning. God you can also finance it if you don't mind. My dad was hospitalized with a mild stroke maybe two days before the wedding. I hurried to the hospital to check on my dad and make sure that he was going to be okay. He was fine and my heart was glad. However, it turned out that he was not going to be released from the hospital in order to walk me down the aisle, but he gave me his blessing from his hospital bed. Well, at least that is how I interpreted what he said. The wedding would have to proceed without him.

God kept speaking and I was too busy to listen. My girlfriends, Cynthia, Anita & Tammy planned my bridal shower, under my direction of course. Thank you girls for everything even the "heart to heart" we had as true friends and sisters in Christ. I will treasure the time we had together that night and hope we will have many more to come. I remember everything you said and everything you did and I know you all meant well, but ... I had a wedding to plan!

I planned everything from the perfect colors, the perfect theme, the perfect cake, the perfect music, the perfect wedding party, the perfect photographer, the perfect wedding coordinator, ushers and decorators, the perfect reception hall, the perfect reception food and catering service, the perfect decorations, the perfect attire. Everyone that knows me knows that I am the perfect planner, with the exception of two days before my wedding my dad who was supposed to walk me down the aisle was hospitalized. Now that was not a part of the plan. Nevertheless, planning is one of my greatest strengths. I might also point out that one of my greatest weaknesses is planning without God!

My special day was also my dad's birthday and I wanted this special day to be special and memorable to me and my dad for that very reason. My lifetime best friend, Pat, was the astonishing Matron of Honor, my oldest girls were my gorgeous bridesmaids, my boys were the groomsmen, handsome ring bearer and ushers, my baby daughter was the beautiful flower girl. I even had a pretty little angel and two anointed praise dancers with starring roles in my ceremony. THE LOVE OF MY LIFE picked his best man and groomsmen. I tried to put my two cents in, but he ignored me.

Anywho, I picked the DJ, the videographer. It was definitely my day. THE LOVE OF MY LIFE did not even need to show up, "Really". No, I am serious this time "Really". I would have been fine with just all that I planned, but you know "I loved that man" so I guess he could come to "My Wedding". I know that I said earlier in the story that I was selfless, but I was totally in the flesh on this one. God did not have anything to do with this one, sorry to tell you. Just keeping it real!

We had our rehearsal practice and dinner. We prepared for the next day which was the wedding. I was exhausted from it all. The next day it was time to get my hair done. Now everyone that really knows me knows that I love to look perfect, especially my hair. I know by now at least one person is saying "This girl wants everything to be perfect. How in the world can she have perfect in an imperfect world?" Atta Girl/Atta Boy. You are good listeners and quick learners. Anywho, if you don't see my hair perfect, know that I am having more than a bad hair day.

I then begin to realize that I had spent all my money in that planning costs to say the least. You have to pay the cost to be the boss and who was the boss? That is right – Me. I asked THE LOVE OF MY LIFE if he had any money and he said he spent all of his money too. So, I now realize the most important thing to me. Note: "Me". The most important thing at this point now to me was that I did not have the money to get my hair done. I had some money, but that was the money I had put aside to get the girls hair done and I could not have my hair done and not theirs so basically I was somehow short of money and if anyone was going to have to sacrifice I knew it would be me because I just could not have the girls looking "crazy by the head at my wedding". So, I began to become anxious and worried, so I did something I don't ordinarily do, I called my mom to explain the situation to her and she said "I will pay for you to get your hair done and that will be my wedding gift to you". I said "Okay, thanks".

Sigh of relief – WHEW. Now I am back on track again, thanks mom. This moment with my mom was memorable for although we have not always seen "eye to eye", she has always been my mom and she has always been there during most of those times in my life that I needed a helping hand. That is how it should be when our children come to us in need. It is supposed to go just like this. I was a very responsible kid that would never really ask for things. I pretty much always handled things on my own, but when I did ask, it was usually a life or death situation or something very serious like "getting my hair done on my big day". Hey peanut gallery, I don't need your comments, this is my story! – laughing out loud.

I would always tell people if I ever ask you for anything never tell me no because it is serious. I would always tell them I very seldom ask for anything that I really don't need. They would always know that I was speaking the truth and I was always good about repaying my debts.

It's the morning of my wedding day. Me and the girls go to the beauty shop to get our hair done. "Come and Get Your Praise On" was the name of the beauty shop. Even the name of the beauty shop had a sentimental meaning to me in regards to the wedding because I was dedicating and committing the wedding that I planned to God - Yeah, no laughing out loud, please, not yet.

I described the "Perfect Look" to my hairstylist, Wanda. She gave me something even more beautiful. She also did two of my daughters' hair, my bridesmaid and my flower girl. In the essence of time, my daughter Che' got her hair done by another hairstylist. She was not pleased because of the style I picked for her. She felt it was old fashioned. The style she wanted was a modern hip look like a "Mohawk with gelled twists on the side" and I wanted a more elegant updo. So Frog, the hairstylist, was caught in the middle of this family dispute and he tried to intervene by talking with Che' to ensure her he would do his very best to give her a combination look of the two different hairstyles and he did. Che' did not even look in the mirror in front of her or the handheld mirror that was given to her when her hairstyle was complete. During this whole time at the beauty shop she was having a complete fit, a full blown tantrum, or a more proper term, a meltdown.

My good friend and brother in Christ, Ed, stopped by the beauty shop to my surprise for I did not even tell him that I had an appointment. I asked him if he was going to the wedding because I noticed I had not received an RSVP from him. He said with a very concerned look "God is not pleased and I do not want you to be disobedient and I love you and God loves you and I cannot lie to you and not tell you what He has given me to share with you". I began to cry real crocodile tears. Everyone in the beauty salon had now gathered around me to minister to me and began to pray that God would open my eyes and that God's will be done and not my own. Yes, we formed a real live prayer circle right in the middle of the beauty shop for I had a praying hairstylist/owner and people who loved me with the love of God and yes God loved me enough to meet me right where I was at. He may not come when you want him, but He is always right on time. Some people I knew and some I did not even know, but we were all connected as family in the spirit right in the middle of the beauty shop in the presence of God. WOW!

I appreciated every prayer and it really meant a lot to me. I truly valued my friendship with my brother in Christ and the blessings that all in the beauty shop had bestowed upon me and my family. I cried and I prayed, but it was my planned Cinderella wedding and story and I was going to finish what I had started. The next chapter would be the wedding, so we shall proceed!

WARNING COMES BEFORE DESTRUCTION

"I have sent also unto you all my servants the prophets, rising up early and sending them, saying, Return ye now every man from his evil way, and amend your doings, and go NOT after other gods to serve them, and ye shall dwell in the land which I have given to you and to your fathers: but ye have not inclined your ear; nor hearkened unto me". (Jeremiah 35:15).

Che' was known to have fits and tantrums all her life, so we let her be. I don't think the fit she was having was only about her hair. Both of my teenage daughters were now not living at home because they could no longer take the stress of it all. They left and when they left they left me to be. I was not "mad at them". I only wished they could have taken me with them. Looking back I see what the devil stole from them that hurt both me and them the most. The devil stole what they treasured in their hearts and that was their love for me and my love for them. You see, I was all my girls had other than God. I brought them up in church from babies to teenage years and they knew God. Yet, I did not teach them about relationship with God because that was something I was still learning. Yes, saved all my life, but not having a relationship with Him.

The only relationship my two oldest daughters had was with me. I was their role model. Their fathers were not active participants in their lives growing up and no fault of my daughters, but my girls still internalized the pain from it all. For many years, I was the only thing constant in their life and now their mama was half crazy so to speak. They tried their best to nurse me back to health, but they got tired and weary. They were children they could not do it in their own strength nor should they have had to do it. I am sure they saw too much, heard too much, experienced too much and lived too much of my hurt and my pain. The devil won that battle, yet he has not won the war.

Nevertheless, this is my fairy tale and I was going to make it Happily Ever After. I was going to be Cinderella, even if I had to pay for it. Believe me I paid for it and it cost way more than the cost of the wedding ceremony! So when our hair was done we arrived at the church. We had two hours to prepare for the ceremony so we had to work fast to do the makeup, accessories, pictures, and start the wedding ceremony on time.

My Matron of Honor was by my side all the way. I never shared with her until years later what took place at the beauty shop four hours before the wedding or anything about what God was speaking directly to me beforehand. I did not want to disappoint her because she always knew from kindergarten that I had "issues" to put it nicely. I wanted her to be proud of me just once in my lifetime. I wanted everyone to be proud of me just once in my lifetime. When I later shared the truth with her about all that God was telling and showing me, she was disappointed that I took her through all of that and that I took myself through all of that without purpose. Well, I really did have purpose; I wanted the approval of others. I guess God's approval was not enough. I guess God's approval was not necessary as long as everyone else approved of me.

Take Note: The spirit of rejection at work. "I AM THE VOICE THAT STANDS AND SPEAKS for the little girl whose mother and father put **IDOLS** before her. The little girl that was never made to feel like she was a special princess by her father nor any male. The little girl whose womanhood was taken from her by someone who didn't even value her enough to take her hand in marriage and say I will love you, I will cherish you, I will honor and obey you all the days of my life, until death do us part. For that little girl, this is your chapter! God is saying to you right now "You are the apple of My eye". The world may have rejected you, but God is saying directly to you right now "The stone which the builders rejected, the same is become the head cornerstone". You may have messed up so bad that you are at the point in your life that you look and feel forsaken, but God is saying to you right now "I am married to the backslider". Come back to your first love, He is waiting on you."

THE MAKEOVER

To appoint unto them that mourn in Zion, to give unto them beauty for ashes, the oil of joy for mourning, the garment of praise for the spirit of heaviness; that they might be called trees of righteousness, the planting of the LORD, that he might be glorified. (Isaiah 61:3).

Applying makeup and apparel to enhance your outer beauty is not the same as allowing God to make you over and enhance your inner as well as outer beauty with his divine power as he gives you a new and clean heart, a renewed mind, body and spirit, a new life in Him.

I normally apply my own makeup and have never really received any complaints. In fact, I have received a lot of compliments over the years regarding my ability to always look my best. I had already enjoyed my half a day at the spa package, a wedding gift from my coworkers, which included a full body massage, pedicure, manicure and deep cleansing facial, lunch and to top that off, a color makeup application.

My special day was important to me and I knew that I could only trust my best friend/ Matron of Honor, Pat, to give me the "Perfect Look". She is an anointed and gifted artist, so

I knew no one else would be able to give me the look that only she could give. She applied my makeup, prepped me and coached me and then she placed my tiara on my head and pinned it in place. I looked in the mirror and sure enough I saw something I had never saw before, I saw a "caramel-complexion beautiful Cinderella". It took all of this planning to make me realize it. Pat even agreed, so I knew it was true and that I was not just imagining it. Of course, it is my special day, who would really have the nerve to say anything different? No really, I did look like Cinderella and I felt like Cinderella.

I still have the pictures to prove it, "but that is another story" why I held on to the invitations, the program, the gifts, the engagement announcements, wedding and honeymoon pictures, the bouquet of flowers, the newspaper announcement articles, the candle that we lit during the ceremony, the decorations, the broom that we jumped over, the bubbles we blew, the rice we threw, the bride and the groom champagne glasses, the knife and spatula that cut/served the cake, the flower girl basket with the flowers, the wedding dress and undergarments, the tiara and all the accessories. Everything that I could salvage and treasure from that special day, I placed in safekeeping for many many years to come and even after that *** TO BE CONTINUED ***. Somehow the top layer of cake got ate by the kids, but Oh well, I was going to hold on to something.

My Matron of Honor and I prayed together and she blessed me on this special day. My good friend Darlene assisted us and helped monitor the crowd that had arrived earlier than expected and was now trying to make their way back to the dressing room to see the bride before the wedding. I was like "Huh? Who really does this? Are you even serious?"

Darlene made sure the kids were dressed in their tuxedos and dresses and that everyone was ready for the ceremony as all my children played a starring role in the ceremony. We started 15 minutes behind my "on-time" schedule, but it was perfect. Everyone was happy; it showed in all their faces except me and Che'.

A SPECIAL BOND BETWEEN MOTHER & DAUGHTER

Me and Che' had a special bond that was very strong. I want to say that it is because I breastfed her, but it was so much more than that. Everything I did not like about Che' was exactly the things I did not like about myself. She was beautiful inside and out. She was very smart, compassionate, and loyal to a fault, head strong, stubborn, courageous and determined. She was relentless. She was not going to go down without a fight. Out of all my kids, if anyone tried to harm me, she would be the first one to step up to defend me. Now I know my kids would fight over this one, but it would be just like Jesus with His 12 disciples at The Last Supper. Out of the 12 who could He really count on when He had to bear the cross? Definitely not Peter, the one that said he had His back.

Whenever Che's friends or my oldest daughter would get in a fight they would always go get Che'. People respected Che' because she was not known to not start a fight only to end one. Che' either through her words or through her actions would put an end to all discord and she would always give you a choice before she acted. She gave you two choices with oftentimes unspoken words to one, get your act together or two, she would get it together for you. That was her attitude. She wasn't violent; she was just determined to be Che'.

As a small baby even before she could talk she would blow big spit bubbles and foam at the mouth and make weird sounds. I nicknamed her Pooh after Winnie the Pooh. My grandmother called her "Hollerin Pooh" because whenever she was not in my care she would cry until I returned. Her other nickname that she acquired from the family was after the cartoon character "Tasmanian Devil". Now I know this was wrong and I now see my error in letting her be called this for words are powerful. At that time I thought it was funny because when she would spit her bubbles and have a full blown tantrum she definitely acted the part of the cartoon character, yet I won't put a name on it I will just say "cartoon character". The daycare teachers were intimidated by this. They would just lie her down on a pillow with a blanket and she was fine as long as everyone left her alone until I came to pick her up.

Fourteen years later, my mother still blames Che' for making her wreck her car in a ditch because she was hollering in the back seat and my mom turned around to try to settle her down and there went the car in the ditch. I don't think my mom voluntarily babysat her since that accident. When Che' was young, since she was so much like me very independent and not requiring a lot of assistance, when she did need attention she had to make a lot of noise to get my attention away from everything else that needed my immediate attention, well at least I thought everything else needed my immediate attention.

I remember one time she was in pain and I nursed on her for days with all kinds of home remedies that my mom had suggested to me. I was one of those mothers that thought I could heal every illness and sickness through home remedies, prayer and faith. She was almost dead after about three days and then I took her to the hospital and they kept her for 10 days and gave her all kinds of antibiotics to restore her back to health. I felt so bad, but I had no idea that home remedies, prayer and faith would not work. I even used holy oil. Her only complaint was a stomachache so I treated her symptoms. Isn't that what doctors do? Well, come to find out after they got done with their complete workup on her, she ended up having to have an emergency surgery.

Later on another occasion, she woke up and both of her eyes were swollen shut. I had learned from my previous mistake with treating her at home with home remedies, prayer and faith, so I immediately took her to the doctor and then to the hospital per the doctor's request. She was in the hospital another 10 days on antibiotics and I labored and prayed in the hospital room with Che'. I anointed her head with oil. I laid hands on her. I sang praises unto God and prayed in the spirit for her healing. She looked up at me and said "Mom, what are you doing?" It was obvious she did not approve of my behavior, but that did not stop me. I was going to "war in the spirit" for my child just as I know she would have done for me. That time she did not need surgery and she has not been hospitalized since. Glory to God! But if she is hospitalized in the future, know that I will be warring again in the spirit for my child right in the hospital room, the waiting room or even in the operating room if I have too.

Years later, God blessed me with the opportunity to witness two of Che's sons being born into the world and only to miss one delivery by 20 minutes because my supervisor was reluctant in giving me time off work and no comment on that one for the one I was 20 minutes late with is the "spittin image of his mama" and he did not even need my presence. He is the one at the age of one-years-old who is walking around giving everyone an "upper cup" if they try to get near him. Nevertheless, God is still God. He saw fit for me to be present to intercede in prayer on her behalf then and He saw fit for her to be present to intercede on my behalf now. She was not going to go down without a fight this time and this full blown tantrum was her way of saying without saying "I am not pleased!"

Yes, me and Che' had some good times together, we often now sit back and laugh at those two previous hospital incidents and the funniest one is when she tells me how I almost killed her by giving her home remedies such as laxatives, pain relievers, fever reducers, soup and juice, vitamins and water trying to heal her naturally.

Through the years we have shared so much in common both good and bad, even the happy pills. I remember one time when we were arguing and I could do nothing else to get through to her. I poured a whole bottle of holy oil over her head and walked out the room and shut the door behind me. She did not come out the room, all she wanted was to be left alone, I guess. I have eight kids now, but out of the eight, Che' is the one that definitely has my heart and my spirit.

It was an honor to have her be a part of my wedding. Even if I had to literally kidnap her from her best friend's house for real and bribe her to participate in the ceremony. I really think she wanted to be there with me and family, but she is so stubborn she would have went to her grave angry or lived with the guilt of not participating in the wedding, so I had to be the more mature one to intervene and humble myself to ask for her participation.

Che' had left the house probably months before the wedding because she could no longer take the pressure that I had placed her under being the oldest kid at home now. She felt the full blow of everything while I was away from home at work, school, etc. She wanted to be a kid, a teenager at that and I wanted to keep her young and sheltered. I needed her help at this time and she totally rebelled against me and I knew I was no match for her so I gave her what my mom gave me "If you can't follow my rules then here is the door ...". Che' got up and walked out the door without a bag or even a coat on her back and never looked back. It was like she was saying and not saying "Thank you, it is about time you saw things my way".

Dang, she makes me sick, I wish I could have done that when I was her age. Me and the kids were standing in the door looking like Mister from the movie Color Purple, watching Che' walk down the street without Shug Avery. I "was not mad at her" I was thinking "Go on with your bad self!"

This reminds me of the one time that I got mad at my mom when I was young and I ran away from home midday. I went to the park and played in the park alone and sat on a park bench and thought most of the day and said to myself "I ain't never going back home!" Well, it started to get dark and as it started to get dark I started to get hungry and nobody can cook like my mama and then I started to get scared for I knew the creatures in the woods came out at night and probably the "Boogie Man". I was so mad at my mama for whatever reason and after a few hours in the park, I didn't remember and as it began to get dark, I didn't even care about the reason. As my stomach started to growl, I said to myself "Get mad, get glad, so sad, I am going home to eat!" I decided I would run away another day, during the early daytime hours of course and I would make sure that I packed breakfast, lunch and dinner and a couple of snacks before I left the house next time. So basically my mom never knew that I had ran away from home until now because she is probably reading this book (OOPS).

Another time when I was mad at my mom and decided I was going to be a little sassy, I said "When I get 16 and get my driver's license and buy me a car I am going to leave and never come back!" My mom just looked at me and did not say a mumbling word and just walked away and let me stand there and absorb what I had just said and what had just took place. I just knew I deserved a slap in the face or something, but she just kept on going about her business and I just stood there for a while thinking about what had just transpired and as the days, months and years went on and everyday life went on, I never forget that encounter and the silent message that she spoke by her nonaction. Well, I turned 16 and I did not have a driver's license and I did not have a car, so runaway Plan B did not work either.

Che' was definitely no match for me because she was successful on the first try. I did not even call the police because I knew exactly where she was at. Right where she felt she needed to be and in the state that I was in then, I knew I could not offer her nothing more than the freedom to find her way. I did not have the time, energy or strength to go after her. Now with my oldest daughter, I was able to drive her to Chicago and leave her with a good friend and then later a grandmother who intervened to help. Everyone knew about Che' and you almost had to bribe somebody to babysit her when she was a baby so you know there were "no takers" for her as a teenager. No Way Hosea! Not that she was a bad kid, she just was "head strong" to put it nicely.

Plus, Che' a/k/a "Little Red Riding Hood from the Hood" knew she was not going to get in the car with me to drop her off at grandmas house in Chicago. She was not going to fall for that "okie doke". I even tried to trick her to get on the bus and go to Chicago for a weekend visit/shopping spree, while all along trying to set her up to stay and live with her grandmother. When she was done visiting and shopping in the Windy City, she left grandma's house and got on the city bus and was on her way back to "Home Sweet Home". In that she had no idea where she was going in the huge city of Chicago, she ended up getting off the city bus and going into a funeral home to ask a complete stranger to use their phone to call home to me collect. When I answered the phone, she proceed to tell me that if I did not come to get her that she was going to walk back home or get back home the best way she can. I thought "Oh My God, they are going to embalm her and place her in a coffin and bury her alive and I have no idea where she is at for I did not even have caller ID".

Well her grandmother intervened again and picked her up from the funeral home and gave her bus fare to get back home and she made it back home safely. I tell ya she is definitely wiser than we thought she was, for she remembered what happened to her older sister when she got sent off to Chicago and it was not about to happen to her. She was not going down without a fight.

I love all my kids dearly and I never ever allow them not to be themselves so my motto was always "You have to live your life!" So Che' was beginning to live her life. Now as a mother I watched over her like a mother hen from a distance for she was only one block away from home. I made sure she had food, clothes, personal care, medical care, schooling, a roof over her head, money in her pocket so that she was somewhat stable. I prayed for her and took her to church from time to time with the family in hopes that she would remember some of what she was taught about faith at an early age. I prayed to God that He would intervene on our behalf, but I never forced her to come home. I always let her know she was loved and she was welcome to come back home at any time, but I never forced her. I knew the prodigal child would return home one day soon, that was my continual prayer then and it remains my prayer today.

HERE COMES THE BRIDE

So the wedding proceeded on, like Madea's Family Reunion, I was the bride and I played the part of Jennifer Lewis, the wedding planner. As I walked down the aisle I kept a fake smile pinned on my face and God was speaking "It is not my will!" I kept listening to the music of Brian McKnight "Still in Love" but God's voice was louder, but how do you call off a wedding that you planned so perfectly and everyone is here even out of town guests?

When I asked my brother in Christ, Ed, this same question at the beauty shop four hours previously, he asked me "Would you rather disappoint God or man?" I guess my answer was "to proceed with the wedding", so the wedding continued and then the ceremony. Everything was beautiful, my best friend/Matron of Honor sang the Lord's Prayer and her and my daughter Krishina, which is also her niece, did a duet of the song "Our Love", their rendition of Natalie Cole. It was just beautiful, so far. No Cut 1, Cut 2, Cut 3 in my live stage production.

Me and THE LOVE OF MY LIFE jumped the broom and then went the recessional, more wedding pictures, the reception dinner with throwing of the bouquet and garter, the best wishes, etc. We had a wishing well and a table for gifts and a beautiful dinner reception that my aunt Dimple prepared. Everything was perfect except "We forgot to put out the mint chocolate lavender and rose colored hearts on the tables (reflecting moment ...). Oh well, good thing we didn't because we needed those to munch on, for the bride and groom ended up cleaning up the whole reception hall and the church in their gown and tuxedo. It was an absolute disappointment that everyone but Darlene, Dwight and Dimple stayed to help clean up after the reception. At the end of the night, I was so exhausted I could have slept in the car all night instead of going to our hotel honeymoon suite. "Planning is hard work and very exhausting … Whew".

Following cleaning the reception hall in our gown and tuxedo, THE LOVE OF MY LIFE and I went downtown to go on a horse and buggy ride just like Cinderella. Remember this is a true story, pay attention! We then went back to our honeymoon suite. I picked a castle lodge hotel, it was part of the theme, of course. It had a lit fireplace, an antique coach, an antique TV and everything antique with extra dust on it, a spiral staircase in the two-story room, shaggy worn carpet and rugs, a full size bed with an antique looking comforter. We looked around the room, took pictures, pulled back and shook the old comforter and layed in the bed for about 1 minute and 10 seconds and held each others hand and looked in each other's eyes and said "Let's just go home". We were definitely not comfortable. We were so tired, so we just went home hugged and kissed each other in our bed, in our home, for the first time as husband and wife and fell fast too sleep. It was perfect and we lived happily ever after ~THE END~ NOT!

When we woke up the next morning we prayed together from that day forward, until … we stopped praying together. When we stopped praying together, the arguments and fights started, the lies started, the cheating started, the stealing started, the suspicion continued, the neglect continued, the hurt, the pain, the sorrow, the depression continued, a revolving cycle. What did I do? I retreated to my four walls. That was easier.

MIRACLES IN MY LIFE

The third near-death experience happened during my marriage to THE LOVE OF MY LIFE. This was a time in my life that for the most part I was so happy. I had a husband. I had a family. I had a master's degree, a job I loved. We went to church together sometimes, we prayed together sometimes. I had just given birth to my first child by marriage. I was no longer committing fornication and living in sin. This child was not a "bastard child" as people who judge would say. I was so happy in my present state when I focused on only that thought, the thought of "I am so happy". My circumstances had not changed. I just decided to only focus on the thought that "everything was perfect and that I am so happy", even though it was not and I was not. Looking back, it was if I was in a trance, under a spell, under hypnosis. It ultimately took God to snap me out of it.

Continuing with my story, the modified G rated version. I brought my baby home from the hospital and he had everything he wanted and needed, the crib, the bassinette, the fancy Fisher Price ocean theme swing that made sounds of the ocean and he could look up and see the fish and sea animals floating above in the pretend ocean water aquarium, the double stroller because I now had two babies to carry and tote around. Yes, two babies on both hips, again! THE LOVE OF MY LIFE had prepared the house for my return home from the hospital. The house was neat and clean. Oh, I hope he hasn't been nervous cleaning. "Lord, please do not let that nervous cleaning be going on again in my life. Lord I know that you honor marriage and that you bless marriages …". The kids were clean. We had a clean refrigerator full of food. My husband was an excellent provider as far as my natural eyes could see.

My God-mom and the kids were waiting my return home with my new bundle of joy. This was the first time that I did not have to drive myself to the hospital to deliver my baby and drive myself and my new baby home after my delivery. See, I am making progress. Hallelujah! So I arrive home to a house and everything is neat, tidy and in place. Note: This is not evidence of divine order – that one was for free!

I begin to nurse and care for my baby and myself just as the hospital staff told me to do when I was discharged. I was going to take 12 weeks of paid time off of work to bond with my newborn baby. The new and improved LOVE OF MY LIFE. He had replaced the old LOVE OF MY LIFE. He was so precious and beautiful. I would not let him out of my sight for one second. I would hardly let anyone touch him or hold him. It would be reservations only to spend time with me and my baby. Even daddy had to make a reservation. I did not want any visitors and I did not want to go anywhere. My baby would have to be placed in a bubble so that nothing or no one could harm him. This lasted about 15 minutes in the real world that it was obvious we were both living in. Pretty soon the other kids welcomed the new addition to the family and you know how i.e. dirty fingers, runny noses, lots of love, hugs and wet kisses, germs and all, all over this new bundle of joy's face.

Oh well, we are one big happy, happy, happy family. I bonded so with my new baby boy that he really did not care too much for THE LOVE OF MY LIFE, for THE LOVE OF MY LIFE did not have mommy's scent, mommy's breathing, mommy's touch or the scent of mommy's breast milk, but THE LOVE OF MY LIFE worked through this and they began to bond, without my permission of course. I really loved the fact that the baby loved me more.

I was going to hold on to him so tight that he could not help but to love me more. I began to spoil him rotten. When you saw me, you saw him. One night I fell fast asleep downstairs on the living room couch. The baby fell asleep nursing on my chest. THE LOVE OF MY LIFE and the rest of the kids were asleep upstairs. What I remember before going to bed was checking my glucose levels like I always do and I remember eating a balanced meal, like I always do and/or a small snack before going to bed to keep my blood sugar levels normal throughout the night. I tried to always eat and drink properly for I was nursing the baby which meant I had to eat and drink extra amounts.

The next thing I remember happening was THE LOVE OF MY LIFE sitting by my side consoling me and giving me food to eat. Per his report, i.e. a granola bar, an orange and offering me juice. I began to wake up to the point where I was now coherent and he was holding me. He appeared very concerned and I said really calmly "What is wrong with you?" and he said "I don't want to lose you, what would I do without you ...?". I thought to myself in partial consciousness "Oh my God, what have you done this time?" He began to explain to me that he had walked downstairs and found me halfway on the coach and halfway on the floor and that the baby was still attached to my nipple and that I was still asleep wrapped up in the blanket and he said "I tried to help you up and place you and the baby back on the couch and you started to slur your speech and make conversation that made no sense".

He said "You asked where each child was, name by name, one by one and I knew something was wrong so I just acted quickly and began to feed you not really knowing what to do, I just acted". He thought he acted in the natural out of adrenaline, but he really acted in the spirit by listening to the voice of God. I listened attentively as he continued to speak and then as I started to become more conscious, my mind began to catch up with what he was saying and I immediately checked my glucose levels and my levels were 36, anything under 60 is a medical emergency and anything under 20 means coma or death. My levels were 36 and that was after the granola bar and after the orange that he said "it appeared that I had just swallowed the orange instead of chewing it". I did not even recall anything he was now telling me.

Remember what I told you about the orange earlier in the book. One single orange will raise your level by "500", so basically in reality I was "negative 500". This was another miracle in my life and God used THE LOVE OF MY LIFE for His purpose and His glory to carry out the miracle. God used THE LOVE OF MY LIFE over and over again in my life in many, many ways to save my life all while the devil was using him to cause me enough heartache and pain, enough to kill me.

My life has been full of miracles each passing day. Each day that I awake I thank God for the miracle of life. I know each day is a gift because each day the devil literally comes in my life to wreak havoc. The devil comes daily to steal, kill, conquer and destroy my life and everything concerning me. All that time I was trying to take my life by suicide, I did not fully understand how precious life really was, but God gave me a clear revelation through all of this.

This above incident happened around Christmas time. It was a few days before Christmas and my family was fussing and arguing about what Christmas gifts they wanted and expected to receive and I interrupted their conversations for it was a "teaching moment". I told them that God had already given them the greatest gift, His unmerited love. I explained to them that He died on the cross for all of our sins so that we could live for eternity in Him. I went on to tell them that they need to stop fussing and complaining about the world's commercialized holiday and start being thankful and grateful to God for all good gifts that He provides us with daily.

I went further to tell them how the devil tried to take my life in my sleep a few nights ago and how God's grace and mercy said NO and how He gave me another chance and saved me just for them for He knew that they could not bear knowing that on this particular Christmas they did not have a mother to love and cherish. God knew that they were not strong enough to go on without a mother who loved and cared for them. I went on to say if there is not one gift under the Christmas tree this year, know that God has already given us everything we need. The house was quiet the rest of the day and night. Oh and there is so much more just hold on, sit back and listen, take a mini break, grab a snack and a drink, get a cup of Joe, some tea, but continue to listen because God is still speaking, catch it in the Spirit and take notes.

I have even witnessed near-death experiences with my children. The first one that comes to mind is of my son Jamari, the first child born by marriage. The one I cherished so because of that very fact. This made no sense but at that time it did not have to make sense. It was my story and I was sticking to it. Our family took a mini family vacation/cheerleading competition event in St. Louis, Missouri. We were at the hotel indoor pool just having fun family time. The older kids were in the 3 feet and dad was in the whirlpool with the two little ones and I was sitting at the poolside enjoying the fun just sitting and watching.

THE LOVE OF MY LIFE waved at me from the whirlpool with the two small babies and as I walked over to him and the babies to see what he wanted he asked if I could switch places with him and get in the pool and watch the kids so that he could go back to the hotel room to watch the basketball game on TV. I was reluctant because I knew I did not really want to get in the swimming pool and I did not even have on a swimming suit. There was no lifeguard on duty, just a pool full of kids and a few adults sitting on the patio chairs by the poolside. Nevertheless, I knew the game was important to him so I agreed and I rolled up my pant legs and got in the whirlpool reluctantly with my 1-year-old and 3-year-old. My 5-year-old, 10-year-old and 11-year-old were in the adjacent pool in the 3 feet. Not one of us was an experienced swimmer, but we were careful. No one had on floaties.

My 3-year-old, Jamari', wanted to play with his siblings and got out the whirlpool and began to walk toward his siblings in the adjacent 3 ft pool. I hesitated and wanted to call him back, but I was right there so I thought it would be okay to ask my 10-year-old son to watch him. I told my 10-year-old son to make sure he stays in the 3 feet with him and to hold on to him tightly and not let him go and he said "Okay". I played with the 1-year-old in the whirlpool, holding him at all times, while keeping a close eye on the others. I began to enjoy the laughter of my 1-year-old and how much fun he was having in the whirlpool. Seconds later, the next thing I remember was this voice that said "Turn around". I turned around and I watched this adult female walk over to the pool. I knew something was getting ready to take place so I began to set myself in motion to act. I had my 1-year-old in my arms and as I set myself in motion to act, listening to the voice within. I began to get halfway out the whirlpool because in my spirit this voice was speaking loud and clear and I looked up and sure enough my 3-year-old was bopping up and down in the water and before I could get to him, for now it was as if my mind was moving but my legs were frozen and could not move fast enough, my heart was pounding faster than my mind was thinking and faster than my legs were moving.

I could see that a little girl, Amaria, one of the cheerleaders in the pool had lifted my son up out the water and handed him to the adult female standing at the side of the pool who had noticed his bopping from afar, before anyone else. What I did not know at the time was this same adult female who was walking toward the pool on assignment by God, had a son who died from a drowning incident at a very young age. God used her mightily to save my son's life along with the help of the little cheerleader in the pool who was just standing by to make the assist. How could God allow someone who lost their child from a drowning incident, save another child from a drowning incident? God is truly amazing to me.

His siblings were right by his side and I was very near but we had taken our eyes off of him while enjoying all of the fun. I immediately grabbed my precious baby by the hand making sure he was okay and making a vow to myself to never, ever let go of him, never, ever again! I then told all the kids to get out the pool. They did not want to, but it was required! My heart could not take what just happened. As far as I was concerned at that point, we would never get in any pool again! To this very day I have only taken my kids swimming maybe once or twice since that incident, maybe. The whole idea of swimming is just not enjoyable to me any more since this incident. This was the same baby I said I was going to place in a bubble so he could not get hurt. The same baby that I made a promise to myself I would not take my eye off of him for even a second. I often relive this incident in my mind.

Growing up in church, I remember hearing the song "His Eye is on the Sparrow" and I have always loved that song and wanted to sing it, but never thought I could sing it good enough. Well now this song has taken on a whole new meaning in my life. Now this song is singing in my mind, heart, soul and spirit. It does not matter if it does not sound right to others for only God can hear the melody in my heart. For I witnessed for myself that "I sing because I am happy, I sing because I am free, His eye is on the sparrow and I know He watches over me".

I know He was the voice that said turn around. Yet I saw my negligence in not having floaties on my kids and leaving my 10-year-old son in charge of his little brother, which is a definite NO, NO to everyone within the sound of my voice. Then I blamed THE LOVE OF MY LIFE for placing me in a position to get in the pool without having on a swimming suit, not being able to swim and leaving me in charge of five small children that could not swim, but it was not fair to place blame on anyone, not even myself.

Even as I reflect on this, I can see God's hand at work. I know without a doubt that I could never have lived through this incident if my child would have drowned on my watch. I would have never lived through trying to place blame on others for not saving my son. I don't believe my son who I left in charge to watch him would have been able to live through the guilt of allowing his brother to drown. I was so traumatized from this one incident, but God used it for His glory because I began to at that very moment witness to everyone I came in contact with about the God I serve whose "Eye is on the Sparrow" and who watches over us at all times and how He saved my precious baby's life and how He will never put more on us than you can bear and how He used a little girl as an angel and a grieving mother as a saint and a hero to perform not only a good deed but a miracle. I will forever be grateful and thankful to God and to them. They were superheroes in the natural and in the spirit at that very moment. What if they had of been too busy to listen to God when He was trying to get their attention, when He was trying to get them to open their eyes and see and open their ears to hear? What if they had of ignored His voice?

You don't know how these two superheroes were affected knowing that they had saved one life. Imagine God placing you in a position to save one life. Heaven rejoices over one sinner coming to repentance. I continue to give God all the glory for saving my child from that day and the days thereafter. I knew one day that I would tell the whole world if He allowed it. I knew if He gave me the ear of the whole world that I WOULD BE THE VOICE to tell the whole world of His goodness. God knew that I would open my mouth and speak. I knew that if He did not open a door one way to let me tell it that He would open one another way. If I could not speak it, I was going to write it/type it. I was going to preach it. I was going to teach it. I was going to sing it and I was going to dance it. My voice would be heard this time!

Somebody's blessing is wrapped up in me opening my mouth for His purpose. I was not going to hold back for I have been pregnant too long. I am full term. My water has broken and I am dilated to 10. If I don't open my mouth this baby won't be able to come forth. I cannot keep quiet any longer. I cannot hold my peace. I won't hold my peace. Something on the inside of me feels like fire shut up in my bones. The anointing is flowing to me and through me. There is an overflow that has now been released to you right now through the very book that you are holding in your hand and reading for I cannot contain it! Release ... in the mighty name of Jesus! Glory to God!

Oh, I am not finished telling about God's goodness. This child that almost drowned at age 3, well ... at age 2, this same child had to be rushed to the ER and undergo an emergency surgery after he suffered an injury playing at home with his siblings. On this incident, I was so upset with THE LOVE OF MY LIFE again for not being there to watch the kids while I worked. I was working from home at the time, but I very well was unable to watch the kids and work at the same time nor was I supposed to be having kids at home while I worked. It was a Saturday and Saturdays are always crazy at my home with all the kids being home and especially when I had to work.

I did not have a reliable babysitter at the time, so I depended on the LOVE OF MY LIFE when he was available and when he was not available the oldest sibling would be in charge of the others, with minimal supervision from me at my workstation. They would mostly watch TV and play games while I worked and I would check on them during my breaks and make sure they were okay and that they ate lunch, had a snack, etc. The LOVE OF MY

LIFE had other obligations; namely, work and he was not able to be there at all times and we did not hire a babysitter to fill in as needed, so we ended up paying a price.

The price we paid was that my son had to undergo emergency surgery. I prayed over him before, during and after his surgery. Everything turned out okay. Thank God. Yet, I blamed myself indefinitely for working that day and not watching over him. I blamed THE LOVE OF MY LIFE for not being there and watching over him. I blamed everyone I could blame even when I knew it was not justified.

I blamed myself mostly for both traumas that took place on my watch, the almost near-drowning incident and the emergency surgery. The very same child born of marriage, the one that I cherished so and vowed and promised to watch over and not let out of my sight, the one that I completely put first in my life and said I would always be there to love, cherish and protect him. He was the "Apple of My Eye", yet, I could not save him, only God could. I lived with the guilt from these two incidents even with the revelations that "God's Eye is on the Sparrow" and the revelation that "God is a Healer, a Physician, a Surgeon" and that He can heal and save. I still wanted to be the hero. I felt like if I could not save everything and everyone then what is my purpose in life? It seemed as if all I was doing was more harm than good.

Another miracle in my life involved an elective surgery with my baby boy. I took him to the doctor and on a routine physical exam they found an abnormality. It was an inguinal hernia and this can either be an elective or nonelective surgery. The specialists and surgeons chose to surgically repair it. I was really not in a position to make a decision in any way because I did not trust my decisions at this time. Nevertheless, I was praying throughout the entire process from beginning to end. Yet, I had a calmness that I did not have in any other children's illnesses in the past. There was something different about my baby boy. He was anointed and appointed by God in the womb.

When naming him, I tried to keep in mind my initials CYH and my best friend Prophetess Kim's name and I came up with the perfect name "Christian Yakim". It means "Follower of Christ, God will Establish". I dedicated this child to God at conception. I said to God "Lord if you want me to keep this baby and carry it full term and care for and provide for this child an entire lifetime on top of everything else I got going on, then you are going to have to keep it because, you know I can't!" Somebody Bless God for the Revelation! Christian Yakim was child Number 8, meaning new beginnings, but I thought I was done with childbearing with child number 7, meaning completion.

I began to be totally dependent on God with this pregnancy. My faith increased tremendously. When I was pregnant with this child I had peace that passeth all understanding. It was if I was carrying the Baby Jesus in my womb. That is how I viewed this pregnancy. One day during a routine OB/GYN visit the sono tech conducted a routine sonogram and her face was just like the face of the doctor that told me that my first son was going to be born with spina bifida and hydrocephalus and that I would be unable to take care of him because he would be mentally ill, developmentally delayed and in a vegetable state.

Well, the sono tech left out the exam room in haste and called the doctor in and he looked at the sono screen and his face turned into the same look as the doctor that delivered my first child and he acted the same way and he said the same thing to me, but it was a different script this time. He said, "I am so sorry to inform you that your baby has fluid on his brain and if it continues to accumulate he may die within the womb due to the fluid crushing the brain, his life expectancy is questionable so prepare for an unexpected outcome just in case. Until then, we plan on following you very closely and we will have you go see specialists for high risk pregnancies, weekly". I really liked and respected my doctor, but I did not even let him finish his report and I did not hesitate. I said with the strongest voice of power and authority that I had within me "God is a Healer!" I said "I have faith in God. He won't put more on me than I can bear and I believe that He is going to heal my baby!" I left out of the office with grace and dignity and I about fell apart on my way home from the doctor that day, but I couldn't there was too much peace on the inside of me. I kept the faith. I kept believing and trusting God. I cried at times, but then I quickly got back in the spirit and stayed strong.

I remember going home that day and telling THE LOVE OF MY LIFE the news. Although I had recently filed for divorce and the divorce was pending, me and THE LOVE OF MY LIFE still had an intact friendship for the kids' sake. The peace of God continued to flow to me and through me during the time of my pregnancy and during the time of my divorce. The peace that passeth all understanding. Me and THE LOVE OF MY LIFE, despite our shortcomings, had a common bond of loving our children and trying to give them the best life possible and the truth of the matter was that I still loved and cared for him dearly. I did NOT file for divorce because I disliked him, listen to me clearly, "I still loved that man" but "I loved God more, much, much, more!"

I have always had the love of Christ in me and I absolutely loved everyone, God was now revealing it all to me. As I walked closer together, hand in hand with God, the understanding was becoming clearer to me. Just because you love someone does not mean that that person is supposed to be your husband or your wife. Only God knows whose set of ribs I belong to, so I rest in an all knowing, all powerful, everpresent God.

I shared with THE LOVE OF MY LIFE the news that the doctor had given me with tears in my eyes and he said "Don't worry it is going to be okay". The way he said it I knew he meant it, but he did not understand my heart. What I was saying to him was "It had to be okay because my heart could not take anymore, not one more thing". My heart could not relive what happened to me 20 something years ago. I just could not do it. I had already endured way too much. No, this could not be so.

I continued to pray and trust God. I talked to a coworker, Carla, about it and she prayed for me. I talked to my family and friends and they prayed for me. I talked to Bishop Davis about it and he prayed for me and then I talked to God about it and He prayed for me! Hallelujah! Catch that one in the spirit! "God prayed for me!"

I went back to my follow-up OB/GYN appointment and there was peace all around me. There was so much peace and I layed on the exam table and the sono tech prepared to do the sono and she did. She left out the room again quickly and called the doctor back in and they both came in the room and I layed down still, calm and peaceful. The doctor looked at me as he placed the instrument down lightly and he looked at me and said with a smile, "Prayer does change things."

You see, I had a praying doctor caring for me during this pregnancy. He believed in the power of prayer and when I told him "God is a healer and that He is going to heal my baby", he did not question me, he simply agreed with me and had hope and faith just like I did and he participated in the process. The bible says "Where two or more are gathered in my name, there I am in the midst." It only took me and the doctor to believe that God could heal my son, but I had so many more prayer warriors on assignment, on post watching and praying, and then on top of all of that God himself was praying for me. The doctor went on to say "You must have been praying because your son is normal, everything is okay." Everyone in the room rejoiced including the baby that leaped in my womb.

It turns out the only abnormality he had was a big anointed bald pumpkin head. He had the family trademark, a big pumpkin head. So, when he was born and he started to be a boy and do what boys do, eat a lot, play harder than they eat and get hurt, I began to confess over his life daily that he was anointed. He received the nickname "Mr. Anointing".

He once got his whole hand stuck in the hinge of a shut door trying to follow me to the bathroom one evening and it was dark in the hallway and I shut the door behind me as usual, not knowing he was right behind me. I turned on the light and opened the door to him screaming at the top of his lungs and saw that his fingers were in the hinges and I immediately prayed over his hand and ran cold water over it, applied ice and comforted him. He was left untouched. No blood, no scratch, no cut, no scar, no bruise. The hand that was bent and bruised immediately became unbent and there was no trace of an injury.

From that day forward I have called him "Mr. Anointing". Mr. Anointing speedily recovered from his elective noninguinal hernia surgery and all of his minor setbacks that he has encountered in life from simply just being a big anointed bald pumpkin head boy. Believe me there were many, many more and God is still a Healer!

SCRATCH IN THE RECORD

Looking back from time to time remembering the very words that **MY IDOL** said to me "Look at this house, you have been here all day and you have not done anything. You have not cooked, you have not cleaned or lifted a finger ... you ... you ... you ..., if you keep this up you are going to lose a good thing. I am going to leave you HIGH AND DRY!" .... SCCCRRRRAAATTTCCCHHH IN THE RECORD .... THE MUSIC STOPS---- COMPLETE SILENCE.

These three words "HIGH AND DRY" cut deep like a double-edged sword, but something on the inside of me rose up and the Rocky music started to play in my head. You know Rocky Balboa in the movie Rocky, well that music was playing in my head. I had a new song playing in my head because the old record that I had played so long in my head had somehow got scratched.

I got up off the coach that I had been sitting on for way too long and I began to walk to the door and I opened the door and I left the door wide open. The gentle breeze was flowing through the house freely. This open door graciously indicated to everything and anyone in the room who needed to exit out of this open door, that now was a good time, because before I could stop myself I had turned around and whoever and whomever remained in the room became my congregation and I began to preach my first sermon with the bible in my hand pointing to the scripture (Philippians 4:19) "My God shall supply all my needs according to His riches in glory by Christ Jesus".

At this point in time, I made an executive decision to go ahead and ad-lib. My bible also tells me that "The God I serve loves me and cares for me and that He will never ever leave me or forsake me and it also says that as long as I serve Him and Him alone, I will never ever ... ever ... ever ... be "High and Dry", Hallelujah! If you don't believe me then take a look at the good book for yourself." I had no takers!

I do believe that I was the fivefold ministry in operation that day. I did everything but pass the offering plate, but it is not too late. That day I stood on the word of God and this day I stand on the word of God. I have not wavered in my faith since that day and God keeps on showing me that He alone is faithful. Oh, let me tell you this is another sermon, "faithful", but I don't have time to preach it today, but you know I am going to preach it for it is in my belly, but for now I will just leave you with this little tidbit, "God is faithful".

The best advice I can give you on this message, you don't even have to buy my CD on this sermon. This one is for free! This message is speaking loud and clear to everyone who needs to receive it. Open your spiritual eyes and ears right now and focus on what I am getting ready to tell you. "If you are ever in a situation in life and the devil pushes your back up against the wall and you cannot move in any direction nor do you even know which direction to move or better yet maybe you cannot even move at all, you are trapped in that very place. I want you to reach for your bible and if you can't reach it call on somebody to bring it to you and then go and tell this same person to open the door and stand back and stand still because the "salvation of the Lord" is getting ready to come right through that open door, you will feel it in the gentle breeze and I want you to go to that same scripture (Philippians 4:19) and "sucker punch" the devil with the word of God. I want you to hit him so hard that you knock him out for the count, "TKO in the name of Jesus". I did it in the name of Jesus and so can you.

When you have knocked him out at the end of the count, I want you to take him by the tail and drag him to that open door that I told you ahead of time to leave open, the one with the gentle breeze flowing to and through. I want you to throw his butt out and shut the door behind him and turn back on the Rocky Balboa music and have yourself a Holy Ghost Party in Jesus Name! I don't have to coach you, prompt you or even tell you when to do it. You will know just when and you will do it just fine.

I can tell you this little secret, your weapon is not your fist, it is not your status in life, it is not your beauty or your charming personality, your loving characteristics and attributes, it is not your personal and professional resume, and it is not running from every situation that approaches you. It is your tongue. There is power in your tongue when you utilize the word of God.

SPEAK THE WORD OF GOD OVER YOUR LIFE AND YOUR SITUATION

When you get sick and tired and sick and tired of the devil kicking your butt you will open your mouth and speak the word of God over your life and over your situation. My anointed baby boy Christian did it one day. One day I arose early as usual and got before the Lord in prayer. I prepared my family for school as usual, just another typical day. I hung up the cell phone early from the Power of Prayerline because it was snowing and I don't like driving in snow and now the police give out tickets for talking on a cell phone while driving and no, I don't have a bluetooth, though I did have a headset. Nevertheless, I had things to do to prepare the kids for school. I did not want to hang up the call, but the situation warranted it.

God was speaking, but I was too busy to listen. I got the kids in the car and got their seatbelts on and was heading to drop them off to school/daycare and then to work. I dropped the kids off at school safely. The roads were hazardous. I decided to take the typical shortcut, the normal way I like to go and God said to me gently, "Don't go that way ...". I did not listen because "I knew what I was doing, I do this everyday, I was like "God, I got this!" I was so confident in what I was doing because this is what I normally do. I assured God that it would be okay. I was explaining to God, as if He was not all-knowing, that it was a shortcut.

God just listened and watched me be rebellious and disobedient. I began to go upwards on the hill. Halfway up the hill my tires began to spin and spin and spin, the car began to swirl. I could go no further I was stuck midway on the hill. I looked behind me thinking I could go backwards and downhill looked further than uphill. I then thought about putting the car in reverse, but I kept looking downhill and it was very steep and I thought "No that would not be wise, I might end up in a ditch or worse, roll the car completely over and no one would even know." I continued to think to myself, "No, that would not be smart."

My next thought was to call the police or rescue workers like the fire department to help us out of our situation or maybe a passerby will stop to help us, maybe. Then I thought "No, they would probably just get stuck just like us trying to get us out." Acting out of fear, I reached for my cell phone to place a call, but decided not to place the call for I thought. "I can surely get myself out of this situation." I am "Super Crystal" like Wonder Woman.

Wait, first before I do anything crazy, I turned around to look at my baby to see if he was safe and in his seatbelt because most times he would not be secure in that he would either get out the seatbelt or he would not be securely positioned in the car seat in the first place. This time he was somewhat secure. At this point it was too late to even worry about if he was secure because I could not do anything but hold onto the steering wheel stuck midway on the hill.

I began to panic and think "If only I had of listened to God when He said "Don't take that turn, don't go that way." Well, anywho, I am going to in my own strength place my feet on the accelerator really really hard and get myself out of this situation. I have been in worse situations than this. I mean I know this is the first time I have ever gotten stuck midway on a hill, but I can do it, right? As I placed my feet on the accelerator, the car began to have a mind of its own. We were now going in reverse sideways, now a 360 degree turn and now downhill. I held onto the steering wheel tightly so that I had somewhat control of the vehicle and I began to pray out loud. The baby, Christian, began to pray with me out loud. I had been teaching him to pray since he was a baby and now he was showing me clearly that I did not have to teach him any longer for he was literally praying out loud along with me and even louder than me.

I was more scared than the baby. I told the baby "Be quiet baby mommy is trying to pray, honey ...". I needed the atmosphere to be still and quiet so I could hear from God. Christian did not listen. He began to cry out to God even louder and now with more force. He said these very words "God Help Us, Honey!" I wanted to laugh so hard, but I was too afraid to laugh, but God heard my little baby's big cry and God began to speak directly to me "He said keep your feet on the brakes lightly tapping the brakes and slowly and I mean slowly coast all the way down the hill, holding the steering wheel tightly and securely stabilizing your tracking and continue to pray and listen and when you get down to level ground continue to praise me and tell the world of My goodness".

During the coast down the hill, I started to feel more confident and I said "Lord I feel like praising you right now" and He said "Now is the time to pray when you get to level ground you can begin to praise". We slowly came to level ground and I proceeded to drive to our next destination with caution while simultaneously giving God all the praise. The gospel music was playing in the car stereo and I was driving and singing and doing a Holy Ghost dance, lifting my hands and working the head, neck and shoulders all from behind the steering wheel.

Just when I thought the "teaching moment" was over, for I had surely learned my lesson from God and I was now rejoicing in the spirit, the baby yelled louder than the music from the third row of the minivan loud enough to get my attention in a baby voice but the stance of a grown man. I turned down my music so that I could hear him speak clearly and he said, "Mommy never go that way again". I knew exactly what he meant, he was saying "Mommy, listen to God and never be disobedient". I caught that one in the spirit. This child knew more about listening to God than I did. That child is truly anointed. That was a prime example of child-like faith in action. Grown adults have to have this same type of faith in order to please God. He does not want us to continue to think we are so grown and so mature that we don't need him for indeed He will allow us to get into situations that will show us that we truly do.

I thank God for that miracle that day because how would my children live knowing that it was just a typical day with mommy dropping us off at school and her last words to us were "I love you and pray" just like always, but the only difference this time was we did not get the chance to hug her and hold her real tight and say "Mommy we love you too and we will pray, promise". God would not allow my children to live with that guilt and the pain from that lost opportunity. He gave me another chance and He gave them another chance to get it right, to say "Mommy we love you too and we will pray, promise" and this time really mean it.

For it is one thing to say something and it is another thing to mean it and do it. That was a test from God and Christian, Mr. Anointing, who just turned 4 years old passed that test. He went to daycare testifying and prophesying about God's goodness. Oh and he did not stop there, the next day when we were en route to the daycare he said to me, just in case I had forgot, because you know the flesh sometimes just does not get it, he said "Mommy, there is still snow on that mountain, don't go that way". I did not say one word, but I caught that in the spirit and I looked at that mountain covered with snow and the flesh was saying again "Go that way it is a shortcut", because the flesh is always warring against the spirit. My spirit, mind, body and soul were in agreement that day that we were only going to take the road that God said was okay to travel for we were in total agreement that any other path would not get us to our destination safely.

One morning, not that long ago, I woke up to a phone call from my God-daughter Nikkia telling me to get ready for church. We had both overslept and had 25 minutes to prepare and get to Sunday school. I was not feeling quite right but I got up and did what I normally do. God spoke to me gently to tell me to check my glucose levels. I wanted to continue with what I was doing and ignore his request, but I didn't for I had learned from timespast the consequences of not listening to God so I stopped what I was doing to check my levels and my levels were 62, which warranted immediate action. All I could do was give God praise and thank him for loving me enough to wake up my God-daughter and tell her to call me to wake me up out of a deep sweet sleep to get ready for church. God on many occasions even used my crying babies to wake me up in the middle of the night and He would tell me to check my glucose levels. God can use whoever, whomever and whatever He chooses to get your attention. What if Nikkia had of ignored God's request? What if I had of ignored God's request? People, please start listening when God speaks, your life depends upon it. Someone else's life depends on it.

Looking back over my life, there has been so many miracles that took place in my life including those that I was asked to never tell. You know those deep dark family secrets that involve someone you trust offending you. Yes, it happened to me too. Well, I won't say the name of the perpetrator of the offense I will only say that he died a horrible death. I really cared for this person. He was not a blood relative, but an adult close friend of the family that we considered a part of the family. He would often give me candy, donuts, special favors like buy my favorite foods or bring home some of my favorite things like ice cream and other nice gifts to just show that he cared. This was a daily thing and I was always thankful and grateful. He really liked me and I liked him a lot. I trusted him and my mother trusted him. My entire family trusted him.

One day my mom was away and it was just me and him alone in the house. I was watching TV, listening to music on the radio, playing albums on the turntable, listening to my mom's old music and singing, dancing and jumping around in my free time as a kid. It was not uncommon for my mother to run her errands and leave me alone. I was very mature and knew how to handle myself while she was away.

It was getting dark and I started to wonder if my mom would be home soon and if she was okay. Just as I was thinking about my mom returning home, the WOLF IN SHEEP'S CLOTHING came in the front room that I was in and said "Let's play a game" and I asked with a "happy go lucky smile", "What kind of game?" He pulled me close to him and said "Give me a kiss" and I looked at him as if I wanted to give him a friendly kiss like one you would give to someone you cared about on the cheek or forehead or like you would give to your parents, grandparents or a family member to show love and affection, but he was trying to give me a very intimate kiss on my lips and even at a very young age I knew this behavior was inappropriate so I turned my head and turned up my nose and said "I don't like kissing" which was the truth.

My paternal grandmother loved kissing and hugging on me and I loved and cared for her too, but I would always try my head and turn up my nose to avoid her kisses. The hugs were okay but kissing, definitely not. I was always like "Yuck". Part of this was because I felt if I loved her or showed affection toward her that would mean I was not being loyal to my maternal grandmother who was my everything and meant the world to me and who I had no problem kissing, hugging and showing affection, but really I think I just did not like kissing or showing affection to others in that way, it was very uncomfortable to me, so you know the WOLF IN SHEEP'S CLOTHING did not have a chance.

He kept trying though. He then said "Well give me a hug" and I said "I don't like hugging either". He then said "Okay, well let's play a game of football" and I said "How do you play that?" A question that an innocent kid would ask when you say you are going to play a game with them. You know those kids that are often left home alone and unattended to and see a game as attention that they are lacking, those kids who live life knowing something is missing, which leads to something being broken. He went on to say "I will get on top of you and we will roll around" and I stopped him in the middle of his game instructions and said "I don't like that game!".

I knew at a very young age that this did not sound like football that involved an actual football. I then went on to say "I don't think that is a game you should be playing with a little girl. I don't like that game!" He then stood over me like a giant and he looked down at me and I looked up to him, it was like my body was stiff and I could not move and there was fear all over me and all around me and without moving one step, I immediately began to get in the spirit and pray and I prayed like my life depended on it.

As a small child with my eyes now looking up to heaven, silently crying out to God for protection, every ounce of fear was overtaken by the power of God within me and I said to him with a strong, powerful voice with force "My mama is in the driveway and she is coming in the house right now and she won't approve of these types of games ...!" He turned around and jumped and ran so fast and set himself in motion to hide, but he could not hide from God. We both saw the car lights flash through the window curtains and heard the car engine in the driveway. My racing heartbeat slowed down to almost a halt. There was a calmness in the atmosphere and my breathing returned to normal. I was very young at that age, but I knew the power of prayer at that very moment. It was just as my grandmother had shown and taught me, but this time I knew it for myself.

My mom came in the house and I remained silent and he remained silent. I later spoke and told my mother on several occasions that "someone" would come in my room and stand over me late at night. She asked me could I possibly be dreaming and surprised by her response I said "No it was not a dream it was real." So I continued to pray and watch. As I prayed and watched and trusted God to protect me, I confidentially shared this same information with my maternal grandmother who believed me at the very first word and intervened in the natural and in the spirit. It never happened to me again as a child.

It happened again later in life when I was in high school, college, and even as an adult. I just assumed this was a normal thing that happened to every girl as if it were somehow her fate. I remember on one occasion in high school when I stayed after school for an extracurricular activity with my mother's permission. She had warned ahead of time about "boys" and how "if they have sex with you one time you will be pregnant". That was the only information she gave me and I really did not even know the definition of sex.

Nevertheless, for the most part, I remembered everything my mother and grandmother told me growing up even when it did not make sense to me I listened and remembered. I was walking down the hallway one evening after school and sure enough there was a "boy". Now I had seen this boy around school and it appeared he was really popular. I was not really what you considered "popular", but I did manage to hang around the popular kids so I guess that kind of made me somewhat popular. Anyways, me and this particular boy never really spoke to each other, but he seemed to be a nice boy. So he looked at me and smiled and I looked at him and gave him a smirk and placed my head back down.

As a small child I was really not that friendly because I remembered the rules taught to me by my elders "Don't speak to strangers." However, this was not the case, for this boy was not a stranger, so I thought to myself it might be okay to just say hello, but instead I just gave him a smirk. I was kind of shy when it came to boys and did not know why so when he spoke to me once again, I just said hello and kept it moving. Plus, we really did not have much to talk about because one, I did not know him and two, he was a boy and mama told me to have "nothing to do with boys" which also meant "have no parts with boys". Which meant to me simply, "don't give them the time of day".

He began to converse with me as I began to walk toward my school locker and get my things to prepare to go home. I had to walk home that day and it was getting late in the evening and mama's standing rule was to be home before the street lights came on so I had to hurry. It was apparent that he was in a playful mood that day as he grabbed my hand and pulled me toward him. I pulled away, turned my head and turned up my nose as he tried to kiss me and I said "Gross". He was persistent and he pulled me toward him again. I resisted again. I then began to look around me to see if anyone witnessed this inappropriate behavior. There was no one in sight. How can this be possible, an empty school building? Surely, we were not the only ones left in the entire school, how could this be so.

He grabbed my hand really tightly and pulled me into a closed stairwell and closed the door behind us and as I began to pull away and tell him "Stop, you are hurting me, let me go." With all the force and the screams that I was exerting, all I could hear was my faint echo back in the empty closed stairwell. I began to get nervous and fearful. I continued to try to pull away with more power and more strength to no avail. He was more powerful and much stronger. For he was a boy and it was just as my mom had said, "boys are stronger than girls and if they ever get you down on the ground it is going to be too late, it is going to be all over with." I knew that it was now too late but I fought with all that I had and I prayed as hard as I could pray and despite it all, I was down on the ground, but I was not going to surrender without a good fight. Oh no, it was not over with yet.

I began to look up to heaven and I cried out once again to God for I knew that no one else had heard my screams. As I cried out to God the stairway door opened and it was the school janitor and the boy jumped up so fast and the janitor said "Are you okay?" as I slowly tried to gather myself, and he looked at the boy in disgust and he grabbed my hand and helped me to my feet and he looked at the boy and just shook his head. The janitor knew me and he knew the boy and he knew that this incident was inappropriate. The kind janitor made sure I got home okay. When I got home from school that day I never spoke a word of this to my mother because I knew she would be disappointed in me "messing with boys". I just kept quiet. The next day, the kind janitor reported the incident to the appropriate authorities at the school and I was called from class to go to the office to explain the situation.

At that time, I really could not speak for myself for I was really traumatized by it all. I had never experienced anything like this and I really did not know how to deal with all the feelings I was having about it let alone explain it to anyone. I said in these very words "He tried to rape me". Now I did not even really know the definition of rape but I had heard about it from others and they informed me that it meant someone having sex with you without your permission. Now call me crazy, but that appeared to be what happened to me "He had tried to rape me". Now, that seems self-explanatory to me.

As I continued to talk to the appropriate school authorities the boy was called into the office in the same room with me and he gave his side of the story and he said "I did not rape her", which was true. The appropriate authorities then asked the boy to further explain the incident and the boy said "It is not as it appears!" This puzzled me greatly and it really made me feel like I somehow could have just imagined all of this, but I knew that was not the case. I did not say one more word. I just kept quiet. I did not even look up. I just kept my head down through the entire meeting. The appropriate authorities continued to talk to the boy and I continued to remain quiet.

The appropriate authorities encouraged me to speak and that if I did not speak that they could not help me. I looked up one more time at the authorities directly eyeball to eyeball and said in all sincerity, "It was just as I told you". The appropriate authorities definitely did not know how to help me for at this time I noticed the appropriate authorities were trying to make a decision that was in the best interest of everyone involved because now it was a matter of this incident being a reflection on the school, the school community, the public eye, etc.

A decision would be made to be in the best interest of all involved and that decision was to be fair and just to all parties involved. The final decision made from that meeting was to give both me and the boy a 1-day suspension from school. We were both informed that "this type of behavior and misconduct" would not be "tolerated" in school. I guess the decision was made based on it was an "alleged attempt to perform sexual misconduct" but since it did "not happen in all actuality" both parties were "innocent until proven guilty". The kind janitor's testimony was not enough. My testimony was not enough. It definitely looked like to me that "this type of behavior and misconduct" was indeed "tolerated in school and in the community" because no one was doing anything to prevent it from happening nor were they doing anything to protect those who it happened to. I just remained quiet. I never talked about this incident to my mother for fear she would not believe me either. I wanted to talk to my grandmother about it but she was not available to talk to me. In fact, she was many miles away. So I began to talk to God about it and He listened and He told me to "hold my head up high and be strong". So, I did just that.

When I went back to school the next day, I did just as God had instructed "I held my head up high and I walked tall and strong." I began to receive mean looks and slanders from the boys cliché of friends, family and others because the rumors were now all around the school of how I was a "mark" and a "trick" trying to get the boy in trouble. I just kept quiet and did just as God had instructed me. The boy never messed with me again and for that I am thankful and I knew God had once again performed another miracle in my life by saving me from this incident because it could have been so much worse had He not intervened and for that I am thankful and grateful. I cannot say that the emotional trauma from all of this did not affect me, but I remembered the saying "whatever does not kill you, will make you stronger", so I looked forward to becoming stronger.

As the years went on I began to feel that this was definitely my fate to have bad things happen to me and no one even believe me and then receive more punishment from the same that I did not even deserve. Yet, I kept the faith in God and continued to live my life. By the time I was an adult, I basically allowed anything and everything to happen to me and I thought to myself "What harm could it be, sin is sin and I was already out of the will of God and God was already not pleased with me, what else could I do wrong, what else could happen, how much lower could I go?" This was an open door to the enemy to bring in alcohol, drugs, sex, lying, stealing, cheating. Sin is sin was my justification.

The devil set everything in motion with these very thoughts playing over and over again in my mind. I started to believe that since "I was at the wrong place at the wrong time" it was somehow my fault. So I accepted what had happened to me and did not view it as victimization although I lived many years to come in the role of a victim.

As these types of incidents in society continued to happen and as these incidents began to touch home and affect the lives of "the appropriate authorities" and others in the world, it was taken more serious and laws began to be implemented to protect innocent victims from such. Terms were established to define different acts of sexual misconduct and in my particular case it was not rape from a total stranger it was "date rape".

Yes, I knew the definition of "date rape" very well but the policies did not apply to me for I just kept quiet. I was silenced by fear, by mistrust, by discouragement, by shame, by hurt, by pain. I had my own personal experience and definition of "date rape". Date rape involved boys and men that I trusted. The boys and men that my mom as a young child used to always warn me about. The very reason she sheltered me trying to protect me from harms way by not allowing me to go to the basketball, football, track, baseball games, or on a date, or to homecoming or the prom unless it was with a girl, or the school dances and the teen clubs unless I was with my big brother, or participate in activities that required a level of maturity that I had yet reached, because I was sheltered in the "safety of my home". The reason she never allowed me to be a cheerleader because "boys were at the game".

I bought into all of this, even her advice to stay away from boys because if I have sex with them just one time I will get pregnant on the very first time. Well, on the "first time" when I snuck out the safety of my home and did not get pregnant, that sort of canceled the validity of her knowledge. From that point on, I felt as she was just keeping the best kept secret away from me. Boy was I wrong.

That same evil, ugly, spirit revisited me again much later in my life, only this time I was the mother. Generational curse in action. This same spirit was now trying to attack my seed. I said to myself, "The buck stops here!" I had already allowed it to happen to me. It was not going to happen to my child. Maybe over my dead body but not as long as I was living.

I don't have to call no names or call anybody out because you knew who I was speaking to then and you know who I am speaking to now. I spoke directly to that spirit and called it out by name. Flat foot, locked and loaded with the power of God and the authority within me and let that spirit know that I had a 0 tolerance when it comes to sexual abuse/rape. I let that spirit know that if anyone ever touched one of my children that they would not have to worry about me calling the "appropriate authorities", they would not have to worry about going to the hospital, or spending one night in jail cell or prison, they would not even have to worry about purchasing a coffin, casket or burial space, because I would personally place them 6 feet under all by myself. The generational curse was broken in that moment!

THE BIRTHING OF MY MINISTRY IN MY HEART – HEALING/TOTAL WELLNESS IN GOD

My heart just cannot take anyone hurting, in pain or suffering, lost or wounded. That is why I confess with my mouth and all my being, believe, receive, claim, own, declare and decree by faith that Healing/Total Wellness in God is my ministry.

I met a new friend on ning.com on my journey. Her name was Donika. Donika is a young daughter of God. Meeting her was like God was showing me and allowing me to relive my youth through her. He was showing me how my life would have played out had I accepted my calling at an early age, well at least this was how I saw it. Donika was presently in nursing school in Atlanta, living at home with her parents and trying to find her way in life by being a good, diligent and faithful servant of God. I believe our spirits connected through divine intervention. Donika and I shared many things in common i.e. a heart for God, a heart for His people, a heart for family, we both had compassion for lost, hurting and wounded souls. We both suffered violence from the world, but were taking everything back that the devil stole from us by force through the power of God.

We both loved Prophetess Juanita Bynum and followed her ministry, her message and her vision. This shared commonality brought us together as online friends. We had an unwritten covenant and bond. We began to share our lives with each other through online fellowship through email, posts and online chats. Me and Donika never exchanged phone numbers or addresses, but we both promised each other that we would not be like others who promised to stay connected, but then later did not keep their promise. As long as there was internet access available we knew would be connected. We never met in person, but we both knew that there was no distance in the spirit.

I mentioned from time to time to Donika that I was going to write this book and that it was my prayer to one day be on the Oprah Winfrey Show and share with the world my love story between me and God. Donika told me that I had so much purpose and she began to prophecy over my life in the spirit. She took it one step further in the natural and put faith in action, she informed me that she had sent an email to Oprah to ask if I could be featured on the upcoming Mother's Day Special on the Oprah Winfrey Show and we both remained hopeful. I then took it even further to contact Oprah myself for her studio was not that far from my hometown and it seemed simple enough to also send her an email and maybe even get a response from her, but that never happened. I remained hopeful and I kept speaking to God about my heart's desire of one day meeting Oprah and one day being on the Oprah Winfrey Show. Notice I did not say "be in the audience of the Oprah Winfrey Show, I said "be on the Oprah Show". Yes, when I talk to God I am very specific.

I have great faith and this great faith does not allow me to just sit around and think and dream. I put my faith in action and act on my thoughts and dreams by faith. I pray without cease and by faith set things in motion in the natural and in the spirit. I was okay when God did not answer right away because I know He is a "right on time God" and so did Donika. We kept fellowshipping and talking about our dreams and aspirations. Donika wanted to meet Prophetess Bynum in person and so did I and we both attempted to contact her on numerous occasions. Donika was successful and she was so excited when she told me all about it and she posted pictures of her experience online for all her online friends to view. I was so proud of her and we both celebrated her experience and I said in my heart, "Wow! Lord, you are faithful!"

I had on many occasions attempted to contact Bishop T.D. Jakes, Joyce Meyers, and Prophetess Juanita Bynum by email. I saw them as great leaders and role models. I just wanted to meet them and tell them how they influenced my life in a positive way and I wanted to talk to them and tell that I admired their anointing and that I too felt I was destined for greatness and wanted to write a book one day just like they had and tell the whole world of God's goodness just like they had. I wanted to share my life story to the world for God's glory.

By faith, I saw myself meeting them in person, but in the natural it had not manifested. When me and may family were featured in Essence Magazine I just knew they would read my article and maybe attempt to contact me, but it did not happen the way I thought it would. Yet, God is still God and I am still thankful and grateful to him for everything and I am still hoping to meet them one day if it is God's will, but if that never happens I just want them to somehow know that they truly have been a blessing to me. Maybe they will read my book one day or maybe someone will tell them or maybe they can just catch it in the spirit and know that they are truly a blessing to the Body of Christ and that God chose them for greatness for His purpose and His glory, just as He chose me and each and every person reading this book for the same reason, "His purpose and His glory". For we are one body in Christ with many members. Nobody has the same purpose, nobody has the same assignment, nobody has the same destiny, nobody has the same anointing. Be comfortable in your own skin in the name of Jesus!

So I say to all of you within the sound of my voice, if I never meet you in person and if I am never able to send you an email or receive or respond to your request, either in person, through mail correspondence, through electronic delivery or telephone service, know that I love you all with the love of God. Know that it is not even about me, it is about God. God has chosen you for His purpose and His glory. Don't get me wrong, I appreciate you for admiring me, loving and caring for me, but I want to show you something even greater than me. I want to show you what is behind my anointing, "what you really see when you look at me", and that is Jesus. When you look at me and through me you really just see Jesus. I am the spitting image of my Heavenly Father.

God wants you to know Him for yourself and that is why He chose me to BE THE VOICE to introduce Him to you. I don't want anyone to think I am perfect because I am going to tell you frankly, because you know I cannot lie, so here it goes. "I sin "ERRRRR" day, "ERRRRRR" single day!" The only time I do not sin is when I am sleep and when I have not yet got out of bed. Let me set somebody free today by being honest and saying, I did not get to this very place in God by doing everything right. I got here by doing a whole lot of wrong. Yet God said, "I can use you because you don't mind telling the truth and getting naked before me and man. You don't mind falling down flat on your back and looking up to heaven and crying out with a loud voice" and saying "Lord, I am a wreck waiting to happen, God help me, please stop by here and save a wretch like me!"

On February 24, 2008, I gave birth with God's help and Donika as the midwife, time of birth – 8:00 p.m., new beginnings, new direction, purpose is birthed to this generation. A Word from the Lord from Donika "God is going to reveal how He will utilize you to kingdom build and birth many nations ...". As I look at my baby that I have birthed, all I can see before me is destiny.

As Donika gives me a word from the Lord, she begins to prophecy to me and I begin to prophecy to her and myself. I begin to confess everything that God had told me, showed me and taught me.

MY PERSONAL PROPHECY TO MYSELF

"This is my bible. I am what it says I am, my life is worth living after having heard the word of God. Faith cometh by hearing and hearing by the word of God. I am the head and not the tail. I am above and not beneath. God said it, I believe it, and that settles it. I will lend and not borrow. I will rise up and not faint. My work for the Lord is not in vain. **MY IDOL** is under my feet and a defeated foe. I am more than a conqueror in Christ Jesus. Count it all joy. Weeping may endure for a night, but joy cometh in the morning. I may have cried many tears in the midnight hour, but God said joy cometh in the morning. So I say, "Good Morning". God is going to dry up every tear, heal me from every pain and sorrow, renew my mind, body and soul daily. My latter years will be greater in Him."

As I continue to speak life to my situation, my heart was comforted and Donika's heart was comforted. We found new hope that the hurt of yesterday is just a vapor compared to the joy of today and tomorrow. God is indeed a restorer and keeper of my soul. I just need to continue to trust Him and obey Him. I just need to believe and trust the God in me. For the glory of God is all over me, the light of Christ is shining to me and through me, even if I cannot see it, others see it. **MY IDOL** sees it and that is why he is so mad. He cannot touch me because my life is in God's hand. I am safe and protected under His wings. He is my refuge in the time of trouble. I am going to keep looking to the hills from which my help cometh. My help cometh from the Lord. I will know and own the power within. How will I know? I will know because God abides in me and me in Him by His spirit.

God is all powerful and so am I. When I allow him to use me as a vessel to do His will, which is now my will, I will begin to have the mind, power and understanding of God. I will begin to look, think and act just like my Heavenly Father. If I go out in my own strength, I will not succeed. If I go out with God's power, I will go from victory to victory.

Knowing and owning the power within will open new doors in my life and close the ones that need to be closed. At this point, I know I have the favor of God and man and that God has given me the grace to handle any situation He brings me to. I now have the wisdom to know if He brings me to it, He will bring me through it. Not by my might, but by His. Any problem or situation that comes my way I will say "God Got Me" and I will proceed and go out knowing and owning it. I will say "Fear get behind me, satan get behind me". I will go out with the peace of God. I will utilize my gifts and the fruit of the Spirit that God has so generously given to me. I am on assignment to birth nations and to raise up disciples and kingdom build with God's help. I am on assignment to heal the sick, the wounded, the broken hearted, to set the captives free from bondage, to find those that are lost and lead them to the Good Shepherd, to bring sinners to repentance through my testimonies, my life experiences, by the Power of God that dwelleth within my soul. It is my desire that none would perish.

THE STORMS OF LIFE

As a small child my family, led by my grandmother, would remain calm during storms by gathering together and praying in the dark for we turned everything off during the storms, lights, TV, phone, etc. God would speak through the sound of thunder and lightning. When God was done speaking, there would be a sense of calmness in the atmosphere. Today, I view the storms of life the same way. I pray my way through every storm. Not that I don't fear the storm just the same, but I have learned to rest in God and trust Him even during the storm.

A lot of people can appreciate the calm before the storm and the passing of the same. Yet few can embrace serenity and peace within a storm. I remember as a small child viewing storms as a good thing. During this time the whole family would give thanks to God for keeping and protecting us in the midst of the storm. During these times together as a family, we would pray in unity to a God that we knew could and would hear us. I personally viewed the sound of thunder and lightning as God speaking directly to me and I would listen attentively. When God would cease to speak, the storm would pass and there would be a sense of calmness all around us. Today, I view the storms of life no different. Right in the midst of my biggest storms, when the storms of life were raging, as I would enter into the presence of God, God would speak. This is how I found my true meaning of peace in the midst of the storm. My prayer for you today is to find your true meaning of peace in the midst of the storm.

As God speaks directly to me and I listen closely to his soft still calm voice, there is peace. Today we are often so busy with our daily lives that we forget to be still and simply listen. My prayer for you today and always is to spend time with God in the midst of your storms in life. He is the only one that can bring you peace right in the midst of your storm. Storms cannot be predicted in advance, but you must have a disaster recovery plan in place in order to weather the storms as you ride the storms out. Your disaster recovery plan should include Jesus. You cannot weather the storms of life without Jesus. You must prepare for the storm by making Christ your life and not adding Christ to your present lifestyle. Begin to renew your mind daily. Christ is not only the remedy to your problems and situations; He is the answer and the resolution. Just as there are mysteries of the kingdom of God that only those that enter into the deep can ascertain, so it is with finding serenity and peace within the storm. My prayer for you today is to seek the word of God as a jeweler seeks jewels. A good jeweler does not just look in one place and give up when he does not find what he is looking for. A good jeweler asks, seeks, knocks, and doors begin to open for him and he walks through those doors and he finds that in which he/she was seeking.

For the word of God is like a hidden treasure that only those who belong to Him and are in relationship with him can dig deep enough to find the true meaning of His parables and can only attain the full wisdom, understanding through application, practice and living out His word. God has spoken in parables so that His children will have to ask Him, seek Him to possess the hidden treasures that they are looking for. They will have to knock so that God will open doors on their behalf. Only those who keep knocking and knocking and knocking shall find the hidden treasures that have already been reserved for them, with their names on it.

No matter what you are facing right now in your life, know that God has already prepared you for the storm. Put on the whole armor of God daily knowing that you are prepared to fight and stand daily because God is with you and He promises in His word that the battle belongs to Him. You just need to fight with the weapons that God has already given you i.e. prayer, praise, the word of God.

NEITHER SHALL THEY DEFILE THEMSELVES ANY MORE WITH THEIR IDOLS, NOR WITH THEIR DETESTABLE THINGS, NOR WITH ANY OF THEIR TRANSGRESSIONS: BUT I WILL SAVE THEM OUT OF ALL THEIR DWELLINGPLACES, WHEREIN THEY HAVE SINNED, AND WILL CLEANSE THEM: SO SHALL THEY BE MY PEOPLE, AND I WILL BE THEIR GOD. EZEKIEL 37:23

Chapter VI

Naked Before God

And the eyes of them both were opened, and they knew that they were naked; and they sewed fig leaves together; and made themselves aprons. And they heard the voice of the LORD God walking in the garden in the cool of the day: and Adam and his wife hid themselves from the presence of the LORD God amongst the trees of the garden. And the LORD called unto Adam, and said unto him, Where art thou? (Genesis 3:7-9).

You cannot hide from God. You cannot play hide and seek with God. When God calls you, you have to come forth. When Adam and Eve were caught in sin in the Garden of Eden, what happened? Were they not found? Yes, they were found, naked and ashamed. When Jonah was caught in sin was he not found, in the belly of a whale? A good parent never takes his/her eye off their child, even if it is only a spiritual eye. You cannot lie to mom just as you cannot lie to God. As a natural parent, you may not see everything in the natural, but if you are attuned to God and your family, you will see it in the spirit. You will see when your child has gone astray, just as God sees His child when he/she has gone astray.

You will know the patterns, your heart will ache, your soul will feel, your mind will sense, your body will be aware, your ears will hear, your eyes will see things from near and afar and it will all be confirmed through the written word of God and through the audible voice of God that your child is indeed standing in the need of prayer. If you are in your rightful place, you will begin to intercede for them because you will know that at this time prayer is best and you will know the value and power of prayer, praise and the word of God. No prayer, no power. No praise, no power. No word in your belly, no power. If you pray you won't worry, if you worry you haven't prayed. This will all make sense to you throughout your life experiences.

God, our Heavenly Father, won't put more on His sons and daughters than they can bear and He will intercede on our behalf through prayer and will deliver us out of every affliction. He will chasten us only when necessary as He remains at our side and continues to nurture us and strengthen our godly character through the process so that we can grow and prosper in the things of God. God knows that the prodigal child will return home one day and He knows the very day and time down to the very second, the location and setting.

So mothers do not lose your mind or your sleep, know that you have a Heavenly Father who sits on the throne, whose eye is on every sparrow and never sleeps or slumbers and is always working things out for your good. Begin to find rest in God. If you have been obedient to God, you can find rest in Him.

COMFORT FOODS FOR THE JOURNEY – GOD CONTINUES TO SPEAK AND GUIDE ME ON THE JOURNEY THROUGH HIS WORD

For since the beginning of the world men have not heard, nor perceived by the ear; neither hath the eye seen, O God, beside thee, what he hath prepared for him that waiteth for him. (Isaiah 64:4).

But now, O LORD, thou art our father; we are the clay, and thou our potter; and we all are the work of thy hand. (Isaiah 64:8).

No story, no glory, no pain, no gain, for every test there is a testimony. Each day is another page in the book of my life. Each accomplishment is a new chapter, loving God *First,* myself and others second, all a part of the process. The greatest gift of all is love/charity and that is indeed my most worthy character and quality.

If you can get through life and never lose the love of God for yourself and others, you have been successful ~cyh~

Know the difference between jealousy and hurt for they both feel the same, but they are different. Know how to handle each respectively. I see my life as a book written and inspired by God. Although satan plays his proper part, I am the leading lady in the limelight. It is no surprise that by faith I presently see it on the top of the bestseller list and I see that scholars from afar will obtain a copy of a love story between me and my first love. The story of how God created, loved, adored and cherished me. A story of how He strategically planned out my life to bring Him glory and how He used me mightily to heal the sick, set the captives free, bring restoration to the land, build up disciples, birth nations and kingdom build.

God has blessed my life so that my cup runneth over. There is no way that I can ever repay Him for His goodness by any act, word or deed nor has He asked for such. Yet, God does require something from me and that is total obedience to Him. I must say that I had to be me through it all. Even the times that I attempted to be someone else or be like someone else it was to no avail. God kept coaching me through the entire process and letting me know that He wanted to use me and only me. I always felt total obedience to God was beyond my reach and when I fell God kept cheering me on and telling me to get back in the race and keep running for the race is not given to the swift but to those that endure until the end. I would often find myself saying to God, "God use sister so and so and brother so and so; they surely could do the job much better than me".

I kept seeing my life struggles in comparison to a competitive game of football and God was the coach. Mind you, I know nothing about football just as I knew nothing about where God was taking me. Now me knowing nothing about nothing has never stopped me before and it has not stopped me from going or telling the story about my journey, so here it goes.

Well, I was on the sidelines on the bench and God needed a player and He thought long and hard and He said "Who can I get to make the final play that will make all the difference in this game?" He looked up and He looked directly at me. Now I had been on the bench for many, many years just watching and I did not miss one play, just watching and cheering every one on from the players to the cheerleaders, I just kept cheering. I had got real comfortable just watching and cheering and even being an active spectator.

A timeout was called in the game and the field was cleared as the coaches pulled all the players in a huddle. As both teams discussed the next plays, it was apparent my coach needed a replacement and he looked over to the bench and He was now looking directly at me and He was walking directly toward me and He said "Are you ready to get in the game?" and I said "Huh – big swallow and gulp" as I tried to clear my throat before answering. Now every one was looking at me, because I was basically just a water girl. I was the one that made sure all the players had their water bottles filled before every game and yes I was on the bench and I never missed one play and I went to all the practices and I knew all the plays by memory, but I had never been in a real game. So, I was like "Huh- big swallow and gulp". Well, I had to be obedient because I was loyal to my coach and the team and I did not want to let them down, but surely the coach could have asked "sister so and so or brother so and so" because they had much more experience and more expertise than me and they have even proven themselves over and over again. They even had a professional business portfolio that illustrated all their great works and their excellent track record and credentials.

Nevertheless, here I go, here I come, I am walking toward the field and getting in position in the game, and the whistle blows and the football is passed and it comes directly to me and I get excited because I know this play for sure, for it is my favorite play and I caught the ball and I ran, and I ran, and I ran, and I ran as fast as I could, I ran and I did not hesitate, I did not stop, pause, look to the left or to the right, I just *HIT IT* and before I knew it I had ran past the end zone and past the goal post and I heard the crowd cheering and I heard over the loud speaker *TOUCHDOWN* and the band and the music played and I guess I was like Forest Gump I just kept on running, and running and running until I was now in the bleachers and ... see, I have gone too far now in the story, I told ya I knew nothing about football but anywhoo, now you can see why I give all the glory and all the praise and all the honor to God for even counting me worthy of the calling – *a big Holy Ghost laugh.*

God has been preparing me all of my life to make the final play in the game, but I kept running away from the calling and hiding behind the other players on the bench just filling the water bottles and making sure the other players had clean towels and making sure everyone else was comfortable and in position, but when God pulled me off the bench for good, all I could see before me was past the end zone, past the goal post and past the bleachers and way past the parking lot. All I could see was destiny.

All my life I had been looking beyond me trying to obtain destiny when God had to speak directly to me and say, "You Are Destiny!" It took more than me just hearing it from God. I had to know without a doubt and believe it without a doubt if I wanted to obtain it. If I had not believed in me like God believed in me, I would still be on the bench. Who else was going to be able to make all the difference in the game in that final play? Well, God could have chose anyone He wanted to and that would have been fine by me, but He loved me so much that He said "My dear darling, come ... follow me". On that very day, I came off the bench and made the commitment to follow Christ and continue on the journey with the final decision to be totally obedient to God as His vessel of honor for His purpose and His glory.

See Prophetess Kim, I finally made the decision God told me to make 12 years ago. I finally made it! Glory to God!

God kept speaking to me and instructing me on my assignment. God kept telling me to "Forgive those who hurt you for they know not what they do. Love them enough to lay down your life for them. Preach the gospel to the nations, just as I did. Let your life be a living testimony just as my life was".

"Then said Jesus, Father, forgive them; for they know not what they do" (Luke 23:34).

Beloved, let us love one another: for love is of God; and every one that loveth is born of God, and knoweth God. He that loveth not knoweth not God; for God is love. In this was manifested the love of God toward us, because that God sent his only begotten Son into the world, that we might live through him. Herein is love, not that we loved God, but that he loved us, and sent his Son to be the propitiation for our sins. Beloved, if God so loved us, we ought also to love one another. (1 John 4:7-11).

And he said unto them, Go ye into all the world, and preach the gospel to every creature. (Mark 16:15).

Now let me ask you, "Is there even a question or doubt in your mind if God loves you? Who would give their child's life to save someone else's? I would not. What about you? But God's love was so unconditional that He did. He loved us that much. Can you imagine that type of love? If you have a relationship with God, you can. Those of the world do not know about this type of love. Therefore, without this type of love, how can they give or show love to themselves or anyone else? Please take note of this question and highlight it for future reference. God will reveal to you the answer to this question during your personal time with Him if you have not received it after reading this book.

Those of the Body of Christ know that God's love is the greatest gift of all and that in order to be like Him we must love and bless even our enemies and those that hurt us and despitefully use us. We must bless them through God's love that dwelleth within us. We must not "shut the bowels of compassion, we must not withhold from doing good when it is in our power and ability to do so".

When you sow love to everyone, you will reap that which you have sown. It is the law of reciprocity in practice. When you give love out it will produce a boomerang effect. The opposite of love is hate. When you hate others, hate comes back to you. Again, "you reap what you sow". If you plant corn seeds, you will get corn as your harvest. If you plant bitterness, jealously, hate and discord, you shall reap the same. So don't be surprised when harvest time comes and you don't receive the harvest you expected. You must be aware of what you have planted. Well you might say "Sister Crystal, I never hated anyone and I never hurt anyone and I never ... but all this happened to me". I will say to you "Go to God and ask him to search your heart and see if you unknowingly sowed a seed in your heart which has produced the harvest which you are reaping". God will show you the very root of your problem and the very thorns that are now choking your fruit.

The bible does not lie and the bible says plainly in (Galatians 6:7-9) "Be not deceived; God is not mocked: for whatsoever a man soweth, that shall he also reap. For he that soweth to his flesh shall of the flesh reap corruption; but he that soweth to the Spirit shall of the Spirit reap life everlasting. And let us not be weary in well doing: for in due season we shall reap, if we faint not".

Looking diligently lest any man fail of the grace of God; lest any root of bitterness springing up trouble you, and thereby many be defiled. (Hebrews 12:15).

He only is my rock and my salvation; he is my defence; I shall not be greatly moved. (Psalm 62:2).

"What a friend we have in Jesus – I am a friend of God". And the scripture was fulfilled which saith, Abraham believed God, and it was imputed unto him for righteousness: and he was called the Friend of God. (James 2:23). Go ahead and get it, the blessings of Abraham!

Thou wilt keep him in perfect peace, whose mind is stayed on thee: because he trusteth in thee. (Isaiah 26:3).

My little children, let us not love in word, neither in tongue; but in deed and in truth. And hereby we know that we are of the truth, and shall assure our hearts before him. For if our heart condemn us, God is greater than our heart, and knoweth all things. Beloved, if our heart condemn us not, then have we confidence toward God. And whatsoever we ask, we receive of him, because we keep his commandments, and do those things that are pleasing in his sight. (1 John 3:18-22).

The LORD is thy keeper; the LORD is thy shade upon thy right hand. (Psalm 121:5).

Order my steps in thy word: and let not any iniquity have dominion over me. Deliver me from the oppression of man: so will I keep thy precepts. Make thy face to shine upon thy servant; and teach me thy statutes. (Psalm 119:133-135).

Except the LORD build the house, they labor in vain that build it: except the LORD keep the city, the watchman waketh but in vain. Lo, children are an heritage of the LORD:

and the fruit of the womb is his reward. As arrows are in the hand of a mighty man, so are children of the youth. Happy is the man that hath his quiver full of them: they shall not be ashamed, but they shall speak with the enemies in the gate. (Psalm 127:1, 3-5).

For thou hast possessed my reins: thou hast covered me in my mother's womb. I will praise thee; for I am fearfully and wonderfully made: marvelous are thy works; and that my soul knoweth right well. My substance was not hid from thee, when I was made in secret, and curiously wrought in the lowest parts of the earth. Thine eyes did see my substance, yet being unperfect; and in thy book all my members were written, which in continuance were fashioned, when as yet there was none of them. (Psalm 139:13-16).

"My daughter, forget not my law; but let thine heart keep my commandments: For length of days, and long life, and peace, shall they add to thee. Let not mercy and truth forsake thee: bind them about thy neck; write them upon the table of thine heart: So shalt thou find favor and good understanding in the sight of God and man. Trust in the LORD with all thine heart; and lean not unto thine own understanding. In all thy ways acknowledge him, and he shall direct thy paths". (Proverbs 3:1-6).

Through wisdom is an house builded; and by understanding it is established. (Proverbs 24:3).

<u>A TWO-WAY CONVERSATION BETWEEN GOD & GOD'S LEADING LADY C</u>

GOD'S LEADING LADY C SPEAKS

"Lord, I am crying out to You like a mother in travail. Why does man lie? Why does man hurt others? Why is man so selfish? Did You not design man in Your own image? What happened Lord? Am I not Your child? Can You not hear me? Do You not understand my heart hurts? Please hear me and help me. Keep me in perfect peace. Whatever it is Lord, please send provision to Your daughter and Your children to help us get through these trying times".

GOD ANSWERS

But he knoweth the way that I take: when he hath tried me, I shall come forth as gold. My foot hath held his steps, his way have I kept and not declined. Neither have I gone back from the commandment of his lips; I have esteemed the words of his mouth more than my necessary food. But he is in one mind, and who can turn him? And what his soul desireth, even that he doeth. For he performeth the thing that is appointed for me: and many such things are with him. Therefore am I troubled at his presence: when I consider, I am afraid of him. For God maketh my heart soft, and the Almighty troubleth me. (Job 23:10-16).

Then shall thy light break forth as the morning, and thine health shall spring forth speedily: and they righteousness shall go before thee; the glory of the LORD shall be thy reward. Then shalt though call, and the LORD shall answer; thou shalt cry, and he shall say, Here I am. If though take away from the midst of thee the yoke, the putting forth of the finger; and speaking vanity; And if though draw out thy soul to the hungry, and satisfy the afflicted soul; then shall thy light rise in obscurity, and thy darkness be as the noon day: And the LORD shall guide thee continually, and satisfy thy soul in drought, and make fat thy bones: and though shalt be like a watered garden, and like a spring of water, whose waters fail not. And they that shall be of thee shall build the old waste places: thou shalt raise up the foundations of many generations; and thou shalt be called, The repairer of the breach, The restorer of paths to dwell in. If though turn away thy foot from the sabbath, from doing thy pleasure on my holy day; and call the sabbath a delight, the holy of the LORD, honourable; and shalt honor him, not doing thine own ways, nor finding thine own pleasure, nor speaking thine own words: Then shalt though delight thyself in the LORD; and I will cause thee to ride upon the high places of the earth, and feed thee with the heritage of Jacob thy father: for the mouth of the LORD hath spoken it. (Isaiah 58:8-14).

GOD'S LEADING LADY C's ANALYSIS

Lord, I will not look back and become a pillar of salt. I will look forward and move forward with You God in Your flow. My midnight will turn into daybreak!

In the bible, Lot's wife disobeyed God and looked back and turned into a pillar of salt. Lot's wife would have had victory in that situation had she obeyed God and kept looking forward. Do not repeat history, do something different, try something different. If you want different results, it is going to take different choices, decisions, actions and experiences. Try God's way, you have already tried your way. When God brings you out of bondage, when God's hand delivers you out of a situation, don't be like Lot's wife and look back. When you are tempted to look back and disobey God's instructions and plans for your life, keep in mind what happened to Lot's wife.

SITTING AT HIS FEET: GOD MINISTERS TO MY WEARY SOUL THROUGH HIS WORD

The fear of the Lord is the beginning of knowledge: but fools despise wisdom and instruction. (Proverbs 1:7).

Behold, I will send you Elijah the prophet before the coming of the great and dreadful day of the Lord: And he shall turn the heart of the fathers to the children, and the heart of the children to their fathers, lest I come and smite the earth with a curse. (Malachi 4:5-6).

Lay not up for yourselves treasures upon earth, where moth and rust doth corrupt, and where thieves break through and steal: But lay up for yourselves treasures in heaven, where neither moth nor rust doth corrupt, and where thieves do not break through nor steal; For where your treasure is, there will your heart be also. (Matthew 6:19-21). *Where is your treasure? Where is your heart?*

For after all these things do the Gentiles seek: for your Heavenly Father knoweth that ye have need of all these things. But seek ye first the kingdom of God, and his righteousness; and all these things shall be added unto you. Take therefore no thought for tomorrow: for tomorrow shall take thought for the things of itself. Sufficient unto the day is the evil thereof. (Matthew 6:32-34).

Grace be unto you, and peace, from God our Father; and from the Lord Jesus Christ. I thank my God always on your behalf, for the grace of God which is given you by Jesus Christ; That in every thing ye are enriched by him, in all utterance, and in all knowledge; Even as the testimony of Christ was confirmed to you: So that ye come behind in no gift; waiting for the coming of our Lord Jesus Christ: Who shall also confirm you unto the end, that ye may be blameless in the day of our Lord Jesus Christ. God is faithful, by whom ye were called unto fellowship of his Son Jesus Christ our Lord. (1 Corinthians 1:3-9).

Who hath saved us, and called us with an holy calling, not according to our works, but according to his own purpose and grace, which was given us in Christ Jesus before the world began. (2 Timothy 1:9).

But sanctify the Lord God in your hearts: and be ready always to give an answer to every man that asketh you a reason of the hope that is in you with meekness and fear. (1 Peter 3:15).

Know therefore that the LORD thy God, he is God, the faithful God, which keepeth covenant and mercy with them that love him and keep his commandments to a thousand generations. (Deuteronomy 7:9).

Grace and peace be multiplied unto you through the knowledge of God, and of Jesus our Lord, According as his divine power hath given unto us all things that pertain unto life and godliness, through the knowledge of him that called us to glory and virtue: Whereby are given unto us exceeding great and precious promises: that by these ye might be partakers of the divine nature, having escaped the corruption that is in the world through lust. And beside this, giving all diligence, add to your faith virtue; and to virtue knowledge; And to knowledge temperance; and to temperance patience; and to patience godliness; And to godliness brotherly kindness; and to brotherly kindness charity. For if these things be in you, and abound, they make you that ye shall neither be barren nor unfruitful in the knowledge of our Lord Jesus Christ. But he that lacketh these things is blind, and cannot see afar off, and hath forgotten that he was purged from his old sins. Wherefore the rather; brethren, give diligence to make your calling and election sure: for if ye do these things, ye shall never fall. (2 Peter 1:2-10).

And we know that all things work together for good to them that love God, to them who are the called according to his purpose. (Romans 8:28).

And I will raise me up a faithful priest, that shall do according to that which is in mine heart and in my mind: and I will build him a sure house; and he shall walk before mine anointed for ever. (1 Samuel 2:35).

Now faith is the substance of things hoped for, the evidence of things not seen. (Hebrews 11:1).

How excellent is thy lovingkindness, O God! Therefore the children of men put their trust under the shadow of thy wings. They shall be abundantly satisfied with the fatness of thy house; and thou shalt make them drink of the river of thy pleasures. For with thee is the fountain of life: in thy light shall we see light. O continue thy lovingkindness unto them that know thee; and thy righteousness to the upright in heart. Let not the foot of pride come against me, and let not the hand of the wicked remove me. (Psalm 36:7-11).

GOD'S LEADING LADY C SPEAKS TO GOD

Search me, O God, and know my heart: try me, and know my thoughts: And see if there be any wicked way in me, and lead me in the way everlasting. (Psalm 139:23-24).

IT'S ALMOST MIDNIGHT ~cyh~

In the stillness of the night I am present in the now knowing and aware that my Lord loves me and cares and is in tune with every part of me even the beat of my heart, He knows when it skips a beat. He allows my body to flow at optimal levels and He enables every part to function in synchrony. It is the work of the Master's hand and for that I am thankful and grateful.

As I await for God to prepare my Adam to meet his Eve I will sit in the moonlight and look up to the stars and as the wind gives off a sacred breeze I will capture the moment and sing praises to His name for orchestrating such a wonderful event. The magical moment in which life will reappear with a zest that only God can impregnate, birth into life, being and existence.

GOD SPEAKS THROUGH OTHERS TO COMFORT MY SOUL

"Your life is like a garden and you shall bloom in June. You are blossoming as we speak. You are on layaway by God and God is preparing someone to get you out. You are going through a healing process. God will complete the work He started in you. Your season is now. You have planted and it is time to reap an expected harvest. Your spirit and your smile let's everyone know about God's goodness and how awesome He is. Hurt no more child. God says hurt no more. Cast your cares on God for he cares for you. He is going to turn your mourning into laughter. God is saying to you "Be still and know that I am God". Prepare your best table for the groom and do not look back".

GOD'S LEADING LADY C SPEAKS TO GOD

Lord, you know my heart, I cannot hide anything from You so I must come to You and just ask, "What kind of man would come into my life to love me and cherish me for the rest of my life and feel the same way about my children who are not his own natural children? What kind of man would not harm them, but bless them in any way possible and respect them and honor them and support them and rear them up in the right way and protect them and lead them and guide them as a godly role model with godly character? What kind of man is this?" Lord, allow me to answer. It is a godly man, a man of virtue, who is fearfully and wonderfully made especially for me by You. Until that day, I will remain a jewel to You Lord the only one who knows my true value and worth as I await the jeweler that You are now preparing to search for one of Your most sought out priceless jewels.

GOD'S LEADING LADY C CONFESSES

I am a "diamond in the rough" waiting on God to finish polishing, shining and refining and when He is done He will place me on display for the whole world to see the beauty of His finished work for His glory. I am the head and not the tail, above and not beneath, I will lend and not borrow. Excuse me devil, I need to change positions. I have been in the wrong position for too many years. I am getting out of my nightmare and getting ready to dream sweet dreams about Jesus and what He is getting ready to do for me. He has already shown me visions as I have rested in the comfort of His loving arms. No more terror by night for me I plead Psalm 91 over my life. I am not "Sleeping with the Enemy" any longer! I am getting ready to enjoy endless sweet sleep resting in Jesus, morning, noon and night. I am going to dream big and I am going to live out my dreams. I am God's queen and not one of your pons or imps. You and your tricks and devices are no match for me because God has given me the authority and dominion over everything, every situation. In Christ I will always win. I will go from victory to victory to victory. I declare, decree and ordain it to be so.

GOD ANSWERS

As it is written, I have made thee a father of many nations, before him whom he believed, even God, who quickeneth the dead and calleth those things which be not as though they were. Who against hope believed in hope, that he might become the father of many nations, according to that which was spoken, So shall thy seed be. He staggered not at the promise of God through unbelief; but was strong in faith, giving glory to God. (Romans 4:17-18, 20).

GOD'S LEADING LADY C SPEAKS

By faith, I will call those things forth which are not as though they were, by the power of God vested in me. By faith I see, believe and receive it. It is so. Now I am going to step on your head devil because you are under my feet and because I have the power to do so in Jesus name.

I am picking up my bed and walking. I am getting into the pool of Bethesda. No one is going to stop me or get in my way. My healing is in the pool. My deliverance is in the pool. I have spent way over 40 years in the wilderness. I am going to push and press my way through the crowd. I have spent way over 40 years in the wilderness. I am going to push my way through the crowd until I reach the hem of His garment and I am going to fall on my face and begin to worship Him. I know if I can just touch his hem that I will be healed, set free, whole, complete in Him instantly in that moment.

PIVOTAL MOMENTS IN MY LIFE THE VOICE SILENTLY CRYING TO BE HEARD

KINDERGARTEN

In kindergarten, I remember an incident on the playground that involved me, another girl and a jump rope. It was recess time and I was playing with my jump rope. I guess this particular girl came up to me and tried to take the jump rope from me and I was not going to let go of the jump rope because "It was mine!"

So I held onto the jump rope for dear life and I guess the girl that was trying to take the jump rope got dragged with the jump rope during the process and suffered minor injuries and consequences as a result. She cried with a loud voice until she was heard. When the recess staff came over to handle the situation, all they could see was me pulling the jump rope and the girl on the ground screaming, so immediately they blamed me for the girl's pain and suffering. Yet, all along I knew I was in the right and that I was just nicely and quietly playing with "my jump rope", just me, God, the angels on assignment and my jump rope.

Now at the time I did not know the principle of sharing because I was indeed the baby in the family and no one really taught or showed me this valuable lesson. So, I had to live out this lesson. I was holding onto the jump rope, by any means necessary. The recess staff tried to get the jump rope from me but I would not let go. How could a five year old girl have so much strength? A grown adult teacher could not get the jump rope from me. She called for backup and now two grown adult teachers could not get the jump rope from me.

I was then pulled by my shirt collar with the jump rope tightly gripped in both fists into the office and the principal asked me what was the problem and I said at the sweet age of five "This is my rope!" The principal then looked at everyone involved in this incident just like I was looking at them, like "What is the problem?" When the recess bell rang I gladly let go of the jump rope and went back to class like nothing ever happened. At the next recess, I did not even ask for the jump rope for I was "so over that jump rope". I then began to play hopscotch just me, God and the angels on assignment and nobody bothered us, only the brave and willing souls like Pat.

Well from that incident at school, I received the respect of not only the school staff but the respect of the other students. I even gained a close friend, Pat, who later became my lifelong friend and she always reminds that the jump rope incident is how she met me. Now that really says a lot about her and why she would even want to have me as a friend. Even when I try to forget this incident ever happened, she vividly reminds me of every single detail. I still love her, dearly.

I believe it was because of my resilient attitude that I received the nickname "Crazy Crystal" in grade school and in high school it changed to "Goofy" and so many more names, some others named me and some I named myself, yet no name other than my birth name truly reflected my real personality for I was far from Crazy or Goofy. I knew exactly what I wanted out of life. It was "Crystal Clear" to me, yet it seemed that everybody else was having a problem understanding it. I remember the saying "It's my world, your just a squirrel trying to get a nut". I think at one point in my life I picked up that concept and bought into that idea, silly me.

FIRST GRADE – THIRD GRADE

Nevertheless, first grade, second grade, third grade were uneventful. What stands out most to me during this time was going to church with my grandmother and learning more and more about God and faith. I remember going to church every Sunday and my grandmother would give me a $1.00 bill and she would tell me to pay my tithes and offering with it. She told me that my tithes were 10% of my income and my offering was any amount I wanted to give over that. So I learned the principle of tithes and offering at a very early age and I took note of it. Every Sunday you would find me calculating up in my head how I was going to spend this $1.00 bill and I imagine my grandma and God were watching me very closely as I calculated.

I loved going to church for a few good reasons 1) to purchase a Welch's grape soda from the soda machine 2) grandma would share her peppermint candy with me 3) singing in the choir 4) passing notes to my friends and that about summed it all up. So every Sunday I was the little girl who held up the offering line, whose whole head and arm was stuck in the offering basket trying to get change for my $1.00 bill because I needed a quarter to buy my Welch's grape soda out of the soda machine that was located downstairs in the church. I would always pay my tithes which was 10 cents and my offering which was 65 cents and I would save one quarter. I heard the preacher say one day "When you get paid make sure you pay God *First*, your debtors second and yourself third, for everyone who labors is entitled to enjoy the fruits of their labor." So, I was paying myself with that quarter that I had labored and worked hard digging to the bottom of that offering plate for.

I would take my quarter and run downstairs to purchase a soda every single Sunday, even if it meant missing the sermon, it was the highlight of my week. It was nice and cold and refreshing. I would gulp it down so fast and then look down to the bottom of the can and turn it up and hold my head back trying to get the last drop out, but when it was gone it was gone. I would then return back to service to cross off the next thing on my TO DO LIST which was asking my grandmother for a peppermint, singing an A & B selection in the junior choir, and passing notes to my friends throughout the entire service and if we somehow got a piece of chewing gum, "Oh Boy" we had a good time hiding our chewing from the ushers or the nosey church mothers in the front row that would turn around from time to time and say "Shewwwww".

We didn't care, we just kept passing notes and chewing gum and playing until the usher was walking in our direction with the tissue for the gum and the new assigned seats for all of us right next to the nosey church mothers who said "Shewwwww" or worse right next to our mama, which in my case it was my grandmother and she was now in the choir stand so you know I wanted to save myself and my grandmother from that embarrassment and the whoopin from the choir stand to the bathroom, so I would always opt for sitting by the nosey church mothers with the tinted blue and grayish hair and the black cat glasses. I know I am not the only one who remembers those black cat glasses that would not only stare at you, they would glare at you, if not look right through you like a magnifying glass. Whatever you were doing or thinking about doing those glasses would deter you. For those glasses allowed those ole church mothers to have 20/20 vision from the back to the front and both sides of their head.

My friends at church had been talking to me about getting a soda for free out of the soda machine by just simply telling Deacon Gibson that I had lost a quarter in the soda machine and he would then open up the machine and give me a free one. So I listened to what they were saying and I thought about it for a while and the next time the opportunity arose, I just so happened to be standing by the soda machine waiting on Deacon Gibson. Deacon Gibson was responsible for a lot of things around the church and I really did not know all of them, but I knew he knew how to open up the soda machine and that was the only important thing to me. So as he was walking by me just standing at the soda machine looking silly I am sure, he walked up to me and greeted me with a smile and asked if everything was okay and I said "I lost my quarter in the machine". Sure enough he then began to open up the machine and give me a grape soda for free. I thought WOW, that was easy, I can do this all the time and get a free soda and save my quarter for some candy from the candy store during the upcoming week.

Well I repeated this "premeditated act" maybe three Sundays in a row and then Deacon Gibson kindly said to me "Now you would not be lying in church would you and I said "Uh, no sir", knowing that I rightly was. He, in disbelieve, continued to tell me about right and wrong and the consequences of the same, in words that I could understand and then he gave me my free grape soda. As I sat in service that day convicted by God and remembering all the words that Deacon Gibson said to me. I knew my grandmother had raised me better than this and she had taught me not to lie and she had taught me not to steal and she had taught me right from wrong too, but I wanted that grape soda so bad and I did not feel like I was doing nobody no harm. You know as a kid we think money grows on trees, so I thought it was more grape soda where those came from.

I continued to think about it all and I felt guilty and ashamed and I decided to do something different. I would start off by telling God I was sorry for lying and then I would start putting my whole dollar in the offering plate to pay him back for those "free sodas" for I knew at an early age by listening to the preacher and my grandmother that the $1.00 bill was all God's money. I knew that even though I was paying myself the quarter, it still belonged to God. I knew God deserved the whole $1.00, even if it meant I had to sacrifice a grape soda. By faith, I knew greater would be my reward for being obedient.

I had heard the preacher say one day "You can't beat God giving, the more you give the more he will give to you." So, I was going to try God and see. So, the next Sunday, I placed my $1.00 in the offering basket and I went downstairs to that vending machine and I spoke to that vending machine and I said "I would like to have a grape soda". I had heard the preacher say one day "You have not because you ask not". I was literally asking that machine for a soda. I then went further and pushed the button on the machine because I remembered the message preached that said "Faith without works is dead" and guess what, I heard a rumbling noise and the can of grape soda was in the dispenser. I looked all around me to see if anyone was going to claim the "ice cold Sparkling Welch's soda" and when there was no takers, that soda was mine. I then went back to service knowing that God was faithful.

I kept placing my $1.00 bills in the offering basket and I kept learning the principle of faith. One Sunday I went downstairs to the soda machine and spoke to the machine and asked for a soda and pushed the button and nothing happened and I began to get discouraged. Yet I had faith so I began to war in the spirit for that grape soda and still nothing happened. Then I just stood there and looked at the soda machine with a sad look upon my face in despair and Deacon Gibson was now walking towards me and said with a smile "Is everything okay?" and I said "Yes" and he asked if I wanted a grape soda and I said "Yes". He then placed a quarter in the machine and gave me a grape soda and I looked at him as to say "I didn't lose a quarter in the machine", but I just kept quiet and said "Thank you" to him and God.

From that day forward Deacon Gibson and I became a team. Deacon Gibson was the best singer and he could even play the piano, so he asked me would I sing a duet with him and he would buy me a grape soda and I said "Yes". The whole congregation loved it. Every chance I got I would say "Yes" to singing with Deacon Gibson. Not that I could even sing all that great, but I did not mind singing praises to God and giving him all the glory, even for my off key notes. I was always shy and would get very nervous in front of crowds but I was very fond of Deacon Gibson and I loved the Lord so half of the time I would be in the choir stand singing with my eyes closed and mouth wide opening, clapping my hands and stomping my feet and it was as if the song in my belly and my spirit would take over my whole body and you would not be able to even tell that I was shy for once things were set in motion there was no stopping me.

Since Deacon Gibson teaching me the little lesson on right and wrong, I never intentionally tried to lie to Deacon Gibson or anyone else if at all possible, because I knew God was watching. Throughout life I just kept giving and giving and giving and God somehow kept providing. From that day forward, I never went one Sunday without a grape soda. I remember the preacher once saying "I have never seen the righteous forsaken or his children begging for bread". Now at that time as a small child I did not know the full understanding of this scripture, but I knew God was faithful in that He never had me begging for a grape soda. I believed God by faith even then.

One hot summer day, I was running around the house playing with my imaginary friends and probably working my mama's last nerve. I ran up to my mom who was trying to rest and stay cool by laying on the floor in front of the fan and I said "Mama, can I have a soda?" for I was thirsty from all the running. My mom said "Baby, we don't have no sodas, mama wish she could have a soda too". It appeared to me that my mama was sad and sorry to inform me that we did not have any sodas. I continued to run around the house like a happy little kid, just playing and playing and playing.

My mom continued to lie on the floor in front of the fan. She had heard my request and knew that she wanted to honor my request. She really at this point did not know what to do because we did not have any sodas in the house and she did not have any money so she did what her mother had told her to do as a small child when you don't know what else to do, she just stretched out on the floor and cried out to God. I just kept on running around the house and playing not worried about a thing. I then got bored playing in the house and decided to go outside for a spell and I opened the front door to go outside and when I opened the door to my surprise there was a box just lying on the porch.

Out of excitement, I opened up the box and looked at the contents and immediately I knew what it was, it was two cans of Fresca soda that were sent by regular mail as samples with coupons enclosed. So, I ran in the house so fast to show and tell my mama, I said "Mama, mama, we do have some soda, look, see, I told you, now we have one for you and one for me". My mama said "From that very day she knew I was special and that God does hear your cry and He does answer in His timing."

When I was more mature, my mama told me that back then we had very little food in the cupboards and that we were living in some hard times with her being off work due to a disability and trying to raise two kids on her own after being divorced twice. As a small kid, I had always thought we were rich, but my mama later informed me that we were indeed poor and that many days she had to go without food just so we could eat. This was news to me because me and my brother wanted for nothing and we ate very well, so the thought never occurred to me that we were poor or that mama had to go without for us to have.

This new knowledge made me more aware of the value of a mother and I did not mind telling anyone. I once wrote an essay in school about my mother's value as a part of a school district wide competition for a "Mother's Day Special". My essay was chosen to be featured in the local newspaper with my mom's picture and my picture. My mom was so proud of me. I remember she was in tears as she read and clipped the newspaper article and placed it in safekeeping and as she told all her family and friends the story. I remember the very words I wrote in the article and it read "My mom is the perfect mother, she loves and cares for me, she feeds and provides for me and she often has to go without for me to have and that is why I believe my mom is a perfect mother". When I was older my mom would always remind me how God supplied our every need back then and there was nothing I needed more than a soda at that time in my life. Praise God!

Not trying to get ahead of myself, but looking back, I remember another teaching moment with Deacon Gibson, n/k/a (now known as), Pastor Gibson. I was pretty much grown at this time and Pastor Gibson was teaching Sunday School. Pastor Gibson was standing in front of the class and I was of course in the back row just listening. Pastor Gibson had the bible and the Sunday School book in front of him and he was sitting down behind a desk lecturing and telling the whole class the Sunday School lesson and I don't remember the lesson but I remember specifically he was telling us what was required of us by God, the "do's and the dont's" all in the book before him.

To me it seemed like the "not to do list" was longer than the "to do list", so I wanted to get this clear in my mind because I knew I was about to mess this all up, so I raised my hand like I was in school and he smiled and said "Yes, Crystal, do you have something to say, you don't have to raise your hand?". I kindly and sincerely asked "You mean to tell me God wants us to do all of this, everything in this book?" Now Pastor Gibson just smiled because he knew I did not mind asking questions to get a full understanding of what was being taught to me, and my heart was pure. I just wanted to get this right so that I did not mess up because I knew about "being good" but I knew nothing about "being obedient", that seemed like it was going to be a lot more work and I did not know if I was ready for that task.

Pastor Gibson responded with scripture to back him up and then he finished with an answer to my question, "Yes, God wants us to do everything that is in this book". There was a long silence in the room. You could hear a needle drop at this point. My body language made no attempt to conceal itself and the big gulp and swallow in the silence of that still room had to have been heard. I did not ask any more questions, because I knew I would not be back to Sunday School until I was 65 years old or older, because there was no way I was going to get all of that right – *a big hearty laugh.* Thank God for His grace and His mercy because both God, Pastor Gibson and I knew I was going to need it.

FOURTH GRADE

Fourth grade was very pivotal in that I had my first black teacher, Mrs. Washington and my first black principal Mr. Hinton. A black teacher and a black principal in the same school was not common back then. Mrs. Washington really favored me and I do believe she saw my potential even back then and she saw how I was very reserved and refused to shine even though the light within me shined so brightly even without my effort. As a small child, I would often articulate and interpret meanings of words and actions and carry out tasks that demonstrated my level of wisdom and understanding reached way beyond my age. I remember on more than one occasion growing up in a predominantly all white neighborhood and trying to fit in.

On one bright, sunny summer day, I remember being bored in the house and wanting to go outside to play with a group of kids in my neighborhood. Now what they were playing was probably not considered a "game" that they should have been playing at that age, but I was just a spectator trying to fit in and they turned around and looked at me and said "We don't want to play with you". I was quiet, but I looked at them as to say "Why" without saying it. They continued to tell me that they did not want to play with me because I was "brown". I then looked down at my skin and for the first time in my life I realized that I was *caramel* by my definition.

Brown, black, Negro, nigger did not seem to fit how I saw myself during that time period of my life. I did not want to be labeled as black, yellow, brown, white, red. I did not want to be called racial names and I was not one to call anyone racial names or any other name than their birth name or nickname. Name calling felt offensive even at a small age. Yet, I was called many offensive names but I remembered what I was taught at an early age "sticks and stones may break my bones, but words will never hurt me" but as I lived my life that was further from the truth.

A Teaching Moment: Don't let someone's opinion of you, define you!

Nevertheless, I gladly left their presence and went back home and sat at the kitchen table watching my mom cook and prepare dinner. This was not the norm, so she immediately knew something was wrong with me and she said "What is wrong?" and I said "Nothing". She kept prying and then I said "The kids down the street don't want to play with me because I am brown". I continued to explain to my mom. "I am not brown, I am *caramel*". She listened in amazement and then she said "How did that make you feel?" and I said "If they don't want to play with me because of the color of my skin, then they were really not my friends anyway". She smiled with approval of my answer and told me that I was very wise and mature beyond my years. It felt good to have my mom's approval but at that age I really did not even know what I had just said but it just felt right and leaving those group of kids just felt like the right thing to do. Growing up, something on the inside of me let me know the correct words to say at the correct time and it just felt right that is the best way I can explain it. My mom just kept on doing what she was doing and I kept on playing with my best friends, my dog Wolf and Jesus. God's handiwork was in progress even then.

I know a lot of parents send their kids outside to play, often just relieved that they are out of their presence, but as parents we need to be mindful at all times where our children are, who they are with and what they are doing. I never told my mom about the games those kids were playing that day but at nine years old I knew it was inappropriate behavior that involved private body parts. Kids are greatly influenced by their peers. Parents remain prayerful and watchful over the children and grandchildren that God has blessed and entrusted you with and continue to leave the lines of communication open with them. If the enemy cannot get you, he will then next try to go after what is most important to you, your children.

Back to talking about fourth grade, as you recall I started off talking about how my fourth grade teacher, my first black teacher, Mrs. Washington favored me, well Mr. Hinton, my first and my last black principal, was another story. I was in his office daily receiving my daily fix, one swat to get me back into shape, two swats if one was not enough. I had three choices daily. Choice #1, get a swat and go back to class and straighten up my act, Choice #2, get sent home to die at my mother's hands and return to school the next day with a behind so sore you could not sit on it, or Choice #3, I could receive both Choice 1 and Choice 2 depending on the severity of my daily behavior.

Yeah there were no in-school or out-of-school suspensions and expulsions back then. It was just corporal punishment or more corporal punishment. If you misbehaved back then you would get it at school and at home and depending on if the neighbor's got wind of it, you might get it on the way home too. Your punishment was your choice, but it was indeed a punishment. No timeouts or slaps on the wrist, that is for sure. I know everybody remembers the long walk to get the switch from the giant oak tree or better yet trying to hide all the belts in the house only to find out that your mother would use a skillet if she had to, and then some of us were lucky enough to escape the extension cords. Thank God I never had to experience that although I was allowed to see the lifetime scars and wounds on others. It really made me sad to see this, but back then mothers and fathers were taught to correct their children by any means necessary. The justification for and saying was "I am going to beat you so that the correctional system don't have to". I was smart, I would always choose Door #1, the swat with a wooden paddle and holes in it or the switch. I knew every other choice was way worse than that.

The bible says "if you spare the rod you will spoil that child" and I guess that is where Mr. Hinton and my mom and many other moms came up with the concept of beating your *caramel* !@# (and I don't mean !@#) until it was black and blue. Then there was the famous mama threat before every whoopin "I brought you into this world and I will take you out!" I would always think is that biblical, where is the scripture on that one? God is a good God, surely He wouldn't have put that scripture in the bible if He really loved me and cared about me and was concerned about me.

Hey, all I can say is it all worked to put the fear of God in us. I would go back to school and class and act like I had some sense, but at the end of the school day it was always the same back in the office. I think I was trying to be the class clown to win the popularity vote, but look at the consequences. Was it really worth it? Would I do it all over again? Yes I must admit I would, only this time around I would be a better class clown. Yes, you already know that I reaped what I sowed on this one with my own children. My grandma and mama used to always say "If the horse paces, the calf is going to trot".

FIFTH GRADE-12TH GRADE

I remember like it was yesterday my 5th grade teacher Mr. Hallberg would always say, or was it my mother, or was it both? I think it was both, "Think before you speak!" Now later on in life I figured out that this was really a good advice, but as a kid these four words paralyzed me. Whenever I was called on to speak, these four words made me literally freeze in position. It did not matter if I was standing or sitting, I would be frozen in position more focused on "thinking before I speak" than actually speaking what I already knew to say.

I did not trust what was going to come out my mouth next and this oftentimes would hinder me from speaking fluently. My confidence was stifled by the effort it took to try to think of words that would illustrate I had indeed "thought before I spoke". Note to self: "When a small child is trying to express himself through words it is a good thing to first listen to what he/she has to say and then to secondly positively instruct he/she and correct him/her only when he/she is in error, but when he/she is just trying to articulate the very words out his/her mouth and he/she is struggling to even speak and express him/herself fluently and you say bluntly to him/her "Think before You Speak!" He/she may just shut down and not say anything for that is much easier and that is just what I did."

These four words made a major impact on my life. To this very day I am afraid of public speaking. I really internalized these four words and it really negatively affected my self-esteem and self-confidence. I never really felt anyone appreciated "my gift of gab" or the power of my spoken words. Looking back on everything that I held inside until this very day, I can see the power of Holy Spirit working in me even as a small child. For I had plenty of things to say even back then, but I held it all in and I am attempting to once again share it now through my writing. It was always easier for me to write than speak. I received excellent grades in English, literature, history, political science and things that pertained to "real life issues" as compared to other required subjects that I really had no interest in. I don't remember ever turning in a writing assignment and not receiving an A grade or a B+ if the teacher had a problem with giving me an A, and that was fine by me because I knew I deserved the A even when the teacher could not give it to me. I remember very clearly all my written papers concluded with talking about my faith and about My God and giving Him all the honor, all the glory and all the praise.

I remember in kindergarten through fourth grade being placed in "special classes" where I received extra help through volunteer tutors who would come in and help me and other students with reading, English, speech. No math which is very surprising because I felt a greater need for help in math than the other subjects for I wanted to make sure I knew how to count my dollars and cents. I remember being a willing participant in my "special classes" but laughing inside because I never really felt special. The kids in the "special classes" were often separated from the mainstream kids and when we returned to class everyone would look up at the "special kids" as we reentered the classroom to rejoin the class. In fact, when you think about it, we were not all that special because we had to complete the same assignments and tests as the mainstream kids to demonstrate we were on target. Speaking for me personally, I knew more than they thought I knew but I was not about to volunteer anything. I simply lived up to their expectations and when I did answer a question and it was correct they were like, WOW! I loved it! A WOW for something that was absolutely nothing to me but a simple answer to the question asked. No biggie, but I accepted the WOWs gladly.

I felt so many times throughout life that I was a better teacher than a student. I never understood why the teacher would ask me a question expecting an answer or have me write a paper and demonstrate that I knew or understood what I had researched. Duh! If I researched it, well of course I know it. I couldn't understand why we could not be on the honor system and just complete the assignments requested on our own, inside the classroom and outside the classroom. I did not feel that was asking too much. When they would ask me a question I felt like "Don't they already know this stuff?" How did they get to be a teacher if they don't know this stuff?" It was as if I thought they needed "special services" instead of me.

I felt like they had some ulterior motive to see what I knew for their own personal agenda. My personal goal was to just sit and listen and analyze everything they taught me, but not to participate. I would always try to find a safe spot in the back to not draw attention to myself, but of course you know that never worked. I only had one question throughout my grade school and high school years and that was "Why can't you just lecture and write on the chalkboard everything I need to know and let me take a few notes and basically just leave me alone?" I just didn't get it! Overall, I was respectful, but my whole attitude was I came to class to be "taught and not to teach!" Yeah, silly to think that a young child would even have that mindset. Nevertheless, I just kept listening and listening and listening and when they called on me I would always shrug my shoulders as if to say "I don't know". Everyone in the classroom would just look at me as if to say "Ugggggh, she does not know anything she is asked". Yet, I knew everything I needed to know because I had the greatest teacher and His name was Jesus.

From 6th grade to 12th grade and beyond I was simply trying to find my way searching and not fully understanding the voice within. God was stirring up the gifts within me even then, yet my mouth was silenced by the four words "think before you speak" that I repeated over and over and over in my mind each time I was asked to speak or each time speaking was required and expected of me. I hope and pray that someone within the sound of my voice now hears me when I say "Care enough to NOT tell someone you love to be quiet in a world where most people don't even have a voice. One day that very person you tell to be quiet may need to speak to you and through you. Somebody has to be the voice of God, someone has to stand for righteousness sake, why not me, you, he or she?"

THE VOICE STANDING FOR MOTHER'S WHO ARE SINGLE-HANDEDLY REARING THEIR CHILDREN AND GRANDCHILDREN WITH GOD'S HELP

Don't get me wrong, I am a mother of eight and sometimes I enjoy solitude and peacefulness just as much as anyone else and not a house or car full of noise, especially meaningless conversation, but when a child is speaking and expressing his/her heart, please listen and take the time to hear what he/she is really saying. Look beyond the words that are coming out of his/her mouth until you connect with his/her spirit. Whether what is coming out of his/her mouth is good or bad, correct or incorrect English, just listen and take the time to hear. Listen closely, very closely; it may be God giving he/she a word just for you or for others. Remember, he/she is a vessel of honor too.

Che'Andrea, named by city manager Andre' Bohannon. Che' was my first child born of marriage and I was so happy for the most part during my pregnancy with her. I prayed over the baby in my womb from Day 1, mostly that she would look more like me than her dad, but I prayed for other things too like that she would be healthy, smart, successful. Che's dad was a nice looking man, but he had some ugly ways and that made me not always see that he was indeed a nice looking man. Nevertheless, when Che' was born she looked just like her dad and I had to squint to see any trace of me and it was definitely a trace. I thought to myself, so much for praying. Yet, I loved her just the same.

We bonded after about two weeks when she started to develop and would open her eyes and would give the biggest smile when you talked to her, I soon realized that although she still looked just like her dad, that we were inseparable. The strange thing is as Che' began to develop more and more, everywhere she went everyone started to ask her "Are you Crystal Holt's daughter?" and she would say "Yes" and they would say "You look just like her". I soon realized that she was beginning to look more and more like me as the years went on and there was no doubt that she acted like me and possessed all my mannerisms, style and characteristics. I guess she was just a late bloomer like me. Looking back, I can honestly say that my children are my blessings and that God used them all in many ways to show me that they were indeed my blessings. I remember on many occasions God used my children in many ways to minister to me. On many occasions, my own children have prophesied to me.

One time when I wanted to just lay down and die and I cried out to God because I was so weary and faint and did not have the strength to go on. I laid on the bed and looked up to God and cried and said "Lord, I don't want to live, please take my life now, I am so tired and so weary, I can't go on, I have nothing to live for". My beloved daughter, Che', probably age 8 at the time, had felt and saw my need and she drew closer to my side and said with tears in her eyes, "Mommy live for me". She slowly walked to the kitchen and brought me an orange and a cup of juice to drink. Oh, don't you know I got up real quick for it only took a word from the Lord, through a child, to turn my situation around. God put it on that child's heart to say "Mommy, live for me" and He did not stop there He said "Feed her". Doesn't that sound like God to say "Feed my sheep"? Then He went further and said "Give her a drink". My daughter was obedient to God's voice at age 8. Hallelujah! If you don't believe me get in your word and go to (John 21:15-17) and (Matthew 10:42) and see it for yourself. My daughter at age 8 was starting her discipleship.

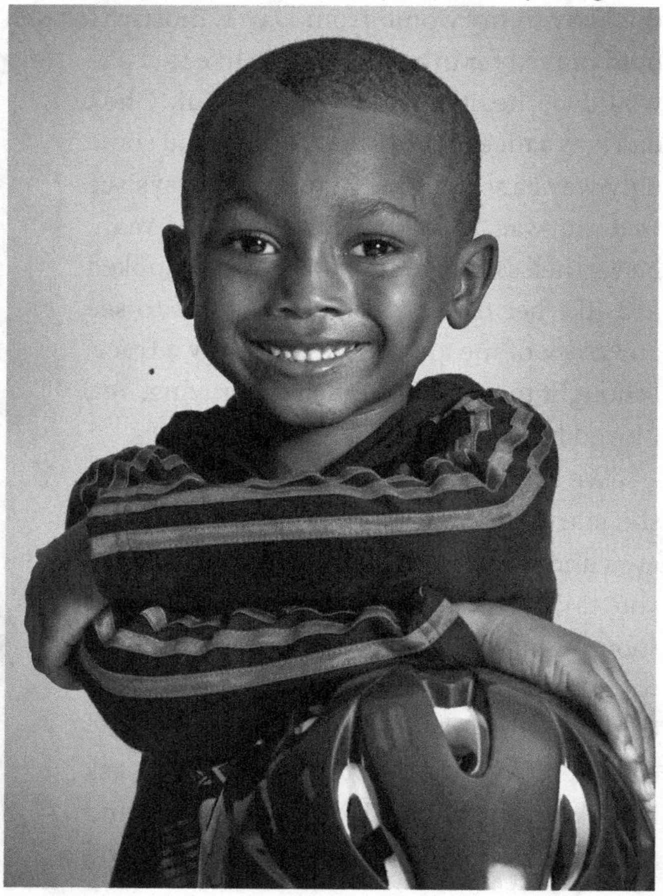

Christian Yakim, "Follower of Christ, God will establish". Christian, my handsome prince, known for his beautiful eyes, breathtaking smile and deep dimples. I remember on one occasion I was preparing the kids for school and I was tired, exhausted and said to God, "Lord, you have to help me; I can't do this for I am tired and I am weary". My 3-year-old child, Christian, walked up to me and I was stooped over at the time at his height level putting on his shoes and preparing him for school and he placed his tiny hand on my head and started to rub his fingers through my hair. This has always been comforting to me and I have no idea why he does this but it appears that it brings him just as much comfort as it brings me.

In this comfort zone, he began to sing praises to God and it sounded a little like this "Praise Him, Praise Him, Praise Him, Praise Him, Jesus Blessed Savior Your Worthy to be Praised". I looked up at my baby boy and I said "Where did you hear that?" and he said "church". I shouted Hallelujah because God is always speaking, even through the mouths of babes. Hallelujah! The atmosphere was then set, prayer had already taken place before the kids even awoke, now out of the mouth of a babe praise and worship had been perfected. As the rest of the kids scurried about you best believe church was in full session. Everyone in the house was singing and joining in on the chorus "Praise Him, Praise Him, Praise Him, Praise Him, Jesus Blessed Savior Your Worthy to be Praised". Praise and worship continued until they reached the school parking lot where I told them what I always say when we part, "Love you and pray". Yes, my children are covered with prayer and sealed with His precious blood every day. I send them to school daily with the weapons of the word of God, praise and prayer.

De'Jonay, named after her dad's name and a combination of the name Deja. On another occasion, I was getting five children ready for church and I was tired again and weary but knew we had to go to church because I needed to be filled for I had felt empty. We got there at 10 a.m. for Sunday School. At the close of Sunday School the pastor did an overview of the lesson and asked everyone this question, "How do you know there is a God?" My beloved daughter, De'Jonay, at 12 years old jumped up in the front row and stood to her feet and raised her hand. She was the only one in the congregation standing so the pastor nodded his head and said "Yes" as he awaited her answer. She said "I know there is a God because He woke me up this morning and He allowed my mother to bring me to church". My heart melted. As everyone turned to look at me, I just smiled and held back the tears and began to hum a little tune deep down in my heart and soul it went like this "Praise Him, Praise Him, Praise Him, Praise Him, Jesus Blessed Savior, You are Worthy to be Praised". You know I am crying and praising him as I write. The Holy Spirit has taken over the pen. I know without a doubt that God is the author and the finisher of this very

book, in the precious name of Jesus! I am just the vessel that He chose to use, that He predestined for His glory.

De'Jonay I must say is the spitting image of her mother. She is an answered prayer. She has such a beautiful spirit that I truly adore. When she enters a room she illuminates it with her inner and outer beauty. She has few friends, but those she has she holds them near and dear to her heart. Some of her peers will never admit it, but they envy her because they don't know her. Anyone that really knows De'Jonay has to love her. She loves the Lord and she knows that God loves her and that he knows her. She knows that He has encamped angels round about her to guide her, protect her and help her through life's journey. Her beautiful smile is just a reflection of what is going on in her inward parts and I pray I live to see what God has in store for her. Her heart is so pure. She is definitely a rare breed. A sought out, treasured jewel. She now calls herself Princess D, but soon she will discover that she is God's Leading Lady D, as she continues to grow into it.

Kha'Leel, God's ordained gift. His name is a combination of Khalil and his father's middle name which is Lee. Kha'Leel, my handsome king, smart, gifted and a wise protector. Born six weeks early due to complications in pregnancy. His father's identical twin. Had I not been awake during the entire delivery and watched everything that took place, I would have sworn that they switched babies with me in the nursery. I could not see me in Kha'Leel even when I squinted. I even checked his ears, toes and fingers. It took me some time to bond with Kha'Leel because I had to figure out some things, like what was I going to do with another baby. Kha'Leel was born "smarter than the average bear". He was very complex to but it nicely. Just when I thought I have him figured out, he would change the rules.

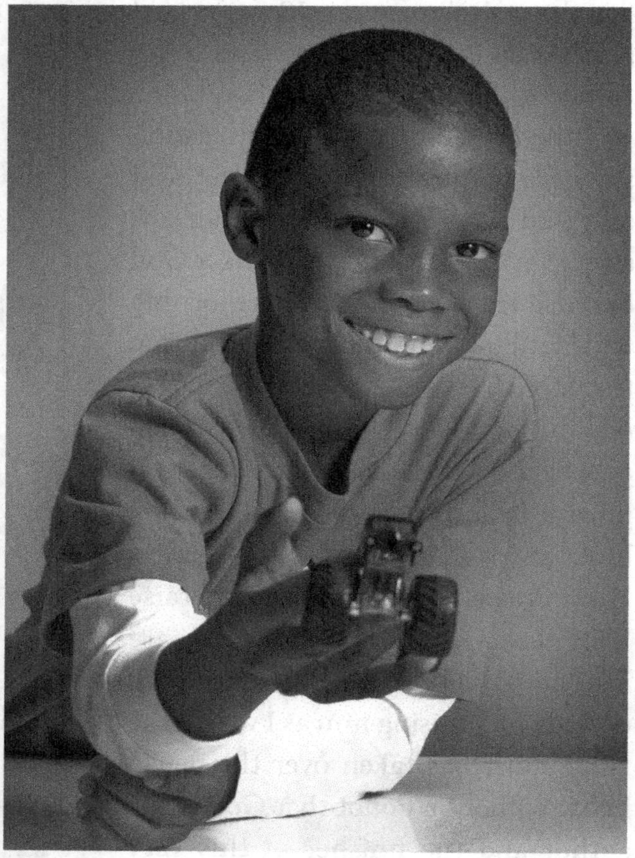

On one occasion, I had to minister to my son Kha'Leel. Kha'Leel often asks questions because he wants to know and understand things in detail. Yes, you already know "he gets it from his mama". Well this particular day he wanted to know "Why do we have to go to church and why do we have to love God?" He just needed a good excuse for me interfering with his playtime. You know he is 7, so he does have a life. How rude of me to impose. He is not the kind of kid that you can give just any answer and he will be quiet. He definitely is not like me in that aspect. You have to convince him why. So I thought long and hard on these two questions and I answered in words that he could understand. Now mind you all the other kids are listening and they might have wanted to know the answer to this question, but they did not ask.

So I turn to Kha'Leel and say "You have to go to church and you have to love God because He first loved you. He loved you even before you were born. All good gifts are from God. When you go to church to see God you get to know Him better and when you pray to God He hears you and He wants to give you good gifts and everything you ask Him for, but in order to receive these gifts you have to believe in Him and you have go to church to see Him and show Him that you love Him". Now I know this is not the best answer, but he is 7, so good enough for now. I know that it was a good answer because Kha'Leel was quiet and he did not ask any more questions, so this was confirmation.

Kha'Leel often opens the bible and reads it. He breezes through it and points with his finger as he reads. He prays on a regular basis, simple prayers on his own like "God help me, bless mommy and daddy and everybody and heal the land, Amen!" or the "Lord's Prayer" with assistance. Whenever he or others have a situation or problem, he is always telling them "Pray to God, He will help you". I know that he knows God is real, even more than Santa Claus, because he has said with his own mouth this Christmas season "There is no Santa Claus" but he has never said "There is no God", so I know my son knows the truth and is walking in it!

Ja'Mari, "means handsome", combination of the name Jamal". My son Ja'Mari is my heart. He is so handsome and lovable. Now most people, like his teachers and daycare staff, probably will not agree, but they don't know the story. Ja'Mari had a rough first few years living through two traumatic events, first having to undergo an emergency surgery and secondly facing a near-drowning incident. Yet, God's eye is still on the sparrow. Ja'Mari sometimes has unnecessary fears and I am not sure why, but I come against the spirit of fear in the name of Jesus because I know the spirit of fear is not from God. I lay hands on my children and anoint their heads with oil daily and my adult children not in the house I simply intercede with prayer. I often tell Ja'Mari when he fears that "God loves you so much that He watches over you at all times. He never takes his eyes off of you and He also sends angels to watch over you and keep you safe. The angels are always watching". I have a little porcelain musical black angel that is watching over the baby Jesus in a manager and I pick it up to show Ja'Mari. He looks and listens. I say to him "This is an angel and you see how she is watching over the baby, he nods his head as if to say yes. Well, this is how the angels are watching over you. You never have to worry or fear all you have to do is pray to God and He will keep you safe and mommy and daddy are going to also watch over you and keep you safe. So stay close to God, the angels and mommy and daddy". He listens and receives it in the natural and in the spirit.

It was confirmed when one day he was talking to his brother Kha'Leel and he said "Kha'Leel you don't have to be afraid because God and Jesus and the angels are watching over you". I turned around and did a double take and Kha'Leel was silent, which is not the norm as I stated previously. I said "Ja'Mari what did you just say?" and he repeated himself and I asked "Who told you that?" and he said "My mommy". My heart and my soul leaped for joy. I gave him the biggest hug and lots of kisses and I said "That is right God and Jesus who are the same person and the angels are always watching over you, so you never have to worry and you never have to fear" and then he followed me around the house the rest of the night and I know it was because of what I told him previously to stay close to God, the angels and mommy and daddy because they are going to also watch over you and keep you safe. Ja'Mari did not fully understand all that he had just said for he indeed had prophesized to his situation and to others, but he had a smile on his face and his heart was glad because he knew that he pleased his mommy and that the hug and the kisses proved it.

Children love to be praised for their goodness just like our Heavenly Father loves to be praised for His goodness. All my children know how to pray. Some seek His face and some seek His hand, but the bible says if you train up a child in the way that he should go he won't depart from it. There are so many seasons in life and we must embrace all of them. I am now in the season where I am embracing the fact that I have trained my children in the way that they should go and I am just praying, watching and waiting for God to do His Work. There is so much power in prayer and no power without it.

Krishina, named after a physician at the OB/GYN office where I was a patient. I later found out that the name Krishina is the combination of the name of a Hindu God. Krishina was my first daughter and I loved little girls so she stole my heart at first glance. What I did not know was that the same thing that brings you tears of joy can turn around and bring you tears of sorrow. As a small child, my mama would always say to me "don't bite the hand that feeds you". I never really knew what she meant by this, but I was soon to learn the full meaning of this as I continued to raise up my children.

I remember oh too well living through the teenage years with my beloved daughter Krishina. Krishina was indeed the most talented and had the most strength, just giving

credit where credit is due and not spiting the others because they are all anointed, but Krishina, the most talented and strongest of them all, took me and herself through "pure hell on earth" so to speak. So many changes, from truancy, failing grades, problems with the school, encounters with the civil and criminal system, basic rebellious spirit at work that is in most teenagers trying to find their way.

It did not help that mom was busy with work, school, rearing up babies and small children, oh yes my hands were full and since she was the oldest in the house I leaned to her for strength. Well a lot of times this causes a child to rebel and I knew this to be true, but at that time I did not know what else to do for it was me and her and the kids and we were a team. Some team members are stronger than others and she was the one team member that I looked to for strength. I know I put way too much on her and I became very dependent on the fact that she was able to do things exceptionally well and I know that I would have not made it at the time had she not been strong.

Looking back, I believe that God wanted me to lean more on Him and less on her. God wanted her to lean more on Him and less on other outlets, but that did not happen at the time. Krishina became very rebellious and due to the stress that I had in my life coming from too many different directions to name, but you can imagine, i.e. children, job, relationships, life, personal affairs, etc., I was unable to handle it on my own. Thank God for the revelation, but even with the revelation, I had no true understanding, so I just continued to live out my life.

When I got to the point in my life when I did not know what else to do, I began to lean more and more on Jesus. As I leaned more and more on Jesus, He began to lead me and guide me in His way. He told me to "Let Go and pray and leave her in My hands". So, with tears in my eyes as I lay across my bed and looked up to heaven and I "Let Go". I prayed to God and I placed her in His hands". When I did just that, there was a sense of comfort as I began to regain my focus by reading different inspirational books and biblical scriptures on raising up children successfully in the Lord. I went out and bought her a bible and different inspirational and life application books to read in hopes she would apply the word of God to her life situations. We went to church on a regular basis. I took her to the pastor for family counseling. I prayed and I prayed and I prayed.

I then confided in a good friend of mine since high school, Crystal, and she offered to help. Crystal lived in Chicago and her and her family were pretty much established there and Crystal informed me that she was in a position to intervene and get Krishina enrolled in a good school so that she could gain a quality education and that there were more positive opportunities and activities available to her. Crystal also advised me that she would be able to keep a better eye on her and that she was willing to help out. Crystal also had two teenage children that she was raising with the help of her husband and God, so she knew what she was getting into. Crystal was my friend since high school and I trusted her so I agreed to the arrangement and I drove Krishina up to Chicago to live with her and family for a while in an effort to save her from the streets in that I knew I had my hands full. Krishina did exceptionally well in Chicago under Crystal's care and began to make a complete turnaround. She was going to school full-time, working part-time and as time permitted, hanging out with a new group of kids that were more goal-oriented and career-focused.

One day when Krishina returned home for a weekend visit, we went to church as a family. As the service was proceeding in the normal course and fashion, the doors of the church were opened, my daughter got up out her seat and walked down the aisle to the alter and it surprised me because I knew she was already a member so I did not know what to think, but I remained in the spirit of expectancy for we all know if you are heading toward Jesus you are on the right track. The pastor was waiting on her like the father of the prodigal son. He had the biggest smile on his face and everyone in the church was now standing, clapping and giving God praise. The pastor asked my daughter if she would like to speak and sure enough she grabbed the microphone and began to give her testimony. Now it was not even testimony service but at 17 years old she had a testimony and it was as follows "I just want to thank God for saving me and I want to thank my mom for not giving up on me and I just want to thank everybody for praying for me". With tears in my eyes, I am writing you to tell you that is not all she said but that is all my mind, body and soul could remember after that I was slain in the spirit, literally!

Oh my God you are faithful. Thank you Jesus. Hallelujah! You word does not go out and return back void. My daughter was delivered and set free that very moment. God knew that would take place even before it happened. So it does not matter where you are at in your process or in your season. God already knows that for every test you go through you are going to and have a testimony for His glory. You might have to take the same test over and over again, but you are going to eventually pass it! I am a living witness. The bible says (3 John 1:2) "God wishes above all things for us to prosper and be in good health even as our soul prospereth". We just have to come in agreement with His will and His perfect plan for our lives.

Jaqi', named after the biblical name Jakeh and a combination of Jacques. Well since I have started, I might as well continue to tell you a little bit about what God has done for me and all my children. Jaqi' whose name was supposed to be Jakeh which is a biblical name. At that time I did not know much about Jakeh in the bible and it was too late to research it because I did not even think about naming him until I was in the labor and delivery room preparing to birth him so time was of the essence. I had my bible with me so I read what I could about Jakeh but still did not know His purpose in the bible. I knew I wanted to name him a name with meaning that was spelled something like Jakeh and pronounced something like Jakeh. So I talked to my best friend, Prophetess Kim, who was present during my delivery and I told her that I also liked her son's name which was Jacques. I then opted for a combination of the two names combined and I came up with Jaqi' pronounced "Jakeh". His middle name is Orlando, named after my father who was very proud that I chose to name him after him. I dedicated Jaqi' to God while he was in the womb.

My pregnancy with Jaqi' was not uneventful in that in the first few months of pregnancy I experienced hemorrhaging and I went to the doctor and they told me I might be miscarrying the baby or that it was possibly two fertilized eggs and that I had probably already miscarried one egg and the other fertilized egg still remained. I prayed that God's will be done. Jaqi' was born perfectly normal. All the hospital staff in labor and delivery just adored him and thought he was so cute while I looked at him and was trying to figure out just exactly what I was supposed to do with a boy. I had no clue. He had a head full of hair, but what was I supposed to do with it? I prayed for my girls to have hair so that I could comb it and put cute little barrettes in it, but Jaqi' got the full head of hair. I thought to myself "Well, I guess this is supposed to come natural so I will try to figure this one out".

This child was born at a time that I was really, really low in spirit and I did not particularly want another child. Although I loved all my children dearly, I was at a place in my life that I could not handle one more setback, disappointment, hindrance, etc. Now although Jaqi' was my second son, he was really the first son that I was able to raise so this was all new to me because I had only raised three daughters to date. Jaqi' came 11 months after De'Jonay and I was already not giving my three daughters the attention they deserved. It felt like I just woke up one morning and said to myself "Dang, I am pregnant again!" Maybe I really did say that, but I still loved my baby I just did not know what I was going to do with him or how I was going to do it.

Jaqi' spent a lot of time alone in the swing in front of the TV and in the bed with me or his sisters enjoying our comfort, but we all did not know how to relate to a boy. I worked 3rd shift so most of my day was spent sleeping, studying, going to graduate school classes and trying the best I could to raise a family with all that I had on my plate. Krishina was in charge while I was away from home and the babies' dad would take over to help out when he got off work. When I would return home to my family in the morning, I would be so weary from a long night's work and after I got the girls off to school, I just wanted to rest. My girls were easy, they were kind of laid back and pretty much "lazy" just like me. We could sleep the day or night away and eat, watch TV, shop, primp in the mirror and pamper ourselves, talk on the phone, listen to music, read a book, and sleep some more. Well, boys are totally the opposite.

Jaqi' however was a rare breed. He was a good baby and never asked for much other than his food on time. So I would feed him and lay him beside me in the bed or coach and turn on the TV to entertain him and take naps in between our ME TIME. Yeah right! He would swing in the swing like he was swinging his life away. You could literally leave him alone and he would not cry until he was hungry or wet. Now I know this was not the best situation for a child, but we all worked together as a family to make the best of whatever life brought our way. Even changing Jaqi's diaper was a learning experience in that as I said before I had only had girls and you know the difference between the two when changing diapers, so let's just say Jaqi' was always a learning experience and full of surprises in his peaceful and solitude state.

He was very demanding when it came to eating though and he still is. I would always make sure he was comfortable at all times. I was not successful at trying to breastfeed him like I wanted to because I could not keep up with his demands. Nevertheless, we soon bonded as mother and son over the next few months and he acquired the nickname "Main Man". Yes, he was my "Main Man". The only man in the house, so you see where this is going. As he began to mature, I placed him in the position of man of the house and he is now still the man of the house at 11 years old.

He loves to eat, sleep, and play sports. He loves video and computer games, gym shoes and nice clothes. He is as strong as an ox when he wants to do something and he is as stubborn as a mule when he does not want to do something. He helps out a lot around the house by taking out the garbage, helping me shovel snow, helping his dad mow the lawn, and helping with the household responsibilities like any "Main Man" would and could. Yet, I learned from past experience that this is not his role even if he is the only "Main Man in the House", it is not his responsibility nor is it his role to be the "Man of the House". Hallelujah for revelation! I get it!

At age 11, Jaqi' still likes his solitude and peacefulness in the comfort of his room where her resorts from time to time. We value his aloneness and when he comes out and wants family time we welcome him and enjoy every minute. He knows the Lord and he often seeks His hand for things like the latest gym shoes and attire and maybe even His face at times, but it's very hard to know because he is often silenced by the hustle and bustle of his other siblings who are way more outspoken. I know he prays when prompted and I know that God hears him. It is my prayer that God will begin to restore everything that was taken from him, even time, attention and love that he did not get because often the squeaky wheel gets the oil. I pray that God will open his mouth and allow him to be confident in the things of God.

Now in the school setting I hear that he is a great comedian, but we seldom see this at home. At home he is "The Main Man", very serious, very focused. Well he plays just like the other kids, but only briefly and then it's back to business. I call him my personal accountant because he can calculate strategically the present and projected needs of the household, mostly when it comes to food or entertainment. He says he wants to be a chef when he grows up, kind of surprising in that I thought he might want to become a professional athlete. When I ask him if he wants to become a professional athlete or a chef, he says, he wants to do both. I will support him in whatever he chooses to do because he is mama's "Main Man".

Mothers, please take notice of your children's different qualities and characteristics, talents, strengths, weaknesses, personalities and behaviors and allow God to reveal to you with full understanding, your purpose in their lives. Your family is your first ministry and nothing else will be successful until you are first successful at home.

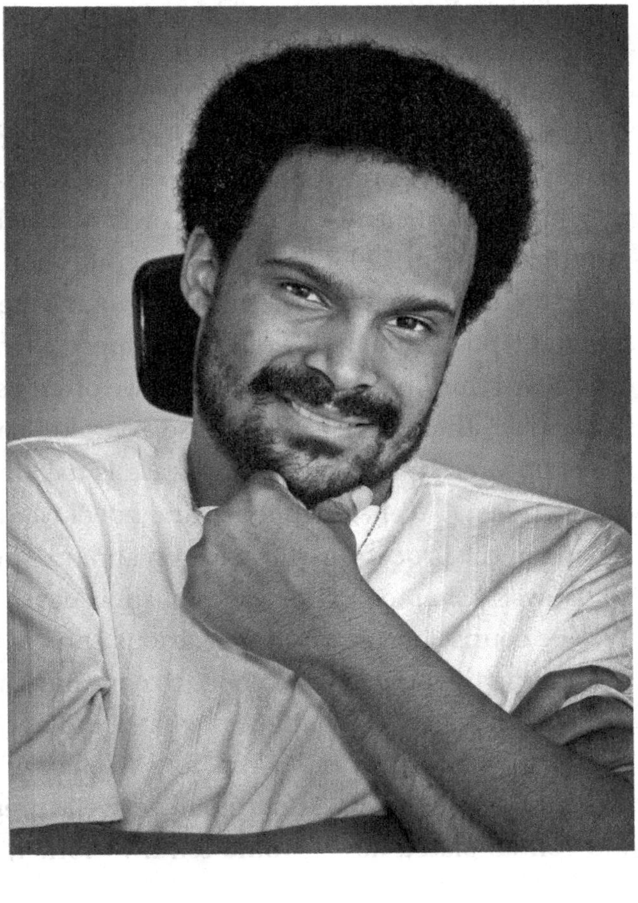

REWINDING THE HANDS OF TIME

Marcus, named by my mother. A combination of Marc and Marquez. Marcus, now 25 years old, is my first-born child. I was 17 years old when I was pregnant with him and 18 years old when I delivered him. I remember as a young teenager, without the covering of my grandmother, I walked away from going to church. My prayers decreased. My personal relationship with God was basically put on the back burner or placed on a shelf to be picked up later. I began to seek the lusts of the world as a teenager, basically trying to find myself in my own strength, my own wisdom and understanding. No vision. No role models. Not a leader, just a follower. I believed in God, but I continued to engage in activities that were not godly i.e. hanging out late with friends, alcohol, sex, drugs, unhealthy relationships, partying, lying, cheating, stealing, and "nothing new under the sun".

One day after school I went to Planned Parenthood with my best friend Nooky to get on birth control. I was learning about the "birds and the bees" and becoming a young lady from my peers who did not even know about the "birds and the bees" and becoming a young lady. You see, my mother never talked to me about the "birds and the bees" and becoming a young lady. I talked to my mother about what I was taught in the world about growing up and becoming a young lady. I would read about it in magazines, watch it on TV, hear the buzz in the media, at school, in the neighborhood, from friends, from boys.

My mother listened even with all the things she had going on in her life, she listened to me, but she never acted. My mom was very protective though, but she was better at reacting than acting. She often put what she called the "fear of God in me" i.e. "Don't do this, don't do that! Do as I say and not as I do! I brought you in this world and I will take you out!" The truth is I often "feared my mother" more than God. This caused me to fill every void with worldly pleasures that I felt my mother was trying to keep from me. I remember saying "Ma, you don't want me to have no fun. You just want me to sit around this house and be like … [You fill in the blank]". I thought to myself, "Why was she telling me to not do it, surely whatever it is must be good?" Remember in the Garden of Eden when that apple looked so appealing to Eve's natural eye? Most teenagers fall into this same trap. We feel our parents are old and miserable and don't know what they are talking about.

Well when I got to Planned Parenthood the counselor did the initial paperwork, screening and physical exam and testing. Me and Nooky waited patiently. The counselor returned to the exam room and said with a straight face "Well it looks like you won't be needing birth control … pause …. with locked eyeball to eyeball contact. You are five months pregnant!" I looked up at the counselor as to say "How?"

I started to analyze everything, "My mother told me not to have sex or I would get pregnant, but I thought it would not happen to me because, "my heart was right". Have you ever heard this phrase or excuse that we often use for not doing what is right, "God knows my heart"? Then there is the phrase every kid has used "Everybody else was doing it", and they appeared to be okay. That phrase is usually followed by the response, "Monkey see, monkey do …". Well, it happened and now I was beginning to live out the word of God and learn it in the process! My first lesson and take home assignment in the School of the Holy Ghost was "Chapter 1: The wages of sin is death".

The counselor discussed the various choices I had available from abortion, adoption to continuing the pregnancy. I chose to continue the pregnancy only because it seemed to be the easiest choice. Oh, but guess what? I did not even know who the father was. Yes, I had to do "eny meny miny mo". Yes, Holy Woman of God was then in an "eny meny miny mo" situation. Nevertheless, I continued with the pregnancy. I went home and I grieved within and contemplated how I would tell my mother, my grandmother, my family, my friends, but I did even better than that. I decided to hide it, I would hide it and then deliver it and then … ? … "there was no then".

One day the opportunity arose as my mother started to become suspicious due to my grandmother's instincts and much wisdom about my appearance and behavior. My grandmother was in town only visiting briefly, but she knew at first glance at me. You know grandmother's know! My mother with fear of the unknown asked "Criss are you pregnant?" I said "Yes, I was raped". Now this was true and false at the same time. For I did say "no", yet all my actions said "yes". I was in places and in situations where I was out of the will of God, where my Heavenly Father said "Do not go!" and where my mother said "Do not be!" So, yes there are consequences and yes this is just one example.

How did I feel about my "no" being taken as a "yes"? How did I feel when I told the appropriate authorities over me what happened to me and they did not take me serious? Am I sorry, was I angry, was I resentful, was I sad? No, I was just plain hurt and wounded. I prayed through every incident and God intervened on my behalf without a doubt in my mind. Yet, disobedience will get you in situations just like this or worse. Did the offenders get away with it? No, the bible says you will reap what you sow and they will reap their harvest if they do not repent and ask God for mercy. They will have little girls and boys and their children and their children's children may very well have to bear the consequences of the sins of their forefathers one day if they do not repent. God is a merciful God and I pray this is not the case, but the bible does not lie.

My mother hugged me and cried with me, but she could not help me. I had to lean on God for healing. Mama could not save me. She could not be my shero. She could not restore me. She thought about it for a while and then she called my father. My father thought the best option would be to terminate the pregnancy. My father felt money could solve every problem. My mother was against this. I had no clue what they were talking about for I had already made my decision to continue the pregnancy as far as I was concerned.

My father loved me dearly and he had good intentions for he knew that this situation would bring shame to me and the family. My father knew that I was too young to raise a child and that I had my whole life and future ahead of me, so he felt money would be the answer, but me and my mother both knew that God was the answer. Oh, it gets better. I show up at my first OB/GYN appointment escorted by my mother and the doctors, nurses and specialists come into the room with the same look on their faces as the counselor at Planned Parenthood so I knew I could handle whatever they were going to say because it was probably going to be the same report "You are five months pregnant!"

Well it wasn't. The doctor's face turned from straight face to "straight face, beet red and there was sorrow and grief throughout his whole body". I looked up at the doctor as he began to come closer to me and held my hand as if to comfort me and himself at the same time and he said "I am sorry. I don't know how to say this. Your baby has fluid in his brain and his spine is not forming properly, it has a hole in it. The doctor continues to describe the abnormalities and deformities in detail to me and adds, the chances of survival are slim and if he survives he may be in a vegetable state." I asked the doctor "What does this mean?" and he further explains "He will be retarded, not able to speak or walk or move his limbs, a vegetable and he further adds, you won't be able to take care of him. He will have to be placed in a nursing facility or you can put him up for adoption to have someone care for him properly or you can think about discontinuing the pregnancy, but you are really far along and you will have to make a decision quick."

My mind was so focused and all I could think and interpret from all of what the doctor had just said to me at the age of 17 was "It's a boy!" So I asked the doctor "It is a boy, right?" The doctor said "Yes" hesitantly and surprised with my question for he did not know why out of all that he had said the only thing I was focused on was the sex of the child. At that time I was more focused on God and what the bible says more than the doctor's report. I thought to myself "God you are a healer. You specialize in miracles. I will continue the pregnancy knowing this". I had bright eyes and a big smile on my face thinking about my baby boy. At this point, it did not matter who the father was because I knew that the bible says "God will be a father to the fatherless". I was encouraged in the Lord for He was with me.

The doctor knew that I did not understand all of what he was telling me in detail because he did not even understand it and he acted as if he had never seen a case like this before and further explained to me that it was a rare condition. All I could comprehend from all of this was "It's a boy! I have to buy some blue clothes and pick out his name".

I began to accept my state knowing this was not my fate. I began to try to take care of myself properly with God, my mother, my family and the support of my friends. I had to give up some things that I loved i.e. I could no longer be a pom pom girl for my coach pulled me aside and in private asked me if I was pregnant and I really wanted to be on the team, so denied it. Looking down at my big belly, in disbelief, my coach went on to say it would be best if you sit the rest of the season out. In the spirit and in the natural, I was trying to figure out all that I was experiencing, but it was too hard to fully understand for I never thought being pregnant would mean having to give up the things I loved and enjoyed like pom poms, the talent and fashions shows, track and other extracurricular activities that I was involved in.

I was really hurt about having to give up pom poms because there is nothing more that I wanted than to be a cheerleader. I had tried out in grade school, but I don't even want to talk about that one and I hope no one even remembers the embarrassment from that one. My mom had finally allowed me to participate in extracurricular activities in school. I had finally come close to being a cheerleader by making the pom pom team. Well, I really was far from a cheerleader, but I had the pom poms. Well I should say I had the pom poms, but not anymore. I had managed to make it almost through the whole season, game after game, routine after routine, practice after practice. We were now at the end of the season and we were working on our final routine and now this.

Although I was discouraged, I continued to go to school. During this pregnancy, I had the opportunity to be a commercial model for a TV advertisement for the local health department. The song that played in the background was "Moody Girl". I was told to act out the part of a young school girl walking along a lonely path while being laughed at by her peers due to her current state of being a young unwed mother and having nowhere to turn and no one to turn to and minimal support and then finding the courage to reach out for help and come to the health department and get the help she was looking for. I was then asked to finish with a big bang by turning around and smiling at the camera and demonstrating to the audience that I had went to the health department and found the help I was looking for and the help that I needed and that I was happy now. This was indeed prophetic.

I became an overnight celebrity through this commercial. Everywhere I went, people were giving me recognition for this commercial and telling me how pretty I was in the commercial and that I looked beautiful pregnant. This really boosted my self-esteem, self-confidence and self-worth. During this time I had a lot of "naysayers" but it seemed like the rest of the world was cheering me on just by this one simple 60 second commercial advertisement. Everywhere I went people were pointing at me and asking me "Aren't you the girl in that commercial?" I would proudly say with confidence and a smile, "Yes". Some people even asked for my autograph and that really made me laugh inside. I never had a pen handy, but I really wanted to give them an autograph and promised them the next time I saw them that I would.

I was encouraged again and it was as if doors began to open for me. I obtained a part-time job as a secretary/file clerk through the school's COOP work program. I worked at the local mental health facility where I was able to indirectly work with patients who were mentally ill and were admitted into the mental health facility because their family was unable to care for them properly. God was showing me firsthand where my son could possibly end up. This made me even more determined to ensure that my child would be taken care of properly.

I am definitely no expert in the area of mental health, but what appeared to me to be missing with these patients was genuine, unconditional love. Some of the patients never received visits from family and some did not even know their family. Some were so medicated they did not even know where they were at. They were cared for as best they could be in a facility, but they lacked love, nurturing, and a friend that sticks closer than any brother. I began to on my lunch hours visit them and intercede in prayer for them. I demonstrated godly love to them through a silent prayer, a smile, a handshake, a walk down the hall with them, a hug, conversation, while all along interceding on their behalf. Most of them did not say much, but others tried to articulate words that often sounded garbled and I would just listen trying to make sense of whatever I could. They enjoyed my company and I enjoyed theirs.

I knew that I was not the perfect candidate to minister to them in that I was an unwed young mother who had fallen short and who was saved by grace, but I said within my heart that I was going to make a difference in the lives of those who are disadvantaged, who are lost, hurting, wounded, who did not have a voice, who were living in pain and oppression. I knew there was a need and in my heart I was willing to be that vessel.

I loved my job. Everyone on my job liked me and was very instrumental in helping me see the positives in me and encouraged me to strive harder and dream bigger and reach higher. I never missed a day of work and I worked hard to do a good job and wanted to please my employer and bless the lives of the patients and those around me.

I had stopped going to church. The church van kept coming and the driver kept blowing the horn in front of my house, but I would not go outside and get on. I would just watch the van pull off from the window. I was ashamed and did not go to church because of shame and I felt that "the church people" would judge me for fornicating and having a child outside of wedlock, but I continued to do God's work. "It was church beyond the church walls".

I woke up early one morning and I had the urge to dance so I got out some of my cousin Tyron's albums and I placed them on the turntable and played them. I began to dance and literally got on the bed and was jumping up and down on the bed like a kid. Looking back, unbelievable but yes, I was jumping in the bed like a kid at nine months pregnant. I was overjoyed and did not know why. I then stopped right in the middle of a beat and rhythm and was bent over due to exhaustion and a burning sensation and an urgency so I thought I had to go to the bathroom and I tried several times in a row, but when I got to the bathroom I no longer had the urgency. I repeatedly kept going up and down the stairs to the bathroom. I then went and layed down on the bed and began to pray "Lord take this pain away, healing in the name of Jesus". I then went back to the bathroom once again and my aunt noticed my behavior and said "Criss are you okay?" and I said "Yes, but it feels like I have to go to the bathroom but I can't". My aunt I believe was washing dishes and dropped the dish in her hand to the floor. She said "Girl, you … in labor … Oh my God, Oh my God, Oh my God". She then anxiously tried to get me together and prepare to take me to the hospital.

I was calm, cool and collective and the music in my room on the turntable was still playing, I mean blasting. I was still ready to dance, but the pain and urgency stopped me, "How dare it". My aunt told me to get ready and she prepared my carry bag with a few things for me to take to the hospital. She then stopped everything she was doing or had planned to do in order to take me to the hospital. You might ask why my aunt? Well, I was under her care during this season for purpose. Me and my mother had our differences regarding my present lifestyle and so I was given the ultimatum "If you can't follow my rules then get out!" Oh don't act like I am the only one that ever heard that ultimatum.

Sometimes you can remember about how you were placed in a certain place, but you don't always have to discuss why. Just know God will always place you in the right place at the right time and with the right people. When it was time to deliver my baby, my aunt

Dimple was right there to take me to the hospital. I was 18 years old getting ready to deliver my first child. I was alone, but not feeling alone because God was with me.

There will be places in life that mama can't go, daddy can't go, grandma and grandpa can't go, auntie and uncle can't go, sister and brother and cousin can't go, your friend and the pastor can't go, but God was with me! My aunt Dimple stood by my side as long as she could. She was a very strong Christian woman and she prayed and she prayed and she prayed and I just looked at her as to say "It is going to be okay". She did her best to hold my hand, stroke my forehead and arm, caress, hold and comfort me, but there was a sense of peacefulness that even she could not give me. God brought peace in the whole atmosphere. I was right in the process of a major emergency cesarean section that was about to take place and I was smiling, cracking jokes and ministering to others about my faith and my total dependence in God. My aunt was humbled by my spirit.

The doctor came in to put me to sleep to perform the surgery and they tried to explain the procedure risks and benefits in detail and comfort me. My aunt, with tears in her eyes, was asked to leave the room. She complied. Now I know how Mary felt when Jesus had to bear the cross for I saw it in my aunt's eyes. The doctor instructed me to breathe deeply into the mask which had now been placed over my nose and he informed me that I would soon fall fast asleep. It seemed like it took a while before I fell asleep. You know I am very strong-willed, so I tried to fight falling asleep as long as I could, but I guess I lost the fight because the next thing I remember was waking up to my aunt leaning over me and trying to comfort me.

The first thing she said when I came to was "Congratulations, It's a Boy!" with a big smile on her face. I said "Nuh uh, I didn't have a baby ... see" as I looked down at my big swollen stomach that was now covered with a sheet. My stomach still looked like I was seven months pregnant. I didn't remember anything. It was as if I had blacked out and came to and I did not feel anything or remember anything other than the doctor's last words to breathe into the mask and them telling me I was going to soon fall fast asleep and my last words were "Nuh uh".

I was still drugged. My aunt laughed out loud at me and my delusional behavior and said "Girl, you are tired, just rest". I rested for a while, but when I woke up I wanted to see my baby. I said to my aunt "Where is the baby?" with the full excitement of a mother who wanted to see her newborn baby. My aunt with a sorrowful voice said "You cannot see him right now the doctors are doing tests and lab work on him and he is hooked up to machines. He is in an incubator". I had no idea what she was talking about. I had no idea what machines he could possibly be hooked up to and had never ever heard of or seen an incubator. My faith was in God so I just knew my baby was fine and I wanted to see him right now.

My patience was beginning to fail, my nerves were wearing thin. I was almost down to my last nerve and I knew it would not be long before the nurses, doctors and staff was going to have to answer me about where my baby was and why I could not see him. I began to ring the buzzer, call the front desk, I needed answers and I needed to see my baby now. I was trying to be calm, but the peace of God had left. My aunt urged me to rest, but instead I tried my best to get out of the hospital bed with my stomach stapled shut with my IV pole in my hand fully standing up in my butt-revealing open back gown preparing to go and see about my baby.

The room was now full of people. The phones were ringing off the hook. Everyone wanted to know about the baby, including me. There was too much time in between before I could see my baby and I was not happy. I cannot recall all the details of this traumatic experience, but what really matters is that you keep your trust in God and not man or you will be disappointed every time.

I was eventually able to see my baby. I remember there was no private time alone to bond. I had to go into the nursery in order to see him. I was unable to hold him, but I held his tiny hand through the incubator. I immediately began to pray and as I prayed "He moved his leg, he kicked, he moved, he kicked". It was a miracle. I was so excited. I thought to myself "The doctors said he would never move, but he was moving as I prayed over him. Thank you God you are faithful!" as I began to praise Him right in the nursery.

The resident doctor on call came in the nursery room as he was making his rounds that day and I told him of the miracle and he said "I know you want him to move, but he will never move, he will be like a vegetable. The movement you saw was just a reflex." I began to cry out to God "Lord I trust you and I believe You, move on my behalf, let him not be a vegetable, let him move, let him live, Lord I trust You". I continued to hold back some of the tears and cry out to God as I held his tiny hand through the incubator.

I was in the hospital for a total of seven days recovering from this major surgery and traumatic event. The normal hospital stay is a maximum of five days, but I was given an additional two days due to high fevers on day five of my hospitalization. The social workers, counselors, nurses one by one came in my hospital room daily to ask me what I was going to do and urged me to strongly consider adoption in that I could not properly take care of my baby and that I needed to make a decision for it would soon be time for my discharge and that the baby would have to stay in the hospital until he was able to be discharged to an appropriate placement. I told them I did not know what I was going to do, but for now I was keeping my baby. They continued to tell me that I was not going to be able to care for him properly and that he would be in the hospital for months. I began to grieve and cry out to God. I cried along with my aunt and she prayed with me, yet she did not know the answer. I asked her what should I do, and she said "Criss, I don't know maybe listen to the doctors and the staff at the hospital". I said "No......................".

I tried to visit my baby in the hospital as much as I could in all my grief. I continued to pray, trust and believe God. My baby was placed in temporary foster care after being discharged from the hospital. I don't remember getting a call and I don't remember signing anything. My mother then intervened and said I have an idea "I will take custody of the baby and then you can go to college. This way you won't have to worry about him being in foster care or a facility or have to worry with the social workers or the legal system. I trusted my mother so I said "Okay".

My mother contacted the social service agency and appropriate staff involved and found out all the pertinent information necessary to arrange for the transition to bring my baby home. I held up my end of the deal and enrolled in college and prepared for my first semester in college by visiting the school with my dad, applying for financial aid, paying tuition and board, school fees, registering for classes, purchasing textbooks and finding appropriate student housing. It was all overwhelming with all that I had going on at the time.

My mother was excited when she came back from the first visit with my baby and the social worker and respite foster parents and she told me that they had named him Christopher and they called him Chris. I was happy and excited to hear everything she said, but what I did not understand was how they could take my baby and not even inform me and how they could not even allow me to name my firstborn child or sign his birth certificate.

I never even got the chance to hold him. I only held his tiny hand from the incubator. I had picked out a name for him, but I was not given the opportunity or right to name him. Although I liked Christopher and the nickname Chris because that was similar to my name and this alone brought me much comfort and I knew it was God's way of showing me that he was still in control for what are the chances of them naming him after me. However, I wanted to name him the name I picked out and held onto in my heart to name him, Marquez Jovan. For nine months as I carried him in my womb, I awaited to name my child Marquez Jovan. My mom said she did not like that name and that we should name him a name with meaning like Marcus. I said "Okay". During this time, my heart and my spirit were speaking louder, much louder than my spoken words. When no one else was listening, God was listening. His ears were open to me.

I continued to bond with my baby in my mother's care and pray over my baby. He was kicking his legs just like I tried to explain to the doctors. It was not a reflex. He was actually kicking his leg. He did not look or act retarded. He was perfect to me. I was able to feed him, dress him, bathe him, comb his hair, play with him. I would read to him because I wanted him to be smart. I was so happy and so proud to finally have my baby back in my arms, really for the first time because in the hospital he was in an incubator. Although he was a few months old now, he had grown so much since I had last seen him in the hospital. He had a full head of hair, but the scars still remained in his scalp from the surgery where they placed his shunt to drain the fluid from his brain and his hair follicles were dead in the area of the incision. He was so precious. I had to be careful with him because he was so precious.

I just continued to bond with my baby and admire God's workmanship. He had everything a baby needed thanks to the donations of federal, state, local and community resources, family and friends. He had age-appropriate toys, swing, play pen, crib, high chair, clothes, diapers, formula, baby food, medical supplies, etc. His favorite toy was a mirror that had all kinds of colorful noise makers attached to it and he would play with the toys dangling in front of him and the noise makers would make different sounds and his face would light up as he looked in the mirror at himself and he would laugh and smile. He really enjoyed looking at himself in the mirror. Everyone was fond of him and thought he was so cute and handsome.

My mother was given temporary custody when he was a few months old, then full custody and then adoption at age 21 years of age. I am talking 25 years later for my son is 25 years old now. In this 25 year process, somehow my rights were terminated from the very beginning because I did not have a voice. My voice was shut by the adversary and the adversary stole my child from me. How? The only good excuse I can give you is "I was out of the will of God".

When you are in the will of God you are protected. I lost that battle and I don't have to tell you all the details how, believe me I did nothing to deserve the pain, the suffering, and the hurt from that very relationship and process other than love a child enough to carry him for nine months and deliver him and then unknowingly allow him to be taken away by a system that does not have the love of God. For a system that has the love of God would not have done this to God's anointed child. "Father, I forgive them for they know not what they do". Yes, through this experience, I understood how Jesus felt on the cross for myself.

Even though my rights were terminated, I continued to visit my child under the care of my mother, but as you know I was not in position as his mother and all I could do was love him through it all. Even if it was from a distance, I still loved my child. I continued going to college and continued to go on with my life, living through the grief and still trusting God. God looked beyond my faults and saw my need. He blessed me with my very first daughter, Krishina. The grief was gone. I had something to live for. She was so full of life. It was me and her in this huge world of endless possibilities, the sky was our limit.

I planned to love this child with all that I had. "God Bless The Child That's Got His Own", that is how I felt. No one was going to take her from me. This child brought me so much joy. My first daughter, she was absolutely beautiful mind, body, soul and spirit. She was beautiful from the top of her head to the bottom of her feet. God is a restorer!

My pregnancy with Krishina went exceptionally well without complications and the doctor had planned to deliver her by normal vaginal delivery, but I ended up having an unexpected delivery by emergency C-section once again but this time it was because somehow between my last visit at the doctor's office and the beginning of full labor, Krishina had decided to turn all the way around into breech position. Yep, that is my Krishina, always expect the unexpected, but she was just perfect!

I remember an incident that happened during my hospital stay. I was feeling all alone in my hospital room. No one standing by my side with a proud look and his chest stuck out passing out cigars and telling everyone he knows, "It's a girl". I was kind of feeling sorry for myself because I was still an unwed mother. I knew life was not going to be easy raising my children without a father. I knew the difficulties and disadvantages I would face not having a husband to lean on, not having someone to love me, care for me and provide for me and my family, not having a father for my little boy to play ball with and my little girl not being able to know the true meaning of "daddy's little girl". Yet, I had a Heavenly Father who said "He would be a father to the fatherless", so I still trusted God.

As I walked to the nursery to see my beautiful baby girl, as I looked through the nursery window she was just beautiful, words cannot describe how beautiful she really was to me, but my heart melted and my spirit was overjoyed every time I looked at her. I noticed another little baby girl in the nursery lying right next to her. She kinda looked like my baby. I had to look twice and think "How so?" I thought to myself she is very pretty, just like my baby, but she had a head full of pretty black curly hair and my baby's hair was black, fine and slicked flat softly flowing to the shape of her face with a little bit sticking up at the top like Alfalfa in the Little Rascals. I had tried my best to put lotion on that piece and brush it down to no avail. Now I was admiring two beautiful baby girls from the nursery window, just as proud and happy as I could be as a mother.

Slowly a young girl about my age or a few years younger walked up right beside me and was now looking through the window with me. She had a very sad look on her face. With a very happy look on my face and a voice full of cheer I asked her "Is that your baby?" and she said "Yes", but with such sadness. I noticed that her spirit was very low so I said to her "She is beautiful". As with most newborns you really cannot tell who they look like but they usually have some features that strongly suggest they look like mommy, daddy, sister, brother, etc. So I asked her in small talk, "Where does she get all that beautiful curly hair from?" She said "I don't know". I then went on to say "Well she sure is beautiful". I continued to admire my precious baby. The other young girl looked as if she had a black cloud all around her but she kept standing in front of the window looking at her baby, not a smile on her face. I continued to talk to her because it appeared she was all alone. Her sorrow really concerned me because I sensed her heart and her spirit and her outward appearance matched everything that was going on in the inside of her so out of concern I continued to talk to her. I then said "I know you are proud". She then said "nothing at all". She just kept her eyes focused looking at her baby.

There was a silent moment and then she said to me "I don't know where she gets her looks from and I don't know where she gets all of her hair from and I don't even know ... who the father is because ... I was raped". I said very sadly "You were raped, how so?" Even though I already knew "how so", I just did not have any other words to say at that moment, but I felt her heart and her spirit. I then just listened as she continued to explain to me "How so".

She said "I was walking home from school one day after practice and I was walking through the alley that I normally walk through to get home from school because it is a shortcut to my house and someone came from behind me and pulled me into a garage and raped me and left me lying on the ground and I later found out I was pregnant and ...". Yes, this was a divine appointment. God was showing me that while I was walking around feeling sorry for myself for what I had been through I had really been through nothing until I had walked in somebody else's shoes.

Yes, I had been raped but at least I knew by whom. Not that it makes it any better but this girl not only was raped, she was raped by a total stranger and then wounded, hurt, abused and left lying on the ground. She then got up and was faced with having to make probably the most difficult decision any young adult would have to make to keep her baby, carry her baby full term and then deliver her baby, name her baby and make another decision to love, cherish and raise her baby. Yes, she was raped, wounded, hurt, abused and left to die that horrible death, but she got up out of the grave that was dug for her by the enemy and she stood up. She may have been weak and weary, but she got up and with everything she had within her she stood up, and she was still standing right in front of the window of the nursery looking at her bundle of joy. The person that hurt her had gone on about his life and had probably not even took the time to look back upon all that he had did, but this little girl just kept standing.

I then began to talk to God silently because I knew the bible says "For where two or three are gathered together in my name, there am I in the midst of them". (Matthew 18:20). There were four people gathered together that day in His name, me, the young girl and our two little beautiful angels and God was in the midst. For I knew that I served a God that sits high yet reaches low and He met us right where we were at that day. She was probably in her room feeling sorry for herself just like I was and God touched her heart like He touched mine and He said "Get up and go see your blessing that is waiting on you in the nursery".

As we stood side by side and looked into the nursery window at our blessings, no further words need to be spoken because God had really showed us that day that He was still God. She was standing just like me and with everything within us we were going to love, cherish our two little angels, despite all we had been through and all that God had brought us out of, we were going to stand and when we could do nothing else we were going to just keep standing. Standing on the word of God in (Luke 1:47-48) And my spirit hath rejoiced in God my Savior: For he hath regarded the low estate of his handmaiden: for, behold, from henceforth all generations shall call me blessed. We were definitely blessed despite our circumstances and God even confirmed it in His word.

I then asked her one last question out of admiration of her strength. I asked her "How did you feel carrying a baby and not even knowing who the father was?" She said "It is not the baby's fault, so I continued with the pregnancy". That young girl was younger than me, but she was so much more mature. She taught me a lot that day, September 19, 1985. I never saw that young girl again, but I just have to let her know and the world know that she was definitely a blessing to me and God is going to restore everything that the enemy took from her, everything! Restoration for the both of us really began that day at that moment. That was just a preview of what was to come if we just hold on a little while longer. God is going to restore! I remained prayerful.

GOD'S LEADING LADY C GOES TO JAIL

No, I did not forget about Marcus. I continued to visit him on a regular basis, but I was unable to raise him for he was under my mother's care and unbeknownst to me the legal documents said my rights were terminated. I had no idea what termination of parental rights meant at age 19 and as a result, I was thrown in jail for the charges of trying to kidnap my own child. Yes, I was thrown in a "real jail cell", sitting, sleeping and eating with other "real offenders" i.e. prostitutes, drug addicts, thieves, robbers. I think I was the only kidnapper at the time, but guess what? God was there too.

God allowed me to minister to the women even in the jail cell. I remember sharing my food with one of the inmates. She must have been hungry because the menu consisted of oatmeal, poached egg and toast for breakfast and white beans and cornbread and sliced peaches for lunch served on a tray right in the privacy/luxury of your jail cell. I remember I passed on breakfast and for lunch I ate the peaches and gave her the beans and cornbread. She was thankful for receiving it and I was thankful that I could bless her with it. Oh my, I was not accustomed to this and I like to eat so I was praying more to get out of jail to eat a good meal than I was to be free, for I knew freedom did not exist beyond these bars for me. I felt more safe in the jail cell. It was a "Hard Knock Life for Me" for real!

You might ask "How in the world" can a young mother who never was in any kind of trouble with the law, a law abiding citizen, a decent girl, respected by her peers and others, who respects her elders, who was brought up in the church, who always tried to do what was right, who loved hard, had compassion for every living thing and would not even step on an ant, or a crack for fear she would break her mother's back, who had always tried to save every stray dog and feed every hungry kid and person in her neighborhood, a generous girl who would give you the very coat off her back, who would give loose change and dollar bills to the homeless on the streets so that they could buy themselves something to eat or drink, a successful high school graduate who made decent grades and had perfect attendance in school, a college student, a girl that works hard at everything she put her mind and heart to, who was gainfully employed, who had reliable transportation, a positive attitude, loyal to a fault, reliable, trustworthy, who never turned anyone away that called upon her for help, and to top that all off she is a Christian.

"How in the world" was she allowed to get in this type of situation where she was now facing a conviction for kidnapping and disorderly conduct? "How in the world" was she now facing the charges of kidnapping her own child that she birthed out of her own womb, that she carried for nine months and labored with, "How in the world" at the sweet, innocent age of 19 did this happen to her? Well, I will tell you ... "Because no story, no glory!"

My aunt Dimple bonded me out on the very next day. I had to stay overnight in jail because I could not be released until I stood in front of the judge during the morning court session. There were no exceptions to the rule. It did not matter that I was a child of the King of kings, Lord of lords. I still had to go through the judge. I now had a court case. My options were to pay a fine and have a criminal record or perform community service work hours and have a record or my last alternative was to be on probation and have a criminal record. No matter what option I took, I was going to have a criminal record. I had no money, not even the money to pay my aunt back for bonding me out. So, I opted for the community service work hours and a criminal record.

As I walked away from the courthouse that day, with tears in my eyes as I cried with my aunt once again, I said to God, myself and to my aunt with such compassion, power and authority, "I won't look back. Lord it hurts me so bad, but I won't look back". My aunt tried to console me by saying "I am sorry for what happened to you, but you don't mean what you say. Sometimes people hurt you, but God will never hurt you ...". I had a deaf ear and a hardened heart. All I knew was I was not looking back. I was going to go forward somehow and someway and I was going to raise my daughter, finish college and be successful. This incident was not going to define me! Well, I hate to say it, but this incident did indeed define me.

You know how people always say they are going to take back everything that the devil stole, well I can say that and mean it, but I will never be able to take back the fact that my firstborn son was taken from me without my permission. I did not have a voice. I was not a criminal. I was a young mother who chose to keep her child at conception, at birth and beyond and a mother who by faith prayed over her son in the womb and through an incubator as she held his tiny hand. A mother who watched onlookers curse her and her baby with hurtful words like "She has a waterhead baby. He is retarded. He is a vegetable. He will never walk. He will never ... she is this ... he is that ... and the words that hurt the most were "She left her baby in the hospital ..." I continued to pray to God because I knew He loved me and He cared even facing the trauma of all of this I knew I was not alone. There was a God out there somewhere, I just knew it.

When I left my child in the hospital in the care of the appropriate authorities, I trusted that they would do what was in the best interest of me and my child. I was 19. I went from math, English, arithmetic and writing to "The Facts of Life" overnight. I complied with every request given. I wanted to be a good mother and a good person. There was nothing stopping me from being that. I continued to do the right thing. I went to college like my parents wanted me to. I worked hard. I stayed out of trouble. I placed my child in the proper care of my mother. I took care of my child with whatever resources I had available to me. I loved him. I bought him good gifts. I spent time with him. Yet, during those three court proceedings, I was asked to speak for myself, without a voice, and sign papers that I did not fully understand at age 19.

"The system" interpreted the papers to me. "The court system, the lawyers, the doctors, the social workers, my mother", you know people you can trust. I signed trusting man and let me tell you just in case you fully don't understand even after I told you and after you have read every verse in the bible and you have been taught the word of God and applied the word of God and you have lived the word of God and have come to the fullness of God,

"Trust no man, only trust God". You know, like all U.S. Treasury Funds say "In GOD We Trust". Please take note of that fact and discern.

I had to live out this truth and it is my heart's desire that no one has to go through the pain that I had to go through to come to the fullness of this same truth. I was not a criminal. I did not deserve to die on that cross. Sound familiar? Jesus said the same things in different words. He said in (Luke 22:42) "Father, if thou be willing, remove this cup from me: nevertheless not my will, but thine, be done". Verse 43 goes on to say "And there appeared an angel unto him from heaven, strengthening him". God sent His word even on this situation. God sent an angel to strengthen me. God assigned angels to encamp all around me to protect me, to help me and to strengthen me on my spiritual journey.

God allowed me to finish college and obtain a job in social work where I witnessed the very thing that happened to me take place in the lives of others. I want you to know without a doubt I was THE VOICE THAT STOOD FOR MOTHERS AND FAMILIES IN NEED. I was the voice that said "No, you will not allow your rights to be terminated. You will plan to work and work the plan. Whatever is required of you, you will do it to save your child". I was the voice that said "We shall reunite the family. Give my client another chance". Even when my family situation was totally messed up, I was the voice that stood in the gap for others. I interceded in the lives of others. I ministered to mothers who were living in impoverished conditions, some who were on crack, drugs, alcohol and even mothers living with AIDS and told them all "This is serious. You don't want to lose your children to the system. Your children need you". I was dedicated and fully committed to fighting for the rights of women, families and children in need. I gave 110% effort to the cause of restoring families with God's help, all while knowing in the natural that I had lost the battle with my firstborn son. Yet in my spirit, I knew I had not lost the war for the real battle belongs to the Lord and if we let him fight all our battles we will go from victory to victory to victory.

I trust God even 25 years later after this traumatic event and know that He is a restorer. I trust God ONLY to restore my life! The first thing I needed to do was forgive every person that hurt me concerning my firstborn son. I then needed to lay my life on the alter of God as a living sacrifice. I needed to place my life in His hands and allow Him to keep it. I needed to kill the flesh daily and walk in spirit and surrender my will to His perfect will and plan for my life. I needed to die to the flesh and live in the spirit. I had to die in order to live in Christ and to live for Christ. This was the first step toward complete restoration.

God is not a man, that he should lie; neither the son of man, that he should repent: hath he said, and shall he not do it? or hath he spoken, and shall he not make it good? Behold, I have received commandment to bless: and he hath blessed; and I cannot reverse it. (Numbers 23:19-20).

Part 2

Take 1, Cut 1 - Looking Back for Purpose

The story continues. Allow me to give you a quick overview to catch you up to speed just in case you somehow got lost in the story thus far. Looking back, August, 1984, six weeks after delivering my firstborn son, I went off to college at the request of my parents to obtain a college degree. I grieved the entire first semester. It was the Fall semester of 1984. At the end of the semester I had all Fs and one B. I received a B in medical terminology. I went home for Christmas and conceived my second child. Same father of my firstborn son, hoping "This time I'll be sweeter, our love will run deeper, I won't mess around, I won't let you down have faith in me, have faith in me ..." you know the song by Angela Bofill "This Time I'll Be Sweeter", well that never happened.

I returned home from college in May, 1985. The city I attended college in only had two practicing OB/GYN. I had a medical card which further limited my care and due to my past medical history, I was considered a high risk pregnancy and had no other choice but to return home to deliver my baby. It looked like I had to put school on hold for at least one semester. In the interim, I worked two part-time jobs and went to school full-time during my pregnancy and three part-time jobs after delivering my baby.

I obtained my first apartment on my own after things did not work out with living with my mother once again, nor my aunt, nor my friends. It was me, God and my baby girl and a utility-included one bedroom apartment with shag green carpet and used appliances as an extra bonus. My personal items and furniture included a boom box, a used mattress only, a used love seat, a black and white maybe 10 inch TV, an alarm clock/radio and just enough belongings to fit in a suitcase for both me and my daughter. Oh, but we were thankful because we had a mop, a broom, a bucket, cleaning supplies and plenty of food to eat because we had food stamps. I had a car that my dad had given me and we had gas and I was working as a cashier at McDonalds, a waitress at a barbeque restaurant and a retail clerk at Bergner's department store.

I would blast my boom box whenever I wanted in the privacy of my own new apartment, just me and my baby, "Awe, this is definitely living!", until the cop knocked on my door and warned me that if I did not turn my music down he would have to write me a ticket. Geez, and this was before I had a 100 watt stereo system, some nerve. OOPS, I guess I must have said "Geez" out loud and received my first citation and the threat that if he had to come back it would be worse. I did not have adequate daycare for my child, but I relied on family, friends and extended family to help and they did for the most part the best they could do. My daughter was never in harmsway at least I hoped and prayed not. She was only a few months old then. While I was away at work I knew in my heart that God and His angels were watching over her for that was my continual prayer.

When my daughter was 9 months old, my grandmother got word of our present state combined with having a court record of being a "convicted kidnapper of my own child and disorderly conduct". She immediately intervened and asked for me to come live with her and my grandfather so that she could help me with the baby and I could go back to college to finish my studies. My grandfather and grandmother did their best to support me emotionally, financially and spiritually even in their absence. They would always send me $20.00 a month to keep money in my pocket just in case. It really helped me learn how to be a good steward of money because I knew I had to make that $20.00 stretch until the next month's payment. They never wanted my pockets to be empty because they never wanted me to be "tempted by the tempter" that they knew would say "If you need such and such, all you have to do is such and such ...". Well at that time I did not quite know how my grandparents knew about "the tempter", but I appreciated their $20.00 a month, their love, their wisdom, their prayers and their protection.

Yes, my grandmother always knew best and that is why she intervened on my behalf once again to ask if she could help. She did not want to force her help on me, but she loved me so and I loved her so, so she knew it was a good chance that I would accept her offer. I did not have to think twice for things seemed to be very unstable around me and it was all I could do to keep it all together. My grandmother had always made me feel special. My grandmother knew without a doubt the anointing over my life. She raised me from birth to 12 years old when my grandfather retired from his two full-time jobs as a laborer and they relocated to Southern Illinois to live out their "Golden Years" in their retirement home. It was the home my grandfather grew up in as a small boy. My grandfather was very proud of his heritage and had plenty of stories to share about it.

My grandmother had brought me up in church from a baby through age 12. Every time the church door opened it was me and her walking in. Every day of the week we participated in church services, bible study, prayer service, midweek service, women's ministry, outreach ministry, Sunday school, Sunrise service, Sunday morning service, Sunday evening service, Sunday night service, Friday night service, choir rehearsal, usher board service, weddings, funerals, chicken dinners, banquets, pastor anniversary, vacation bible school, etc.

I was her prayer partner and she was my prayer partner. When she got on her knees I got on mine and I remember always looking around to see if she had got back up yet and it seemed like she would never get up and I would fall asleep right on my knees waiting on her to finish praying and when she was done she would gently place me in the bed and cover me up with a blanket. When I would wake up in the morning she would be back on her knees praying again. I would just lay in the bed until breakfast was done because that way too much praying for me. She was my covering and I was hers. She was never alone and I was never alone. We were connected in the spirit and in the natural. She would always tell me "If I fart you are going to smell it". Yes, my grandmother had her way of speaking truth so you could understand it, but I would not let her out my sight.

If she grabbed her coat, I would grab mine. The rest of my cousins could not stand me half the time because of how I acted toward my grandmother and since I was the baby, well let's just say I got it "real good" when grandma was not looking or around to protect me, but I had a way of screaming from the top of my lungs and they would leave me alone too. Now sometimes when grandma did get away and left me home alone with my grandfather and my cousins, I had "hell to pay", but as much as they could not live with me, I knew deep deep deep down inside that they loved me and could not live without me.

I remember they would always tease me about many things and they were all funny, but the funniest two things that I can remember them teasing me about was one, the fact that I could not drink from a glass. I was known to be drinking and the next thing you know the glass would shatter into pieces. My cousins were looking at me like I was the "Bride of Chuckie" who just so happened to love eating glass. There would be glass everywhere and my grandmother would never fuss, she would just shake her head and clean up the mess. I fortunately never got cut or injured in any kind of way. My cousins would just laugh and laugh and laugh and tease me indefinitely. So my grandmother then began to intervene and cover my shortcomings by buying all plastic cups and serving only the glasses to guests, but my cousins would then just find something else to tease me about. They did not have to try that hard either for I was always "special".

The second funniest thing I can remember is one day we were all sitting on the porch eating watermelon. This was back in the day when they did not sell seedless watermelons. I was about maybe 6 or 7 years of age at the time. Somehow I swallowed a watermelon seed and I kind of overreacted and my cousins caught on to the fact something was wrong with me because I was acting like I was choking because the seed almost went down the wrong way but I managed to cough it back up and it felt like it got stuck in my throat. The only cousin that was paying attention to me while I was choking as the others just kept on eating, said "You didn't swallow that watermelon seed, did you?" and I looked real dumbfounded but you know I can't lie, so I said "Yes" and my cousin jumped up and said "I am tellin, I am tellin, I am tellin", and he ran in the house and told everyone that I had swallowed a watermelon seed.

I slowly followed behind him and went into the house to see what the big ruckuss was all about and he went on to explain to everyone how I swallowed the watermelon seed and now everyone in the house chimed in on the fun. My older family members, cousins, brother, auntie all began to tease me that now I am was going to be pregnant and they went on to explain how the watermelon was going to grow in my stomach from that one seed and that I was going to have a huge watermelon belly and a big watermelon baby ... I just lost it ... I started screaming and hollering "Mama, I don't want to be pregnant and I don't want to have no watermelon baby" and the whole house was laughing out loud at me, Oh, my God! Let me get back to the story because my book will never end talking about my youth and my fun times with my cousins.

Another important fact I forgot to mention was that I spent most of my youth sleeping because whenever I would get in trouble or whenever they really just wanted to get me out their hair, which was a lot. My grandparents would either whoop my butt and/or send me upstairs to the bedroom to take a nap. Here is the famous saying that I heard at least three times a day, 10 a.m., 1 p.m. and 4 p.m. ,"Go to bed, ain't nothing wrong with you but sleepy". Now, I was obedient and I listened and I took the three naps a day as requested, but I would often think "I ain't sleepy I just woke up" but I knew it was no use fussin for I had a standing naptime appointment. It was if everyone was saying and not saying, "Talk to the hand and just go to bed", while looking directly at me as I walked what seemed like a mile as slow as I was walking upstairs to the bedroom. Now, when I did get up in age and my grandparents wanted me to get up out of bed and do "something", I was like "I'm sleepy, I just need to go to bed" and they would always say "You lazy scound bugger you" and they would just laugh and laugh and laugh at me not even realizing that they "created the monster" and that they would be lazy too if they slept most of their life away. I believe the good Lord knew even then that I needed to rest up for the years to come for I definitely don't have the luxury of resting now.

My grandmother was very loving and kind, but she was also a disciplinarian and an enforcer. I got a whoopin every single day before sunset. I even had to go out to the backyard and get my own switch from the tallest tree in the yard. It seemed like it reached as high as heaven. I thought it was the Jack and the Beanstalk tree. However, I knew as much as she whooped my butt, she loved my butt. I lacked nothing, missed nothing, I was complete. As long as I was under her care, I was covered.

I trusted my grandmother and she trusted me. When she offered to care for my child, she was also saying without saying I want to take care of the both of you. She did not want to take from me she wanted to give me more than I already had. What happened miraculously in the process was my grandmother sowed a seed of love by caring for me and my 9 month old baby, but she reaped so much more in return. My grandfather signed off on everything my grandmother approved of and he was blessed as well. That little baby girl restored so many years onto their life, maybe not in number of years but in the liveliness of their spirit. They both felt young again and they were so happy to care for another baby in their golden years and they enjoyed her company to say the least.

My grandfather would go out in the yard and work like he was a young man again, chopping wood for the stove, cutting grass on acres of land with a push mower, feeding every stray animal in the woods and the pet cat, dog or whatever he would take in temporarily to nurse back to health. He would fix things that did not even need to be fixed and he just kept busy. He would then come in the house and clean up for supper and would help my grandmother with the baby while she prepared the meal. He would then sit down at the table and enjoy his wife and his little baby girl. They called her "Krishy". It was "Uh Krishy" to them.

My grandmother worked around the house, cleaning, washing clothes, cooking, caring for the baby. My grandfather would sweep and mop the floors as needed to help my grandmother out. He would also wash dishes from time to time but he seldom cooked. He thought he could make some "mean Jiffy cornbread muffins" though and he would be so proud of himself too, and of course you know me and Krishy helped him eat them so that he could feel extra proud. I never told him that they never really had any taste to them. He just kept on baking them and me and Krishy just kept on helping him eat them. My grandmother would just watch us in admiration for our effort. She never ate one muffin because she knew better, but she never said a mumbling word. My grandfather would run all the errands with my grandmother because she never took the time out to learn to drive a car. My grandmother handled all the personal affairs of the household through the telephone or through mail correspondence. My grandfather handled all the business affairs of the household in person. While my grandfather handled the outside affairs of the household, my grandmother would run the inside affairs of the household. She did not need the internet, cable, computer, cell phone or a microwave. She was Ole Skool. Everything was made from scratch, breakfast, lunch, supper and dinner and dessert. She even cleaned Ole Skool, no Molly Maid or Stanley Steemer required.

Although they were living out their retirement years, my grandparents began to live again because they had something to live for. They were not retired, they were revived. They went to church together. Krishina loved to go to church with my grandmother and sing in the choir just like I did. They ate together. They played together. They prayed together and they stayed together. My college was only 20 minutes away so I would visit every weekend, when school was not in session or basically whenever I had reliable transportation. We were one big happy family. I can honestly say, the happiest times of my life were being with my grandparents down in Southern Illinois. No worries and no problems, just fresh air, soul food, rest, relaxation and more and more rest and more relaxation and more fresh air and more soul food. I have so many fond memories.

Krishina was a good baby. She was no problem. The worst thing she ever did was chase flies to eat them. I know yuck right, but what else did she have to do in the back woods. There was no daycare or social activities. She had to make her own fun. She ran upon a snake once trying to play with it. She was making up a bunch of noise on the porch just playing with her little friend the snake. My grandfather heard all the commotion and he went to check on her and he said "Jesus" as he quickly grabbed the baby and yelled "Inez, come and get this baby she out here playing with a snake". My grandmother quickly swooped the baby up and shut the front door. My grandfather went out the back door and came back in the house with a shotgun and came back to the front porch and that was the end of that! My grandfather's shotgun reminded me of his favorite pastime. My grandfather was a Western movie fanatic and I think even in his old age "he thought he still had it going on" when he would pick up that shotgun.

My grandfather was very wise. He was pretty quiet for the most part, but every now and then you could not get him to shut up especially when he was telling you a story. I guess that is where I get my story telling from. Anywho, he knew how to get his point across without saying much. One day I called myself "smelling the musk under my arms" and I raised up to give my grandmother a piece of my mind. She did not approve of me taking the baby in and out of the house in all types of weather because she once had a baby that died from pneumonia.

Well my attitude was "This is my baby and I will do what I want to do with my baby". Of course, I never said those words out loud for I knew better, but I thought it. I never really disrespected my grandmother in any way for she was my heart. She was my everything. I will never forget, the worst thing I ever said to my grandmother one morning when she was cooking breakfast. I was mad because she was trying to teach me how to be a good mother, but it felt like she was treating me like I was an irresponsible kid, and she said to me "You ain't gone learn how to take care of no baby until you kill one!"

My grandmother had two children die when they were very young. One died due to rheumatic fever and the other died due to pneumonia and it really affected her greatly. During that time common illnesses like the flu, pneumonia, rheumatic fever, polio, etc. went untreated and/or were untreatable. This was the reason for her being overprotective of the ones she loved. She was really trying to help me, but I had a total attitude "smelling the musk under my arms". She had something for my attitude and she said "Well, you grown so I can't tell you nothing, but since you so grown I guess you won't be having breakfast this morning" and with my stomach growling knowing that I wanted some of her melt in your mouth pancakes, I acted without thinking about the consequences. Without giving her eye contact, in a voice loud enough that it was now no longer considered mumbling, trying to hold back the very words, but to no avail because I was now fully in the full flesh and unable to return to the spirit. I said "I don't like your nasty Bisquick pancakes, anyway ... HMPH!"

My grandmother was in tears, but she turned her whole body all the way around with her back to me so I could not see her sorrow, but I saw it and I felt it and I heard the sniffles as she tried to hold back the tears. I was in tears on the inside as I looked at her because I never ever, ever wanted to hurt her. I held my tears back as I headed out the door to my car so that she could not see me crying. Before I left out the door my grandfather who was sitting in his favorite chair, watchful and fully aware of what was going on, had stood up and basically took off his house shoe and he had raised the shoe in the air as if to hit me with it, but he didn't. I shrugged my shoulders as to say "You can't whoop me, I am grown ... HMPH!" Know that I did not say it, believe me, because he would have beat me down with that raggedy house shoe.

My grandfather stood strong and tall with broad shoulders and said with authority, without raising his voice "You better watch out for that bear down the road". I looked up at him with wide eyes with fear and trembling wanting to ask him "What bear, where ...?" but I was grown and grown folks "Ain't even scared!" and they definitely don't ask questions because that would make too much sense, that would require too much wisdom and understanding for a "grown young adult". He further said "You gone keep on with that attitude until you meet your match. Go on and go out there, you gone run into that bear down the road and you gone lose that attitude and don't think I am coming to save you either."

As I drove down the street in tears knowing that I had hurt my grandmother's feelings and disappointed my grandfather, I was very careful, watching out for the bear that my grandfather had warned me about. Now, granddaddy a/k/a "daddy" in all his wisdom knew it was not a real bear in the woods. He was talking about something much greater. He was talking about life was going to teach me some sense. Life was going to teach me wisdom and understanding, that was the "bear" that he was referring to. Me, in all my smarts and wits, a "college student, smelling the musk under my arms and thinking that I was grown and that you could not tell me nothing", I was actually looking to my left and right, in front of me and behind me for a real live grizzly bear.

Now laugh if you want, but my grandparents lived deep in the woods and their next door neighbor was miles away, there was one cop in the town and he was also the sheriff, the firefighter, the judge, the deputy and the mailman, all at the same time. They had a population of probably 120 people and it seemed like most of them were my family, a Dollar General store, a trailer ice cream shack/food grill/candy store, one grocery store and one gas station/convenience store and you had to drive miles to get to everyone and everything. There were no pay phones or cell phones back then so if you ran out of gas on your way to town ... What? I guess you could get on one of the farm horses or mules and ride them to town but I advise you not to get out your car and walk because there would be a hungry coyote or dog waiting on you or worse the real live grizzly bear that I was now searching for in every angle. So I thought for sure the bear would get me somewhere in between my grandparents house and town where I was heading.

The bear did not get me then, but it sure got me later. My grandfather would always grin when he would tell the grizzly bear story because he knew whoever he told it too would be naive enough to believe it every single time. That grizzly bear story still works to this very day even on my own kids. My grandparents were speaking the truth even then, but I was just not getting it. By the way, just thinking about how good my grandmother's pancakes were just makes me want to cry. Nobody made pancakes like my grandmother. I wish I could take back the hurtful words I said to her, but I learned the hard way that you cannot take any words spoken back. That is why the bible teaches us in Psalm 39:1 "I will take heed to my ways, that I sin not with my tongue: I will keep my mouth with a bridle, while the wicked is before me". The bible goes on to say in James 3:8 "But the tongue can no man tame; it is an unruly evil, full of deadly poison".

I know somebody is saying "She should not have said that to her grandmother". Well believe me, I am so sorry for those very words and I truly know my grandmother forgave me and God even forgave me and then eventually I maybe even forgave myself and I learned from that mistake and it is my prayer that you too will learn from my mistakes. What I don't want you to do is judge me, because when you do, you are really judging yourself because like my grandfather always used to tell me when I felt self righteous he would say "You just keep on living". If you keep on living you will see a lot of things take place in your life that you believed would never happen or should of never happened.

I kept living and my baby girl Krishina ended up in the hospital with pneumonia just like my grandmother said would happen if I did not listen and that is why she had went out of her way to teach me what was right in order to prevent it from happening. Guess who was the first person I called from the hospital room? Yes, you got it, my grandmother. She did not hold a grudge or say "I told you so". She just told my grandfather to warm up the old pickup truck and they were going "41 MPH on the freeway trying to get to their baby". It was a 20 minute drive going the normal speed limit which was 55 MPH and minimum 45 MPH, but my grandfather was going 41 MPH. Now I know you are thinking well that ain't fast at all, but anybody that knows my grandfather knows that he does not go no faster than 20 MPH in the fast lane in town or out of town. So, he was flying at 41 MPH on the freeway trying to get there as fast as he could and he did and when he got to the hospital he made sure everyone was okay and then he got right back in the old pickup truck and drove 20 MPH in the middle of the road guaranteed, all the way back home with my grandmother. God healed Krishina from the pneumonia and she was never hospitalized again, thank God.

My grandmother loved my daughter even more than me. She raised her just like she raised me until my daughter was 3 years of age. She was fully committed to her God-given assignment. My grandmother did not stop doing her Father's business until her health began to fail. When my daughter Krishina was 3 years old, my grandmother had a mild stroke and my grandfather asked that I intervene to help out and I did. I did everything I could to help.

I never thought God would take my grandmother from me because I thought He would never place more on me than I could bear and I could not bear that so I trusted Him. Now, at age 21, I had the grief of the past, losing my firstborn son to "the system" and the grief of possibly losing my rock, my grandmother presently facing me. Yet, I still trusted God, so I continued on with God's help. I started going back to church and taking my daughter with me. I continued to pray even if it was just to pass my exams and to intercede on an as needed basis for myself, others, people, things and situations I faced along the way.

During my time of grief, I met a guy in college that caught my attention. He appeared to be nice. He looked like Al B Sure. Well let me say, he told me he looked like Al B Sure and I believed him. I will give it to him he was a close runner up back in the day. He was a business man with a business plan. I should have asked for his business plan in writing, but anywho. He was THE MAN OF MY DREAMS, nevertheless. Could God have sent me an angel? Where did he come from and what took him so long? These are the questions I asked myself back then. Well things began to move quickly. It went like this fornication, marriage, birth of my third child Che'Andrea and then some. I ask you, "Does that sound like God set this situation up nicely or was this something we both did in our own strength?" Well, nevertheless I loved this man. He was THE MAN OF MY DREAMS. He was the father of my child and now my husband, so I plan to make it happen.

Somehow it did not happen the way I had planned "I take this man to be my lawfully wedded husband, to trust, to love, to cherish until death do us part ...". No, it was more like "I take this man to be my "awfully" wedded husband ...", "I love you as far as I can throw you ... until death do us part ...". Now that was a joke. "I trust you as far as I can see you and as long as you don't go around the corner, I trust you". Now I am still joking because my first husband and I are still friends, but I am just speaking truth. We exchanged our vows one unto to another, but we really had no clue of what we were doing and what the end result would be. I can tell you that God was still God even in that situation.

I remember getting pregnant and Che'Andrea's father saying to me "Is it mine?" I was very hot headed back in the day and I did not think first, I just acted. I got on the phone and made my appointment. I said to myself, "Well if it ain't yours, it ain't mine!", because I knew from the last two kids it was "mama's baby, daddy's maybe", so I made an appointment to abort the pregnancy. I was four months pregnant and the abortion clinic told me I would have to pay extra money because I was more than 12 weeks pregnant and they scheduled my appointment and gave me specific instructions and directions. I was not going to deliver another child without a father being there to help raise it. I had my money, reliable transportation and everything I needed to get the job done. I called upon a friend to go with me because I was instructed not to come alone. It was a two hour drive. My good friend Monica agreed to accompany me to the appointment.

So, I packed my bags to go. There was nothing stopping me. I would get up bright and early in the morning and off we would go. Yes, it happened that fast. I woke up and was on my way out the door and when I opened the door it was the MAN OF MY DREAMS saying "I am sorry about what I said to you the other day. I didn't mean it. I know that's my baby, where are you going with the bag?" Now this was back in the day when I did not have a home phone or a cell phone, no text service, no pager, no computer, no internet, no cable, no walkie talkie, no voice mail, no email, no social network, no yahoo chat, no regular mail. I had to go all the way to the post office, a P.O. Box, just to retrieve my mail. No daily newspaper delivery service, not even a door bell. I had a 19 inch color TV with three local channels that were fuzzy without an antenna, so basically no communication, but God can meet you right where you are at without all of that!

I dropped the bag and he held me and I held him and of course you know over the next few days we made up, married and eloped and had our honeymoon at McDonalds. We did not go through drive-thru, we went in and sat down to eat. It was so romantic. I had to drive him across the state border because he was a minor at age 19. I also had to pay for the marriage license, the marriage ceremony and honeymoon, because he had yet to implement his business plan. Anywho, we walked out the courthouse and he said now you are Mrs. !@#. I said "No I ain't, I am Crystal Holt". Out of order in the courthouse courtyard and the marriage had just begun.

This takes me back to the memory of my mother once telling me that I too was a scheduled abortion appointment. Me and my mother had an understanding and I never judged her regarding this, for I understood her heart and spirit. I knew in the spirit she did not want to abort me, but in the natural she knew she could not handle one more thing, so she went to the doctor to get some medication that would terminate the pregnancy. She took the medicine that the doctor prescribed and guess what, 43 years later I am still here writing and telling the story about God's goodness, grace and mercy. All that medicine did was act as a placebo as she carried, delivered and birthed destiny from her own womb in May, 1966 for God's Glory, Hallelujah!

So as a young woman living out my own destiny, but not fully knowing the fullness therein, I was so happy to be married and to tell everyone about THE MAN OF MY DREAMS. I would say "This is my husband …". We looked so good together too. I didn't mean to spite him back at the courthouse courtyard and I think I hurt his feelings, but I worked hard to get a name I was proud of and I was proud of my name and now he wants to change my name, HMPH! Oh my, did I have a lot to learn.

We remained married from May, 1989 through Spring, 2003, when I divorced him ONLY to marry my second husband. Smart move huh! Yes, you can see that I still was out of the will of God doing things that were not decent and not in order, satisfying my needs, the lusts of the eyes and the lusts of the flesh. Putting God on a shelf and utilizing Him only when I needed Him. So the story continues … not decent and … definitely not in order.

For the steps of a righteous man are ordered by the Lord and when you are not living righteously your life will reflect the same. Just know that your steps will be out of order, you will be out of order, your life will be out of order, you will be going through a revolving cycle because when there is a calling on your life, that calling does not go away you just have to catch up with it and surrender to it.

To everyone within the sound of my voice, God is calling you even as I speak. He is calling you and saying "Come …", it is up to you to listen to the call and take heed to the call. God loved you so much that He said "Leading Lady C write this book so that I can get their attention. If I can't get their attention one way, I will get it another way."

I said "Lord, why do I have to get naked and tell the whole world all about my business, what if they judge me and talk about me?" God answered and said (Isaiah 53:3-12) "He was despised and rejected of men; a man of sorrows, and acquainted with grief:", "He was afflicted, wounded, bruised, oppressed, thrown in prison, stricken, smitten, and He still had to die on a cross after all of that to please His father". Go read the scriptures for yourself. He did all of that for us, why would we be selfish and try to hide all the things that God brought us out of, all the things that God has done for us just to save our reputation. At this point in my life, I really don't carry about my reputation and what man thinks about me.

I am only trying to please my Heavenly Father, so if telling you the truth makes you feel less of me, know that you are really just digging your own grave and that you are going to eventually fall into it for I have decided that I am going to be obedient to God and if He says tell it, I am telling it. If He says don't tell it, I won't put my mouth on it! I am only trying to please my Heavenly Father and I am on assignment by Him to bring His people to repentance so that they can be saved, delivered, set free, healed and made whole so that He can use them to do kingdom business. It is not about you. It is definitely not about me. It is not about your business or my business. It is about God's kingdom business.

I wish somebody could have got naked for me so that I could have caught it in the spirit! No, a lot people are hiding their skeletons when they need to "come out the closet". A lot of people are sweeping things under the rug when they need to clean up the mess under the rug and clean the rug and bless somebody. A lot of people are walking around acting like everything is okay and like they got it all together saying things like "I am blessed and highly favored, praise the Lord saints". These same people you better not follow them home and open up their closets and/or lift up their throw rugs, because you don't know what is going to come out. Now don't get me wrong I don't mind telling people "I am blessed and highly favored", because I am.

If we serve God and He is First in our life, then we are blessed and highly favored, but I care enough to go even further than that and just get naked with the whole world and say "I personally have not been saved all my life, but God saved and delivered me and brought me out of every affliction". I don't mind telling somebody "I can't keep me, but God can keep me". I don't mind telling somebody "There is some things about me that I am not pleased with, but God is not done with me yet, so don't count me out the race". I don't mind saying "I am only blessed and highly favored only because of His love, His mercy and His grace". I don't mind telling somebody that "I have to stay in God's presence, it is a necessity for me to stay before the Lord to remain worthy of my calling, for without Him I can do nothing". I just don't mind "being real". So if me "being real" offends you, then close the book now because I am getting ready to get naked and real with you and I apologize in advance. I am getting naked and real for "My Daddy". I don't mind telling people "I was messed up, but God cleaned me up for His glory!"

Part 3

Take 2, Cut 2 - Once upon a Time ... Writing & Rewriting My Story for God's Glory

Sometimes in life I viewed my life experiences as playing the cards I was dealt. With this mindset, I placed God in a box. In so doing, I placed God in a position in which His hands were tied and even though he wanted to bless me beyond my imagination, he could not release all blessings unto me because I was not quite ready to receive them. Although I didn't like the cards I was dealt in life, I didn't want to sacrifice what I needed to sacrifice in order to receive a new deck of cards to play. In fact, I did not even have to sacrifice that much, because God kept speaking to me and telling me that obedience is better than sacrifice, but the flesh cannot receive the things of the spirit. So what I did was in all my strength, I kept on trying to be in control of my destiny and not allow God to be in control of my destiny.

The truth of the matter is God is in control regardless of whether we want to believe it or not. I just kept on living my life and writing and rewriting my story, but God's Mighty Hand was at work just as my hands were at work. For God in all His wisdom, power and understanding held the blueprints of my destiny tightly within His hands and he knew I would eventually have to come to Him and seek Him with my whole heart for the answers to my questions, for instructions on my journey and for directions on the path before me. He knew eventually I would get tired and weary enough that I would have to come to Him and sit at His feet and listen to Him. Then and only then would I be able to see clearly what he wanted me to see all along. God knew when I began to have total faith in Him and keep Him *First* and trust Him and only Him to write my story that I would then be content with just living out the story, but I was not there yet. I still wanted to write and rewrite my story and have some type of control over my direction in life, but what I was really doing is only delaying the process.

So here we go again, another time around, with me attempting to tell my story. Looking back, summer, 1989, new college graduate, newlywed, pregnant, two children, one that I am not caring for who is in my mother's care. I returned home from college to be with THE MAN OF MY DREAMS in Chicago, Illinois, "The Windy City". We were going to plan and start a life together "Happily Ever After ...". Although the beginning may have not got off to a good start the ending would surely be "Happily Ever After ... like a fairytale".

This fairytale lasted about two weeks in the real world. I was starving in Chicago. We had limited resources like i.e. food, water, shelter, clothing. Need I say more? We did not have an apartment. We moved from place to place to whoever would open their door to us and be kind enough to feed us. Need I say more? We did have a lot of delicious fast food, ethnic foods, soul food, food carts, family restaurants and fine dining, etc. available to us and "my mouth would water every time we passed by them". Need I say more? We did not have the luxury of opening up the kitchen cabinet and taking out a clean bowl and a box of cereal and pouring the cereal in the bowl and turning around to the refrigerator and opening up the refrigerator door and reaching inside the refrigerator for the full carton of nice cold milk inside and taking the milk out of the refrigerator and shutting the refrigerator door behind us and pouring the milk in the bowl of cereal and going to the kitchen cabinet drawer and pulling out a clean spoon and sitting down at the kitchen table in a kitchen chair and saying "MMM Good". I was starving! Need I say more?

Now, in a big city like Chicago it is like New York "it never sleeps" so there was plenty for us to do and plenty of time to do it, but there was no stability. I was pregnant, unemployed, beating the streets daily to find work and hungry. Not a good look, I must say. I was like Dorothy in the movie Wizard of Oz thinking and singing "When I think of home I think of a place where there is ... food". All I could think about was "When I think of home, I think of a place where there is food!" I had a car and I had gas so "Home Sweet Home" here we come. Well you might say "What about THE MAN OF YOUR DREAMS? I shall say "Anywho". I loved THE MAN OF MY DREAMS very dearly, but I did not sign up for that so I had to sign out. Oh, we can stay married and that was fine but I was like "Got Milk?" I got back home and I was full, fat and happy once again.

My dad allowed me and my daughter to live with him until we got on our feet. He put a roof over our head and fed us. I remember his famous fried tacos, fried pork chops, fried potatoes and onions, mouth watering meatloaf, barbeque chicken, fresh fruit and vegetables from the garden, fresh seasonal fruit on the counter, iced homemade lemonade, squeezed fresh orange juice, Stafford's Dairy fruit punch, dinner rolls, strawberry shortcake, whipped cream and vanilla ice cream for dessert. Yeah, this is definitely home for now. We went to church together as a family and we prayed together as a family and we trusted God in all things. One Sunday during church service, I went to the alter for prayer and a minister at the church, Rev. Steve Humes began to pray and prophecy over my life. He asked if I dreamed and I said "No, not really". He said "God has heard your cry and He is going to answer and you will dream and interpret dreams and God is going to reveal everything to you" and he smiled and I smiled and walked back to my seat.

The very next day, Monday morning, I hit the pavement to obtain work. I was seven months pregnant. I obtained temporary work the same day through an agency as a receptionist/secretary. I could not understand how I could just walk into the agency and be "hired on the spot" and in Chicago I walked the streets for weeks to obtain work, to no avail. That just did not make sense to me. Nevertheless, I worked full-time in this capacity until I delivered my baby, Che'Andrea. I had great temporary positions at city hall in the mayor's office and in the development office, a local law firm, an insurance agency, University of Illinois College of Medicine. I loved every job and was glad to have the opportunity to work, make a living and enjoy such diversity of meeting different people and getting a lot of experience under my belt.

THE MAN OF MY DREAMS later came to reunite with his family in my hometown and we obtained our first apartment as husband and wife. I helped him obtain a job right away as a janitor at Mister Donut, n/k/a (now known as), Dunkin Donuts. He kept making excuses for not finding work and we were driving down the street one day and I saw a big sign in the window that said "Now Hiring". So I asked him to pull over and go in and talk to the people and he said "They not gone hire me. I am not trying to be no janitor. I am a Business Man with a Business Plan" and I said "If you don't work, you won't eat!" School of the Holy Ghost at work! He was a "growing boy" and he liked to eat, so he did not hesitate to comply.

I stayed in the car while he went inside and applied for the job and he was "hired on the spot". He only made a little over minimum wage, but that was fine. He made about $100.00 a week net and I only asked "The Business Man" to give me $60.00 for the household bills and I paid for everything else. He spent his free time hanging out with his "business associates" playing basketball, and taking me to and from work and the kids to and from school which now makes no good sense because we had two cars. HMM, Anywho. Don't think I am sleep on this one now. If you don't get this one, I will send you a private email. No, I am just kind of kidding, NOT!

I was so comfortable in my marriage that most of the time I would ask him to drive me to work because I was always oversleeping and running late and he drove so fast like a maniac and I drove like a little old lady driving in the middle of the road with both hands on the steering wheel. I knew if I let him drive he would make up the difference in driving time and I would possibly get to work on time. Now sometimes it took me longer to wake him up than it would have taken for me to drive myself to work for he slept like a bear hibernating for the winter.

Back to what I was saying, don't think I forgot. You will notice I shift gears a lot in my mind, but know that I stay on the same track. Just hold on and keep listening. Then, there were times that he volunteered or insisted on driving me to and from work. Now listen to me clearly, if your man insists on taking you to work and picking you up from work and it kind of appears to you that he may be trying to just show you chivalry and you say in your mind "Awe that is so sweet". First, do a little "self-check". Ask yourself these simple questions, say "Self, do I have a valid driver's license? Self, do I have a reliable car with gas? Self, am I capable of driving myself?" If you have answered yes to all of the above questions, I want you to now discern in your spirit and know that the correct answer is "This makes no sense!" Let me share a little secret with you that I found out about the hard way. It ain't about chivalry, silly girl, he don't want you to warm up the car on your lunch break and catch him in the ... (You fill in the blanks). Okay, I could go on, but I am done here. Let me get out the flesh and back in the spirit and move on.

He kept his used hoopty parked most of the time, but it was always clean and pretty much in good running condition and he kept his hair "did" and he stayed well groomed, so I was happy to have a "hunk of a husband" and I truly loved him and he was the father of my child so we tried our best to make it. We even went to church sometimes together as a family and he seemed to pay attention and enjoy the service because I would oftentimes turn and look at him to see if he was awake and listening real good and he was "Awe ain't that sweet?", but things were out of order still because God was not First in our lives. We were living our lives and having a lifestyle together as husband and wife, but God was supposed to be First in our life and our lifestyle. A threefold cord is not easily broken, not a twofold cord. To make a long story short, the fights and arguments continued, the in and out of jail for domestic violence and plain childish mischief continued. The rest is just a mess so no need to bless it with words.

I then packed everything I could pack in a clothes hamper and told THE MAN OF MY DREAMS I was going to wash clothes. We did not have a washing machine or dryer so this was just another typical day. He did not ask any questions, very comfortable in his present state whereas, I lived in constant fear and uncertainty most of the time. I gathered up the kids and we got in the car. I went to my father's house to wash me and my girls' dirty clothes and we did not return! I guess when it came night THE MAN OF MY DREAMS began to worry but this was the time before cell phones and pagers and we did not have a home phone so he jumped in the hoopty to find me and I was right where I needed to be, safe in the shelter of my natural father's care and my Heavenly Father's arms folding our nice and clean clothes and placing them in the nice and clean dresser drawers in our nice, clean and comfortable bedroom.

So then of course the apartment was given up due to no more payments. Now THE MAN OF MY DREAMS was without a place to stay and my dad was not going to support a grown man, so THE MAN OF MY DREAMS decided to stay with the "business associates" that I assume he met in his capacity of "Business Man with a Business Plan" and that worked for a while and when it no longer worked, he shortly returned home to Chicago. I stayed with my father for about six months. Enough time to save up enough money to get my first and last month's rent and deposit together for a new two bedroom townhouse apartment for me and my girls.

In 1990, I obtained my first full-time permanent job as a legal secretary at a local law firm working Monday through Friday 8:30 a.m. to 5 p.m., no weekends or holidays, competitive benefit plan including medical benefits, flexible spending account, 401K, paid vacation and sick time, yearly raises and bonuses, all-inclusive catered Christmas dinners at the finest restaurants in town, wonderful gifts and special favors on Secretary's Day, at Christmas or just because gifts to show that my hard work was appreciated. I was paid $330.00 a week net starting out. My kids were in quality daycare. Life was grand. I purchased my first brand new car a white Honda Civic. I managed to get a decent two bedroom townhouse apartment. Me and the kids were going to church on a regular basis. All our needs were met, everything was falling into place for us finally. We had plenty of resources.

Now we were still out of the will of God because He was still not First in our life, but thank him for His mercy and grace. I was now 25 years old, living life to the fullest, partying, my heart was merry. I now had a good man, we were dating. A baller, shot caller. I now had the luxury of going out to eat, going on family outings and family vacations, going to the movies, shopping sprees, concerts. OOPS wait, I still have a husband. UH, that's right. UH OH! Oh well, out of sight, out of mind! The bible says in (Ecclesiastes 7:2) "It is better to go to the house of mourning than the house of feasting". This was a lesson I had yet to learn.

In 1992, I went back to college to finish up my schooling in social work. My plan was to obtain a BA degree in Social Work. Well I had to modify my plans based on the fact that this particular major was only offered 30 minutes away from where I lived basically in another city and I had to think about the commitment, travel time, transportation, costs and the inconvenience of it all. So I decided to attend a local college where I could obtain reduced tuition, evening classes, and online classes in a setting that worked around working students' schedules.

This particular school and major met my needs. I majored in social justice. A combination of social work and criminal justice combined. After finishing up my courses I planned to go into the social work or criminal justice field. So I set out to accomplish this endeavor. I excelled beyond imagination. My GPA remained above 3.5 at all times. I would only accept As and Bs. If I got a C there was a problem and I did not mind speaking up about it. I was committed to this and I worked hard, long hours to achieve it and of course you know my good man helped, oh and yeah, and God too. Notice the order. Yes, still living life out of order.

I relied on my family, extended family and friends to accomplish my life goals and aspirations as well as cooperative employers. I had everything in place just perfect, the favor of man and God. Again, notice the order. I sometimes felt guilty being away from my kids a lot because most of my time was spent going to work, classes and then there was study time and homework, but I felt my kids would understand and see me as a role model and would benefit in the long run. I felt if I did positive things in life they would do greater. So I continued on the path that I was going. Hindsight is better than no sight at all.

In 1994, I graduated with Honors with a BA Degree in Social Justice. I was so proud of my accomplishment and gave God all the glory throughout the whole two years of study for He completed every assignment, every paper, every test. It was definitely not in my own strength that I made it. Not only did I make it, I made it with honors. There was a national recognition book that everyone who graduated with honors could pay to have their picture published in this book so that the whole world could see you graduated with honors. It was my prize possession in addition to my college diploma which by the way are now both packed up in storage somewhere for the moths to eat.

THE MAN OF MY DREAMS was now facing federal charges and he was sentenced to a five year prison term. I always tried to talk to him about living right and doing the right thing. I know no one is perfect, but I would always tell him "There is a way that seemeth right unto a man, but the end result is destruction". (Proverbs 14:12). I knew the end result, but I could not live his life for him. All I could do was continue to try to live right. I kept encouraging him to not chase money because the bible says in (Proverbs 23:5) "for riches certainly make themselves wings; they fly away as an eagle toward heaven". I kept encouraging him to seek the kingdom and His righteousness and all things would be added unto him. He listened, but he chose to do things his way.

So THE MAN OF MY DREAMS was now off to prison. My little girl would not see her father until she was 7 years old. I could not do the prison visits for my heart could not take losing another person I loved so I did what I normally do. I did not look back. I couldn't look back because it hurt so bad. The man I loved dearly, THE MAN OF MY DREAMS was going to be gone from my life for five years and even more for unknown to the both of us, in the years to come, due to again ungodly decisions and choices attempting to chase money once again, he would serve another five year term on top of the first term which would include a loss of 10 years total that we would never be able to take back.

Now I know I said I had a good man and I loved him dearly as well, because he comforted me and cared for me and loved me and my children with all that he had and he came into my life at a very crucial time, but I made a vow before God with my husband. I had a binding covenant with my husband, still. Nevertheless, I continued on the path that I was going, not looking back, out of the will of God with **MY IDOL** leading the way. I was going to find "Happily Ever After even if I had to pay for it ...." Well let me tell you, I did just that. I paid for it! Except it was not with money, it was with my life. It cost me my life!

In 1994, upon graduating from college, I worked an internship as a juvenile probation officer. I then obtained a summer job as a youth outreach worker and months later a permanent full-time position as a youth outreach specialist. I worked with children and families providing educational and recreational activities through outreach opportunities. I really enjoyed my job and I had a passion for helping families.

I wanted to reach more diverse populations and make a bigger difference in the lives of families, so I applied for a job as a foster care caseworker in 1995. I worked in this capacity for one year. This job required me to travel back and forth to Chicago for home visits, sibling visits, court dates, etc. three or more times a week. I would have to arise early for work to get on the expressway before rush hour traffic, sometimes 3 a.m. in the morning and leave my children in someone else's care until I returned which was usually late at night, sometimes 10 p.m. or later only to turn around the next day and do the same. The pay was $10.00 an hour/$21,000.00 a year. It was a salary job, no overtime, but travel expenses were paid and mileage reimbursement. Any overtime hours could be taken as flex-time which meant you could take time off during the work week as time permitted. So there was a lot of flexibility with this job, but it was definitely not a job for a single parent. So, I basically just worked on getting experience under my belt. The job itself was really stressful to me in that I really internalized everything and when cases were lost in court, you know I grieved.

I had now broken up with **MY IDOL** and now I had a new **IDOL**. OOPS wait, I am still married and still out of the will of God ... Dang! Yes, **MY NEW IDOL** knocked on my door as an "Angel of Light" and asked "Can I be of any help?" I cracked the door open and kindly said "No". "He said, "Well, if you ever need me, I just wanted you to know that you can just call me, for anything, Really ....". "Awe, wasn't that sweet?"

So I decided to pursue other career and other personal options. It was in my family's best interest that I did so, so I thought. I found myself taking care of other families' needs and other families' children and my very own children were basically fending for themselves. When I say that I don't mean they were neglected or abused, but I mean I was spending so much time away from home, working long hours, having to travel back and forth out of town handling my work caseload, i.e. court cases, doctor visits, school conferences, meetings and more meetings, appointments and more appointments. By the time I got off work and got home, I had nothing left in me to ensure that my children's needs were met other than their basic needs of course like food, shelter, clothes, school.

Anything extra was extra and not always available to them. For example, helping them with their homework, giving them a bubble bath, reading them a bedtime story and tucking them in bed at night, kissing them and hugging them and telling them I loved them when they woke up every morning, or even taking them to fun activities like a girls day together and showing them that they were me and God's special little princesses. I did take my kids along with me on my business trips sometimes and they enjoyed it, but still I did not have the quality time available to spend with them that was required and that they deserved.

In July, 1996, I obtained a job at a hospital as a medical secretary. This was so much better in that it was basically a "9 to 5" job with no weekends or holidays. I was able to spend more quality time with my family and take care of all of our needs. The pay was $9.00 and hour with overtime pay and an excellent benefit package including family benefits, tuition reimbursement, and advancement opportunities. My girls now had good quality daycare and schools and I was able to participate in all their school and recreational activities. My girls were in private jazz, tap and tumbling lessons. I was so proud of them. Yet I was still out of the will of God, so you know what comes next. Yes, consequences that were not favorable. I really don't even have time to share it all, but let's just say I made some major decisions and as a result of the major decisions that I made on my own free will without asking God *First*, the private lessons of tap, jazz and tumbling were now extra and I, without God's help, made an executive decision to downsize everything extra. Not a smart move in the long run.

One thing I learned from this experience is kids need to be involved in something positive and surround themselves with peers who are doing something positive. They need a skill, talent, trade, etc. and if you cannot personally teach them then the best thing to do is get them involved in programs, groups, teams or networks that can. Whether free public services or private or by obtaining scholarships available to you, but the worse thing you can do is not give your children the opportunity to utilize their gifting or allow them the opportunity and then take it away from them for no good reason. Even if it means you have to sacrifice yourself temporarily, don't sacrifice your children's future! Again, hindsight is better than no sight at all. I thought we could not afford the luxury of extras, but I soon found out that we couldn't afford not to!

Children are your blessings this I know, but five in a row back to back without God *First* in your life is like playing "Russian roulette – a potentially lethal game of chance". For your body was not designed for this type of stress. Then you add on to that the fact that you still have limited resources, limited time and limited support, and you are still out of the will of God. Yes, "You definitely have your hands full".

That is a phrase that makes me cringe. I mean my hair sticks up on top of my head when somebody says that to me. Know that! When I go out in public with all five of my anointed praise dancers that is the phrase I always get. "You sure have your hands full". I cringe every time and I think to myself "Well you don't so why don't you just roll up your sleeves and help out". Now I know this is not godly thinking, so what I have done is renewed my mind to view this phrase as a compliment.

You see when I only had my two wonderful girls Krishina and Che' and we would go to church together or out to eat or anywhere in public, people would always say "Your children are beautiful and they are so well behaved" and this would always make me feel so good inside and I would just smile knowing that at home this was not always the case, but for the most part they were good kids 95% of the time. So that was spectacular, but granny and mama always said "the children get weaker and wiser" but I think she meant "the children get worser and worser". Not to claim that on my kids, but five kids in a row back to back and the last four boys, Oh my God! Yes, they are too wise, they are so wise that they have placed me in the category of "Stupid!" I had no clue how to handle them other than stay on my knees and before the Lord for strength, guidance, protection, provision and basically everything.

So in saying all of that, I can attest to the fact that "children are your blessings because they will keep you on your knees". I often reflect back on my life and say "I wish the "system" would come and get the last three "Hebrew Boys", Kha'Leel, Ja'Mari and Christian, so that I can rest, but you know I don't mean it. Just like I can't live with them, I can't live without them. Now when their father has them for arranged weekly and weekend visits, I do my best to try to live without them indeed, trust! Even if it means that every now and then I have the luxury of taking a "Calgon bath" with lit scented aromatherapy candles surrounding the tub. As I lay back my head in the tub and pretend that I am on a tropical island away from all the cares of the world, OOOH WHEE, Yes, I definitely know how to do me! I don't have no problem doing me!

MY PERSONAL PRAYER

Lord, I know that You are a restorer. Restore everything that the devil stole from my children's life, their latter days shall be greater in You. I speak against the enemy's plan to kill, steal, conqueror and destroy them. Thank You Jesus for blocking every weapon formed against them. Thank You for Your love, grace and mercy. Thank You for bringing about salvation, deliverance, freedom and healing in every area concerning my children and my family. Yet, do not allow the enemy to even think he is going to get away with what he has tried to do or what he has done for he shall surely pay. Every predator, every pedophile, every demonic spirit, every evil worker shall be brought to nought by the power of God! Yes, Yes, Yes, I am speaking to you and you know who you are. You pon, imp of the devil. Oh yes, I forgive you according to God's word, 70 x 7, but I also intercede in prayer for you right now for Your deliverance. I am obligated to tell you by the gift that God has deposited in me to speak the word of God over you in truth with the power and authority of God within me. I declare, decree the word of God will not go out and not perform what it was sent out to do, Amen!

I SEAL THIS CHAPTER CONCERNING MY BELOVED CHILDREN WITH GOD'S WORD

Dearly beloved, avenge not yourselves, but rather give place unto wrath: for it is written, Vengeance is mine; I will repay, saith the Lord. (Romans 12:19).

Then said he unto the disciples, It is impossible but that offences will come: but woe unto him, through whom they come! It were better for him that a millstone were hanged about his neck, and he cast into the sea, than that he should offend one of these little ones. (Luke 17:1-2).

Upon the wicked he shall rain snares, fire and brimstone, and an horrible tempest: this shall be the portion of their cup. (Psalm 11:6).

Part 4

Take 3, Cut 3 - I Love You on Purpose

Looking back, THE LOVE OF MY LIFE, what page are we on now, is there enough time and room in this book to talk about him? Yes, THE LOVE OF MY LIFE, he was everything I desired, in that season of my life. At that time in my life, I loved him to death, on purpose. I loved his dirty "draughs". He could do no wrong in my eyes. It was a good thing I was blinded and could not see. OOPS, did I say that out loud? Total sarcasm, but true. Maybe, I should recall my thoughts that I just spoke out loud. I mean this with all sincerity and I will never ever disrespect anyone on purpose and I will always love everyone on purpose, but I will not lie and I cannot lie. However, I can speak the truth very well. So if you don't want the truth, don't ask me anything! Today is your lucky day though because I feel the need to give you the truth, for free, without you asking.

I just want everyone to know that I loved THE LOVE OF MY LIFE from the bottom of my heart, deeply and dearly. I am going to go greater than that and talk Real Talk to everyone in the sound of my voice. Yes, I AM THE VOICE that will be heard. I am not holding back. I am going to speak loud and clear. The devil is a liar! He shut up my mouth way too long. There is deliverance in your voice. When you speak power into the atmosphere you create the atmosphere. There is power in your words. Remember that! Now back to the issue at hand. As I said before and I cannot say it enough, I loved THE LOVE OF MY LIFE more than anything and everything! I repeat, "I loved THE LOVE OF MY LIFE more than anything and everything! Again, I loved THE LOVE OF MY LIFE more than anything and everything!"

You know this phrase constantly played repeatedly over and over again in my mind, so don't get upset and say she keeps saying that get on with it already. This phrase just kept playing in my mind over and over again. It played like a broken record from 1995 to present until God had to literally shake up the very ground that I stood on and allow me to fall flat on my face and repent.

He spoke to me over and over again. He rebuked me over and over again. He corrected me over and over again. He comforted me over and over again. He provided for me over and over again. He healed me over and over again. He kept me over and over again. He protected me over and over again. He dried my tears over and over again. He gave me joy, peace and love, over and over again. Even God gets tired of foolishness. For over 14 years that same broken record played in my mind "I love THE LOVE OF MY LIFE more than anything and everything". If God was not a gentleman He would have just said "SHUT UP!"

IN 2007 GOD FURTHER SPEAKS …

Turn ye not unto idols, nor make to yourselves molten gods: I am the Lord your God. (Leviticus 19:4).

Ye shall make no idols nor graven image, neither rear you up a standing image, neither shall yet set up any image of stone in your land, to bow down unto it: for I am the Lord your God. (Leviticus 26:1).

And I will destroy your high places, and cut down your images, and cast your carcases upon the carcases of your idols, and my soul shall abhor you. (Leviticus 26:30).

The idols of the heathen are silver and gold, the work of men's hands. (Psalm 135:15).

For every one of the house of Israel, or of the stranger that sojourneth in Israel, which separateth himself from me, and setteth up his idols in his heart, and putteth the stumblingblock of his iniquity before his face, and cometh to a prophet to enquire of him concerning me; I the Lord will answer him by myself: (Ezekiel 14:7).

My obituary reads, Crystal Y. Holt, Sunrise March, 1995 through Sunset … - Over 14 years. This love affair turned into so many things. I totally lost my mind and myself in the process. I gave up everything, even my mind, body and spirit to hold on to this love affair if that is how you describe it. Now don't get me wrong God designed us to love. There is nothing wrong with that. We must love everyone with the love of God. Yet, God gives us the type of love that we can only have for Him and Him alone, and the type of love we can only have for our husband and that our husband can only have for his wife. This type of love that belongs to a husband and wife only belongs between husband and wife. You know the apple of his eye and the apple of her eye. To love, to cherish, in sickness and in health, rich or power, better or worse until death do us part. It does not belong between, husband and wife and mistresses or wife and husband and other "generous gents", or husband and wife and other extramarital affairs involving single, married, divorced, or separated individuals.

I know that I am about to step on somebody's toes but I don't care. Call me rude like that! Oh, I am going to take the time to break it down. It only belongs between husband and wife. In marriage, a threefold cord consisting of God *First*, and then husband and wife is not easily broken. The knot that ties this marriage together is God. This knot, union of marriage, can only be tied by God and it can only untied by God. You don't have the power to tie it and you don't have the authority to untie it.

God hates divorce! You can only ask God to untie the threefold cord for two permissible reasons and those reasons are 1) if your spouse commits adultery, i.e. marital unfaithfulness or 2) if he is an unbeliever and he leaves the marriage, i.e. abandonment. Now even with these two "way-out clauses", you can choose to remain married and forgive your spouse for his/her infidelity and God honors your choice and your decision. However, should you choose to take either "way-out clause", God honors that too because God values and loves you as a person and is not in favor of keeping a legal vow at the expense of someone being abused. If you don't know the definition of abuse, then please look it up in a dictionary. Unfortunately, I lived out the definition of abuse without having to research it! Now giving you any more details than that would not be about bringing God glory, so I will hold my peace for now, can I get an Amen?

Nevertheless, you do not have the power or authority to keep your husband, just as your husband does not have the power or authority to keep his wife. Only God has that power and the authority to keep two married people married. It takes keeping God *First* for a marriage to withstand any circumstance and any situation with the bond holding you together being the value and love for each other that God has placed in each of you. Your marriage will unravel right before your eyes if you try to keep it together by yourself without God being First and in the midst.

Marriage is not easy, but it is well worth it! Both husband and wife need to do their respective part in the marriage because marriage is ministry. The wife needs to minister to her husband as a "help meet", loving him, honoring him and giving him due reverence. The husband also needs to minister to his "help meet". The husband in his rightful position as the "Head" needs to wash his wife with the word presenting her faultless before God our King. He needs to be a provider and a wise protector for not only his help meet, but the entire household. When the husband is in his rightful position as the Head, everyone and everything else receives the overflow, but it starts with God *First* and it continues with God *First*. Only then can the saying "Behind every good man is a good woman", vice versa, be true.

God's word says "That which I have brought together let no man put asunder!" Before you ask "Why Did I Get Married?" and before and after you see the movie by Tyler Perry "Why Did I Get Married, part 1 and 2", I would ask that you now do a relationship check by asking yourself this question "Did God bring me and my significant other together?" God don't bless no mess! If your relationship looks like a mess then know God is not in it, so you should not be either! Only relationships that are built upon a solid foundation in God can bring Him glory. Yes, I am talking about me, but you can apply it to your situation if the need be. Yes, my life was messy, my house was messy. It was out of order. THE LOVE OF MY LIFE tried to keep it together. He worked long hours at work. Well, at least he said he worked long hours at work. He worked two and three jobs to take care of the things he needed to take care of. Well, at least he said he was working two and three jobs to take care of things he needed to take care of. Call me naive, but I believed everything he said, even when I did not believe it! I was convinced beyond a doubt that he was THE LOVE OF MY LIFE, period. That was my story and I was sticking to it!

I worked 1st, 2nd, 3rd shifts working around my families' needs, so that we did not have to pay the expensive cost of childcare for it was over $500.00 a week. God sent provision through divine intervention even during this time of disobedience. I was so tired and so weary during this time. I called on the pastor, my mother, those close to me to tell them I needed their prayers and I needed their help to figure out a way that I could get some rest. My health was not optimal and I was getting little rest and my physical and spiritual diet and exercise was unhealthy and unbalanced.

So, I was basically not taking proper care of myself, my loved ones or others. Knowing I could not longer do it in my own strength, I began to reach out for help. My mom referred me to an old friend of hers named Ms. Ida Lee, also known as Ms. Ida. She spoke very favorable of her. I was very nervous because I am the type of mother that would never leave my children with someone who I knew nothing about, but at that time I was desperate. So, I called Ms. Ida and spoke to her and she asked me what exactly I needed and I told her. I poured my heart out to her and I told her "I am just so tired and I need some rest, any hours you can work will be sufficient. I really do not have a lot of money but I can pay you $100.00 a week; so, basically for $100.00, whatever you can do. She said "That is fine, do not worry about the money just pay me whatever you can. You just drop the baby by my house tomorrow and you get some rest." I said "Thank you so much and God bless you for helping me."

So, this was the start of my new family in God. For whoever began to bless me and my family became my new spiritual family that I knew God had blessed me with. You see, God will be a mother to the motherless, a father to the fatherless, a sister to the sisterless. Ms. Ida became my God-mother and she taught me so much about how to not only know God and to have a relationship with him, but how to do what God requires us to do and that is bless others with our gifts. Ms. Ida had the gift of nurturing and caring for others with the love of God. She could run a whole household, even if it was not her own, by the power of God. She would teach my kids about God and teach them how to pray. She would anoint their heads with oil and pray over even the food she cooked and served them. No demonic spirit could coexist in the presence of Ms. Ida.

She set the atmosphere in my home as she sat on the couch watching TV, playing with the kids or resting while the children were asleep. She was a praying babysitter. I never wanted to call her my babysitter even though she worked in that capacity. The title babysitter did not fit her because she did so much more than babysit. So I began to call her my second mom and she officially became my God-mother. Just as in the presence of both my natural grandmother and mother, I would call my natural grandmother "mama or granny" and my natural mother "my other mama a/k/a ma". Each granny, ma and Ms. Ida had their rightful place in my life and in my heart.

My son Kha'Leel was six months old when Ms. Ida began to care for him. She would watch him during the day while I slept because I worked 3rd shift. Ms. Ida eventually began to care for all the kids during the evening hours as well and the babies' dad would take over when he got off work and he would watch the kids at night while I was at work. Ms. Ida did an excellent job with the kids. She came at a perfect time in my life and we came at a perfect time in her life. I sensed that the devil was also speaking to her just as he was speaking to me. The devil was saying to her "Your this, your that and … look at you now … where is your God?" Ms. Ida is a very strong woman of God with great faith, but at that time she was transitioning and did not know exactly which way she was going. So when I called and asked for her help she knew God had given her an assignment and she got up from her stagnant place and began to work. For the harvest is plenty but the laborers are few. She did not have a job at that time, but now she was gainfully employed for God's purpose and that purpose being to bless my life, my children and the lives of many more families to come. What an assignment. She knew only the beginning of it, but God knew the end. She was faithful, loyal, loving and kind.

One day the enemy showed his ugly face and said "You cannot afford to pay $100.00 a week. You need to cut some expenses and it looks like it's going to be child care because your bills are piling up and …." So, I began to talk to the LOVE OF MY LIFE and ask for his opinion and help regarding this situation. The LOVE OF MY LIFE informed me that he did not have any more money to give me for child care for he was already struggling trying to make ends meet. This was the trick of the enemy because we both worked full-time and overtime.

At that time, we did not see where this was going. I had a creative idea to put Kha'Leel in a daycare program that was subsidized based on income and basically I would pay a small portion of my income. I looked at this as if it would be a savings, HMMH. Then I thought, well I could keep him here at home with me and I could sleep when he naps. So I discussed with Ms. Ida my situation and she said "That is fine, you are going to put him in school?" and I said "Yes" and she said "That will be good for him …". She said that with her mouth and she meant it, but her spirit was speaking much louder saying "Now Lord, what am I going to do?" It hurt me to tell her this because I really wanted her to continue to care for my family. I wanted her to continue to be the rock that we could lean on for strength. I wanted her to continue to intercede on our behalf with every gift that God had deposited in her, that was the truth, but me and the LOVE OF MY LIFE were now struggling personally and financially. I assume it was because we were shacking, not married, out of the will of God, and there are consequences. This is just an example of them.

I did manage to get Kha'Leel in a licensed/quality daycare center full-time, but it seemed that his behavior was not acceptable. He was kicked out of several daycare settings before we found one that would work with him for in the transition process he was diagnosed as having a learning disability and he required special services. This explains why I was so tired and weary working 3rd shift at night and trying to care for him during the day and get some sleep. Oftentimes, I would wake up to him engaged in some dangerous activity and have to intervene. That is why I was so desperate to find help and I found that help with Ms. Ida and then **MY IDOL** convinced me to send my help away by convincing me that I could no longer afford to pay. The truth was soon revealed that I couldn't afford not to. I know that I am talking to myself right now and that nobody within the sound of my voice understands what I am really trying to say. I pray this is not the case. Wake up people and know that the enemy is always at work trying to sabotage God's plan for your life in many ways. Wake up and take notice. Don't give the enemy even a small crack to come in, remain watchful and vigilant.

After Ms. Ida stopped caring for the kids on a regular basis, things began to fall apart all around me and my family, "Effective Immediately!" It was as if someone pulled the rug from under our feet. Me and THE LOVE OF MY LIFE continued to do the best we could with what we knew, but God still was not First in our lives. By the grace of God, Ms. Ida continued the relationship she had with me, Kha'Leel and the family, filling in only as needed. She then began to work on the things she had put off in her life like going back to school to get her college degree, participating in various activities in the community, i.e. voting booths and other community events and functions, being actively involved in church, being actively involved in her own personal ministry which involved providing a group setting for women whose children were victims of violence. She facilitated this group so that women could come together and fellowship and could get the help they needed through learning and applying biblical principles for daily living and gaining healthy social skills through educational and recreational activities.

Ms. Ida had lost two children due to violence. Kha'Leel brought her restoration, a six month old baby boy to love and cherish and care for. He very much reminded her of one of her sons that she lost due to violence, but she never shared it with me until later when it became quite apparent. Kha'Leel loved cars just like her son. Ms. Ida bought Kha'Leel his first toy car and he would carry that car wherever he went. He would even sleep and bathe with that car, never letting go of it. She bought him his first book and read to him. She told him about God and taught him how to praise and pray even before he spoke his first words. She fed him just like she fed her own son. She cared for him just like she cared for her own son. Then one day, Kha'Leel was taken out of her care to go to school. Now what would she do? I will tell you what she did. She began to live! She no longer sat on the couch and played with children and cared for children and watched TV, and remained stagnant. God elevated her and said "Well done, thou good and faithful servant: thou hast been faithful over a few things, I will make thee ruler over many things: enter thou into the joy of thy Lord" (Matthew 25:21). Hallelujah!

Ms. Ida shortly thereafter graduated with her first college degree. She is presently still working on her second degree. I made a personal commitment to help her in any way possible in all her endeavors and I know she is very thankful and I am thankful and grateful to be able to bless her just as she blessed me. Not always in monetary, but in time and through the love of God. We definitely blessed each other and we still bless each other as family. We often set aside one day a month to have lunch together and we continue to fellowship with each other as time permits and we really enjoy each others company. So,

MY IDOL did not win this battle nor the war. The bible and Ms. Ida taught me that we are our brother's and sister's keeper. I remember Kha'Leel at age 6 asked Ms. Ida for her phone number and she wrote it on a tiny piece of paper and stuck it in his pocket. From that day forward, Kha'Leel has never lost Ms. Ida's number and he calls her whenever he feels the need. This is so strange because he does not even know his home number or any other number, but he definitely has Ms. Ida's number memorized. Ms. Ida gave him the nickname of "Mr. Professor". Knowing that child, he probably has her number on speed dial.

Now I am going to continue talking and you will see that it will begin to sound like a broken record, but one thing will remain constant and that is the fact that God was not First in my life. Yes, I am sorry. Yes, I regret. Yes, I went through unnecessary heartache and pain because God was not First in my life. I knew better. THE LOVE OF MY LIFE may have not known better, but I did. But I loved him so. I thought if I do this and if I do that I could. I thought if I looked right, if I smelled right, if I walked right, if I talked right, if I was educated, if I made a lot of money, if I had a nice house, if I had a nice car, if I popped out five kids for him, if I cooked the best food for him, if I cleaned the house for him, if I rocked his world, if I, if I, if I, if I …(You fill in the blanks). Where is the God in all of that?

Just like you are not saved by your works but by grace, your marriage should not be saved by "works" but by grace. Amen! I am going to start a Hallelujah praise all by myself on that one. Catch that one in the spirit. I am sick and tired of marriages failing because people think they have the right to look to their spouse to fulfill their needs and to fill every void. The devil is an absolute complete liar and I AM HERE ONCE AGAIN WITH THE VOICE THAT WON'T ACCEPT A LIE. Let the truth be told and let the truth stand!

There was so much hurt, so much pain all because I was out of God's will. A lot of times I looked back over the years and I thought to myself maybe if I coulda, woulda, shoulda I could still be with … I could still be in that … I could still have …, then I regain my focus and know that "It was not God's will!" I could go on and on and on and we would come up with the same case scenario "It was not God's will!" If the words out of my mouth don't give God glory it is best to remain silent. I guess I will take my mom's and Mr. Hallberg's advice on this issue. Think before you speak. The bible says "Everything done in secret shall be revealed and everything done in the dark shall come to light" (Mark 4:22, Luke 12:2) so I remain silent this time only, if you believe that! Ha!

I will say this, in his own special way, THE LOVE OF MY LIFE loved me dearly. He even introduced me to the 50/50 motto when it comes to relationships. What that means is if you have a bill we split it 50/50. If you go to the grocery store it is 50/50. If you do anything for each other it is 50/50 or if you do anything for the house or the kids, it is 50/50. Now here is the trick, the twist to it. If he leaves his wallet at home and you are in the line at the grocery store, it is "I owe you". If his check from work is short and the bills are due, it is "I owe you". If he is running low on cash, it is "I owe you".

Nevertheless, when it came to fixing around the house, cleaning the house, making his famous breakfast pancakes, eggs, bacon, sausage and Grand biscuits, taking care of the kids, taking the kids to school, picking up the kids from school, taking the kids to fun activities, mowing the lawn, washing and detailing my car, washing the clothes, decorating the house, taking his family out to dinner and to the movies (everything you are supposed to do as a husband and father), he really tried to show me he loved me. I will give him that. Every woman's dream I know. Yet this particular woman, with a calling on her life, required only one thing. "Total submission to God *First*", and then all the other extra stuff was very much appreciated. Real Talk!

I was "totally submitted to loving THE LOVE OF MY LIFE". I thought I really loved THE LOVE OF MY LIFE, but really I didn't because I did not even love myself. If you don't love yourself, you cannot possibly love anyone else. I did not love myself, because if I loved myself how did I lose myself? Here is my next question, if I really loved myself, why did I not put God *First*?

To tell the truth, because you know I can't lie. I was more in love with the obsession that I loved THE LOVE OF MY LIFE than the reality of it all. Obsession is not love. If you were to ask me "Crystal, how do you love him or better yet, why do you love him?" there would be a long pause. So if you ask yourself the same question, "Yes, I am talking to you now. We are off of me and it is time for you to disclose. Ask yourself this question, "How or why do/did I love the person I am with/was with in the past, present or thinking about getting with in the future?" If there is a long pause, well then know you too are out of the will of God.

Looking back, I can see and tell you why I was so obsessed and it was not that my heart was not right. I was holding on for dear life to people, places, things and memories for purpose. I had the tendency of making things that I cared about **IDOLS** that I literally worshipped so to speak. I mean how else can I explain it.

All of my "emotional roller coasters" consisted of trying so hard to hold onto something so that I would not lose it. Even the things I needed to lose I held onto. I became a pack rat in the natural and in the spirit. I was determined not to have to grieve over another loss. That was the bottom line. No pain, no gain. Better to have loved and lost than to never have loved at all. This is BS also know as "incorrect thinking". Now you know Holy Woman of God cannot curse, but I do believe in utilizing appropriate acronyms as needed Sugafoot!

Oh let me go back and tell you about Holy Woman of God before she got saved, sanctified, justified and filled with the Holy Ghost, because I know ya want to know all the "juicy juicy on Sugafoot". Well here it is so you don't have to waste your time calling the tabloids. Remember you heard it from me first. If my man told me he was stepping out late at night to go get some butter pecan ice cream because he had a sweet tooth, I would be just as nice and would wait until he got around the corner and I would step out for the whipped cream to go on top of the butter pecan ice cream and when he got back he would be looking for me.

If he got up in the wee hours of the morning, on a morning creep, to get a pound of bacon, I would be just as nice and wait until he turned the corner and I would burn rubber in my car going to get the dozen of eggs to fry with the bacon. When he got back he would be looking for me. It was all good with me back then.

When he would tell me he was going to wash his clothes at the laundry mat I would say, "Awe that is so sweet a man that washes his own clothes" and when he turned the corner I would be going to the bowling alley with my spare tire and surprisingly run into this same man that said he was going to the laundry mat to wash his clothes coming out of the adjoining theater with his sidekick. At the end of the day, I would not be worrying about if he used Downy in his rinse water. Now this really happened during this season with THE LOVE OF MY LIFE, so don't get lost in the words, stay with me! If he told me he was going on a road trip, "business trip", to the Dirty South. I would be just as nice and wait until he got around the corner and I would go to Chicago via Miami via the Caribbean and when he got back he would be looking for me. This incident also really happened during this season with THE LOVE OF MY LIFE. I came back home singing, "I shot the sheriff, but I did not shoot the deputy". HMPH!

He could do what it do, because I was going to make it do what it do! Back then, a man to me was nice, but not necessary! Those were the days when my name was not God's Leading Lady C, it was Flygirl C and I still have the fond memories, the pictures, personalized license plates, the leopard and zebra attire, the platform shoes and accessories, etc. to prove it. So you see, I don't hate the player, I hate the game, because the end result is destruction.

Well enough about the old me. Please, no one take notes on my past mistakes and fall short like I did. Now that I am a woman of God, it is all about Jesus and my life is so much better. I am overjoyed in my spirit and its overflowing to you. It is all about the love of God, so you know I am going to tell you with love. If you are in a relationship that does not glorify God, I will repeat so that those who are slow readers and slow thought processors of what they have just heard or read can catch up and get this. If you are in a relationship that does not glorify God, you are stuck. You are "Stuck on Stupid!" Just like I once was. *I LOVE YOU ON PURPOSE* and that is why I cannot let you stay stuck. I AM THE VOICE THAT STANDS for all that are stuck on stupid, because I too was once lost and now I am found giving God all the glory and all the honor and all the praise for my true deliverance.

The truth of the matter is the bible says "You have to lose your life to gain it". Well that is not what I was doing. I had it all backwards. I was trying to keep my life and not allow God to give me the life He wanted me to have. Our thoughts are not His thoughts and our ways our not His ways. Like my grandfather used to say a long time ago about the parable of the snake "You can pet a snake and care for a snake, but when it bites you don't be surprised when blood is running out your wound and the snake says to you; "Well, you knew I was a snake". The snake did exactly what snakes do, they bite. That can be applied to a dog too ya know, but I came up with dog version of the story, not grandpa.

But back to the matter at hand, it is really not important how you look at what happened to me in my past. What is important is that you look at the patterns in my life. Out of the will of God, putting **IDOLS** (people, place and things, my job, my family, my friends, my relationships, my entire life) before God which is the same as serving **IDOLS**.

You might say, well how are you serving **IDOLS**? You are serving **IDOLS** by looking to them for provision. You are allowing **IDOLS** to meet your needs and to fulfill every void instead of God. Only God can complete you. If you want Nothing Missing/Nothing Broken Complete in Him to be your stance, you have to go to Jesus just as you are. He is the one who can heal you and make you whole. It is that simple. Do not make it complex. This is biblical principles for dummies. I have broken it down for you to fully understand and there is so much more.

Don't think this was a quick fix. Don't think I put a Band-Aid on this wound and it miraculously healed. No, I went through pure hell on earth before I got the revelation! I am not so high and mighty that I don't admit that all the mistakes were mine. I allowed it to happen. I knew better and now you know better. When you know better, you are required to do better. You don't have any more excuses. If you choose to stay in your mess well Praise God, I will await your book. That is if you live to write it. It is my prayer and my hope that all would be saved. That all who lack anything will ask God for provision and that He will not only give them the wisdom and knowledge to get it, but the vision and plan of action to implement it and the understanding to keep it. It is my prayer that none shall perish.

REPENTANCE PRAYER

*Lord forgive me, I repent right now in dust and ashes for sinning against You, for putting **IDOLS** before You, for mishandling, hurting or offending anyone that You sent in my life, anything that You sent in my life that I mistreated in any way because of my disobedience to You, please forgive me. Everything that the devil had me do for evil and fall from Your grace, Lord forgive me right now and turn it around for Your good. Lord, thank You for Your mercy. Lord, as You forgive me for my trespasses, I forgive my debtors for their trespasses and most importantly Lord, I forgive myself. Touch my heart and touch their hearts right now in the name of Jesus and bring true healing and deliverance and restoration in every area, according to Your perfect will. Lord, I receive true healing and deliverance right now and I thank You for true healing and deliverance by Your power and Your might. Amen.*

INTERCEDING FOR FAMILIES

I rebuke every spirit that comes against families. Every spirit that comes in to bring division and discord within families I come against it in the name of Jesus. People wake up and realize where you left off. You left off when you did not keep God *First*. It was not the fact that you were not pretty enough, strong enough, talented enough, educated enough or even good enough. It was the point that you were out of God's will when you did not keep Him First and there are consequences. All the stuff you endured in your past and are enduring now is just a consequence of the sins you committed and the generations before you committed by not keeping God *First.*

Oh, I hope I am helping somebody today. I hope you are not at a point in your life that you feel you cannot be restored because I know that the devil has been whispering in your ear and lying to you way too long just like he did me in the past. You have been a slave to the adversary too long. God said in His word you are free from the bondage of sin. When you humbled yourself and repented before Him, He forgave your sins and blotted out all your iniquities. Stop listening to the enemy. Your life depends on it. Your family's life depends on this very word. Keep God *First*! Commit all your ways to Him, all your living. Commit everything you got to God. Dedicate it to God. Your family, your marriage, your job, your ministry. God will keep it. Do not give satan any room to stay in or even visit your life.

Anytime you are disobedient to God's word you open the door to the enemy and he will come in and wreak havoc every single time. Get this revelation now in Jesus Name! How much do we have to go through or lose before we get this revelation? The infamous question my best friend, Prophetess Kimberly, would always ask me "Crystal, what is it going to take?"

I did not pour out my dirty laundry before you for you not to be saved, delivered and set free from bondage. Not only do you need to be saved, you need to be sanctified, justified and filled with the Holy Ghost. You need to put on the whole armor of God daily and fight for everything you have and everything the devil stole. It is not too late. Get up from your defeated state and fight! Use what God has given you. Use what He has deposited into you.

Take notice of all your strengths and start there. He has given each and everyone of us different gifts. Whatever you love and are passionate about, that is where you start. There is nothing too big or too small for God. There is nothing to hard for God. He has all power in His hand. Yet, you have to take the steps that He ordered to obtain it. Walk into it, crawl into, just don't give up. Get up, do not die there. This is not another inspirational pep talk. This is my life that I have unfolded before you. I have lived every word, every sentence, every paragraph, every word of God in this book I have lived it. I had to get naked before God and man just so that you could live and not die.

PROPHETIC WIND

I am coming against the root of every fowl spirit in the name of Jesus that has got you down. I come against the root of every sickness and illness that has you burdened. I come against the root of everything that has attacked your mind, body and spirit and has you bound. By the power of God I speak life to your situation. I speak the power of God over your situation. I am sending you a fresh wind, a fresh anointing through His word. There is power in my tongue. I speak life and the word became flesh. Let the word of God arise up in you right now. Open your mouth and speak to your situation and begin to move forward in the things of God. Get up off your couch, get up off your bed, get up out your house and stand on the power of God within you. God deposited everything within you for your journey. You just need to get up and activate your faith to get it to operate within you. It is already in you. You don't have to look for it or seek anyone out to give it to you. You already have it deep down on the inside of you.

Open your eyes in the name of Jesus. You are no longer blinded by false belief and doctrine. You have heard the truth revealed in the flesh by God and now by me. God loved you so much that He told me to visit you today and tell you the truth. Yes, I know you have been hiding, but God knows your secret hiding place. So where natural eyes could not see, He went out like a good parent would do and sought you out. He wanted you to know the truth because He knew that satan had been whispering all kinds of lies in your ear in your secret hiding place. Get out of that secret hiding place that the devil set up so nicely for you to die. Get up and know that you are found by your Heavenly Father who loves you and cares for you. No more hide and go seek for you. No more peek a boo. Come out by the power of God vested in me. Come out! God wants you to come forth into His secret place where you will be safe within His loving arms. "He that dwelleth in the secret place of the most High shall abide under the shadow of the Almighty" (Plead Psalm 91 over your life).

Here is the truth! The truth is that God reigns and therefore you reign as a child of the King, but in order for Him to reign you have to keep Him on the throne. I am sending angels to encamp all around you right now. Do you feel the fire of God throughout your body right now? When you do, you will feel a sense of warmness, a comfort from within. That is Holy Spirit at work. Continue to pray, praise and worship God and let Holy Spirit do its work!

Begin today to confess the word of God over every situation you are facing. Begin to plant and nurture the seeds of faith and God will yield the increase. Your life will never be the same because you won't look back like I did in my story. You will keep looking forward to destiny before you. Yes, God has placed destiny before you so there is no need to look back. You don't have to clean up that place where you were at. You are moving into a new place. You are moving in a new direction in God. You can place a "Sold" sign in your front yard because you are now "Sold Out to Jesus"!

You don't have to clean up that marriage you walked out of or that husband or wife that walked out on you. You don't have to pull them back. You don't have to win them back. Their chapter in your life is over! I come against the root of that stagnant spirit in the name of Jesus! Move on to the next chapter with God. You are not alone for God is with you. Hold on to His unchanging hand and don't let go. You are not traded in like a used car. Here is a little secret that only God knew, "You are set apart by God for purpose". Yes, they hurt you but it is not over until God says it is over. You don't have to seek vengeance because vengeance belongs to the Lord. Don't worry about what happened to you or your loved ones even down to your very children being harmed and hurt by the curses of your wrongdoings and the generations before you wrongdoings, just Let Go and Let God!

God is getting ready to do a new thing in you. You cannot put new wine in old wineskins. Don't try to pick up the old pieces of the puzzle and put them back together, God has changed the pattern and design. Thank Him in advance for His mighty work. He knew that you would come to this very place and it would feel as if your back was against the wall and that you could not go backwards, forwards, nor would you know whether to look to the left or right. He knew you would get to the place when it seemed like there were no answers and nobody could help you. He was waiting on you to get to this place. Now He can use you. Yes, you are right where He has always wanted you to be in your rightful place, a place where He can use you as a vessel of honor. You know God once used a donkey. I know you think more of yourself than a donkey. God even once used a prostitute. Don't try to clean yourself up before you come to God. You can't clean yourself up. Allow God to make you over and wash you as white as snow. Put your confidence in God, and not **IDOLS**. God can and he will help you.

Yes, the devil left you feeling like you were all used up, depleted and defeated, but God heard your cry, even your silent prayers and He has stepped in, showed up and is getting ready to show out in your life. When you began to praise Him anyhow, right in the midst of your mess, you moved God. When you just broke out in total praise despite your circumstances and situations, God stopped what he was doing and said "Wait a minute, that is my child crying out for me. He then began to open up the windows of heaven and pour an overflow of blessings unto you. He began to speak and say "Come Forth My son, My daughter, My child, I can use you!" Remember, the stone that the builders rejected, God made that same stone the Head Cornerstone. Amen! Hallelujah, Glory to God!

Oh, let me tell you, you definitely don't know the cost of the oil in my alabaster box. I am going to continue to sit at His feet and anoint His feet with the oil and cleanse His feet with my hair and tears for He alone is worthy! Know that I am writing right now filled with his Holy oil. I am writing, typing and praising God right now telling Him how awesome He is. He is actually writing this book. I am just the vessel He chose to use. The devil had my mouth shut but God said "Get up, don't you bow down, stand up and stand strong for I am with you. Take in a deep breath and inhale and exhale and now open your my mouth and speak!" Thank you Jesus, Hallelujah! God is telling you right now to "Open your mouth and speak". The devil has had you quiet too long. Speak the word of God over your life right now and keep speaking. Never allow the enemy to close your mouth again. There is power in your tongue. Declare and decree a thing in the name of Jesus and it shall be established unto you. I did not say that, God said it, turn your bible to (Job 22:28). Praise Him!

Behold, the LORD hath proclaimed unto the end of the world, Say ye to the daughter of Zion, Behold, thy salvation cometh; behold, his reward is with him, and his work before him. And they shall call them, The holy people, The redeemed of the LORD: and thou shalt be called, Sought out, A city not forsaken. (Isaiah 62:11-12).

On January 1, 2010, in total obedience to God, I wrote THE LOVE OF MY LIFE a letter asking for forgiveness and telling him that I forgave him. I released him from everything I held in my heart that did not glorify God. He accepted the letter and I know he cherished it by his unspoken words and his humble spirit. I then began to pray and intercede on his behalf out of obedience to God and at his personal request.

On January 17, 2010, God brought about restoration in this relationship and we sat down and had a nice heart to heart. In spoken and unspoken words we both forgave each other completely and said we were sorry for placing each other in a position to fulfill each others needs and fill the voids only God could fill. God brought us to a humble state in which we both could receive the revelation from Him directly and we knew without a doubt that it was God. You see, THE LOVE OF MY LIFE recently gave his life to Christ and God gave him a new mind, body and spirit and he became a new creature and all the old things had passed away and the new things became new and he was able to humble himself and come to me and just simply say "I am sorry". He said so much more, but I just needed to hear those three words and it was not the words it was confirmation because God had already told me that he was sorry and that he did not know how to fix it. So, I humbled myself and said to him, "You don't have to fix it. Only God can fix it and know that I am sorry too and I still love you and I will always love you with the love of God and I know that you will always love me the same". The devil lost this battle. Victory was ours. Yet, we must always know that we are at war against the enemy. He is always waiting for an open door, a leak, a crack to get in. Remain watchful and vigilant!

Now in closing this chapter of my life for the very last time, it feels as if a huge burden has been lifted. I pray to God that I did not offend anyone and if I did I ask for your forgiveness right now with God as my witness. It was only my desire to tell you the truth and shame the devil who is the author of all lies, confusion and discord. The truth shall definitely set you free. I am free and I hope you are now too. *I LOVE YOU ON PURPOSE!*

I SEAL THIS CHAPTER OF MY LIFE WITH GOD'S WORD.

Touch not mine anointed, and do my prophets no harm. (1 Chronicles 16:22).

Take heed to yourselves: if thy brother trespass against thee, rebuke him; and if he repent, forgive him. And if he trespass rebuke him; and if he repent, forgive him. And if he trespass against thee seven times in a day, and seven times in a day turn again to thee, saying, I repent; though shalt forgive him. (Luke 17:3-4).

Then came Peter to Him and said, LORD, how oft shall my brother sin against me, and I forgive him? till seven times? Jesus saith unto him, I say not unto thee, Until seven times: but, Until seventy times seven. (Matthew 18:21-22).

THE DIFFERENT SEASONS & CHAPTERS OF MY LIFE
A DIARY BETWEEN ME & GOD

To every thing there is a season, and a time to every purpose under the heaven: (Ecclesiastes 3:1).

MAKING IT EASY FOR THE CLEANUP WOMAN/MAN

Thank you God for turning my midnight tears into daybreak, my tears of sorrow into tears of joy, mourning into laughter and dancing.

Anyone can produce a baby but raising them and bringing them up in the Lord takes a man and woman of God not just an egg and sperm donor. If you love someone you invest in them your time, your money, your support, your resources, you give 110%. It is not conditional it is from your heart and it has no limits. It is the type of love that God had when he allowed his son Jesus to die on the cross for our sins. That type of unconditional love that lasts through the seasons, through the storms, through good times and bad, through sickness and health until death and only death separates us.

The saying that "People come into your life for a reason, a season or a lifetime, some are branches, some are limbs and some are roots". Lord, allow the man of God that comes into my life be a root and what you bring together, let no man, not even me, put asunder. Lord, I pray that it is an everlasting love, forever and ever. Lord, prepare me for my king. Fill me with your Holy oil so that my lamp will not go out before, upon and after his arrival. Until then, you will be my King of kings, Lord of lords. Just as nothing can separate me from the love of God, nothing will separate me and my king that you prepare and send especially for me from the love that we will share together as husband and wife, Mr. and Mrs. Man/Woman of God, in Jesus Name. Amen!

It seems as if it has always been the case that there has always been something or someone ready and available to be the "cleanup woman/man" but if you take care of your king or queen the way that God has designed and equipped you to do, then the "cleanup woman or man" will remain unemployed. Nevertheless, Hallelujah Anyhow!

ENCOURAGING SCRIPTURES

THE LORD is my shepherd I shall not want. He maketh me to lie down in green pastures: he leadeth me beside the still waters. He restoreth my soul: he leadeth me in the paths of righteousness for his name's sake. (Psalm 23:1-3).

And God said, Let us make man in our image, after our likeness: and let them have dominion over the fish of the sea, and over the fowl of the air, and over the cattle, and over all the earth, and over every creeping thing that creepeth upon the earth. So God created man in his own image, in the image of God created he him; male and female created he them. And God blessed them, and God said unto them, Be fruitful, and multiply, and replenish the earth, and subdue it: and have dominion over the fish of the sea, and over the fowl of the air, and over every living thing that moveth upon the earth. (Genesis 1:26-28).

Now the God of hope fill you with all joy and peace in believing, that ye may abound in hope, through the power of the Holy Ghost. (Romans 15:13).

This I say then, Walk in the Spirit, and ye shall not fulfill the lust of the flesh. For the flesh lusteth against the Spirit, and the Spirit against the flesh: and these are contrary the one to the other: so that ye cannot do the things that ye would. But if ye be led of the Spirit, ye are not under the law. Now the works of the flesh are manifest, which are these; Adultery, fornication, uncleanness, lasciviousness, idolatry, witchcraft, hatred, variance, emulations, wrath, strife, seditions, heresies, Envyings, murders, drunkenness, revellings, and such like: of the which I tell you before, as I have also told you in times past, that they which do such things shall not inherit the kingdom of God. But the fruit of the Spirit is love, joy, peace, longsuffering, gentleness, goodness, faith, Meekness, temperance: against such there is no law. And they that are Christ's have crucified the flesh with the affections and lusts. If we live in the Spirit, let us also walk in the Spirit. (Galatians 5:16-25).

For HELP, S.O.S. - 1-800-JESUS -When you call on Jesus the devil must flee, but he will be back so put on the whole armor of God so that you may be able to stand through every test that comes your way from the adversary. Call on the name of Jesus as often as you can for there is healing in His name. There is deliverance in His name, freedom in His name, power in His name. Whatever you are going through Jesus is the answer. Every situation you are going through, go to the word of God for an answer. God speaks audibly and He also speaks through His word.

FIGHTING BACK *- Women's Health Awareness ~cyh~*

Why not take care of the body that God has blessed us with. We only get one body in this lifetime. Our bodies belong to God, the Holy Spirit dwells within, our bodies are God's temple, made for honor and sanctification. Be ye holy because He is holy. Our bodies were designed in His image.

Maintain a well-balanced lifestyle. A well-balanced lifestyle includes taking care of our mental, emotional, physical, spiritual, financial and social health. Physically by obtaining and maintaining ongoing optimal health care. Spiritually by spending time with God and reflecting on our God-given gifts, purpose and destiny. We are "God's Leading Ladies" (T.D. Jakes, 2003), His "Trophy Women" (J. Jakes, 2006) on assignment by God to reach nations, birth generations and go into the byways and highways in the kingdom preaching the gospel. We must first start charity at home and then spread it abroad. Think of your body as "the home you live in". Begin to take care of your home!

Individually and collectively we can make a difference for God's glory. We must be assertive in researching qualified medical providers and affordable insurance plans and schedule routine medical annual exams and checkups including dental care, vision, podiatry, gynecological exams, breast exams, etc. We need to ask questions of our medical providers such as what we need to do to maintain an optimal health status. We need to ensure we ask our medical providers what lab work we need to obtain on the basis of age/gender/race/family medical history. We need to ask questions about how to develop healthy eating/exercise and sleep habits. We need to develop and incorporate a healthy lifestyle that incorporates healthy diet and exercise regimens. Prevention is better than intervention. So let's take a proactive approach versus a reactive approach when it comes to our health and our family's health with the goal of improving our overall well-being and obtaining and maintaining Total Wellness in God.

CONFESSION IS GOOD FOR THE SOUL

If we confess our sins, he is faithful and just to forgive us our sins, and to cleanse us from all unrighteousness. (1 John 1:9).

Lord forgive me, I do not know how I got here and do not know where You want me to be at this time. Please cover me with Your precious blood and place a hedge of protection around me until You move me to my rightful place in You. Amen.

In God is my salvation and my glory: the rock of my strength, and my refuge, is in God. Trust in him at all times; ye people, pour out your heart before him: God is a refuge for us. Selah. (Psalm 62:7-8).

For I know that in me *(that is, in my flesh,)* dwelleth no good thing: for to will is present with me; but how to perform that which is good I find not. For the good that I would I do not: but the evil which I would not, that I do. Now if I do that I would not, it is no more I that do it, but sin that dwelleth in me. (Romans 7:18-20).

There is therefore now no condemnation to them which are in Christ Jesus, who walk not after the flesh, but after the Spirit. For the law of the Spirit of life in Christ Jesus hath made me free from the law of sin and death. (Romans 8:1-2).

Jesus loves us so much for there is no greater love than Jesus laying down His life for our sins so that we can not only live, but live life victoriously. We are not only victorious in every situation and everything, in Him we are more than conquerors. We must continue to pray, believe and remain hopeful, working together individually and collectively making a difference. God says in His word that you are a leader and not a follower. Leadership makes all the difference because when the head has the mind, heart and spirit of Christ, everyone else receives the overflow. Choose this day to be the head and not the tail.

When you are in God you are joint heirs to His promises. Do not let the devil torment you and make you beat yourself up, because God's mercies are new every day and God's mercies endure forever and ever and ever. So the next time the devil pays you a visit, tell him that he was not invited to your Holy Ghost party and just starting dancing and praising God and thanking Him in advance for delivering you from your affliction, whatever you are going through. Thank Him for setting you free from bondage, whatever you are in bondage from. Thank Him for healing you and making you whole, healed from whatever you have allowed to afflict, break and shatter you.

By faith remain rooted and grounded in God, until you cannot be moved. No matter what storms of life come your way, stand on the Rock knowing that there is peace, there is refuge, there is joy, there is happiness, there is love, there is everything you need in God. Do not look back but look forward. Do not let your state be your fate. Hold on, press, PUSH (pray until something happens), fight like your life depends on it, fight like you are fighting for a loved one or friend as if their life depends upon it. Do not just fight and swing amidst, but come with boldness and force with the power of God backing you.

Proceed to take your rightful place in the kingdom knowing that the devil is defeated and under your feet always because the mighty God that you serve has already paid the price on the cross. Know that your name is already written in the Book of Life. Your mansion is already prepared for you in heaven.

Tell the devil he is not going to hinder you getting home to your mansion. Tell the devil you are going home to see your loved ones and friends who have gone on before You. Tell the devil, "Get behind me satan, I rebuke you in the name of Jesus. I have on the whole armor of God and I am standing knowing that God is getting ready to use me in a mighty way. As soon as you send your weapon, God is going to block it. As soon as you devise a tactic or plan, God is going to send provision. There is nothing that you have that I need or want because I belong to the King. I am His child and I am not walking to and fro like a lost child or sheep. He met me right where I was at. I have a Good Shepherd who loves me and cares. Ye though I walk through the valley of death I shall fear no evil.

He saved a wreck like me so that I can go out and tell the world of His goodness and with everything that I have it shall be done in Jesus Name. I am not only going to fight the good fight of faith to save my soul and my loved ones and friends, I am going to preach the gospel in the byways and the highways, I am going to tell everyone I know, every one I come in contact with about Jesus, my personal Savior. I am going to make it a point to tell the world that the devil is defeated and that God reigns supreme in heaven and earth. What a mighty God we serve. For I am blessed to be a blessing. Hallelujah!"

Grace be to you and peace from God our Father, and from the Lord Jesus Christ. Blessed be God, even the Father of our Lord Jesus Christ, the Father of mercies, and the God of all comfort; Who comforteth us in all our tribulation, that we may be able to comfort them which are in any trouble, by the comfort wherewith we ourselves are comforted of God. (2 Corinthians 1:2-4).

Now then we are ambassadors for Christ, as though God did beseech you by us: we pray you in Christ's stead, be ye reconciled to God. For he hath made him to be sin for us, who knew no sin; that we might be made the righteousness of God in him. (2 Corinthians 5:20-21).

I will bless the Lord at all times; his praise shall continually be in my mouth. My soul shall make her boast in the Lord; the humble shall hear thereof, and be glad. O magnify the Lord with me, and let us exalt his name together. I sought the Lord, and he heard me, and delivered me from all my fears. (Psalm 34:1-4).

Keep thy tongue from evil, and thy lips from speaking guile. Depart from evil, and do good; seek peace, and pursue it. The eyes of the Lord are upon the righteous, and his ears are open unto their cry. The face of the Lord is against them that do evil, to cut off the remembrance of them from the earth. The righteous cry, and the Lord heareth, and delivereth them out of all their troubles. The Lord is nigh unto them that are of a broken heart; and saveth such as be of a contrite spirit. Many are the afflictions of the righteous; but the Lord delivereth him out of them all. He keepeth all his bones; not one of them is broken. Evil shall slay the wicked; and they that hate the righteous shall be desolate. The Lord redeemeth the soul of his servants; and none of them that trust in him shall be desolate. (Psalm 34:14-22).

BUT I SAID UNTO THEIR CHILDREN IN THE WILDERNESS, WALK YE NOT IN THE STATUTES OF YOUR FATHERS, NEITHER OBSERVE THEIR JUDGMENTS, NOR DEFILE YOURSELVES WITH THEIR IDOLS: EZEKIEL 20:18

Chapter VII

Redemption from the Green Monster

Everybody who walks in the flesh is prey to the green monster. Envy raises its eyebrow to everyone and in this mindset you begin to view others who appear to be doing better than you. The saying "The grass is not always greener on the other side" is so true. If you do not believe me just walk across the street and bend down real low and see how green it is. No, literally you do not have to do that, just ask your neighbor genuinely and sincerely, "Is your grass really greener?" You may come to find out that all this time your neighbor was saying the same thing in their minds about your grass. This may be the beginning of a wonderful friendship and an opportunity to fellowship with others about the Lord. The devil wants us to be divided and envious and jealous of others, but God wants us to love one another with a godly love and in so doing we represent His children. The bible tells us to love our neighbors, so why would we be jealous of them? Well, my dear friend, I must say this type of attitude and behavior is not of God, it is the enemy at work once again.

For the bible says, "Fret not thyself because of evildoers, neither be thou envious against the workers of inquity. For they shall soon be cut down like the grass, and wither as the green herb. Trust in the Lord, and do good; so shalt thou dwell in the land, and verily thou shalt be fed. Delight thyself also in the Lord; and he shall give thee the desires of thine heart. Commit thy way unto the Lord; trust also in him; and he shall bring it to pass. (Psalm 37:1-5).

The steps of a good man are ordered by the Lord: and he delighteth in his way. Though he fall, he shall not be utterly cast down: for the Lord upholdeth him with his hand. I have been young, and now am old; yet have I not seen the righteous forsaken, nor his seed begging for bread. He is ever merciful, and lendeth; and his seed is blessed. (Psalm 37:23-26).

The mouth of the righteous speaketh wisdom, and his tongue talketh of judgment. The law of his God is in his heart; none of his steps shall slide. The wicked watcheth the righteous, and seeketh to slay him. The Lord will not leave him in his hand, nor condemn him when he is judged. Wait on the Lord and keep his way, and he shall exalt thee to inherit the land; when the wicked are cut off, thou shall see it. (Psalm 37:30-34).

God is our refuge and strength, a very present help in trouble. Therefore will not we fear, though the earth be removed, and though the mountains be carried into the midst of the sea; Thou the waters thereof roar and be troubled, though the mountains shake with swelling thereof. Selah. (Psalm 46:1-3).

Be still and know that I am God; I will be exalted among the heathen, I will be exalted in the earth. (Psalm 46:10).

Cast thy burden upon the Lord, and he shall sustain thee: he shall never suffer the righteous to be moved. (Psalm 55:22).

As for me, I will call upon God; and the Lord shall save me. Evening, and morning and at noon, will I pray, and cry aloud: and he shall hear my voice. He hath delivered my soul in peace from the battle that was against me: for there were many with me. God shall hear, and afflict them, even he that abideth of old. Selah. Because they have no changes, therefore they fear not God". (Psalm 55:16-19).

MY PERSONAL PRAYER

Lord search my heart and know that I strive to be more like You daily. If I fail charge it to my mind and not my heart. I have good intentions in all that I do even if my actions don't appear to line up with the same. Lord forgive me for I am sorry. Lord I repent and want You to know that I love You and I need You. Lord I cannot make it without You. Thou the world turns its back on me I know that you are still there with open arms. You are a friend that sticks closer than a brother and I thank You. The world can be a lonely place, but with You I am filled with love and everyone else can see Your light shining through me as they receive the overflow.

Lord do not take Your goodness from me, please always dwell in me through Your Holy Spirit for I can do nothing without You. Thank You for saving a wretch like me and delivering me and setting me free and making me complete and whole in You. In the mighty name of Jesus I rebuke every spirit that is not of You. I bind it and cast it out into the sea of no return. In the name of Jesus it is so. From this day forward I will not put anything or anyone before You. You and You alone are the Captain of this ship, the Pilot of this aircraft, the Potter of this clay.

Lord make me an instrument of Your will today and always. Where you lead me I will follow. Lead me and guide me and cover me with Your precious blood. Put a hedge of protection around me and my family as we go forward with You. Block every weapon that the enemy is preparing right now. As we speak, he is trying to launch another one. I know that Your word says "No weapon formed against me or my family shall prosper". God You are my help in the time of trouble. You are my refuge. Lord, you have not given me the spirit of fear or jealousy. So I am sending everything You did not give me back to satan. He can take back all of his tricks. I do not belong to him. The DNA test came back today. I am 110% positively Jesus Property. Satan there is none of you within me so you have no power to possess this vessel. I belong solely to God, Amen!

FOR THEY THEMSELVES SHEW OF US WHAT MANNER OF ENTERING IN WE HAD UNTO YOU, AND HOW YE TURNED TO GOD FROM IDOLS TO SERVE THE LIVING AND TRUE GOD. 1 THESSALONIANS 1:9

Chapter VIII

Another Day's Journey

"It's another day's journey and *I'm glad. I'm glad about it. I'm glad. I'm glad about it. So glad. I'm glad about it. It's another day's journey and I'm glad. I'm glad about it. Don't you know that I'm so glad to be here". Now I know exactly what this song means. As a little kid growing up I did not. Lord, I am so glad to be here. As I meditate on Your scriptures day and night, I am inspired and encouraged. I will keep Your words and hide Your words in my heart.*

Keep me as the apple of thy eye, hide me under the shadow of thy wings. (Psalm 17:8).

Let the words of my mouth and the meditation of my heart be acceptable in thy sight, O LORD, my strength, and my redeemer: (Psalm 19:14).

My God, my God, why hast thou forsaken me? Why art thou so far from helping me, and from the words of my roaring? (Psalm 22:1).

I continued to trust God! I kept praying ... I kept seeking His face ... I kept believing... I kept reading and speaking His word over every situation I faced ... and God kept answering in His word and in an audible voice.

Wherefore seeing we also are compassed about with so great a cloud of witnesses, let us lay aside every weight, and the sin which doth so easily beset us, and let us run with patience the race that is set before us, Looking unto Jesus the author and finisher of our faith; who for the joy that was set before him endured the cross, despising the shame, and is set down at the right hand of the throne of God. For consider him that endured such contradiction of sinners against himself, lest ye be wearied and faint in your minds. (Hebrews 12:1-3).

According as he hath chosen us in him before the foundation of the world; that we should be holy and without blame before him in love: Having predestinated us unto the adoption of children by Jesus Christ to himself, according to the good pleasure of his will, To the praise of the glory of his grace, wherein he hath made us accepted in the beloved. In whom we have redemption through his blood, the forgiveness of sins, according to the riches of his grace; (Ephesians 1:4-7).

I am crucified with Christ: nevertheless I live; yet not I, but Christ liveth in me: and the life which I now live in the flesh I live by the faith of the Son of God, who loved me and gave himself for me. (Galatians 2:20).

For if, when we were enemies, we were reconciled to God by the death of his Son, much more, being reconciled, we shall be saved by his life. (Romans 5:10).

Now unto him that is able to do exceeding abundantly above all that we ask or think, according to the power that worketh in us, (Ephesians 3:20).

Give everything to God in prayer and be persistent. By faith, believe and know that He can do exceeding abundantly above all that we ask or think and He will do just that.

April 19, 2008, I am still on the battlefield for my Lord. There is so much going on in my life. I cannot keep up with everything. I am so glad that all I have to do is follow the Lord's lead. I know sometimes I think I have to do everything on my own but the fact is during those times I think I am walking alone, He is really carrying me for I can do nothing without Him. I lean not to my understanding today and I trust God in all things and in all situations. What a mighty God we serve.

Friends come and friends go for different reasons, purposes, seasons and some stay throughout a lifetime. There is one friend who stays closer than any brother and that is Jesus. He promises to never leave us and never forsake us and we can trust Him in that He cannot lie. So I will cling to my Friend until the very end in hopes that I will hear Him say like He said in (2 Peter 1:17) "This is my beloved Daughter, in whom I am well pleased". That gives me so much hope as I await hearing my Savior say that He is well pleased with me. Just as He endured what He did during His time on earth fulfilling His Godly purpose and destiny just for me and His own Father kept encouraging Him by saying in (Matthew 17:5) and (Mark 1:11) and (Matthew 3:17), "This is my beloved Son, in whom I am well pleased". I too aim to do a good work on this earth in hopes of hearing my Heavenly Father say those same words to me.

This brings me back to the mother in me, I was just thinking what if I said these same words "This is my beloved son/daughter, in whom I am well pleased" to my own children and to my children's children, I can only imagine what an impact that would make on their life. WOW, what a revelation!

FOR THE IDOLS HAVE SPOKEN VANITY, AND THE DIVINERS HAVE SEEN A LIE, AND HAVE TOLD FALSE DREAMS; THEY COMFORT IN VAIN: THEREFORE THEY WENT THEIR WAY AS A FLOCK, THEY WERE TROUBLED, BECAUSE THERE WAS NO SHEPHERD. ZECHARIAH 10:2

Chapter IX

The Upper Room

Lord, I need You and *cannot make it without You. Lord, be near and dear to my heart. Lord, hear me when I call. Lord, hear my cry and answer. Do not let me stay in this place and under this type of stress longer than I have to, for I am tired and weary. Lord, please send me some help. Please send me some relief. Please send angels on assignment to encamp around me. I cannot handle this alone. Lord, please send Your comforter. Thank You in advance for provision. Thank You for making a way out of no way. Thank You for deliverance. Thank You for freedom. Thank You for protection, thank You for redemption in Jesus Name. I need You Lord right now and I know that You are going to move according to my faith so by faith I receive a miracle, an answer to my humble prayer, a blessing in due season. Lord, allow blessings to flow into my life right now, rivers of living water, in Jesus name, Amen.*

Walking in the Spirit makes all the difference in your life. When we are walking in the Spirit you are joyful and fulfilled. When God guides and directs us we use are God-given gifts to glorify Him and not ourselves. When we walk in God's power we keep in step with God's plan and not our own. We implement God's agenda and not our own.

People who walk in the spirit do not seek the approval of the world but the approval, direction and correction of God. They are in tune with heaven. If God does not say move they do not move. When God says move they comply. They do not compromise the truth. They live according to every living word of God. They are dedicated, loyal, diligent and committed servants of God. They come out from among the things of the world. They do not teach false doctrine based on seeking approval. They do not seek personal gain. They do things out of the love of God within them. When they see others in need they provide and share what God has given them. They seek God *First* for wisdom and guidance in every situation. They are on assignment by God and do not neglect their God-given gifts and abide by Godly principles and standards. They know the consequences of not walking in the spirit and walking in the flesh is death. Individuals walking in the flesh are ruled by ungodly spirits such as deception, fear, unforgiveness, witchcraft, **IDOLATRY**, etc. No child of God should be overtaken by these spirits because God has given us the power over every demonic spirit.

Behold, I give unto you power to tread on serpents and scorpions, and over all the power of the enemy: and nothing shall by any means hurt you. Notwithstanding in this rejoice not, that the spirits are subject unto you; but rather rejoice, because your names are written in heaven. In that hour Jesus rejoiced in spirit, and said, I thank thee, O Father, Lord of heaven and earth, that though hast hid these things from the wise and prudent, and hast revealed them unto babes: even so, Father, for so it seemed good in thy sight. All things are delivered to me of my Father: and no man knoweth who the Son is, but the Father; and who the Father is, but the Son, and he to whom the Son will reveal him. And he turned him unto his disciples, and said privately, blessed are the eyes which see the things that ye see: for I tell you, that many prophets and kings have desired to see those things which ye see, and have not seen them; and to hear those things which ye hear, and have not heard them. (Luke 10:19-24).

THAT THEY HAVE COMMITTED ADULTERY, AND BLOOD IS IN THEIR HANDS, AND WITH THEIR IDOLS HAVE THEY COMMITTED ADULTERY, AND HAVE ALSO CAUSED THEIR SONS, WHOM THEY BARE UNTO ME, TO PASS FOR THEM THROUGH THE FIRE, TO DEVOUR THEM. EZEKIEL 23:37

Chapter X

The Value of a Mother

This chapter is dedicated to my daughter Krishina who made all the difference in my life in 2008 by giving me the revelation of the value of a mother. Krishina, God knew from the beginning of time the value of a mother. I want you to treasure this chapter and know that I wrote it especially for you and know that it applies to me as a mother, you as a mother, your sister as a mother, and every mother and for everyone who has ever cared enough to love, nurture and raise a child. I know you have heard the saying "Anyone can make a baby but it takes a real man to be a father and a daddy". I believe this to be true but I would like to add onto it and say "A boy is not a man. A real boy is not a real man. It takes a man that loves God *First* and puts God *First* and that possesses the Love of God to make a lifelong commitment to make, love, cherish, nurture and raise a successful child by bringing him/her up in the Lord". A lot of individuals are just not equipped for the job so we must continue to pray for those individuals that "God will turn the heart of the fathers to the children, and the heart of the children to their fathers". (Malachi 4:6). God said it in His word and I believe it.

God designed women for purpose and destiny to carry out His heavenly and earthly plans. It was no mistake, no mishap, no misunderstanding. God knew exactly what He was doing and all His plans were well thought out, each and every detail. Indeed, everything in this world has meaning and value. The value of a mother is infinite, unlimited and priceless. In fact, most mothers do not know their true worth/value. Yet, God knows our true worth/value!

God only allows the *woman* to carry and bring human life from the womb. Man was not given this privilege. Isn't that amazing? How wonderful are His works. Some people may think what a disadvantage it is to be female and as a woman I can understand that, but God does not think that way. Just look at how Jesus valued His own mother Mary. "Blessed art though among women, and blessed is the fruit of thy womb" (Luke 1:42). Luke 1:45 further states "And blessed is she that believed: for there shall be a performance of those things which were told her from the Lord".

Mary, Jesus' mother is our role model. Look at mothers throughout the bible and how God valued them and spoke highly of them. Look at the story of the Virtuous Woman in (Proverbs 31) and how in verse 30-31 it says "Favor is deceitful, and beauty is vain: but a woman that feareth the LORD, she shall be praised. Give her of the fruit of her hands; and let her own works praise her in the gates". Look at the favor God gave Sarah and how He blessed her womb at a very late age.

I AM THE VOICE SPEAKING TO MOTHERS ... Mothers/women we must redefine how we see and value ourselves and make sure that it lines up with the way the bible says we should see ourselves and the way God sees and values us. Know that God designed you for His purpose and destiny and be fruitful and multiply just as He has asked us to do in His word. Fruitful means to produce fruit, spiritual fruit.

For the women who do not have children, know that there is work for you to do as well and that you too can be fruitful. There are so many young girls and boys that need to be loved, cherished, nurtured, taught, mentored and brought up in the Lord, what are you really waiting on? May God begin to open your minds, hearts, and your homes to the possibility of making a positive difference in a child's life. Maybe you don't have the time to commit to parenting full-time. Just begin by making yourself available to spend time with a family in need or a child in need. Give of yourself and your time and your resources as the Lord leads.

Your blessing may very well be waiting on you, but you will have to activate your faith in that direction to receive it. I can say that because I truly wished I had of had someone be available for me. I prayed to God for provision and He did answer in His timing, I just wish more people could hear the gentle call and the gentle nudge of God "asking servants to serve" families in need. There is a tremendous need!

<u>HELP WANTED! HELP FOR MOTHERS IN NEED IS IN HIGH DEMAND!</u>

In today's recession there is no such thing as no work available for "the harvest is plenty yet the laborers are few". In fact, if we are doing kingdom work we are indeed in a progression. Get up from your present state and begin to do God's work. Don't let the devil defeat you in your thoughts by saying we are in a recession and then you begin to act accordingly. Know your true worth and value and begin to walk in it. When you begin go seek the kingdom and His righteousness, God is going to begin to supply all your needs according to His riches in Glory. Remember, it is a faith walk. Begin to walk toward your destiny.

I just want to share with you a very special Mother's Day 2008 from my eight little blessings, now ages 23 through 2 and two grandbaby boys and many more to come. It is a combination of purchased and homemade treasures that they made at school and home that most definitely brought a smile to my heart and face.

"Blessings from the Whole Family: Special wishes just for you on Mother's Day. You have a special touch, warmth and understanding and it is thanks to you I feel loved every day. Happy Mother's Day, Signed, Orlando Holt a/k/a Dad."

"Happy Mother's Day – Thank you for buying me things and cheerleading. I'm sorry I thought you were kinda mean so I will help you on Mother's Day. Signed, De'Jonay."

"Mommy's Special Day Coupon. Entitles bearer to fun time with Mommy. Signed, Kha'Leel Holt."

"My Mom is Special! My mom's name is Crystal. She is special because she plays with dogs. I like it when my mom help the dogs go to the bathroom. My mom can do many things! I think she's best at catching a cat. My mom has a pretty smile! I like to make her smile by telling her I love her. Signed, Kha'Leel."

"My Mom is as Pretty as a Sheep. My mom is smart! She even knows how to fly a kite. I'd like to tell my mom that I love her and thank you. Signed Kha'Leel."

"My Mom is Special! My mom's name is Crystal. She is special because she works on her computer. I like it when my mom let's me play on her computer. My mom can do many things. I think she's best at working on her computer. Signed, Ja'Mari."

"My Mom is as Pretty as a Princess. My mom is smart! She even knows how to go "boo boo" in the bathroom. I'd like to tell my mom I love her. Signed, Ja'Mari."

"Happy Mother's Day, I Love You, Signed, Christian."

"Happy Mother's Day, This is for all the mothers who didn't win Mother of the Year. Hang in there. Better luck next year, I will be rooting for you. Signed, DeJonay Holt."

"A combined Mother's Day/Birthday basket of pineapple flavored shower gel, body lotion and bubble bath. Signed, Che'Andrea and Krishina."

What my children did not know is that on Mother's Day 2008, I was so happy and content in my spirit. I thanked them for the cards and gifts and let them know they meant so much to me. However, one month later, on Father's Day there was a sadness that came all over me. This sadness I really cannot explain, but it brought me to tears and as the first tear fell from my face, I sat down on the couch to collect myself and pray. My little ones were playing about as kids do, not even noticing my sadness.

There was a knock on the door and then the doorbell rang. It was my oldest daughter Krishina. I quickly gathered myself and wiped away the tears as I opened the door. She had a card in her hand and she informed me that she would not be able to stay long but she just wanted to drop off the card. I had no idea why she would be dropping off a card for me for it was not a special occasion. I thanked her for the card and as I began to read the card my heart melted and I tried my best to hold back the tears. It was my very first "Happy Father's Day Card for Moms" and it read: "You hear a lot of talk these days about children growing up without a father without this and without that. You hardly ever hear about the mothers who, in spite of everything, raise their children to be strong, to believe in God, to work hard and to make their lives worthwhile. That's the story I'd like to tell because that's how you raised me. In spite of it all, it's our story. I made it because of you.

Have a Wonderful Day." *"Thank You for being strong enough for 2! Love You Mom, Signed, Krishina, Happy Father's Day (from all of us)."*

Krishina and I only visited briefly. As I walked her to the door and as we exchanged our goodbyes, I thanked her again. I then shut the door behind her and walked back to sit on the coach and began to cry all over again as I read the card over and over and over again. The tears then dried up and the sorrow lifted. Only God can heal every wound in His special way. God's timing is just perfect!

I guess I was sad because I was living out the role of mother and father at the same time and my soul was sorrowful in that I thought my work was in vain. Simple cards not only allow you to be acknowledged, they show respect and they show you that you are valued. What a minimal price to pay for someone who you love and know to be irreplaceable. We must always love, cherish and respect our mothers, for if it had not been for our mothers who brought us into this world with God's help, well you and I both know we would not exist.

Let us no longer take our mothers for granted. Remember the sayings "Even the smallest gesture may be the grandest intent". "You may be just one person in the world but you may mean the world to just one person". I know my children know I love them dearly and there is no perfect mom, dad, sister, brother, family or person, but what is perfect is God's Love and God's Love has always been the center of my life, so I know they had to receive the overflow. *"Thanks again Krishina. Love you so much, always, Mom."*

NEITHER SHALL THEY DEFILE THEMSELVES ANY MORE WITH THEIR IDOLS, NOR WITH THEIR DETESTABLE THINGS, NOR WITH ANY OF THEIR TRANSGRESSIONS: BUT I WILL SAVE THEM OUT OF ALL THEIR DWELLINGPLACES, WHEREIN THEY HAVE SINNED, AND WILL CLEANSE THEM: SO SHALL THEY BE MY PEOPLE, AND I WILL BE THEIR GOD. EZEKIEL 37:23

Chapter XI

2007 The Year of Completion, a New Beginning, New Doors Opening

God promised in his word in (Isaiah 1:19) "If ye be willing and obedient, ye shall eat the good of the land". I would like to share with you my year of completion, my new beginning, and new doors opening in God. It was an opportunity to start over and walk daily by faith, trusting and believing God for everything. As I walked on the barren land under my feet, I looked up to the hills from which my help cometh and I lifted my head and my hands towards heaven and began to worship my Heavenly Father, for He alone is worthy.

As I looked all around me it was as if heaven and earth agreed because all I could see before me was all that God had promised me if I keep Him *First* and if I be willing and obedient.

On August 17, 2007, my family and I moved into our brand new two-story construction single family home built from the ground up. We prayed over the land daily even before the ground breaking and we continued to pray every day thereafter. This was definitely our Year of Jubilee. We had sacrificed so much and set aside everything that God had instructed to set aside, believing and trusting God that we would one day experience our Year of Jubilee and God is Faithful, because "We Are Here!"

I had lost so much over the years and now had to lose even more and leave even more behind in order to go forward with God into my new promised land, my new promised future in God, enjoying the land of mild and honey and eating the good of the land. The land that He promised was given to not only me, but my entire family. Everything I had to leave behind, I count it all dung. One thing I held onto and never lost and always treasured throughout the years was the fond memories. The memories of good times captured in special memorable moments, the pictures, cards and gifts I received over the years from loved ones and friends. From thank you cards to congratulations cards to happy birthday cards, mother's day cards, valentine's cards, Christmas cards, etc.

I want to take this time to thank everyone who helped me make it to and make it through my Year of Jubilee. It was definitely not easy as I thought it would be. I remember having to sacrifice even food to pay off some of my debtors so that I could obtain the prize before me, but God sustained me. I remember the individuals who fed me physical food and spiritual food through their love, their kindness and even their time. During those times, I was indeed weary, but you strengthened me. Thank you for ensuring me that I was not alone. Thank you for believing in me. Thank you for supporting me. Thank you for your encouraging words and for letting me know that you admired my hard work and tenacity. Thank you for pointing out my strengths even in times when I focused only my weaknesses. Thank you for letting me know that you admired me for one, taking pride in helping myself first and secondly, for not being too prideful to ask and accept the help of others.

It was not an easy thing for me to do to open up my heart to people after being hurt so much throughout the years. However, I trusted man once again, but most importantly I really trusted God. You see through it all, I received the revelation that God blesses people through people. I discovered through it all that God does not literally pour money down from the sky like I had imagined, but that God chooses the people he wants to use to bless others. I am so thankful and grateful that God chose you to bless me and because of your obedience to His call, I am truly blessed and highly favored and this Year of Jubilee proves it!

As you already know, through it all, I continued to let everyone know that God was my source for He was. I cannot stress enough to you that the road that was before me was not an easy road to travel. When I was a babe in Christ, I thought the closer I got to Christ the less troubles I would have, but as I matured in Christ I soon realized that to whom much is given, much is required.

I remember on the day of the closing on my home, at the title loan company. It was my first closing, my first home. I sat in the room of what felt like the elite of the world, sitting at a large round table of people with a 20+ page document to read and a pen for everyone to sign it. I had feelings of joy, fear, happiness, excitement and more fear. As I thought to myself, I began to ask myself these questions "Why, would I be afraid? God had brought me this far why would I be afraid? I had believed and trusted God this far, why was I now afraid? Everyone believed in me, why was I afraid?"

I knew God was with me, but I did not feel I could do this alone and I was correct. I could not do it alone. The truth is even at the closing there was still a void within me and I wanted someone in the natural with me to share my joy and celebrate my success. God began to speak to me and comfort me through the closing and assure me that He was with me. I began to talk to God and I said "Lord, I don't think I can do this" and He said "You are correct, you can't do this, but I can".

Throughout the entire process of building my new home, I had convinced myself that I had contributed in some way to the process, but all I had really did was keep God *First* and be willing and obedient and God did the rest. He set everything in motion from the first phone call to the real estate agent, the calls to the lenders, the preapproved loan, the hiring of the contractors, the blue prints and floor plans, the interior and exterior design, the appliances, through the choosing of individuals that He was going to use to sow into my life and bring about an expected outcome, so I was correct in saying that I could not do it.

As the 20+ page document was being passed around the room and I was asked to read and sign, I read everything line per line, word per word and as I held the pen in my hand to sign, I hesitated. The figures on the paper did not look like the figures I had agreed upon in the initial contract. I immediately remembered what I learned in my home buying classes to read everything before you sign it at the closing and if the figures did not match the originally agreed upon amount, then it was a "No Deal". So after reading everything thoroughly, while holding back the tears, trying to keep my hand from shaking due to nervousness and my feet from "shaking in my boots" due to fear, I took a closer look at the bottom line figure and again it was not the amount I had agreed upon beforehand, so I did something I don't normally do.

"Shaking in my boots", I sat up tall and strong and with the boldness of God I for the first time in my life stood up for myself and said "These are not the figures we agreed upon!". Yes, in a room full of the elite, I stood strong with God backing me. Now, all eyes were on me. God continued to speak to me and through me and the title loan company representative began to explain to me the reason for the change and I said politely "No, I would like the amount we agreed upon to be reflected in the document before I sign".

The title loan company representative walked out of the room to speak with the proper personnel to see if it was even possible to change the prepared final document. There was a small wait and everyone in the room was quiet except for small talk. A sense of calmness came over me and I was no longer "shaking in my boots". The title loan representative returned to the room and sat at the round table and handed me the revised/corrected final document for review and signing. As I looked at the document, sure enough it was the original agreed upon bottom line figure. Me and everyone in the room had witnessed the favor of God and man and God's faithfulness.

I held back the tears and tried to maintain a confident posture, but even after the title loan company representative had changed the figures to reflect the figures we agreed upon originally, there was a little voice inside of me wanting to yell out and say "I can't do this" but the voice of God spoke louder and said "It is Already Done!" So as the appropriate signatures were placed on the final document and as it was being passed around the table, I was handed the final signed and authorized document and my first set of keys as a new home buyer/owner of my first brand new construction home and congratulations from everyone in the room, something I had never experienced before. I had never experienced the true meaning of congratulations, just in case you missed it the first time I said it.

In all of my accomplishments I had never heard or felt "Congratulations!" I may have received it, but I never heard or experienced it. The best I can explain it is if I had a deaf ear and possibly blind eyes. A lot of times in life things happened to me and I just went through the motions and did not embrace the moment. I was constantly chasing the wind on many occasions trying to pursue happiness, but this time I was not chasing, only capturing and embracing the moment with joy. I was experiencing it and living it. I had planned on living in the celebration for eternity.

At this time in my life the words "Congratulations!" meant so much to me. As I drove home to open the doors of my new home, escorted by one of the lenders who worked diligently to help me find resources for the down payment on my home, her name was Michelle. Michelle and I were going to be the first ones to open the door to my new home. Thank God she was with me because I really did not want to be alone in this experience. Although I knew God was with me in the spirit, in the natural I did not want to walk through the doors of the "Promised Land" alone. I wanted to experience this moment with someone and Michelle was the willing and obedient vessel. So as we approached the door, I had the new key in my hand and I had on "My Big Girl Panties" and I placed the key in the door and I was so nervous that I dropped the key in front of the door instead of placing it in the keyhole and me and Michelle just laughed and laughed and laughed.

All the fear and nervousness had gone now because it was just one of those moments that laughter overcame the fear and nervousness and now there was just joy unspeakable joy and laughter. As I bent over to pick up the keys from off the ground, it was indeed a "Kodak moment". Who gets "the key to the kingdom and drops them?" Who drops "the key to a brand new construction home, the Promised Land that God had blessed her and her family with?" The answer is God's Leading Lady C. I had successfully completed, with God's help, the entire process of closing on a brand new home and God leaves me alone for one second to do something simple on my own like simply open up the door and I drop the key and can't even open the front door. WOW!

Michelle and I just laughed and laughed as I tried to regain my composure. You just had to be there to see how funny it was. Anywho, I finally managed to open the door, this time with God's help, and Michelle gave me my first gift for the home it was a candle and card and I placed both of them on the fireplace mantle. Just walking through the home you could feel the presence of God. It was as if God had already done the walkthrough and had already blessed, anointed and ordained the dwelling place. As I continued to walk through each room of my brand new home that I must say was three times larger than the home I had left behind, I knew what was now required of me and that was to continue to keep God *First* and remain willing and obedient. I now knew all of God's promises firsthand and by faith I stood on His word that said "I shall eat the good of the land".

As the months passed by, I remember looking back briefly where I had came from out of Egypt and quickly renewing my mind to the present, but still experiencing the same fear that I had at the closing of the home of not being able to do things on my own. I would oftentimes in my flesh revert back to trying to do it on my own and not fully trusting God and the patterns and consequences were all the same.

So, one day I called my mom for a pep talk and she told me these very wise words "God did not give you all those children to not provide for them. God is going to provide for you just so you can provide for them. He is more concerned about them than you." It clicked. Those words were confirmation. God had blessed me to be a blessing to my children. God was going to take care of me and everything concerning me. I no longer had to singlehandedly take care of me or anything else. I no longer had to act as if I was God for truly I was not. I get it! All I had to do was continue to keep God *First* and remain willing and obedient. God had already said at the closing "It Is Already Done!" So, in Jesus name, It Is So. Hallelujah!

I remember looking back for purpose over my life there were times when the cupboard was bare and I struggled to put two ingredients together and prepare what had to be considered a meal in order to feed my family. I remember the times when my family and I were evicted from our home due to not being able to afford the payments. I remember the times when we had to live temporarily in shelters and bounce from house to house trying to keep a rough over our head and make ends meet, sometimes living in unsafe and uncomfortable and impoverished conditions and doing things illegal and unethical just to get by and now God had blessed us to live in a dwelling place where He provided us with manna daily and our cup was overflowing, the cupboards were overflowing, we lacked nothing, we desired nothing, we wanted for nothing, we had all we wanted and needed. Yet, we desired more and more and more of Him.

We were now both blessed and filled! God promised in His word in (Matthew 5:6) "Blessed are they which do hunger and thirst after righteousness: for they shall be filled". Yes, God has His way of getting you right to the point in your life where all you desire to do is hunger and thirst after righteousness, in your rightful place in Him. Below are just a few cards and words of encouragement that helped me stay focused and on track for God's purpose during this season of my life, my Year of Jubilee 2007-2008.

"Congratulations on Your New Home, May happiness and contentment always be at your door! Signed, Love, Carla Johnson & Family."

"Congratulations on Your New Home, May happiness and contentment always be at your door! Signed, McFarland Braggs, Robin Berry, Arthur Welch, Michelle Sanders & PCCEO."

"A New Home, A New Beginning, Wishing You Happiness .... And many new memories in your new house. Best Wishes. Signed, Aunt Armenta & Uncle George."

"From Your Friends At AFE Construction, Inc., Building relationships with customers like you is the most rewarding thing we do. Happy Holidays Wishing You a Very Merry Christmas & a Blessed New Year. Signed, Tommy & Monica Arbuckle & Staff of AFE Construction, Inc."

"Merry Christmas Mom, I Love You, You Got Me, Signed Khaleel Holt."

"Thanks for all your help and especially for getting my Jeremy to school every day. Thank you. God bless you and your kids. Enjoy the little gift from us. Signed Angela Green."

"Thank You. Crystal, thank you so much for your baby gift. I guess being a mom yourself you knew exactly what I would need. Hope you are all doing well! Signed, Thanks again, Jess & Max."

"How to Make A Beautiful Life, Reflections For A Daughter On Her Birthday, Love yourself. Make peace with who you are and where you are at this moment in time. Listen to your heart. If you can't hear what it's saying in this noisy world, make time for yourself. Enjoy your own company. Let your mind wander among the stars. Try. Take chances. Make mistakes. Life can be messy and confusing at times, but it's also full of surprises. The next rock in your path might be a stepping stone. Be happy. When you don't have what you want, want what you have. Make do. That's a well-kept secret of contentment. There aren't any shortcuts to tomorrow. You have to make your own way. To know where you're going is only part of it. You need to know where you've been too. And if you ever get lost, don't worry. The people who love you will find you. Count on it. Life isn't days and years. It's what you do with time and with all the goodness and grace that's inside you. Make A Beautiful Life ... The kind of life you deserve. Signed, Happy Birthday, Your Mother."

"For God so loved the world that He gave His only begotten Son ... May you be blessed this Christmas by the greatest gift ... the greatest giver – Jesus. Signed, Love, Glenda Allen & Family Merry, Merry, Christmas."

"Bold- Radiant – Glamorous – Girl, you're all that and more. This birthday's looking just too good on you. Signed, Jim Allen."

"Peace on Earth – May the special gifts of health, peace, joy and happiness be yours throughout the year. Signed, I love you Sis. I hope God blesses you with all you need & deserve in the year to come. Have a Wonderful Holiday Season. As Always, Heidi."

"Merry Christmas – As bright as the star on the top of the tree … hope that is how your Christmas will be. Signed, Dan & Rhonda Ruffin."

THAT YE ABSTAIN FROM MEATS OFFERED TO IDOLS, AND FROM BLOOD, AND FROM THINGS STRANGLED, AND FROM FORNICATION: FROM WHICH IF YE KEEP YOURSELVES, YE SHALL DO WELL. FARE YE WELL. ACTS 15:29

Chapter XII

The Breakup ~cyh~

Dear Crystal,

I am writing to tell you that it is over between me and you. You no longer belong to me or me to you. You can no longer trust me or depend on me. Actually you never could. All those times that you thought I was faithful was a lie. I only deceived you. You see, my sole purpose in your life was to steal, kill, conquer and destroy you. Yes, I lost and you are more than a conqueror so I hope you live happily ever after because I am going on with my life. I do want you to know that I have someone else. Sorry I will not be available for you any longer. Do not look for me to satisfy your needs nor supply your needs for I am unable to grant any of your wishes or desires in that I am not number one in your life nor are you number one in mine. Actually we have nothing in common for what does darkness have in common with light. We have never really had anything in common. Absolutely nothing. I guess this means that you will no longer invite me to your pity parties and we will no longer be able to live a life full of fun and adventure and vanity. I guess you outgrew my sinful nature and your mind is renewed as you replaced the old man with the new man in Christ. I envy you as I once was right where you are at and will never again be able to be where you are right now. I won't be given another chance as you are. I thought I had you fooled. I guess the ditch I dug for you I fell into myself. It is with deep regret that you discovered who you are and will no longer except the label of victim I had given you. I will really miss how I tricked and deceived you and tortured you daily. What fun I had destroying everything your heart desired and everything you held near and dear. There is just one thing that I regret and that is not being able to destroy your soul. You never allowed me to have that. I guess you were stronger than I thought and wiser than I predicted. Your prayers must have been more powerful than I thought. Your faith must have been greater than I had imagined. Your God must be more sovereign than I had expected. Well like I said what is done is done and if I were you I would not look back because if you do I have 1,000 more demons that will be waiting to help me finish the job. I have never loved you and will never be your friend. So don't give me that line "maybe we can just be friends" trying not to hurt my feelings. Actually I am your enemy, so remember that the next time you think about giving me another chance to prove myself. Why you ever trusted a snake I do not know.

That is like trusting a dog that you know will bite you. You should have known that from the beginning of our relationship. You know what, I never thought you were smart at all, but I guess when you operate in God's wisdom, power and understanding and the fact that you have a heart, mind and body of Christ, well you are no match for me. Well all those promises that I promised you remember that I will never fulfill them. Those were lies too. Yes another trick of the enemy. I am the father of all lies. It was so funny how you believed it would be a happy ending with me. Oh, do not feel sorry for yourself, you were not the only one. I have tricked so many people, so many I can no longer keep track of. Only the strong survive. God must have really loved you so much that He saved you because if it were not for His grace and mercy, you and I would have had a future together. He sure knows how to mess up a good thing for me. Well no need to reflect on that. I am sure you're satisfied and content and complete in Him. You are satisfied and content aren't you? Because if you are not I will always be waiting on your feet to slip. I will be forever vigilant and roaming about the earth to and fro just waiting on you to fall into the traps I plan on setting before you in the present and in the future. I know that no weapon formed against you will prosper but that is not going to stop me from forming them, launching them and trying. You see, I know a good thing when I see one and you are a good thing. What we shared together was a good thing, so I won't quit without a fight. So bye for now, but it is not over until God says it is over and I have a deaf ear to him anyways so remember I will be waiting for you to mess up like I have always done. Remember that the next time you become weak in your flesh and allow the desire to sin and/or remain in sin manifest itself, I will be right there. I will also go so far as keep track of every sin you have committed in the past and from this day forward and bring them all back to your remembrance. I won't be like God and throw them in the "Sea of Forgetfulness" to never remember again. Oh no, I am not that forgetful or forgiving. Everything you did wrong in life I have kept a journal of and I can remind you of it at any time. Everything you did, how you did it, when you did it, where you did it, why you did it and who you did it with. So go on with your life, but be careful on your journey. You make sure you do not burn the bridge between me and you. You never know when you might want to return. Signed, The Devil, Lucifer himself!

AND THEY THAT ESCAPE OF YOU SHALL REMEMBER ME AMONG THE NATIONS WITHER THEY SHALL BE CARRIED CAPTIVES, BECAUSE I AM BROKEN WITH THEIR WHORISH HEART, WHICH HATH DEPARTED FROM ME, AND WITH THEIR EYES, WHICH GO A WHORING AFTER THEIR IDOLS: AND THEY SHALL LOTHE THEMSELVES FOR THE EVILS WHICH THEY HAVE COMMITTED IN ALL THEIR ABDOMINATIONS. EZEKIEL 6:9

Chapter XIII

The Breakout

Adversary who? "He is not even a "convo". I am so over him. Let's move on, keep it moving!"

Yes, it is Saturday once again. I remember growing up Saturday was a wonderful day. My grandmother would be cooking in the kitchen, breakfast, lunch, supper, then dinner with dessert and then nighttime snacks. What a life! Now I am in my grandmother's position and I cannot supply the same. I am like "Microwave Queen or Super Sandwich Maker". What is the difference? Well I will tell you. My grandmother was a full-time stay-at-home working mother, she had God and a man of God. I am a full-time career woman/full-time working mother and I have God. I am fully aware that the same God that my grandmother relied on to supply all her needs according to His riches in glory is the same God yesterday, today and tomorrow and as He was faithful and just to my grandmother, He is going to be the same for me.

With that being said, as God continues to supply all my needs according to His riches in glory, I am therefore obligated to God to make sure I supply all of my children's needs. To me that means make sure I give my children the quality of life that demonstrates they indeed have kingdom blessings. I remember telling my son Kha'Leel one day when dropping the kids off to school to "be good". I tell all the kids daily to "be good" but I find myself having to repeat the instruction "be good" to Kha'Leel on most days for he seems to have a hard time grasping the definition, to put it nicely. The kids were all quiet except for Kha'Leel, from the third row of the minivan he began to declare and decree these very words "I am blessed!"

Thank God the car was in park, because I turned around to do a "double take" and ask "What did you just say?" Not that I was deaf, but I just wanted to make sure I heard correctly. He repeated himself. He said "I am good and I am blessed". It was definitely another teaching moment, once again. I said "Yes, you are good and you are blessed. You are blessed because you are good and you need to continue to be good and do good things to stay blessed. God wants us all to be good and blessed. The opposite of good is bad. God does not like when we are bad because when we are bad we are not blessed, we are cursed. The devil was bad and now he is cursed." The car was completely silent.

I further asked "Do you know what cursed is?" No one answered. I went on to say "When we are disobedient to God and we do not listen to Him and do the things He wants us to do like be obedient and listen to our parents, our teachers and those that have authority over us then we are cursed and life will not be well for us." Everyone remained quiet and their little eyes and ears took it all in as they got out the car and went to class. From that day forward, Kha'Leel never stopped testifying to everyone within the sound of his voice that he was more than good, he was blessed! I am not mad at Kha'Leel at 7 years old, he knows he is good and he is blessed. Hallelujah!

It is really hard to walk in my grandmother's shoes. I have tried all my life to be the mother she was to me to my children. What I have discovered is that God gives us each our own destiny and we cannot walk out anyone else's. So, in doing my part, I do my best being a good mother and as Kha'Leel would say "A good and blessed mother". I often find myself not having enough hands, strength, patience or time, but I continue to do my best knowing that God is going to do the rest. Why? Because, I know who I am and whose I am. I belong to God. I am God's property and because I belong to him, I am equipped for my God-given destiny.

I strive to be organized and manage things within the realm of my natural and spiritual abilities utilizing Godly principles, always. I often bargain shop and watch for sales, use coupons, food banks, thrift shops, clothing pantries, donations, practice good stewardship, practice recycling and ecofriendly techniques. I teach my children not to waste and be good stewards of their resources and to save and have a "rainy day fund" in place. I teach them to share and give to others. I also try to teach them to love and respect themselves and the things that God has blessed them with including, but not limited to, one another, a beautiful home, etc.

So overall, I believe by faith we maintain a well-balanced Godly lifestyle. No it is not a life of luxury nor a lifestyle of the rich and famous, but it is a fulfilling lifestyle and a life worth living in God. God definitely gives us our daily bread and supplies all our needs according to His riches in glory and when He gives us extra favor and fulfills our wants and our heart's desires, we are just even more thankful and grateful.

I also practice good time management techniques. I have a daily, weekly, monthly and yearly calendar. If something ever happened to my calendar system, know that "This world would not be a better place". So, remain prayerful for me. I keep a watchful eye on my calendar and make sure each and every second of my time is accounted for. No "time wasters".

Everything in my life has a time, even this book that I am writing. I have a deadline that I am striving to reach. Yet, our time is not God's time! In writing this book I found myself putting a lot of unnecessary pressure on myself in order to complete the assignment before me, but God was still God and He was working things out during the entire process. What

I was learning through the process was that He simply wanted me to first totally surrender to Him and it was then and only then that He was able to begin to take me higher and higher in Him.

Nevertheless, working within the realm of my time and money budget, I was often let me think of a nice word - okay, "driven". That is just a nice way of saying "When things are set in motion, there is no stopping me". Now this is a good thing if you are going in the direction that God wants you to be going and doing the things that God wants you to be doing, but I am sure you know the flip side of this as evidenced in this book. Yes, it is all about God's daily agenda and not my own. Back to what I was saying, "I have a time and money budget". When shopping whether for food or clothing or running errands, everything has to be done within two hours maximum. Daily meals that take two and three hours to get done are not within my time budget. Clothes, shoes, purses, accessories, makeup, hair, skin and nail care that cost more than $50.00 or take more than two hours to find and purchase are not within my time and money budget.

Now I love to cook and I can cook pretty well, no complaints to date. However, compared to my grandmother I am definitely the downgraded version of Aunt Jemima and Betty Crocker. I do cook big meals on holidays and maybe even on Saturdays and Sundays. You know those meals that seem like they take all night and all day to prepare. Yes, way over my two hour time budget. I am just being real. My dear grandmother, cooked every single day, four times a day, six days a week, no cooking was done on Sunday because it was the sabbath day so we would usually warm up leftovers or my grandfather would pickup a bucket of chicken with all the fixins from KFC or we would go out to eat at Bishop's buffet.

My grandmother had a structured/organized weekly schedule that consisted of church services Sunday through Thursday. Now Friday and Saturday was considered the "sabbath days for shopping" mostly because my grandfather got paid every Friday and when my grandfather got paid, "Granny got paid" and when granny got paid, everybody in the house got paid. "When Granny was happy, everybody was happy" and Granny was happy when she was shopping. Fridays consisted of taking the bus downtown and shopping at Bergner's, Sears, Woolworth, Kresge's, Grants, the nut shop and Saturdays consisted of grocery shopping at Del Farm. I remember the grocery bill was always $65.00 even and I don't care what items had to go back, my grandfather would not budge a penny over. My grandmother used to "huff and puff" because of his rigid $65.00 rule, but it did not bother me that much because I always managed to put my corn curls in the basket first so that they would not forget the necessities.

My grandfather was proud to work all week and bring his paycheck home to take care of his household and his family. Yes, that is a Godly man not a "Goodly Man"! That is how their marriage lasted until death do us part. Divorce was unthought of back then, something to think about men and women of God. God wants us to take care of home first. When we take care of home first everything else and everyone else receives the overflow. "Thus saith the LORD, Set thine house in order for thou shalt die and not live". (Isaiah 38:1).

It is my prayer that my children view the little things that I do now as grand, so I must hold on to see what the end is going to be. Maybe one day they will sit back and say their Saturdays were wonderful and maybe their memories will be grandiose about me being "barefoot in the kitchen, without me being pregnant", and maybe they will have stories to tell their children from their eyes and not mine.

MY PERSONAL PRAYER

Lord, help me keep my eyes on You. Help me continue to seek Your face and not Your hand. Allow me to stay in Your presence despite my present situations and circumstances. Let me remember that I can create the atmosphere in which I presently exist through Your Holy Spirit. Allow Your Holy Spirit to orchestrate the flow of Your permissive will as I surrender my submissive will. Give me a revelation of what it is You want me to see, hear, know and feel. Let me continue to say yes to Your will and Your way. Let me continue to be blessed so that I can be a blessing. Allow me to intercede for others and to love and forgive others just as You love and have forgiven me. Give me fresh oil, a fresh anointing, a fresh breath from You. Give me Great Faith, the type of faith that can move any mountain, situation or problem that comes my way. Give me the peace that passeth all understanding. As I hold on to Your unchanging hand, allow me to be transformed into Your likeness, for purpose, for destiny, for Your glory. Allow me to give life and to live life abundantly. To birth nations, to impregnate and give birth to ideas, inspirations, dreams, and aspirations, through enrichment and enlightenment opportunities in You. Lead me down the path of righteousness for Your namesake. Amen.

CINDERELLA MISSES THE BALL

Now you have heard of the story of Cinderella and how her wicked stepmother and stepsisters treated her and how one day her fairy God-mother intervened and granted her wish and her dream came true to go to the ball where she was driven in a carriage with white horses and she wore the finest gown and array of accessories including glass slippers. When she walked into the ballroom every head turned. She was beautiful for the first time in her life inside and out and it was a look of confidence that covered her and brought forth an astonishing glow as she walked down those spiraling stairs to the ballroom floor. The onlookers despised her beauty. They were filled with envy and surprise. How could this be so? How did she get to the ball? In that moment of time until midnight, it was as if "time stood still" for Cinderella.

What about the other handmaidens that were not allowed to go the ball? You know the ones that have a wicked stepmother and stepsisters just like Cinderella and are placed in servitude positions and feel like the "have nots and have beens". The ones that look and feel like time spent, the ones who spend all of their days and nights wanting and never receiving, who spend all there time giving and never getting anything in return, the ones who spend all their energy on others and never obtaining appreciation, the ones who are ever learning and never actually grasping the knowledge, wisdom and understanding of truth. What about them?

Well, I will tell you about those handmaidens. Those handmaidens never make it to the ball. In fact, they miss the ball. Oh don't feel sorry for them. They don't need your sympathy. They only desire empathy because God has hand delivered each one of them a personal invitation to a RSVP/VIP event in the Upper Room. The Upper Room has a 7+ star rating, whereas the ballroom is only a 4.5 star rating. Yes, these handmaidens are called "God's Leading Ladies".

"God's Leading Ladies" come in all different shapes and sizes, all different races and colors, economic statuses and classes, different backgrounds and educational levels. Yet they have one thing in common, they seek God's face and not His hand. They just want to spend time with Him in His presence. If He never decides to bless them again they just want Him to know that as long as they can stay in His presence they will be just fine. They view life as worth living. They view life as worth giving. They don't mind being His servants, His handmaidens for His honor and His glory.

They don't wait on prince charming to come and complete them. They know that only God can complete them and fill every void. They know they are the "apple of His Eye" and nothing else matters during their moments alone with Him. As God draws them nearer and dearer to His heart their spirit connects with Him and forms a bond that is inseparable. A bond that no one can pull apart. Nothing can embrace, replace or penetrate this union. It is for eternity. They will never be the same. They will never return to life as it was before. Their latter days will be greater and their former days are nothing more than a vapor.

They have hope, peace, love, assurance, serenity, faith, endless fruit of the spirit dwelling within them. They have rivers of living water flowing to them and through them. They glow with the light of God that penetrates from deep within. They radiate God's glory for the whole world to see. They don't really care at this point whether or not they are wearing the finest ballroom gown or glass slippers or whether they are escorted by a prince. These leading ladies are covered with God's precious blood. They are covered with His love. They are wearing the whole armor of God. They don't look to man, they look to Him. They lean on Him. They depend on Him. They trust Him and only Him. Their faith is in Him and only Him.

There is no greater joy to God, their King of kings, than to know that His leading ladies are walking in spirit and truth as they continue in His word, as they continue on the path of righteousness that He has set before them, as they continue to walk in faith, as they continue to pray, believe and trust God who is the author and finisher of their faith. Oh, how they know without a doubt that "It is not the end of story, but only the beginning in God", for they are renewed daily by Him.

So what they missed the ball! They did not miss their divine appointment with destiny. God has predestined them for destiny. God has ordered their steps. It was God's plan for them to miss the ball, so that they would not miss their higher calling, so that they would not miss God, so that they would not miss their divine appointment with the King of kings. Oh, the angels rejoice in heaven knowing that they did not miss their divine appointment with God. For God and God alone has prepared a VIP table before them in the presence of their enemies. God chose them to be a royal priesthood made for His honor, glory and purpose. They are "Designer Originals" resembling their Heavenly Father, walking in the fullness of Him through the byways and highways, God's true runway models.

Yes, who can find a virtuous woman for her price is more valuable than silver and gold? Well you can find her in the Upper Room. She is wrapped up in God's loving arms, under the shadow of the Almighty and you will have to go to Him and through Him to find her. She was sad when she missed the ball, but He turned her sadness and mourning into dancing. He turned her midnight into daybreak. Now she is singing praises unto Him. Her cup runneth over. Her joy is full. Surely goodness and mercy shall follow her all the days of her life in Him. She now knows without a doubt why she missed the ball and she is now content in her mind, body, heart and soul that in God everything happens for a reason and not by chance.

How marvelous are God's works! No one but God knows them from the beginning to the end and from the end to the beginning. These women know that they are wonderfully and fearfully made. They will no longer allow the destroyer to come into their homes and spoil their goods. They know that God has encamped angels around them. They are covered with a hedge of protection and they know that the destroyer cannot spoil their goods unless they allow him to enter in and guess what? These leading ladies homes are now "Under New Management". Yes, God/the New Manager has changed the locks and threw away the old keys and satan and his pons and imps are no longer welcome to visit. Somebody say "Locked Out, Locked Up and Locked Down!" Yes, God has locked up the "pure gold" and sent away the silver and platinum, for there was no room in the Upper Room for anything less than His very best. Yes, nobody, no one is getting in, unless they go to and through God *First*!" Now, God's Leading Ladies, stomp the devil under your feet on that one with your "gold slippers". Hallelujah!

THE BATTLE BELONGS TO THE LORD

Lord, please show me where I went wrong so that I may remain and always be close to thee. Lord, accept my true confession "Thou the seasons change one thing remains the same and that is hurt. I know it happened to me and I suppressed it and tried to forget it and act like it never happened but it did happen and it did hurt me really bad, that I remember. Lord heal me and make me whole. Only you can do it. I trust you Lord! I love you Lord! Set me free, deliver me, save me! I cry out to you Lord!" ~cyh~

Though the seasons change one thing remains the same and that is hurt. Why do I allow **MY IDOL** to trick me every time? Time after time after time. Why do I fall repeatedly when he attacks my mind and my body? I know from past mistakes that when I fall I am entangled in his traps and handled with the least of care. I know that he only comes to steal, kill, conquer and destroy those that he preys on and whomever he can employ along the way. As I continue on my path with him, he changes the road and signs to make me ask him for direction, guidance, protection and safety, but he never offers me anything good. I always end up having to go back to my First Love, My King, My Lord. His name is Jesus, Jehovah Jireh, My Provider. Yet, I still do not know why I get distracted, lose my focus and get off track and fall into sin every single time.

Why does hurt have to exist? Allow me to try to answer, "So that God can show Himself strong in our weakness". God is going to rise up when we bow down. When we bow down before the King of kings, he is going to show Himself strong in our weakness. The bible declares it to be so. God is faithful. He is able. He can do all things. We can do all things through His power, His understanding and His wisdom. We do not have to win the battle for The Battle Belongs to the Lord. We just have to fight. Fight like our life depends on it, because it does.

GOD SPEAKS

For Zion's sake will I not hold my peace, and for Jerusalem's sake I will not rest, until the righteousness thereof go forth as brightness, and the salvation thereof as a lamp that burneth. And the Gentiles shall see thy righteousness, and all the kings thy glory: and though shalt be called by a new name, which the mouth of the LORD shall name. Thou shalt also be a crown of glory in the hand of the LORD, and a royal diadem in the hand of thy God. Thou shalt no more be termed Forsaken; neither shall thy land any more be termed Desolate; but thou shalt be called Hephzibah, and thy land Beulah; for the LORD delighteth in thee, and thy land shall be married. (Isaiah 62:1-4).

THE BEST IS YET TO COME

The everyday monotony gets old. Yet, I know that God won't put more on us than we can bear. God knows the story from the beginning to the end, so we must trust Him. In good times and bad, happy and sad, sickness and in health, for better or for worse until death do us part, like a good marriage except with God, our First Love, our First Husband, we shall never be separated, divorced or abandoned, mistreated or mishandled. He said in His word "Thou shall no more be termed Forsaken; neither shall thy land any more be termed Desolate; .... For the LORD delighteth in thee, and thy land shall be married". God is always with us and for us. No matter whether we feel it or not. Even if we can't trace Him, we must trust Him. He is there and He is watching over us, always. God said it in His word and He won't take it back!

So, we must remain thankful and grateful that we have a Heavenly Father whose "Eye is on the sparrow", who never slumbers or sleep. Even while we are resting in our beds, He is making provision for the next's day's purpose for our lives. When we awaken to our morning cup of coffee, when we put on our clothes, when we get in our cars to go to work or school and we are in our right mind, we need to thank God that all body organs are functioning at optimal levels. Because some people do not wake up and some do not wake up in their right minds. Life is so precious it can be taken in a second. We must fulfill our God-given destinies while we have time. Tomorrow is not promised to us, but today is a gift from God, so let us embrace it with a heart of thanksgiving.

Seek God daily for direction and He will show you the way. Go through to get to, but whatever you do, do not quit. You are on assignment. Your next opportunity is around the corner. You have to pass the next test in God and you will pass it. It is just a matter of time, don't give up. Somebody's blessing is connected to you passing the next test. If you get out the race they will not be blessed. Keep going. Keep running for Jesus. Why? Because your comings and your goings are blessed in God, proceed my sisters and my brothers. You may think that God has brought you a mighty long way, but the Best Is Yet To Come!

ENCOURAGE YOURSELF IN THE LORD

So, now the news is out and everybody knows that I am writing a bestseller book. Everyone and I know that it is God inspired. Yet, I do not know the time limits regarding the same. This is an uncomfortable state yet I am still overly excited in that I know it is just like the development of a child in the womb from conception to the actual birth and thereafter. It is a process. Each day is a new page on the tablets of my heart. Each situation is a different chapter. Each circumstance is a new subheading. Each problem is a prefix and each answer is a suffix. Sometimes I think the story will never end. Life seems to be a mystery, like an ocean treasure. Each day you never know what the tide will bring in yet you wake up each day to new surfaced treasures. We do not know what tomorrow holds, yet with embrace each day anew. In seeking out each day we find that which we did not get a chance to enjoy yesterday.

What does this mean? It means that God knows the beginning through the end and that we have a special place on this earth to fulfill God's purpose which includes our heart desires. This book is my heart's desire so I declare and decree in Jesus name that it shall come to pass! We just need to speak to our Creator and our Maker on a regular basis and make sure we are in agreement with His perfect will. Do not worry and fret over what tomorrow may bring, because today is sufficient in its own. Do not worry about what ye shall eat or drink because God promises us our daily bread and that in itself is more than enough. We are blessed to bless others. So, when we are in our rightful place in God's flow receiving the constant favor of God, well it is seems to be self explanatory.

We are blessed and highly favored. It does not matter if it does not look like it or feel like it. It is so! I am so excited today that God chose me, that He predestined me. He could have picked anyone else but I am His chosen one, a royal priesthood designed specifically and accordingly to His heart's desire to do a good work in the kingdom. It was prophesized that I would birth many nations. It is in His word that I will birth many nations, how do I know because I am heir to Abraham's blessings. So I am going to get my blessing and I plan to bless everyone I come in contact with, because I know it is going to be too much for me to contain. My storehouses are already full and God is speaking an overflow as we speak in the spirit. How do I know? Because, I am listening to His voice, what about you? Are you listening to His voice? If you are you can hear Him say "Overflow ... as I blow a fresh wind unto you ... receive it by faith in Jesus Name!"

If you accept what the devil gives you, what he is whispering in your ear and placing before you to trick and deceive you, you will be in a constant state of lack. You will live on "Skid Row Street". You will have no inner peace, but a constant inner storm. How do I know? I know, because it was not that long ago that I lived there. I was there and God changed my address. God changed my residence to "Authentic Street". God said "You are authentic! Your anointing is Authentic! You live on Authentic Street!" The devil is trying to tell somebody that they live on "Skid Row Street". God is trying to shift you and move you to "Authentic Street". Take heed to His voice and continue to ignore the devil. Hallelujah! When the devil shows his ugly face, begin to send out a roar cry unto your Heavenly Father. The enemy has to flee when you begin to cry out to God with your whole heart, sincerely. Stop worrying about who's looking or how you are looking, just get in His presence and cry out to Him. Yes, now you have entered into a secret place. God is getting ready to hide you as he communes with you. It is about relationship in this place, not religion.

In this secret place, God will begin to teach you His word and how to apply it. In this secret place, you will begin to accept the word of God and what He has in store for you. You will know without a doubt that you can live life abundantly and you will begin to live the life that He alone designed and planned for you. You will know that He shall and He will supply all your needs according to His riches in glory. You will no longer let your bank account balance limit you. You will no longer let anyone define you or set expectations for you. You will only strive and aim to meet God expectations of you. Your altitude in life will be declared and decreed by God. God's plan for your life will be implemented through His preapproved unlimited resources. Begin today to walk toward your God-given destiny. Start walking right now. You won't know whether or not God has a ram in the bush for you if you are not walking toward your destiny. God may have placed a ram in a bush around the corner from your home, but you wont find it if you stay in the house. Get out the house and get to your destiny.

Satan wants you to remain in bondage. God says you are free, free in your mind, body and soul. You are walking in victory in God. There is no failure in God. Your success rate in God is 110%. So those things you have been putting off in your past because of fear, complete them now in Jesus name. Lay your cares upon God and continue the course with joy and grace. Don't let your fears keep you in bondage another second. God has not given you the spirit of fear. He has given you the spirit of love, joy, peace and a sound mind. Continue the course with the fruit of the Spirit within you. Yes, it is within you my dear friend, my sister, my brother.

Though you may be weary, weak and even tired, don't faint. Continue the course with God's strength, power, wisdom and understanding. Do not let the naysayers stop you. They want your anointing! Do not let jealous people hinder you. They want your anointing! Do not let unbelievers define you. They want your anointing! Reposition yourself in God and redefine your stance and with the love of God let them know that it is through God that you live, breathe and have your being. Let them know you are too blessed to be stressed. Let them know that you are too anointed to be disappointed. Continue to praise and worship God for He alone is worthy. Let your heart be glad when you think of His goodness. In these trying times, do not quit and do not give up the faith. Continue the course with grace. Continue on the course like you know, that you know, that you know, that you know, you are a king and queen of God.

God has promised you that He will deliver you out of all your afflictions, trials and tribulations. It is your time. You cannot afford to miss this opportunity. God is a man that cannot lie. God loves you. It is okay to accept His endless love. His love is not like the love you have experienced in the past from man. The kind that loves and leaves you. No God is not like man. God loves you and He promises to never leave or forsake you. He loves you so much that He wants to give you everlasting life and not take your life. He does not want you to lack anything. He wants to give you His very best. Ask yourself this question "Do I want His very best?" If you answer yes, begin to seek His face to obtain it.

He does not want you to compromise. He wants you to obtain what He has in store for you. You will have to come to Him in order to receive it for He is a gentleman and He won't force Himself on you. He is waiting on you to knock so that the door will be opened. He is waiting on you to seek Him so that you will find Him and all that he has for you. He is waiting on you to ask so that He can give it to you. He wants to give you everything that your heart desires, everything you deserve and so much more.

It is not going to be easy. It is not an easy walk in Christ. A lot of times you won't know how God is going to bless you from day to day. A lot of times you may not even know your next step on the path. You may not even know where the resources are coming from, but you have to have faith and believe and trust that God can and He will bring provision from the north, south, east and west directly to you. Your blessings are going to come in many ways, more than you and I can number or imagine. Be assured and know that you won't miss any of your blessings. Your blessings have your name on it. You will soon see. Keep the faith and never doubt. Until it manifests in the natural, keep the faith and know without a doubt that in God, all things are possible.

Let me reassure you that there have been many, many times in my life that I prayed and I prayed for provision and I wanted a door to open and I thought I needed a door to open, but it did not open. I just kept praying and believing. I was so low in spirit, but I kept seeking God. There were times in my life that I truly wanted a blessing that I felt was good for me. Something I wanted to attain, obtain or achieve that just felt right, but it did not happen the way I had planned. I became discouraged, but I still trusted God and knew that He knew what was best for me. God will always open the right doors and close the right doors in your life at the right time. You can count on this!

You may say to yourself well I do not have the time to do this or that. Do not worry God will put you in position. He can restore the time you lost. God even has the "Hands of Time in His Hand". He can turn the hearts of kings. Can you imagine a priestly blessing given to you by a King? Prepare to receive what is yours. There will be times in your life that you may feel like you will be dead and gone before you receive all that God has promised you, but as He awakes you each brand new day, just begin to thank Him for he alone is worthy of all the honor, all the glory and all the praise. Your blessings are in your praise, don't miss them. God still specializes in miracles and things impossible. He wants to give them to you. If you can really be honest with yourself, you can look around you and see miracles every day. Continue to believe by faith. Faith is the substance of things hoped for, the evidence of things not seen (Hebrews 11:1). Keep hoping for even those things that you can't see!

Yes, you will lose things along the way in order to gain what is rightfully yours in God. Some people have been laid off from their jobs because God had a better plan for their life. Some people have lost their jobs because God had a purpose for their life. "Many are called but few are chosen", I was born for greatness. I was called and chosen to do a great work in the kingdom and I pray that you can believe that you were too. So "think it not strange when the fiery darts are thrown" your way. Just know they won't prosper.

When God closes a door, do not fret. Just begin to thank God because your blessing is within reach. Just keep on praising Him and worshipping Him. Do not let the devil know that you are upset or offended. Praise God through good times and bad. When the new door opens just walk in or run in, which ever you prefer, knowing that God alone has brought you to and through, has brought you out and is now walking right beside you holding your hand as you walk or run into and through that new door that He and He alone has opened for you.

There are some things that happened to me in life that let me know without a doubt there is a God and so shall be your story as you continue on your Christian journey. The bible says that "every knee shall bow and every tongue shall confess that Jesus is Lord". We are not a minority in Jesus, we are a majority. Every unbeliever will one day know the God we serve. So "choose ye this day who ye shall serve". The invitation is always open. Come to Him just as you are. He is awaiting with open arms to embrace you and wrap His loving arms around you. You will be safe from harmsway in His arms. Come in from out of the storm, He will protect, comfort and provide for you. What a mighty God we serve.

God will meet you right where you are at whether it is at the crack house or the white house, a tavern or bar, the club, the gambling boat, the street corner, the jail cell, the prison cell, the hospital bed, a homeless shelter, a rundown efficiency apartment, etc. God will meet you with open arms. Whenever you call Him, He will be right there. He may not always answer in the way that you would want Him to, but He is a right on time God.

You will hear Him and He will hear you because the bible says "my sheep hear my voice and a stranger will they not follow". God knows that each and everyone of His sheep, even the sheep that may have been scattered away from the herd, but He is looking high and lo for those lost sheep. God wants His sheep to come home. He wants the prodigal sons and daughters to return home. He is waiting on us.

No one but God knows the time when He will return for us, but He wants us to be ready today for tomorrow may be too late. May we live each day like it is our last so that we will be ready. What this means is to do unto others as we would want them to do unto us. What this means is to love your enemies and do good to those that hurt, use, despise and persecute you. What this means is to be your brother and sister's keeper. What this means is to visit the widows and children and orphans. To give to those in need. To open our hearts to others and our homes to those in need. To feed the hungry. To provide the basic necessities for body and spirit, spiritual and physical needs of one another. Why tell everyone about the God we serve when we do not have the heart of God nor the mind of God. How can we draw believers to God when we act nothing like our Heavenly Father. i.e. we preach about God but live a life far from what the word says. As believers we should practice what we preach.

The bible says to visit the widows, children and orphans. That means to make sure they are taken care of. That does not mean to take from them by not providing their basic needs and only giving them lip service. "Lip service is pimp service", a wise woman once said. The Body of Christ needs to reach out to the lost and take two fishes and five loaves of bread and do as Jesus did provide for a hungry nation seeking to be filled. That is our mission. That should be our vision. That is what Jesus did. He came on this earth to save us. We should therefore do what He did to save others.

We are His disciples. I know the devil has been whispering in your ear saying "God only had 12 disciples and they were male (no pun intended)". Tell the devil to "SHUT UP!" Tell the devil that God told you "A disciple is one that walks to and fro on this earth preaching the kingdom of God with the Gospel of Christ and witnessing to others about the goodness of God. We need more workers because "the harvest is plenty but the laborers are few". We need more saints walking in truth and more about their Father's business than about their own personal agendas. How can we bring others to Christ when we are a total mess ourselves? The church doors should always be open to everyone, not just believers, not just those that look the part. The church doors should be open to everyone for we are all God's children.

God accepts us as we are and so should His church. It is His church. It is not our church and it is not our pews. It is not our pastor. It all belongs to God. Everything belongs to God. I hope you are getting my point. We can scare people away by being unfriendly and unwelcoming and darn right evil. I know from personal experience on numerous occasions where I felt like I was unwelcomed in church and that is very hurtful.

Yes, there are some in the Body of Christ that can hurt you just like there are some in the world that can hurt you. In fact, sometimes it seems like "church hurt" can feel worse than "world hurt". You might expect the world not to be right and do right, but when you come into the church house and expect the presence of the Lord and liberty and you get "sister so and so with an attitude or brother so and so with a chip on his shoulder and church folk talking about you like a dog behind your back", where is the God in that?

Call me crazy, but I just expect to be treated right in the house of God. I expect me and my family to be welcomed in the house of the Lord and greeted with a friendly kiss, hug, handshake, smile or nice gesture and I expect to be included in all the activities of fellowship with other saints, isn't that what family does? We are a church family, correct? We are one body with many members. I hope I am not talking to the walls and that everyone within the sound of my voice can still hear me. If not, "Hello walls! Amen walls!" Seriously, I believe we all can work together in unity as a church family making a difference within the church walls and beyond the church walls. God's word says "There is one body, one Spirit, even as ye are called in one hope of your calling". (Ephesians 4:4).

Just like everybody cannot be in the pulpit, everybody cannot be in the nursery or usher board or deacon board or on the mother's board or in the choir or on the praise team. We can't all be praise dancers. We can't all play musical instruments, etc. We all have different gifts and with these gifts we can all participate instead of spectate. The bottom line is we need to love one another and respect one another and not covet each others natural and spiritual gifts. The Body of Christ needs to look so good that even nonbelievers will be compelled to come into the house of the Lord and see for themselves what they are missing out on.

The Body of Christ should not look like or act like the world. We should love one another with the love of God. When was the last time you told your sister or brother in Christ you loved them with the love of God and meant it? I am not talking about that "God Bless You" phrase. You know who I am talking to and what I am talking about when I say some say "God Bless You" and "Go in Peace" and go so far as to greet their neighbor with a friendly hug and kiss, but really can't stand them. If you don't know what I am saying, ask somebody in the world to interpret it for you. Yes, one thing I like about the people in the world is they will "call it like they see it" and I ain't mad at them!

When was the last time you told a sinner you loved them with the love of God and meant it? Remember love is an action word, it is not enough to say it, you have to show it. When was the last time you prayed for someone? When was the last time you fed someone who was hungry or provided water to someone who was thirsty? When was the last time you ministered to someone in need? When was the last time you gave someone your coat or a pair of shoes that was without? This is not extra; this should be done on a daily basis. What would it be like if God took a day off? God is always at work in our lives and we should always be at work doing kingdom business and blessing the lives of others.

While I know we are not God and we are human and that we do have some limitations in that we must eat, sleep, work, rest, etc. Nevertheless, in all of our waking hours we must do everything unto the Lord. Everything we do should be to give God glory. One must constantly do a self-check and ask themselves "What have I done today to give God glory?" One must also keep their personal relationship with God intact so that others can see the light of Christ through them.

The Body of Christ should not strive to obtain worldly riches. We should be looking for kingdom blessings. We are not to strive to get comfortable on earth for we are only visitors here. God will be returning soon for us. Oh don't get me wrong, I can see myself now driving in my pink Denali truck all laced in chrome and my breathtaking mansion home, circle driveway, professional landscaping that offers the luxury of an indoor and outdoor Caribbean oasis that includes 2 swimming pools, a Jacuzzi, hot tub, palm trees, gazebo, the finest patio furniture, the perfect atmosphere of peace, tranquility and serenity, all within a private paradise, and the wish list goes on and on, but now let me stop daydreaming and get out the fantasy and back to reality and live in it and thank God for the minivan and two-story home with the curved driveway! Don't laugh at me or feel sorry for me because we won't be able to take our fine jewelry, designer fashions and accessories, BMWs, Mercedes, Cadillacs, Lexus, Porsche, half a million, million and billion dollar fortunes with us to heaven. Our soul will be the only thing getting into heaven. In heaven we will have a new mansion with streets paved with gold, a new beginning, a new life. Everything we leave behind will not matter.

So we must not put our trust and our heart into worldly gain that is temporary. We must place our hearts and our minds on things that are eternal. I hope this all makes sense because it did not make sense to me until this point in my life. I remember chasing dreams and opportunities for personal gain that were not in any way to bring glory to God. Looking back now on those very things, I feel they were to only bring me glory, but that is okay. We have not because we ask not. We know not because we seek not. Now that we know better we must do better.

When you come into the full knowledge of God you have no excuse to live the life that you used to live. You must now reposition and redirect yourself so that you can make choices and decisions that line up with the word of God, constantly, daily and on a regular basis. Renew your minds daily. Kill and make a righteous resolve with the flesh daily. What this means is anything that is not of God, do not engage in, participate in or cooperate with sin. Do not get comfortable with worldly things.

Do not make it a point to associate with worldly people and hang out in worldly places that do not give God glory. If you go in a club to pick up some chicken livers, chicken gizzards and/or chicken wings, with extra sauce and pickles on the side, and minister to people along the way and then get out, well that is okay. Please, don't lose your focus on the way out the club and end up in the middle of the dance floor doing the electric slide. If you do, chances are you will show up at church the next morning with that same spirit on you. Don't be surprised if you get caught doing those same dances moves from the night before during praise and worship service. You have been forewarned, don't blame me when everybody in church is looking at you like you crazy when what you call praising God turns into a combination of the electric slide dance moves, clapping you hands, stomping your feet, snapping your fingers, rolling your neck, back, hips and rump and dropping it like it is hot all at the same time. The only way you can avoid this embarrassment is if you opt out of the electric slide for a few drinks at the bar and after a few drinks you find yourself asking the person sitting next to you, "How many is a few?" and you end up spending the night slumped over the bar counter and missing Sunday service. Either way, you won't bring God glory. Just stay out the club, please!

If you go on the gambling boat and minister to someone about being a good steward of the money that God has blessed them with and then get off the boat, well that is okay. Please do not lose your focus and end up staying on the boat and gambling your tithes and offering, your mortgage, your car payment, your utilities payments, your alimony and child support payments, etc. That will not give God glory and you and your family, the pet dog, cat, bird and fish will suffer. Some people may be big winners and say well I will pay my tithes and offering and give some of the money to the church when I win. Well what will you do when you lose? The bottom line is, none of it is God's best or way of gaining a good thing in Him.

Personally, I am not afraid of speaking truth. It is necessary in this time and season when some put all their effort into covering up and watering down the truth. God is not pleased. God hates falsehood and so do I. Let's begin to live in the truth and walk in the truth. God has revealed it to you over and over again, what is it going to take until you get it? Meditate on (Psalm 119:103-104). "How sweet are thy words unto my taste! yea sweeter than honey to my mouth! Through thy precepts I get understanding: therefore I hate every false way".

If that man or woman calls you in the middle of the night and asks that you come over and pray for him/her, well utilize the five senses that God gave you and I hope you know that you have just been "booty called" instead of "pranked called" and I hope you have sense enough to rebuke that devil in the name of Jesus and then hang up the phone and rebuke the devil in you for answering the call in the name of Jesus!

God's way is the only WIN/WIN situation. You are 110% sure to win in Christ. Do not gamble your life away. Do not take chances that can be detrimental to your well-being. In the natural you obtain insurance for your worldly possessions. In the spirit God is insurance for your earthly and heavenly possessions.

Now, I do not know who made me go off on a tangent or even why I went off on a tangent, but I am now coming off of my soap box. Nevertheless Lord, I allowed Your Holy Spirit to have its way. That might have even been a sermon I just preached, hard to tell at this point. Ooh weee, I feel much better getting all that off my chest. Praise the Lord Saints! Are we even on the on the same book or have I started a new book? Hallelujah Anyhow! Oh yeah, this subheading was "Encourage Yourself in the Lord". Well I don't know about you, but I feel encouraged and I feel better, so let's move on.

AND WHAT AGREEMENT HATH THE TEMPLE OF GOD WITH IDOLS? FOR YE ARE THE TEMPLE OF THE LIVING GOD; AS GOD HATH SAID, I WILL DWELL IN THEM, AND WALK IN THEM; AND I WILL BE THEIR GOD, AND THEY SHALL BE MY PEOPLE. 2 CORINTHIANS 6:16

Chapter XIV

Reminiscing on the Past

In life I tried many things. I wanted to be a lawyer so that I could have success, wealth and power. I wanted to be a supermodel to obtain a glamorous lifestyle filled with wealth, fortune and fame. I wanted to be a police officer to obtain wealth and power. I was not successful in any of those career paths, because that was not my destiny. I have had a heart's desire to write every since I was a small child. If you gave me a tablet and a pen or pencil, I would write until I could write no more. If you gave me a computer, I would type until I could type no more. It was my passion. I excelled in it. I would write poetry, journals and books. I would treasure my writings and keep them in safekeeping, never throwing them away or losing them. My writings were very special to me. I held on to the tablets of my heart knowing that one day my voice would be heard. Words are so powerful.

The words in my heart are God-inspired. I have the heart, mind and spirit of God and God has anointed my mouth and my hands for His glory. I often encourage others through words. I write to encourage others. I write to comfort others. I write to inspire others and the passion I put forth in my writings bless others as well as myself. Each one of us has God-given gifts. Whatever our God-given gifts are, we have a passion for it. I do not like public speaking and I do not think I am good at it, but what I am good at I know. I know exactly what I am good and bad at and that is because I have tried it. If you don't try you will never know your potential and if you don't try with God's help you will never know your full potential.

With God's help, we need to try different things and then focus on our strengths while acknowledging our weaknesses. We need to give more attention to our strengths on a regular basis to be walking towards our destiny. God is leading. We just need to follow. Faith without works is dead. We must have faith and we must work toward our goals in order to achieve our goals in life, our dreams, our aspirations, our God-given destiny. Let's start today walking and working toward our God-given destiny. We have infinite possibilities in God.

RESTORATION *~cyh~*

Where there is hate, allow me to only see love;
Where there is sorrow, allow my heart to be filled with joy;
Where there is confusion, allow me to have peace that passeth all understanding;
Where there is division, allow unity within my soul;
Where there is evil, allow me to dwell in the safety of Your arms;
Where there is fear, allow me to have safety within Your hedge of protection;
Where there is lack, allow provision to fall from the hills;
Where there is doubt, allow faith to be developed through trials and tribulations;
Where there is discouragement, allow Your grace and mercy to comfort me;
Where there is insecurity, allow me to feel secure in Your hands;
Where there is weakness, allow Your strength to lead and direct my paths;
Where there is darkness, allow Your light to shine to and through me;
Where there is a need, allow me to be the vessel You use for Your honor;
Where there is trouble, allow Your words to bring assurance;
Lord continue to restore me each day.

CRYSTAL Y. HOLT'S SURRENDER'S PRAYER *~cyh~*

Lord my burdens are heavy yet Your ways are light. Lord, if it be thy will, please send me the provision I need to withstand the tests in life. I know that You hold me accountable to take care of what You have provided me with yet I lack wisdom, understanding and power without You. Lord draw nearer to me as I apply my face to heaven. Lord, send a word that will renew my spirit, mind, body and soul. Trouble is all around me, yet I seek a word from You that will carry me through as it has in timespast. I am tired and weary Lord and I know You know just how much I can bear, but I do not and that is why I often wonder. Lord I am trying my best to trust You with all my heart, mind and soul, but the days, months and years are passing and I do not know where I am at in the process. Am I on target? Am I even in the race? Only You can answer these questions as You know every strand of hair on my head, the frame and the length of my days. The inferior and exterior portions of my body were designed by You. You even know my inward parts, You and only You. Lord, I surrender, let Your will be done in my life. Lord, last but not least, please help me Lord to understand the magnitude of it all. Amen!

GOD ANSWERS .... A WORD FROM THE LORD...
SUMMING UP THE WHOLE MATTER

"Sing, O barren, thou that didst not bear; break forth into singing, and cry aloud, thou that didst not travail with child: for more are the children of the desolate than the children of the married wife, saith the LORD. Enlarge the place of thy tent, and let them stretch forth the curtains of thine habitations: spare not, lengthen thy cords, and strengthen thy stakes; For thou shalt break forth on the right hand and on the left; and thy seed shall inherit the Gentiles, and make the desolate cities to be inhabited. Fear not; for thou shalt not be ashamed: neither be thou confounded; for thou shalt not be put to shame: for thou shalt forget the shame of thy youth, and shalt not remember the reproach of thy widowhood any more. For thy maker is thine husband; the LORD of hosts is his name: and thy Redeemer the Holy One of Israel; The God of the whole earth shall he be called. For the LORD hath called thee as a woman forsaken and grieved in spirit, and a wife of youth, when thou wast refused, saith thy God. For a small moment have I forsaken thee; but with great mercies will I gather thee. In a little wrath I hid my face from thee for a moment; but with everlasting kindness will I have mercy on thee, saith the LORD thy Redeemer. For this is as the waters of Noah unto me: for as I have sworn that the waters of Noah should no more go over the earth; so have I sworn that I would not be wroth with thee, nor rebuke thee. For the mountains shall depart, and the hills be removed; but my kindness shall not depart from thee, neither shall the covenant of my peace be removed, saith the LORD that hath mercy on thee. O thou afflicted, tossed with tempest, and not comforted, behold, I will lay thy stones with fair colours, and lay thy foundations with sapphires. And I will make thy windows of agates, and thy gates of carbuncles, and all thy borders of pleasant stones. And all thy children shall be taught of the LORD; and great shall be the peace of thy children. In righteousness shalt thou be established: thou shalt be far from oppression; for thou shalt not fear: and from terror; for it shall not come near thee. Behold, they shall surely gather together, but not by me: whosoever shall gather together against thee shall fall for thy sake. Behold, I have created the blacksmith that bloweth the coals in the fire, and that bringeth forth an instrument for his work; and I have created the waster to destroy. No weapon that is formed against thee shall prosper; and every tongue that shall rise against thee in judgment thou shalt condemn. This is the heritage of the servants of the LORD, and their righteousness is of me, saith the LORD." (Isaiah 54:1-17).

Thank you Lord for answering. ~cyh~

A PONDERING MOMENT

A former employer once said to me "You do not get paid to think". He said it in a joking way and I know he was being sarcastic; however, knowledge is power and knowledge is wisdom when you apply it. I must admit over the years I have done a whole lot of thinking, but if you do nothing but think, you will never obtain your dreams, goals and aspirations. Take one day at a time, step by step in God and you are guaranteed to get to your destination.

I always try to begin and end every plan of action and direction by saying, God willing. I must tell you that God is willing, if you are able. If you are not able, then know that God is not willing. God will equip you with whatever you need to do, which is your God-given assignments. God does not want us to do everything. He only wants us to only do our God-given assignments. So we need to go to Him in prayer and ask Him exactly what those assignments are. If something seems impossible and you do not feel that God is willing, go in prayer and ask Him and He will answer. When He answers you will know what to do and no one will have to tell you. Take note of what I have just said "No one will have to tell you". God is going to tell you first. When someone else tells you, it will only be confirmation.

AND THEY SHALL RECOMPENSE YOUR LWEDNESS UPON YOU, AND YE SHALL BEAR THE SINS OF YOUR IDOLS: AND YE SHALL KNOW THAT I AM THE LORD GOD. EZEKIEL 23:49

Chapter XV

The Synopsis

In 1989, I returned home from college in Southern Illinois to deliver my third child upon completing my studies. I obtained a full-time position as a legal secretary for a very successful law firm. Life was grand. Four years later the firm downsized and since I was the last one hired, well you know the story, I was the first one laid off. Thankfully, I was given a nice severance package and was able to rebound by returning to school to complete my BA degree. I worked several different jobs to gain experience, maintain a living and find my way through life's journey; namely, secretary, youth outreach worker, youth outreach specialist, probation officer intern. I even pursued a job as a police officer and firefighter recruit.

Yes, I know, what was I thinking? I passed the police officer written and physical exam and went through the first and second interview and was placed in a pool for hire. I passed the firefighter written exam and successfully bombed the physical exam so no need for an interview on that one, right? Yet, I had a wonderful time trying to pass the firefighter physical exam and if nothing else I was in great physical shape after that one. Know that if I were called to the scene of any crime in progress or a kitty stuck up in the tree or a even a bush fire, I would be the first one to call 911 on behalf of the victims. Oh and I would go further than that I would pray for them and me until helped arrived and thereafter. Again, what was I thinking? God did not tell me to be a police officer or firefighter, nor did He even place the desire in my heart. HMMM, something to think about, huh?

In 1994, upon obtaining a BA degree in Social Justice, I successfully obtained a job as a foster care caseworker and worked in that capacity for about a year. It was then that I realized I wanted so much more out of life. I wanted to meet a greater need in the community, in society, in the world, not knowing that God had another plan, for He was preparing me to meet a greater need of the kingdom.

So I returned back to school to work on my MA degree in Human Development Counseling. I worked full-time as a medical secretary, then medical transcriptionist and went to school part-time at night and/or weekends, while simultaneously raising my children, taking care of my family and living out my different individual desires/dreams and aspirations. No "Happily Ever After" in this fairy tale, I guess you could call me a mover/shaker. Life was still grand!

My last semester in graduate school was very difficult in that I was diagnosed with Type 1 diabetes and had to seek immediate medical attention which was the first time in my life that I realized that I was not Super Woman and that I was not designed by God to be Super Woman. Nevertheless, with God's help, I graduated with honors, with a MA Degree in Human Development Counseling in 2001. Anybody surprised? I was. Although at that time in my life graduating from undergraduate and then graduate college seemed like mountaintop experiences, I now know that it was deep in the valley, in the deep trenches, where I grew and excelled the most.

In 2010, with God's help, I am simultaneously writing my bestseller book and preparing to obtain my credentials to be a licensed professional counselor. This is my heart's desire now and becoming a bestseller book writer has been my true heart's desire from the very beginning. Yes, I have experienced some delays and major setbacks on my journey; nevertheless, God is still God! I am still on track for Jesus with my "eye on the prize". I had to go through all of the above to actually find what I wanted out of life, who I am, whose I am and what I am actually made of. This in itself is a milestone experience.

I am presently a full-time working mother of eight beautiful children, five boys and three girls, ages 4 through 26 years. I am also a grandmother of five beautiful grandsons, ages 6 months through 5 years and God has given me the grace to handle it. I plan to take one day at a time with God as my guide. I am walking daily by faith, trusting and believing God for everything. I know in Him there is no failure. So it is with great confidence that I can say "The Best Is Still Yet To Come!"

CONSIDER GOD'S SERVANT JOB

Then Job answered the Lord, and said, I know that though canst do everything, and that no thought can be withholden from thee. Who is he that hideth counsel without knowledge? therefore have I uttered that I understood not; things too wonderful for me which I knew not. Hear, I beseech thee, and I will speak: I will demand of thee, and declare thou unto me. I have heard of thee by the hearing of the ear: but now mine eye seeth thee. Wherefore I abhor myself, and repent in dust and ashes. (Job 42:1-6).

CONSIDER GOD'S SERVANT CRYSTAL

Lord, I have heard of Thee by the hearing of the ear: but now mine eye seeth Thee. Wherefore I abhor myself, and repent in dust and ashes.

MY PERSONAL PRAYER

Lord, my heart is sorrowful for man knoweth not what they do. Like Your servant Job, I too am Your servant and tragedy is every present, yet mine eye seeth Thee. Trial and tribulations are near, yet mine eye seeth Thee. I have found favor in your sight for you have given me peace in the midst of the storm. Seasons come and seasons go, yet I know You are the same God, yesterday, today and tomorrow. You alone have remained constant. You are the source of my strength and my joy. Though tears flow from my eyes like a well of everflowing waters, I know that You are not a high priest that cannot feel my infirmities. I will continue to seek Your face and trust You. Everything that I am presently going through and have been through I know that it was for my good. I know that You are building my Godly character and strengthening me and molding me like a potter molds clay. Lord I thank You, Amen.

GOD'S LEADING LADY C SPEAKS TO GOD

Never will I compare what I am going through to the trials of Your servant Job but thank You for giving me the spoken word to minister to my present circumstances to know the same God that brought Job out of his trials and tribulations will bring me out of mine. Sometimes, I find myself wanting to do the very thing that Job did when he was afflicted. I have felt discouraged and felt like cursing the day I was born. I have felt like hating man for what he has done and continues to do, but I am too much like You Lord and I find it to be impossible to hate when there is so much of Your love dwelling within me. Lord, I want to be more and more like You each day.

Therefore, I must forgive. I must continue the course with joy and grace. I cannot blame man, because those that hurt me were just on assignment by the enemy walking to and fro seeking whom he may devour. Those that hurt me sole purpose was to do the work of the enemy that sent them. Why would I think it would not happen to me when the very thing happened to You Lord and my brother in Christ, Job?

Never can I think that I am too good to experience afflictions for I know that no one was more righteous than You Lord. Yet, You endured the cross for my sins and the sins of us all. There is no greater love. So when I am sorrowful and feeling unloved, I know that I have a Heavenly Father who loves me unconditionally. A Heavenly Father who is always there, always near, always wanting me to experience His very best. So the joy that remains in me is the joy in knowing that You are the center of my joy! You are the center of my life! The joy of the Lord is my strength! I cannot remain defeated for I know that in You I am more than a conqueror!

When my life is out of balance and I think about You and Your faithfulness, everything seems to just fall into place. When I put You First in my life, there is no imbalance. There is only an imbalance when I go out in my own strength and try to do things according to my own will, in my own strength. That is the reality of the whole matter. You keep showing me this over and over again, but I guess I am not getting it. Lord, You are a lifestyle and not just a decision, choice, pastime or hobby. Following You is a full-time job plus overtime with maximum benefits, 365 days of the year. I am on assignment for You Lord, 24/7. Just as Your servant Job did not give up and he did not curse You and You blessed him tremendously in that his latter days were greater, so shall be my portion.

MY PERSONAL PRAYER OF FAITH AND PSALMS

I am going to continue the course and I am going to hold on to God's unchanging hand. Lord, I will seek You in good times and in bad, in happy times and in sad, in storms, at war and at peace. When the sea is raging and when the waves are calm, I will seek You. When I do not know what today may hold nor what tomorrow may bring and resources are limited and few, I will seek and trust You, because You promised in Your word that you would provide for me daily and give me my daily bread.

You have always kept Your promises and I know that You are faithful. You alone are worthy and I will continue to give You all the honor and the praise. All the credit for my success belongs to You Lord. I am Your servant. I remain humble and prayerful because I know Your ear is attuned to my cry. Your eye is always watching over me and I know You know every turn and twist I take on the journey. Every step I take You are with me. When I can no longer walk, I know You will carry me. Amen.

What a mighty God I serve. When the world turns against me I can say "Greater is he that that is in me than he that is in the world" (1 John 4:4). *When I am afraid I can say* "Ye, though I walk through the valley of the shadow of death, I will fear no evil: for thou art with me; thy rod and thy staff they comfort me" (Psalm 23:4).

I can proclaim and declare the word of God and have victory in every situation knowing it is already done! As I begin and end each day with the Lord's Prayer (Matthew 6:9-13), *I can walk in victory knowing that it is already done. I can begin to count my blessings, one by one, knowing it is already done. I can go ahead and get the blessings of Abraham knowing it is already done. I can go ahead and walk by faith forward on the journey in the spirit of expectancy know that the only sacrifice You require of me is that I have faith that You will provide a ram in the bush, and while I walk by faith, all I have to do is know that my God can and will perform it because He is God and because He loves and cares for me and wants to show His love to all whom believe and rely totally on Him. It is a relationship based on the principle of love. God's love has no limits! Lord, I love You more and more each day and I know that You love me. It is a beautiful love and a wonderful feeling of being in love with You.*

Lord, I know that "You wish above all things for me to prosper and be in good health even as my soul prospereth" (3 John 1:2), *so why do I continue to be sad and sorrowful? Allow me to answer. I know the devil preys on those who are weak and are not utilizing the principles of God on a daily basis, who are not putting on the whole armor of God and speaking life into every situation with the power, understanding and wisdom and strength that has already been given to them from the beginning of time for it is already theirs to have. They just need to acknowledge, believe, receive, claim and own the power within.*

I know that I should not be walking around like a child without a father, when I am royalty, the child of the King. I know that I should stop allowing **MY IDOL** *to whisper despair in my ear when my God is able to bring me out of every affliction.*

Lord I know You want to whisper in my ear in a small, still, gentle voice that only Your sheep can hear, but **MY IDOL** *is trying to distract me in so many ways so that I will be so out of touch with You that I cannot hear You, but Lord I can hear You say* "Hold on my dear child, you will hear me when I speak. I will get your attention. I will speak directly to you and through you. For now, just be still, and know that I am God!"

Lord, I can hear you. Thank You for answering me. I will begin to worship and praise You in advance and bless You with the fruit of my lips. Lord, I thank You for holding me in Your loving arms. Thank You for comforting me. Thank You for keeping me. For everything You have done I give thanks. I will continually thank and praise You, for You alone are worthy. Lord, I can hear You say "Beloved, no matter how sorrowful and sad you feel now, know that everything will work out for your good. Weeping may endure for a night, but joy cometh in the morning, just hold on". *"Thank You Lord, I love You so much and Good morning ...".*

REBUILDING AND REPOSITIONING ME

God is rebuilding and repositioning me. He is redefining me for my good and for His good. God is preparing me to minister to others. Through my life experiences, He is giving me the very words to say and the very actions to do. "I will overcome by the words of my testimony". My life will be an example to others. I have lived every word that has proceeded out my mouth and I am forever thankful and grateful. **MY IDOL** thought he left me dead, but every time he knocked me down I got back up stronger.

The enemy did not know that it was "ride or die with me". He did not know that I was a "Soldier in the Army of the Lord". He took my kindness for weakness. I allowed him to come into my life and cause me to fall time after time again, but that is okay, because I am back up now on my feet, ready for battle. I plan on fighting for Jesus for life. I am in my army tank right now. Me and Jesus side by side, ready for battle. I plan on riding with Jesus for Life!

I am honored that God chose to utilize me as a student servant in the School of the Holy Ghost probably because He knew I would make it my goal to go out and recruit others to kingdom build. God knew I would move forward with the anointing that He has placed over my life. God knew that I would be willing and obedient and build up leaders even greater than me. This is why the adversary has tried all my life to abort the assignment, from the first day of conception and thereafter. Satan knew that God was going to use me to reach nations. The enemy knew that he would not be able to overtake "God's Endtime Army", the remnant that God has prepared for such a time as this.

God is shaking up the atmosphere like an earthquake, hurricane, tsunami, etc. He is rebuilding in places He wants to build and tearing down places that need to be torn down.

Yet, His remnant will not be moved. His remnant will remain intact for they are rooted and grounded in Him. They are locked and loaded and ready for battle. They have on their whole armor and they are not playing with the devil. He is no match for those that worship God in spirit and in truth. All I can say is "devil get ready for the Big Payback!" Yes, I now know that I was "Set Back to be Set Up for the Big Comeback!" Thank You Lord for the revelation!

I thank God for the opportunity to carry out the assignments that He has placed over my life. I am indeed a success story in Jesus. He has ordained me to do a good work in the kingdom. He has prepared me to do a good work. No one else can teach you your destiny and purpose greater than the creator. As I allowed Him to lead and guide me daily, He has instructed me throughout the journey. When I look all around me I can only say "Thank You Lord" for I know that it was none of me, I have definitely come this far by faith.

AFTER THE DANCE

My journey has been that of a love story with my First Love, Jesus. He is the first man that ever loved me unconditionally. That is why He and He alone is my King, my Lord and I am His handmaiden, queen, God's Leading Lady C. As a young lady, I was never really asked to go to the homecoming dance or the prom, but if I were asked I would have went and I probably would have danced. I know that sounds strange, but I often think about the times that my mother did not allow me go to a dance because of my level of maturity. Then I think back to the times when she did allow me to go to the dance and I had to go by myself or with other female friends who also had to go by themselves and I would stand on the sidelines and watch others dance and/or I would end up holding up the walls most of the night saying to myself "I wish someone would ask me to dance". Very seldom was I asked to dance. On those few occasions I was asked to dance, I would either politely say "No" or I would somehow find the strength and courage to say "Yes" and then slowly proceed to the dance floor astonished, but it was far and few. For the most part, I have always had a very shy spirit which never allowed me to be free to dance.

I sometimes think about my walk with God as if He invited me to the dance, as if He took me to the dance and as if He taught me how to dance. I can just imagine Him picking me up for the dance and me being dressed in my best attire. For the exterior design, the perfect smile, style/look, dress, shoes, accessories, makeup, hair and fragrance. For the interior design the perfect inner/outer radiating glow, mannerisms and etiquette. Yes, the essence of a lady at work wanting her King to always see her at her best.

As my King approaches me and says "Would you like to go to the dance with me?" I would say to myself "Wow, I can't believe He asked me to the dance". I would begin to get excited like a high school girl who has just been asked to the dance. I would begin to tell everyone I know who invited me to the dance.

I would recall the story as this. "On the day of the dance, He arrives at my door. He greets me with a friendly kiss and hug and my parents quickly come in the room and look at us together and they immediately approve of what they see. Looking at Him is so glorious. I can hardly take my eyes off of Him. I cannot help but stare at His face.

He gently grabs my hand and places a corsage on my arm, something I never experienced. He tells me how beautiful I look and how honored He is to escort me to the dance. I am more excited than He could ever be and way more honored than He could ever imagine. For in times past everyone passed over me and never thought about asking me to the dance, but not Him. He cared about me and He was concerned about me and on top of that He gave me my first corsage and told me I was beautiful and that He was honored to escort me to the dance, what a gentleman.

When we arrive at the dance we make a grand entrance. It is obvious that everyone is pleased. We look around the room and the room is filled with fun and laughter and the sound of music and love seems to fills the air. The mood is perfect. He looks over at me and says "Would you like to dance?" I pause before I respond in total surprise because it just dawned on me that "I don't even know how to dance". I nod my head "Yes", really meaning "No" and He graciously holds my hand and walks with me, side by side, to the middle of the dance floor. My heart is racing, my chest is pounding for "I really truly don't know how to dance".

He begins to move to the left and then to the right and He notices that I am still standing still and He now knows exactly what to do. He then comes closer to me and softly whispers in my ear, "Don't worry, I will teach you how to dance, just follow me". He begins to show me and tell me as He continues to whisper in my ear in a still, soft, gentle voice so that no one can hear that He is giving me my first dance lesson. I begin to follow His lead, step by step as onlookers look on. I was so nervous and afraid that everyone would notice that I could not dance. He senses my fear and holds me closer to Him as if to cover me, comfort me and reassure me that I am not alone in this. His body moves with mine slowly to the rhythm of the music. I move with Him. He did not go too fast or too slow, it was just perfect.

We had the perfect rhythm, sequence and harmony. As the music played He continued to show me every single move. He was the perfect dancer. How could I get so lucky on my very first date with Him? It was now as if I was floating on air as He lifted me up and twirled me around still keeping the beat of the rhythm and never losing step. I continued to follow His lead on every step while He continued whispering in my ear "To the left, to the right, stand still, pause, proceed, move forward, turn around, etc".

As I allowed the music to take over my mind, body, spirit and soul, it was as if we became one together. I began to embrace the moment. It became more natural to me than rehearsed. As I began to follow His lead, it became easier to hear, feel and understand the process of dancing to His flow. My attitude was now that of a dancer. My steps began to flow beautifully with His. The music became an uninterrupted melody and we danced the night away. I never knew dancing could be so much fun and could feel so good. I never even imagined I would be able to dance let alone be a good dancer.

As the onlookers and bystanders from afar and near continue to watch us dance together so magically, they did not know or understand all the choreography that went into the dance. They did not see that it began even before the very first time our eyes met. You see, even before He asked me to the dance He knew I was "the one" and I knew "He was the one". It is kind of hard to explain it, but it was like a vision in a dream. Yet, I never knew the fullness of what it all entailed. I never new that He would ask me to the dance and that He would then take me to the dance and that He would then show me how to dance. I never saw that coming. I knew in my spirit that I desired to experience this moment, yet I did not know the time or the season.

What the onlookers did not know is that it did not happen overnight. It was a process. I did not just show up at the dance and then walk on the dance floor and start dancing in my own strength and talent. As everyone continued to look and admire the beauty of our orchestrated steps, they appear to desire what we share together. I have seen that look before, for it was not too long ago that I walked in their shoes as an onlooker and I too had that same look and said to myself "When is my turn, when will I get my chance to dance?" To be honest, I really did not know that I would ever dance. Yes, I was once just like them, always looking and hoping and waiting on my turn and my chance to dance.

I pray that one day they will be asked to the dance just as I was and I pray that they will say "Yes". I pray that they will be ready to go to the dance, that they will be willing to learn how to dance and that they will indeed dance. My life will never be the same after this dance for it is not every day that a young lady such as myself gets asked to the dance by a King. How do I know He was a King? Because no one else has ever been able to make me feel like a "Queen for a lifetime". He is definitely a King!

I pray that one day I can teach others to dance just like He taught me, but I will only teach them what He has taught me and I won't try to change the steps or the moves, for everything He taught me was perfect. Until then, I will continue to dance whenever He asks His queen to dance, always remembering that He cared enough and was concerned enough about me to escort me to my first dance and that He placed my first corsage on my arm and told me I was beautiful and that He was honored to escort me to the dance. I have felt like a queen from that day forward. He alone is worthy of all honor and praise. He is the only one who took the time to teach and show His Leading Lady C how to dance.

In my Christian walk, I know that I am a forerunner in the race and that many will follow after me, but it is important for me to always remember and teach those that choose to follow to always know that God is the one who leads, not I. If I try to lead others in my own strength, they will fall in error and so will I. It is important for me to always remain a student servant in the School of the Holy Ghost so that God can continue to teach and show me exactly what I need to know to lead His people. It is important to me and God that lives, generations, and nations be saved, healed, delivered, set free and made whole by the power of God for the advancement of His kingdom. Bless God of whom all heavenly blessings flow!

A CRY FOR HELP

"The righteous cry, and the LORD heareth, and delivereth them out of all their troubles. The LORD is nigh unto them that are of a broken heart; and saveth such as be of a contrite spirit. Many are the afflictions of the righteous: but the LORD delivereth him out of them all." (Psalm 34:17-19).

FAITH WORKERS, MY MODIFIED RUTH AND NAOMI EXPERIENCE

Over a year has passed since I restarted writing this book and to my surprise my Ruth and Naomi experience has come to pass. Praise God. You see I was once in the position of Naomi, widowed and in despair. Not by the death of a spouse, but by the death of a relationship through divorce. I was like Naomi, in desperate need of help. I, like Naomi, had gone out full and returned home empty. I was not without children but I was empty. I was bitter. I felt forsaken in that I believed that everyone I had taken care of throughout the years, loved ones, friends, acquaintances should have been there for me in my time of need. Let's not forget the church. I thought it was biblical that "the church" was supposed to look after the orphans and widows. Well that did not happen the way I thought and I felt so alone and helpless.

I felt victimized instead of victorious. So, I began to isolate myself and I did not want anyone to follow me for I was returning home to a familiar place, within four walls, where I could wallow in my sorrow and despair. This place was comfortable in that I knew it oh so well. I did not give up hope. I did not stop loving and believing in God, but I felt God in all His power and might had done bitter with me. I began to quietly confess "Do not call me Crystal call me "Mara" for the Almighty hath dealt very bitterly with me". (Ruth 1:19-21). Onlookers looked at me as if to say "Can that really be Crystal? She looks like Crystal but she has changed a bit through the years, through the seasons, I remember when she used to look like ...". I silently responded within "I went out full, and the LORD hath brought me home again empty: why then call ye me Crystal, seeing the LORD hath testified against me, and the Almighty hath afflicted me?"

I believe some of us get to the point in our lives when we do not feel or look our best. Yet in God's eye, we are still "The apple of his eye". If we remain in His unchanging hands, if we hold on to the true vine as the branch, we will shine through even the darkest times. When all hope appears to be gone, we have to continue to believe that God is going to turn our situations around and that He is going to see us through. We have all His promises to stand on so that we don't get weary in well doing, so that we continue to run the race and not faint. God has promised in His word that he is going to strengthen us. We just have to believe and have faith and stay in the race.

God is going to send people like Ruth into our lives to comfort us, to glean in the fields of our lives and collect bit by bit. People who will give us new hope, life, strength, to walk each step of the way with us. People who love us and who care for us when we grieve and people who will encourage us when we feel despair. Yes, it is always nice to have someone in the natural, whether it be a husband, a good friend, or companion, but God is always everpresent. He is omnipresent. Anything we need Him to be, He is. God is really all we need, but God loves us so much He grants us our heart desires and so much more. He wants to be our everything. God does not want us to place **IDOLS**, people, places or things before Him, and that is why He is not always quick to act on our behalf until He can trust that we will indeed keep Him *First.* It is only when we begin to seek Him *First* and Keep Him *First* that He adds all things unto our lives.

In the story of Ruth and Naomi, Naomi really did not want to be alone. She isolated herself because she did not want others to know she needed them, but God searched her heart and looked beyond her faults and saw her needs. Naomi prayed to God to help her through this state. She did not know how to deal or handle the situation she was facing. She planned a pity party for herself and she did not want to invite anyone to her pity party. Has anyone been there? This is where the devil comes in to remind us of our current state. "Where is your God now the devil may say?" Well, I am a living testimony that God is right there.

You have to trust Him even when you cannot trace Him. Sometimes He wants us to go through different situations for our good. You do not know how you are going to benefit from your experiences or how others are going to benefit from your experiences, but God does. You do not know always how you are going to bless someone by going through your trials and tribulations, but you do know it is going to be for your good because the bible says so.

Naomi lost a lot in her lifetime yet her latter days were greater in that she gained so much from her life experiences because she continued to live and not die and hold onto the true vine. Ruth gained so much from Naomi's experience because she continued to live and not die and hold onto the true vine. These two women also held onto each other. They were both destitute and desperate for in those times a woman without a man was destined for failure. Kind of sounds like today's times, huh. These two women pulled together and clung together in their weakness, looking to the same God for provision and they obtained refound strength and hope. God heard their cries from heaven and He began to open doors for them and place people in their life like Boaz who blessed them beyond measure. God made a way out of no way. When God is for you, who can be against you? Naomi and Ruth's latter days were indeed greater.

I thank God for my Naomi/Ruth experience. I was right at the end of my rope so to speak where I felt like giving up but did not know how for I knew God's word. God's word was deep down in my belly. I had tasted His goodness. His Holy Spirit dwelled within my soul. I did not know how to quit or how to give up. Every time I felt like giving up God said "Don't Give Up, Don't Quit". As God continued to encourage me, I continued on the journey. I had heard the preacher say one day that "there was no way I could fail in Christ for in Christ there is no failure". Yet, my circumstances looked and felt like I was a done deal! When I felt like I had lost it all, I kept the faith! I kept believing and trusting God! I kept calling on His name! I kept standing on His word! I kept seeking Him early in the morning! I kept PUSH-ing (praying until something happened)!

God began to whisper in my ear in a calm and quiet voice as He gently held me close in His arms. He said "My dear child, I love you and I want you to have and experience My very best. I wish above all things for you to prosper and be in good health just as your soul prospereth. If only you would trust Me and place your faith in Me and only Me and surrender your will to My perfect will. Then and only then will you see that "I AM THAT I AM" (Exodus 3:14). Then and only then will you know that I can and that I am able to bring things to pass in your life exceedingly, abundantly above all that you could imagine or ask. For My thoughts are not your thoughts and My ways are not your ways, but you my dear just simply have to trust Me".

With all the strength that I had left in me I said "Okay". Yes, I was so weak and weary, that all I could say in my prostrate state was "Okay". God had humbled me to a state where all I could do is look up to heaven and say one word "Okay". Now do not think I said "Okay" and then everything changed that second? No, "faith without works is dead. God just wants us to first say "Yes" and He will do the rest. After we say "Yes", God will begin to order our steps and give us specific instructions to follow in order to carry out His Master Plan. At that present time in my life, I needed help with my five anointed praise dancers, a/k/a, my children, ages 11 and under. "I had my hands full" and I was weary, mind, body and soul. I keep pushing, praying and pressing in the natural and in the spirit, but it just seemed like I was getting nowhere.

Even when everything around me said "What you are attempting to do is impossible". I knew God's word said "all things are possible", so I treaded water even when I could not swim. I kept treading even when it felt like I was sinking. I just held on like God had just thrown me a floatie when I could no longer tread. Most times I had to "encourage myself in the Lord". I had a praying grandmother, I had a praying mother, I had a praying aunt, I had a praying father, I had praying children, I had prayer warrior friends and church families, we just kept on praying and believing and then one day God spoke. He said "Call Irene at Crittenton Centers".

Crittenton Centers is a local child care facility that provides quality care services for children ages 7 and under and to families in emergency/crisis situations. The agency has qualified staff trained to care for your children by providing food, shelter, support and services aimed at helping families in need. I had utilized the Crittenton Centers daycare and their Crisis Nursery for quite sometime. Dan, who was supervisor of the Crisis Nursery was very instrumental and helpful in providing services to me and my family in our times of need. Yet, they did not always have enough time, space or staff available to meet the greater needs of their clients and the community at large. Nevertheless, they did an excellent job and the best that they could do for me and many others and for that I am so thankful and grateful.

So I called Irene who happened to be one of my old friends and sister in Christ. She was working as a family specialist at Crittenton Centers at the time, and I simply asked her if she could help me in any kind of way. I told her I was in crisis and I really needed her to intercede on my behalf. She was eager to help and we talked and troubleshooted together about different options.

She referred me to a friend of hers who she strongly recommended would be a good resource to help me with my children. Her name was Nikkia. She was a young Christian girl, a dedicated and committed servant of God, Sunday School teacher, choir member, director of the children's choir at church, college student, fiancée, manager of a fast food restaurant. She was the type of person that I was honored to meet. So we met and the connection was divine.

She seemed to be more eager and willing to help me than I was in getting help. For help to me meant "someone picking you up to drop you back down even further". I had asked so many people to help and they had disappointed me, so I was kind of scared to ask yet I was at a place I knew I could go no further without supernatural intervention.

You see, I had prayed so hard for a miracle that when the miracle was staring me dead in my face I did not recognize it. Now that is the thing with me. It seems it always happens that way. God does not give me any type of clues when He is going to bless me for He knows if He does I will probably mess it all up. He only blesses me and then keeps on blessing me, in His timing. No questions, no explanations. The bible says on this matter, "And the cities that are inhabited shall be laid waste, and the land shall be desolate; and ye shall know that I am the LORD". (Ezekiel 12:20). My Naomi experience definitely allowed me to know the Lord thy God. Yes, there is no doubt in my mind that God worked it out and turned my situation around and I just give Him all the glory. Everything that has happened to me in life, whether good or bad, I thank God for everything and give Him all the glory for He alone is worthy.

Nikkia and her fiancé Troy, a/k/a, Boaz in this story began to minister to me and help me and my family. They let me know that they were honored to do their part and happy to do their part all for God's glory. They let me know that helping children and families and people was their ministry.

The best part is not only did they do it out of the kindness of their hearts, they practically volunteered most of their time and spent their hard earned money and their own resources unselfishlessly just to be blessing to me and my family. I offered them money most of the time and most of the time they refused. I had explained to Nikkia from the beginning that I really did not have a lot of money, but I was wiling to pay her for her time and help and she said "Don't worry about the money. I will accept whatever you can afford to pay". Now doesn't that sound like God? Remember earlier in the story Ms. Ida said the same thing to me when she first intervened to bless me and my family years prior.

I thanked Nikkia and Troy and let them know how thankful and grateful I was to have them in my life and they assured me it was their pleasure and that whenever I needed them to call. They kept their promises. They showed up on time. They remained constant. They compelled me to have hope and believe that God is not only faithful, He is able. They restored my joy. They took the kids off my hands and allowed me to receive physical and spiritual rest. I mean good rest. I would often just lie in my room with the doors closed and listen to Nikkia and Troy run my whole entire household. I was playing possum for sure. Then I would come out the room to grab a bite to eat and they would always say "Now, go back to bed and get some rest". You know I did. OOOH WEEE, this is living! I even took bubble baths, snuck in a movie here and there, all on their watch. I was like a little kid again. Just resting and enjoying life once again. God is a restorer!

Nikkia and Troy invited me and my family to attend their church, Gospel Experience Church, the church of power, compassion and praise. So, I attended their church one day and was welcomed by all members of the church with such appreciation and gratitude. I wanted to be among saints that had a desire to help others and a commitment to live a godly life by example. I wanted to be around people who were not only hearers of the Word, but doers of the Word. It did not take long before me and my children felt right at home where we belonged and we decided to become members of Gospel Experience Church under the leadership of Pastor Richard K. Hammond.

God wants us to love Him and to love others just as He loves us. He commands that we love our neighbors as much as we love ourselves. That says a lot. When you have it within you to do good and you don't do good, is that giving God glory? I think not! We are to even bless our enemies. That says a lot. God makes it clear just how we should act towards believers and nonbelievers. Yet we often fall short.

Well Brother Troy (Boaz) and Sister Nikkia (Ruth) did not fall short. God was well pleased and I know He is going to bless them beyond measure. I cannot wait to see what the end is going to be for them. They began to take my children to Sunday school, church, Chuckie Cheese, McDonalds, Cici's Pizza, Perkins restaurant and different recreational and educational activities. They began to teach them manners and grace and show them how to be respectful and well mannered and behaved children in public and at home, all the things that I could not do in my tired and weary state. They even taught them how to be responsible for cleaning up after themselves. Something I did not always enforce and that did not help my weary state for I would often tire quickly from trying to maintain all the household responsibilities in my own strength.

My children loved Troy and Nikkia and the attention they were receiving and so did I and I often would tell them and mean it? "Stop spoiling us because we are not accustomed to getting any type of help". I continued to tell them that I did not want these special privileges to ruin us. I told them "You cannot quit this job until my kids are grown so don't think about leaving us now". We would all laugh, but I was serious. Well Nikkia and Troy in all sincerity assured me that I deserved it and the kids deserved it and for the first time in my life I understood it. I do deserve it. You know why? Because I am "God's Leading Lady" and I deserve God's very best, my children deserve God's very best. No longer call me "Mara", call me God's Leading Lady C, because God has blessed my latter days and they are greater. What a wonderful testimony. Praise God!

ANOTHER DAY, ANOTHER CHAPTER, ANOTHER SEASON

It is so easy to praise God when things are going right, to trust Him when the skies are blue, to worship Him when the storm is calm and there is peace in the atmosphere. Oh, but when the rivers are raging and the tide is coming in and it looks like it is going to be a flood we often run instead of worship. We often cry, whimper and complain instead of giving Him thanks and praises for all that He has done and for all that He is about to do. God is not like man, He does not go when the going gets tough. He does not sneak out the back door when we need Him. He does not leave or forsake us. Man is not reliable for in his heart and mind he says "I love You Lord, I put no one before You, You alone I shall serve whole heartedly", but when there are more bills than money, woe unto our foolish hearts for we begin to look for ways and resources to manage and cope that do not always line up with the word of God and I am not only talking about those Check into Cash establishments. Yes, you are in church worshipping and praising God on Sunday, but when you get home and look at your mess, you try to think of ways to compromise all that you have learned, and the rest of the week you negate everything that you know is right.

For that which I do I allow not: for what I would, that do I not; but what I hate, that do I. If then I do that which I would not, I consent unto the law that is good. Now then it is no more I that do it, but sin that dwelleth in me. For I know that in me (that is, in my flesh,) dwelleth no good thing: for to will is present with me; but how to perform that which is good I find not. For the good that I would I do not: but the evil which I would not, that I do. Now if I do that would not, it is no more I that do it, but sin that dwelleth in me. I find then a law; that, when I would do good, evil is present with me. For I delight in the law of God after the inward man: But I see another law in my members, warring against the law of my mind, and bringing me into captivity to the law of sin which is in my members. O wretched man that I am! who shall deliver me from the body of this death? I thank God through Jesus Christ our Lord. So then with the mind, I myself serve the law of God; but with the flesh the law of sin. (Romans 7:15-25).

I know this story and these scriptures too well and that is why I am writing about it. I have been here too many times so now God wants me to tell the world that I have victory through Him. I do not know how God is going to do it, but I know that He can. When your back is up against the wall and there are no means to an end, you won't be able to go backwards into your mess for God has cleaned up your mess and He has shifted things. He has changed your altitude and latitude. He has severed and loosed every tie. Now all you can do is keep your back up against the wall looking forward and look to the left and the right, but you cannot move. You must remain still. Not because you choose to remain still, but because you do not know the next move.

You may be an adult or child, but you do not know the next move. Is this a good place to be? Oh, yes. Does this feel like a good place to be in? Oh, no. Rest in God in this place. Stay in God in this place and you are going to see your Heavenly Father show up and show out! You are going to know without a doubt that it was God and God alone. God is going to show you that He loves you so much that this time He wanted to do it all by Himself, without your help.

<u>HAPPY VALENTINE'S DAY 2009, LOVE, JEHOVAH JIREH, YOUR PROVIDER</u>

I will share with you a little story that lead me to this conclusion. My resources were low. My support system was much better, but still I knew that without God I could do nothing. So with my few resources I tried to manage things with God's help. I filed my income taxes and was expected a nice refund. Well they decided to audit my records and place a freeze on my account. Then they took out what I owed them. So, I called to check and see when I might expect the remaining refund and they said another freeze was placed and they asked me "Do you own a business?" I said "No". They said "We will be in contact with you".

Now the bills were piling up and I did not know what to do. It was only a matter of time before the matter was going to necessitate some type of intervention. So guess what I did? I looked to the hills from which my help cometh and I began to seek God wholeheartedly and do not think I sought Him without asking, "Why me Lord?" and wanting to cry like a baby and wanting to have a tantrum like a 2 year old, but this time I actually did not. I simply thought in my mind and knew in my heart that God was Jehovah Jireh, my Provider. God knew I was serious this time, for God knows your heart and He knows your thoughts even before you think them.

I began to talk "real talk" to Jesus in this humble state and said these very words. *"Lord, I know about Your servant Job, but I do not want to be like Your servant Job. I don't want to lose everything before I gain more. I want my latter years to be greater, but I do not want to go through all that Job went through to attain it. Lord, I want the glory without the story."* God continued to listen and encourage me. I said *"Lord, give me a sign that you are going to get me out of this mess."*

God continued to love me through all of this. God spoke and said "Do the things which I ask you to do. I said *"but God ..."*. Have you ever been there saying "but God ...?" Have you ever walked in my shoes and been under the pressures I was under? God kept speaking "You know what you are supposed to do; you are the only one delaying your blessing in that you are not doing what is required of you". So I listened and I began to do some of the things that were required of me since it looked like I had no choice.

One thing I knew I was supposed to be doing is writing this book. So I began to write again. I said maybe I wont get out of this situation today, but I will write every day about my troubles just like they did in the Book of Psalms and I will write about God and how He was so merciful to get me out. I want the whole world to know that God is faithful and that He alone is able. I want the whole world to see the glory of God in my story. So bless God and Amen as I continue to write about My God.

Valentine's Day 2009, "Lord I thank You for keeping me and loving me everyday 24/7 and celebrating me everyday 24/7. I know that man made Valentine's Day and that You designed me for someone special that You are preparing for me right now. I receive this person by faith and I celebrate our unity and until then I appreciate and cherish that You are the apple of my eye and I am the apple of Your eye. Happy Valentine's Day and thank you for continuing to do a great work in me and through me for Your glory! Hugs and Kisses, XOXOXO!"

I BEGIN TO PROPHECY TO MY SITUATION
I SPEAK LIFE TO THE SPIRIT OF DEPRESSION

Lift up your heads O ye gates; and be ye lift up ye everlastings doors; and the King of glory shall come in. Who is this King of glory? The LORD strong and mighty, the LORD mighty in battle. Lift up your heads O ye gates; even lift them up ye everlasting doors: and the King of glory shall come in. Who is this King of glory? The LORD of hosts, he is the King of glory. Selah. (Psalm 24:7-10).

Release everything you are going through right now to God and give Him praise. Do not hold on to the old when God is doing a new thing in your life. Your breakthrough, blessings, healing, peace and joy are in your praise. Lift up your heads O ye gates; and be ye lifted up ye everlasting doors and the King of glory shall come in!

I SPEAK LIFE TO THE SPIRIT OF LONELINES

Who shall separate us from the Love of Christ? shall tribulation, or distress, or persecution, or famine, or nakedness, or peril, or sword? As it is written, For thy sake we are killed all the daylong: we are accounted as sheep for the slaughter. Nay in all these things we are more than conquerors through him that loved us. For I am persuaded, that neither death, nor life, nor angels, nor principalities, nor powers, nor things present, nor things to come, nor height, Nor depth, nor any other creature, shall be able to separate us from the love of God which is in Christ Jesus our Lord. (Romans 8:35-39).

Stand through life obstacles and oppositions remembering that in Christ you will always come out flourished, equipped, and empowered to live a victorious life. You will go from victory to victory to victory and everything in between is just the process. God has everything worked out perfectly and He knows the beginning through the end, so just rest in Him and remain in His resting place!

IMAGINE ME *~cyh~*

Imagine me, living a life of victory, walking daily by faith and trusting God for everything.
Imagine me, not knowing what today or tomorrow will bring, but knowing that
God has His eye on the sparrow and knowing that He also watches over me.
Imagine me, arising early in the morning while everyone else sleeps
to be in His presence, seeking His face and not His hand.
Imagine me, finding comfort and joy throughout all my trials and tribulations in His
loving arms. Imagine me, drawing nearer to Him as my closet friend. When the enemy
comes in like a flood, He raises up a standard for He is my refuge, my fortress.
Imagine me, when the storms of life seem like they will never end, He gives me peace in
the midst of the storm for my God is sovereign. He delivers me out of all my troubles.
Imagine me, when I am worried and distressed He brings me rest and assurance
in a way that no man can do. He is the keeper of my soul. I shall forever give Him
praise. I shall forever thank Him for allowing me to live out my life for His glory.
Imagine me, living a fantasy life of abundance while in reality
actually having a life of abundance in Him.

Oh how I know trouble, hardship, persecution, famine, nakedness, danger and the sword, but God still is my rock. I am still here to tell the story for His glory. **MY IDOL** thought he had sifted me as wheat, but I am still more than a conqueror in Christ Jesus not because of my works or my merits, but because of His grace, His mercy and because He loves me and cares for me.

Imagine me, being so loved by God that He gave his only begotten son to die on the cross for the forgiveness of my sins, for my salvation, for me. That is the greatest love. It brings a smile to my face and my heart knowing that I have tapped into a love so rich. Some may never find a love like this, but I am thankful that I have and I won't let go. I will never be lonely again, for I am not alone. God is with me. Nothing and no one will ever separate me from the love of Christ. How awesome is that?

THE EFFECTUAL FERVENT PRAYER OF A RIGHTEOUS MAN AVAILETH MUCH

Confess your faults one to another, and pray one for another; that ye may be healed. The effectual fervent prayer of a righteous man availeth much. (James 5:16).

After this manner therefore pray ye: Our Father which art in heaven, Hallowed be thy name. Thy kingdom come. Thy will be done in earth, as it is in heaven. Give us this day our daily bread. And forgive us our debts, as we forgive our debtors. And lead us not into temptation, but deliver us from evil: For thine is the kingdom, and the power; and the glory, forever: Amen. (Matthew 6:9-13).

And Jabez called on the God of Israel, saying, Oh that thou wouldest bless me indeed, and enlarge my coast, and that thine hand might be with me, and that thou wouldest keep me from evil, that it may not grieve me! And God granted him that which he requested. (1 Chronicles 4:10).

"Greetings Apostle/Mother Cauline. I am in need of intercessory counseling and prayer. I am presently experiencing job stress and family stress as I am a divorced singled parent. I won't complain because I know God is keeping me, but I just wish I could stay in His rest. I lay my burdens down at the alter and then days later go back and I pick them back up and then worry sets in. It is a revolving cycle. My prayer is that I can find rest in Him and continue resting in Him and finish the course with joy. I have so much to be thankful for and I am. I pray without cease for provision and God provides daily. He is faithful."

The above is an email that I sent to Apostle Cauline of Endtime Army. It was the beginning of a new divine connection in God. I was asking her to intercede in prayer on my behalf because I felt like God was silent at this time and I really needed to hear him. What I did not understand was that I was just too busy, busy, busy again, like Martha and not sitting at His feet like Mary to listen. So I kept on being busy, busy, busy and I kept praying and asking others to intercede on my behalf. God kept speaking to me in many ways, but I could not hear him for I was too busy, busy, busy.

When I received a response from Apostle Cauline, it was quite surprising. She said "I have been expecting you. I sent a friend request to you months ago and you never responded, but God told me you would be contacting me and I thank God that you did because there is work to do". She began to minister to my heart and to my soul. She began to give me a word from the Lord. It all made sense now. I do recall receiving her friend request, but I ignored it because I was just too busy, busy, busy. God had been trying to reach me in many ways, but I just kept being like Martha, busy, busy, busy. Sound familiar or am I the only one?

"Sometimes I get sorrowful when the world makes me feel like I am not complete. Not that I need the world's approval or validation, but here is an example. I have been on my job for 13+ years with no worries or problems, but now I am starting to feel incompetent. I find myself trying to attain a production and efficiency level that seems almost unreachable. I have talked to my supervisor and other coworkers about it and they encouraged me to keep trying. I guess I have no choice. I know with God's help all things are possible. So I pray and I have faith that God will work it out just like He has in the past, somehow, someway, but that does not take the worry and concern away for I really want to do my best and I know that God expects me to do everything to glorify Him and if I don't make my production or meet the expected efficiency level, does that bring him glory? That is the question."

"As a mother I love my family and I know that my children are my blessings, but oftentimes I become weary so I pray and I have faith that God is going to give me the grace to handle it and He does, but that does not mean that at times I feel it is too much too bear. God knows the beginning through the end, but I just wanted to share this with you for I sense that you possess godly wisdom and are in a position to help me see what God sees and what I need to see and know today, tomorrow and always. Thank you my sister for listening and God Bless You."

The above quoted words are two emails that I sent to my sister in Christ, Prophetess McCoy, of Endtime Army. She responds with a word from the Lord and great encouragement. Thank you sister. Love you and God Bless You. I then say to myself, "I will continue on the journey!"

SEEING MYSELF AS GOD SEES ME, THE TRANSFORMATION

As we become more Christ-centered and kingdom-minded our desire should be to see as God sees, with clarity, with our spiritual eyes and to hear, with clarity, what thus says the Lord with our spiritual ears. God speaks in many ways. We just need to be attuned to Him. This comes with relationship with Him. In order to receive revelation from Him, we have to continue to be in relationship with Him by reading His word, prayer, praise and worship and by setting aside a time in our busy schedules to be in His presence. How can we be like Him if we don't get to know Him? We need to not only know him for who He is, we need to get to know His ways and His way of thinking and doing things. We need to know His love for us and how He wants us to love others the same, believers and unbelievers.

As we dedicate our lives to Him and allow His Holy Spirit to lead and guide us we will begin to fulfill our purpose on this earth with the comfort of knowing that He has already went out ahead of us and prepared the way. On our journey we will need to let the light of Christ shine through us so that others can see. We can accomplish this by being spirit led as we begin to speak and sow into the lives of others for kingdom purpose. God will show us how to draw others to Him.

We don't have to worry about getting cleaned up to come to Him because He is not interested in our outward appearance. He searches the heart. He is more interested in knowing that He can trust you to do His work and that you have a heart for His people, than He is in your status, your gifts/talents, your qualifications, your resume, your repertoire. God can anoint and appoint whomever He chooses to do His work.

God wants ordinary, common people after His heart who are seeking His face and not His hand. When we seek God's face, we find His heart and we tap into purpose and as we commit to purpose, we become instruments of His perfect will and not our own personal agendas. It is not about building churches, it is about building the kingdom through building the children of God.

It starts with building God's people and not tearing them down. Those that have the heart of God can do this with ease for He has equipped them to do so. They have spent so much time with Him that they know how to go out and be fishers of men (Matthew 4:19), just like their Heavenly Father. It is our Christian responsibility to teach others how to live victoriously through faith in Jesus Christ. "We are the light of the world. A city that is set on a hill cannot be hid. We have to let our light shine before men, so that they may see our good works and glorify our Father which is in heaven. We are the salt ("the flavor") of the earth. But if the salt ("the flavor") has lost his savor, wherewith shall it be salted?" (Matthew 5:13-16) Those that follow Jesus are like salt. We are called to make a difference in the world.

I thank God for being God. In the different seasons in my life I have had been blessed with the opportunity to witness God for who He truly is and witness to others who God truly is. He has been my:
Jehovah: God
Adonai: Lord
Jehovah Elohim: Eternal Creator
Jehovah Jireh: The Lord will see or provide
Jehovah Nissi: The Lord our Banner
Jehovah Ropheka: The Lord our Healer
Jehovah Shalom: The Lord our Peace
Jehovah Tsidkenu: The Lord our Righteousness
Jehovah Mekaddeshkem: The Lord our Sanctifier
Jehovah Sabaoth: The Lord of Hosts, our Deliverer
Jehovah Shammah: The Lord is present
Jehovah Elyon: The Lord Most High
Jehovah Rohi: The Lord my Shepherd
Jehovah Hoeenu: The Lord our Maker
Jehovah Eloheenu: The Lord our God
Jehovah Eloheka: The Lord thy God
Jehovah Elohay: The Lord my God

TABLETS OF MY HEART

HOMEGROWN – Midwest meets Midwest, Saturday, August 29, 2009 and Wednesday September 2, 2009. Saturday, August 29, 2009, My 21st college class reunion in Chicago. I stayed for about an hour or so just long enough to greet everyone with a friendly hug and kiss. I then embraced the opportunity to recapture my youth and my youthful desires in the time that God had bestowed upon me. It was a beautiful experience. I have never felt so much love, life, happiness and freedom mixed in one. Wednesday, September 2, 2009, a day spent doing what I enjoy, modeling and being photographed. On the above two occasions, the glory of God illuminated through my inner spirit and was portrayed in all the images taken of me by my good friend, anointed photographer, Chas Richardson. He has the God-given gift to capture the supernatural through photography and reveal it in the natural.

I will praise thee; for I am fearfully and wonderfully made: marvelous are thy works; and that my soul knoweth right well. How precious also are thy thoughts unto me, O God! How great is the sum of them! If I should count them, they are more in number than the sand: when I awake, I am still with thee. (Psalm 139:14,17-18).

I posted the finished work on Facebook under the photo album entitled "Midwest Meets Midwest". I wanted everyone to celebrate life with me. Something I found hard to do in the past. My photo album read as follows:

"I would like to first and foremost thank God for allowing me to embrace my heart's desire of modeling in my starring role as God's Leading Lady C. God miraculously planned this one out to perfection and I am living in the Celebration. I would like to thank Chas Richardson, skilled photographer, my life-long friend. I would like to thank my loving daughter Krishina who styled my hair with her God-given artistic gift of hairstyling. She knows that when mom gets her hair done something big is about to take place. I would like to thank my God-daughter Nikkia for allowing me to borrow her shoes and accessories. I would like to thank my little ones for spending time with their wonderful father so that mommy could have some long overdue Me Time. Last but not least, I would like to thank all of my FB family for your ongoing love and support. I must say I felt like Cinderella for just one moment in time. It was even better than I had imagined."

On the last picture of the album, I left everyone with a cliffhanger that stated "Some love to envy and some love to be envied!" with a double back turn and a smile. God's Lady C walked out her destiny on this one. All praises due to God and all the glory belongs to Him.

You see looking back on my personal Cinderella story where I experienced the hate and bitterness of a wicked stepmother and wicked stepsisters, not that my experience was the same, but I felt what Cinderella felt so many times, hurt, abuse, neglect. Yet, God is a restorer and in that moment in time in Chicago, I felt something magical happen. Alone with God once again looking out upon Lake Michigan as far as my eyes could see with my bare feet in the sand, I lifted my eyes and hands to heaven, declaring and decreeing that my latter days were greater and promising to never again look back upon my life the same.

I am so thankful that I captured this moment through pictures so that the world could see what I saw. Pictures to me are like a 1000 words. I have a massive collection of pictures that I have accumulated over the years and I value each one. I will always treasure that moment in time in Chicago. I felt free. I felt beautiful. As I walked in the water on the shoreline on Lake Michigan, as I experienced the wind beneath my wings and as I looked up to the skyline, I thanked God for another opportunity to experience the beauty of His handiwork. There was a release in my spirit that was captured in each picture. I was not worried about anyone or anything. It was my time with the Lord, my Prince Charming, as He escorted me to the ball that I never got invited to, the ball that I was never allowed to go to, and the ball that my wicked stepmother and stepsisters thought I would never be able to attend. God's Leading Lady C finally made it to the ball with her King. Yes!

As onlookers and passerby's on the beach looked on, I can only imagine what they thought, but at that moment it really did not matter for what God put in motion was completed and I know that He is not done yet for eyes have not seen nor ears have heard what God has in store for me. This moment made me appreciate the meaning behind the song by Mary Mary, "It's the God in Me" for it truly was not me it was the God in me all along shining for His glory. Thank You Mary Mary for singing that song to encourage others in the Lord and thank God for blessing you to be a blessing to the kingdom.

Oh and it gets better. I was reunited with a long lost friend on Facebook who I discovered loved God just as much as me. I also discovered that we had similar heart desires to live for God and to magnify God and give Him glory and to spread the gospel to the world. We both felt that if God would allow us to have the world's ear by any means necessary we would speak the truth. The passion for God was so evident in the man of God's speech. His presence was so powerful and his words had such magnitude. As he ministered to me and I ministered to him it was as if God placed us in the same place at the same time. It was apparent that we both had been in the same hiding place for many years, hidden under His wings.

It was then that I realized something great, when you are seeking God you find exactly what you need. I had wanted many things in life, but what I needed and desired was already in place for me. So, I began to take all of this in at face value. I learned from timespast not to get ahead of God so for that moment, I decided to just rest in Him. At 43 years of age, I had finally learned how to do just that.

It seemed as if while everyone else around me was experiencing a recession, I was experiencing a progression. It was my season of renewal. God had prepared me for such a time as this. Wonderful, Great Architect, WOW, His Master Plan was perfect. He indeed knew the beginning through the end. He finished before He started! God is magnificant!

I could go on and on and never end when it comes to talking about His goodness. I remember the days when I was ashamed of having eight children and even desired not to have the burden at times. As a small child, I always dreamed of having ten kids, five girls and five boys, but that was because I watched The Brady Bunch daily and a big family looked easy for Carol because she had Mike, Alice, the butler, and she was a stay home mom, etc. Not that I did not love my children, but it takes great strength and courage to raise a big family, something I did not believe I had. Yet, God knew what He had placed in me and He knew that one day I would realize it too. Life has a way of showing you what is important and what is not and what is important to me is family whether small, medium or large. It is my most valuable possession! With this newfound knowledge I decided I would see my children as God sees them in good times and in bad times.

So now I declare and decree "Happy is the man that hath his quiver full of them: they shall not be ashamed, but they shall speak with the enemies in the gate". (Psalm 127:5).

That is exactly what I am doing. So for all those that don't value me and my eight anointed and appointed children and five anointed and appointed grandsons and say I have missed my mark or even skipped a beat, I will say "God Bless you, I am right where God wants me to be".

The Lord placed in my spirit "Lo, children are an heritage of the Lord: and the fruit of the womb is his reward". (Psalm 127:3). I concur! I am blessed and highly favored in the Lord today and the fruits I bear confirm it to be so. Lord, I will continue to trust You. I have tried my way and now I choose to try Yours. Glory to God!

Thank You father for choosing me. Thank You for naming me Crystal. Crystal means transparent. You designed me so that brilliant light could illuminate through me. You wanted everyone to see through me so that they could see You. Hallelujah! What an honor. It is no wonder **MY IDOL** tried to kill me in my mother's womb and throughout my lifetime. It is no wonder he has been on assignment to abort the destiny that You have placed within my womb to be birthed in Your timing, but Your grace and mercy said "No". Thank You for Your grace and Your mercy. For Your mercy endureth forever. Your grace is new each dawning day. Thank You Lord.

Thank You for not allowing death to visit by door. Thank You for not allowing sickness to dwell among me or my family. For I declare and decree healing by Your stripes even before the diagnosis. As the doctors continue to scratch their heads and wonder, I tell them, "All is well by faith". When the lab tests are in and they are optimal levels I say "God is a healer". I will believe the report of the Lord that says "I am whole". I will praise You, honor You and magnify You forever. I will tell everyone of Your goodness as long as You allow blood to flow through my body. As long as You give me a voice and mind to speak, I will speak. Your name I will proclaim, confess and profess. Thank You Father, Thank You. Thank You. Thank You.

September, 2009, a friend of mine/sister in Christ, Christine, contacted me to give me a word from the Lord. She had a vision that she received in a dream and was led to tell me for she did not understand why she was dreaming about me and why she had the vision for we really did not talk that much outside of church activities and Christian fellowship. The vision was as follows. "I see a large gathering of women, artwork. Do you do artwork?" I said "No". She continues, "You are wearing the colors yellow and black, a checkered print. There are two dogs, one is a mean dog that is growling and snarling and it looks like he is injured and has hurt his foot. He is trying to get in the room, but the door is shut."

I then begin to try to interpret the dream to better understand what she is telling me so I say to her "I believe the dream represents ministry. I believe God has given me a ministry to minister to the sick, lost, hurting and wounded souls. I believe it is healing and deliverance ministry that you see." I thought to myself the mean dog is probably **MY IDOL,** but if he hurt his foot I really don't want to help him. So, I thought to myself, I do not like this interpretation for I wanted a happy ending. So, I gave her another interpretation. I, so badly wanting a "Happily Ever After" ending, changed the dream interpretation again to "It is a bridal shower and the wedding is going to be on an island, a cruise ship on the ocean. She interrupts and says "I did see an island and the ocean… but …". She persisted in saying "It looked like two mean dogs and one was injured ...". I interrupted and said "It was probably two men fighting over me … laughing out loud." She laughed with me as she continued to interpret the dream and said "One has a beard and one is without a beard and they are arguing." I said to myself "Who are these men?" even though I knew. I also knew that dogs do not have beards. I then asked her "Who won?" She said, "I don't know, that is all I can remember". I thought to myself these are questions that God will reveal in His timing.

Thank you Sister Christine for your obedience in giving me that revelation and sorry for misinterpreting it to meet my needs in my own strength. At that time, I thought I knew what was best for me so I acted in the flesh again ("somebody say again ….") believing that "A girl has to do what she has to do!" as I proceeded to go out shopping for the yellow/black checkered print and found it too, believing that if I purchased it I could help bring this prophecy to pass. Yes, still trying to help God out and not surrendering to the process.

You see, this is how I always get in trouble, trying to help God out. I oftentimes try to figure out God's master plan. I really mean no harm, I just always try to analyze things and I am often just curious about how He is going to do things and in what manner and yes I too become impatient. God simply wants us to trust Him and believe that He can perform what He already wants to do on our behalves without our interference. When we activate our faith we show God that we trust Him and we believe Him. Without faith, it is impossible to please Him. When we constantly try to figure God out and help God out, we are not using faith and we are frustrating Him and slowing Him down. Real Talk!

OUR SOUL & BREATH ARE IN HIS HAND

But ask now the beasts, and they shall teach thee; and the fowls of the air, and they shall tell thee: Or speak to the earth, and it shall teach thee: and the fishes of the sea shall declare unto thee. Who knoweth not in all these that the hand of the Lord hath wrought this? In whose hand is the soul of every living thing, and the breath of all mankind. (Job 12:7-10).

This scripture was a relevation to me. I am so amazed because we oftentimes take life for granted. Knowing that our very breath is in His hand makes us realize that our next breath is not promised to us if not for His sovereign grace and mercy. If we are willing and obedient God has so much in store for us, yet the opposite of this is not so promising. We really need to get the full revelation of God's word and know that if we want to continue prospering even to the very height, width and depth of each hour, minute and second and our next breath, we need to thank God for everything even the fact that He continues to be the Keeper of our soul. We should find much hope in this.

MY QUESTION TO GOD

Who can find a virtuous woman? For her price is far above rubies. The heart of her husband doth safely trust in her, so that he shall have no need of spoil. She will do him good and not evil all the days of her life. She seeketh wool, and flax, and worketh willingly with her hands. She is like the merchants' ships; she bringeth her food from afar. She riseth also while it is yet night, and giveth meat to her household and a portion to her maidens. She considereth a field, and buyeth it: with the fruit of her hands she planteth a vineyard. She girdeth her loins with strength, and strengtheneth her arms. She perceiveth that her merchandise is good: her candle goeth not out by night. She layeth her hands to the spindle, and her hands hold the distaff. She stretcheth out her hand to the poor; yea, she reacheth forth her hands to the needy. She is not afraid of the snow for her household: for all her household are clothed with scarlet. She maketh herself coverings of tapestry; her clothing is silk and purple. Her husband is known in the gates, when he sitteth among the elders of the land. She maketh fine linen, and selleth it; and delivereth girdles unto the merchant. Strength and honor are her clothing; and she shall rejoice in time to come. She openeth her mouth with wisdom; and in her tongue is the law of kindness. She looketh well to the ways of her household, and eateth not the bread of idleness. Her children arise up, and call her blessed; her husband also, and he praiseth her. Many daughters have done virtuously, but though excellest them all. Favor is deceitful, and beauty is vain: but a woman that feareth the Lord, she shall be praised. Give her of the fruit of her hands; and let her own works praise her in the gates. (Proverbs 31:10-31).

GOD ANSWERS

Delight thyself also in the LORD: and he shall give thee the desires of thine heart. Commit thy way unto the LORD; trust also in him; and he shall bring it to pass. (Psalm 37:4-5).

But seek ye first the kingdom of God, and his righteousness; and all these things shall be added unto you. (Matthew 6:33).

MY PERSONAL PRAYER

Father, I know that I have broken Your laws over and over again by trying to obtain my heart's desires and bring things to pass in my own strength. Help me to trust You even when I cannot trace You. Help me to seek Your face and not Your hand. Help me to seek Your kingdom and Your righteousness. Help me Father. It is me, Your daughter, once again standing in the need of prayer. Have mercy on me Father once again. Amen.

RELATIONSHIPS 101 *~cyh~*

(CURRICULUM DESIGNED WITH WOMEN IN MIND BUT MEN ARE WELCOME)

I digress again and again and again, a revolving door, yet God is still God!

The Charmer. He is smooth and silky. He looks good. He smells good. He talks good. Feels good. He says all the right things. He does all the right things. He makes you feel like a woman. He walks right. He talks right. He appears to be almost perfect. You leave his presence remembering **"what he did"** and you ask yourself these questions.

Was he really my prince charming that swept me off my feet?

He took me on a carriage/buggy ride with a white horse, could he be the one?

He took me to a 5+ star hotel with wine, candlelight, fine dining, chocolate heart candies, should I give in to the feeling?

He bought me long stem roses, Godiva chocolate, treated me to a day at the spa, could he be the one?

Could God have sent me an angel of light?

The Deceiver. He is slick and cunning. His outer appearance is not as attractive as what is coming out his mouth. He makes promises that he can't keep. He tells you half truths but since you know nothing about him you won't discover what you need to know until its too late. This is what he specializes in "deception". He preys on victims that don't ask questions and just allow whatever happens to them to happen. He is very insecure and loves to gain control and overpower his companion to increase his confidence and desire for control. You leave his presence and what you remember is not what he did but **"what he said"**.

He said "I was beautiful, the woman of his dreams".

He said "I was everything he prayed for".

He said "I was a dime".

He said "I was the bomb".

He said "I am the best he ever had".

He said "I remind him of Janet Jackson. Am I really as pretty as her?"

He said "I got "flava", I wonder what flavor he thinks I am?"

The Opportunist. He is not very attractive. Your attraction to him is his "so called" knowledge and his "so called" confidence. He is a "so called" entrepreneur. He talks fast. He talks a lot. He is a professional hustler. He does not let you get a word in and when he does you tell him way too much. He keeps track of everything you say because he has a plan. He plans to take the "opportunity" to get what he wants from you. It is NOT about love, it is about the "opportunity". You have something he needs. You leave his presence thinking **"he has what I need"**. He is skilled with selling himself, i.e. professional businessman.

He is good with his hands.

He has his own business. He is an entrepreneur.

He knows how to fix things.

He knows how to work on cars.

He has a nice place and it is nicely furnished.

He has a nice car and he plans to … (you fill in the blanks).

He appears to be loving and caring.

He said "Anytime I need him to call him he would love to help me".

He said "When he gets out of (jail, prison, debt, etc.), he is going to marry me".

He said "When he gets a divorce he is going to marry me".

He said "He wants me to have his baby because he loves me".

He said "I am the best".

The User: He comes in all different shapes, colors and sizes. His main objective is to get what he wants. He does not want to make a commitment. He just want you to be available on an as needed basis. Oh, he cares about you don't get me wrong. He cares that you will be there when he needs you. You leave his presence thinking **"This is as good as it is going to get, I might as well compromise. It does not look like there are many fish left in the sea"**. Users prey on victims because they are victims themselves. Misery loves company.

He said "If I don't give him "none", he will go somewhere else and get it".

He said "If I let him borrow some money he will pay me back (when – You fill in the blanks) he gets his check".

He said "His wife don't treat him right".

He said "He just wanted a friend because he is trying to get over his past bad relationship where his girlfriend dogged him out".

He said "I was everything he misses at home and he just needs a good friend by his side".

He said "He does not know how he is going to make it because all his bills are overdue and he lost his job because of "The Man" or "The Woman" was against him".

He said "He can't imagine life without me and that he just has to have me, but he said I have to get a babysitter for my kids first".

He said "He will help me pay for a babysitter for my kids if I need him to, but I definitely have to get one because we cannot take them with us".

The Self-Righteous: He knows the word of God. He knows how to pray. He knows about the basics of religion, but has not quite figured out that they apply to him also. He is always right even when he is wrong. He always talks about improving and changing things. He is very focused and determined on his own personal agendas. You leave his presence feeling like **"you are glad you left his presence so that you can actually hear yourself think"**. You then start saying things to yourself like, **"I would rather have a "bad boy" that a "self-righteous goody two-shoes"** who is stuck on trying to fix me according to his idea of perfection that by the way does not having anything to do with the word of God. Everything he tells you and does, just line it up with the word of God and you will see the difference. Just pray, watch and pray some more for the Self-Righteous man.

He said "God has been saving me for 20 years for you".

He said "He was attracted to me because I am a Woman of Virtue".

He said "I am Queen of God and that my words are powerful".

He said "He has his own house, his own car, his own this, his own that, his, his, his, his ..."

Okay people, well I know you can relate to one of the above categories and examples. Believe me, you can do your own chart, graph and analysis, but it all boils down to this Matthew 6:33. All of the above categories are timewasters. We need to be good stewards of everything that God has given us and for me, time is the most valuable possession. Why waste your time in ungodly relationships. God has you set apart for a reason and that reason being His purpose. Seek Him and His righteousness and He will add all things unto you. You no longer have to go looking for people, places and things to be your **IDOLS**. Put God *First* and keep God *First* until He releases you to your husband or wife to be!

COURTSHIP ASSESSMENT TEST *~cyh~*

If a man of God knocks on your door and tells you anything that God has not already confirmed in your spirit, immediately ask him for three forms of identification including a driver's license, work ID and checkbook. Make sure everything on his driver's license is correct. If he does not have a checkbook make sure he has an active major credit card that has not exceeded its credit limit. You may have to call customer service to verify this information. If everything seems to check out okay stay at your front door, one foot in the door and keep the door partially open and partially closed. After you have confirmed that everything has checked out correctly, you may begin to ask specific questions to complete your Courtship Assessment of the individual in question. Ask him if he is saved, sanctified, justified and filled with the Holy Ghost.

If he smiles and there is a long pause, know that he is a Charmer and kindly shut the door.

If he stutters and then answers quickly, know that he is a Deceiver and kindly shut the door.

If he pauses and looks confused, know that he is a User and kindly shut the door.

If he looks surprised and then gives you a long drawn out speech and adds three biblical scriptures to it know that he is Self-righteous and kindly shut the door.

If he happens to answer you correctly with a straight face and a stern look of confidence and you discern that he is genuine, sincere and that he truly is an honest man, then kindly invite him in and ask if he would like something to drink i.e. water, tea, coffee, soda or juice, wine if it is not Sunday. Begin to inquire about his career, his life in general conversation without prying too much. Ask him about his family, his dreams, his aspirations, where he lives, where he was born, where he grew up, what schools he graduated from, what year he graduated from high school, his age, weight, height, blood type, his highest level of achievement, his college aptitude score, his IQ status, his educational and work experience, etc.

If he still seems genuine, sincere and appears to be truly an honest man, continue to talk and ask him if he would like something to eat i.e. snack, appetizer, sandwich, or dessert. Ask him would he like a refill on his drink. As he is eating and drinking, begin to talk to him about his 5 year and 10 year projective goals and plans and inquire as to how he plans on implementing his said projective goals and plans. See if he offers any information regarding i.e. furthering his education, advancing up the career ladder, advancing in ministry, a good business proposal or plan, a creative idea or witty invention, settling down, getting married and starting a family, building a home, purchasing a pet, purchasing a motor vehicle. Find out specifics like whether he plans to purchase a sports car, sedan, luxury, SUV or minivan. Find out if he has plans to travel and what countries, cities or islands are on his itinerary.

If he still sounds sincere and genuine in all his answers and you truly believe that he is indeed an honest man. Ask him the following additional questions which should complete your Courtship Assessment Test: What is your FICA score, what is your credit score, have you ever been in foreclosure, have you ever filed bankruptcy or Chapter 13 or Chapter 7 or Chapter 11 (*you don't even have to know what these chapters mean just ask quickly, time is of the essence), have you ever been more than two months late on any bill, have you ever been convicted of a felony or misdemeanor, been on probation, have you ever been hospitalized, have you ever tested positive for any communicable disease or STD, what is your HIV status, do you have proof of this status and have you been tested within the last 6 months and if so can you show proof, ask him what he feels about sex outside of marriage, ask him is he up to date on his medical and dental exams and all immunizations, ask him is he current on all his medical lab work, testing and screening, ask him does he have a retirement plan, 401K, burial insurance, life insurance, homeowner's insurance, flood insurance, earthquake insurance, long-term disability insurance, medical and dental insurance, car insurance, stocks and bonds, CDs (and not the CDs for pictures, music or movies), ask him does he have a will and power of attorney for property and health care. You may have repeated several questions and asked them twice, but don't worry, just stay on track and continue.

Now, hopefully now you can still say that he is a genuine and sincere and truly an honest man. Here is a for sure way of finding out. If after you ask him all of the above questions he says, really nicely, "Why do you ask?" Just pause for a couple of seconds and move in closer to him until you are right at his side and hold his hands within your hands and look him directly in the face, eyeball to eyeball and say "God gave me five senses and I plan on using every single one of them". ROTFL (rolling on the floor laughing). I love ya with the love of God on purpose, and "you know this" that is why I can just be real with you - a big Holy Ghost laugh.

Now I am not going to waste my time or paper on making this a chapter in this book just know that I have tried every category and example above in Relationships 101 and it did not work. I then took the final exam, the Courtship Assessment Test, and passed it with a 110% grade, an A+. So if you are really serious about finding a Woman of God/Woman of Virtue/Virtuous Woman or a Man of God/Man of Virtue or a Boaz, then go back to the instructions that God has given you in Hs word in Matthew 6:33. Better yet, I will just copy and paste it until you get it.

If you need extra credit take home work you can study My Life Application Study Guide. My Life Application Study Guide says in a nutshell, "Leave All Stray Dogs At The Pound!" or was that a wise woman who said that? Lord, let me stop trying to lie and "sugarcoat" this message. Here goes nothing, "I said it! Now! I am the wise woman that said it, but a wise woman probably once thought it! So, again, the devil is a liar, not me! Hallelujah!

Time out for looking for Mr. Right and Mr. Right Now! It is time for you to let God send the one, not the two or three or four or five you have picked out and picked up along the way. It is time for you to allow God to choose what is best for you and prepare him and send him your way. It is time for God to send the right one He wants in your life and take out the wrong ones that He does not! Case closed, end of story! Stop getting ahead of God and falling short by engaging in unhealthy and ungodly relationships that lead to fulfilling sinful pleasures and worldly desires. Stop fornicating! "Why would he buy the cow when he can get the milk free?" Why would Mr. Right take your hand in marriage if he can get all the benefits of marriage without the obligations and responsibilities that the covenant of marriage holds? Close your legs and open your eyes and ears, God is speaking to you right now!

Stop looking to man and look to God! Stop listening to man and listen to God! You don't need a suga daddy/pimp/trick daddy. You have a Heavenly Father who can supply all your needs. That is something your suga daddy can never do. Your suga daddy needs Jesus probably more than you. Don't get it twisted suga mama! Yes, I said it and I meant it and I won't take it back! Matter of fact, I am going to add more to it! I won't take back the truth, because I know it will set you free just like it set me free.

Oh, I am done for now and I hope I did not offend anyone, but I had to get that off of my chest. I feel so much better now, but I am tired now. I need to rest. I think I will go take my family to Disney World after this book is published, because ya done wore me out! I have so much more to say, but I won't get ahead of God. Ya just gone have to wait on the next book. Know that I am going to tell everything God says to tell you as He gives it to me and everything He says to not tell, I am going to hold my peace.

Everybody who really knows me knows that I am the best secret keeper and if you tell me to keep it a secret, you won't hear it from me. Oh no, I am not one to gossip, no siree, you won't hear it from me, but if you tell me to tell it, well put it like this, I can show you better than I can tell you. In the natural I am kind of shy with a timid spirit, but in the Spirit I am bold as a lion, a real big loud mouth! I won't shut up talking about Jesus! I have truly been nice here, that is because I am prayed up. I prayed without cease to God daily that this book be written in His words and not mine because if I had my way, I would have gave it to you straight no chasers, but I don't know if it would have glorified God. Anywho, I think I managed to stick of few lines in every now and then. Thank God for His grace and His mercy for not deleting and editing out those few lines I stuck in there. Hallelujah!

If God gives me ear to hear it, the microphone to speak it or pen and paper to write it, or a computer to type it, know that I am going to speak it, teach it and preach it in the pulpit, in the choir stand, in every pew, in the church parking lot, in the streets, in the byways and highways. I will no longer be quiet. I will no longer let the devil shut my mouth. What goes on at home won't stay at home no longer! No, that is not going to work for me any longer. I come against the spirit of deception in the name of Jesus, for nothing should be going on in private or public that does not glorify God, whether it is in the streets or between the sheets. My grandmother used to always tell me "Charity begins at home and spreads abroad". God is going to ensure that the love of God within me dwells among me and throughout His kingdom. If I continue to be willing and obedient to God, I shall inherit the good of the land and everything and everyone connected to me shall receive the overflow.

But seek ye first the kingdom of God, and his righteousness; and all these things shall be added unto you. (Matthew 6:33).

But seek ye first the kingdom of God, and his righteousness; and all these things shall be added unto you. (Matthew 6:33).

But seek ye first the kingdom of God, and his righteousness; and all these things shall be added unto you. (Matthew 6:33).

I hope you get it now, because "I am going Green". No sense in wasting any more paper on this one topic.

If you don't get it by now, just write it out 100 times until you get it. Use paper and a No. 2 pencil with an eraser just in case you make a mistake and have to rewrite something.

The next time a man comes in your face and drops you a line ask him to recite (Matthew 6:33). If he answers correctly, conduct the above Courtship Assessment Test. If he answers incorrectly, have him write (Matthew 6:33) 100 times until he gets it.

Now men don't get mad at me because I am not a sexist. I love everybody. I am just sick and tired of "silly women", including me. I have to do this because I want you to truly have a true Woman of God/Woman of Virtue/Virtuous Woman one day. You will never ever get her if she keeps falling for these stupid traps that the enemy is setting right in front of her face on a consistent basis, even daily.

The bible even says "she is the weaker vessel" (1 Peter 3:7), so I am just trying to help the women out. You know that I am not lying when I say this. I have personally had my share of and have gone through too many Charmers, Deceivers, Users and Self-righteous men and I have had it up to here! I am telling the truth and shaming the devil. Straight is the narrow gate and you can't go around it. You cannot obtain kingdom blessings by using worldly principles. You have to use godly principles. It is God's Way or No Way!

For example, a married man comes to a woman and promises her dinner, movies, a night of wine, cheese, poetry and dance, a dress, a nice hairdo, salon nails and all she has to do is ... basically all she has to do is lose her soul by being with him. Basically all she has to do is fornicate, commit adultery, and lose her soul in the process and maybe even her life or someone else's life. That is all she has to do. So she thinks about the offer and she says to herself what? Well first she thinks "That sounds like an offer I can't refuse". She then does one or two things. She either says "Yes" or "No". Her No answer is based on she has godly morals and standards and she won't compromise. No means, "No I will not compromise, I will not settle, I will not lower my standards. I will not disrespect myself or his wife. I will not disappoint myself or God. I will be a Virtuous Woman. I will be a Woman of Virtue. I will be a Woman of God. Satan you go back to the pit of hell where you came from I rebuke you and I curse the spirit of lust and seduction from the root in the name of Jesus, get behind me. Matter of fact I am going to just stomp you under my feet."

Her "Yes" answer is based on she is a victim of her current circumstances. The devil preys on silly women like this. "Yes" to her means, "Well, one time won't hurt anything and I do need the comfort of a man, that would probably make me feel better, I am kind of lonely. I could use some tender loving care. It would be nice to get out the house for a change. It would be nice to be pampered by a man, even if it is somebody else's husband. I deserve to get my hair and nails done and go to the movies and dinner and shopping. We are just going to be good friends. It is just the movies, dinner, dance and poetry. It is not like we are going to sleep together. There is nothing wrong with a little fun every now and then." So then they end up going back to the hotel adjacent to the restaurant where they had dinner at and adjacent to the lounge where they enjoyed wine, cheese and poetry. She feels like a queen in her new dress, her new hairdo and her new salon nails, all done up to perfection. When they get to the hotel room he has rose pedals spread from the front door to the bed and bathroom, more wine, candlelight and chocolate, he runs her a bubble bath and her heart melts. She now realizes she has gone too far to turn back, so now the wages of sin are death for the both of them, no turning back. Yes, Holy Woman of God (ME) has been there way too many times and have gotten too many T-shirts to prove it! I know you are probably thinking "I can't believe it!" Well, so did the fly on the wall that witnessed it, but unfortunately did not live to tell it!

Now you see why I have to go to the extremes to explain why it may take someone writing it 100 times over and over again to get it. It is not about calling nobody out, because this applies to male and female, all races, all cultures and nationalities. God does not discriminate. His law applies to us all.

I am not sexist; there are silly women out there too. They can write (Matthew 6:33) 100 times over and over again until they get it. Do you absolutely think I am single with eight kids on purpose? Come on now, you know better than that! I think NOT, but I have birthed too many Ishmael's in my lifetime and now I plan on utilizing (Matthew 6:33). I don't want No More Counterfeits! I want nothing less than my Isaac promise! I want my Boaz! I am sick and tired of falling prey to satan's traps and devices.

I WILL BE THE VOICE THAT STANDS UP AND SAYS (Matthew 6:33) IS FOR REAL! It is not a lie! I have tried everything under the sun and now it is time to get that scripture deep down in my spirit and if the only way I can get it is by writing it over and over and over again and having everyone I meet write it over and over again 100 x 100 times, then I will be glad to do just that.

If you cannot take God at his word then "you are a fool and I will just have to shake the dust from under my feet" and move on to the next territory that God has for me to conquer. I am only trying to share with you some valuable truths that I had to learn the hard way. Never ever sin and fall short of the glory of God if at all possible trying to obtain your heart's desires in your own strength. The devil is way to deceitful and cunning. You won't get away with it! There are dire consequences.

You have seen examples in the bible in the past and in the media in the present. I won't say any names, but you know about those individuals that "did things in the dark and it came to light for the whole world to see". Satan even tried to tempt God. You can't do it in your own strength. Stop trying to be God and bring things to pass in your life. Let God be God. God does not need our help! I cannot stress this enough. Learn from the stupid mistakes I have made over and over and over again in the past. I learned from them and that is why I can teach them to you in hopes that you will pass the next test.

God gives us His word to lead and guide us. He communes with us through His word, through His audible voice, through prayer, through praise, worship, through people. We are equipped with everything we need so why do we veer from the truth and get off track every single time? When you stop to think about it, it really does not make sense, now does it?

<u>THE PATTERNS IN MY LIFE</u>

It seems as the same patterns keep reoccurring. Let me go back to the creator and ask where I missed Him. Obviously I left off somewhere for if I was walking with Him and behind Him, where did I miss it? As soon as I figure this one out I will be delivered and set free from this pattern and be able to get to my desired destination.

From this day forward, I will utilize the godly wisdom and apply godly principles only in my life. God is my source not man. I will no longer look to man to fulfill the promises of God. If I can believe it and see it with my spiritual eyes, I can by faith obtain it in the natural. So I confess "I do not possess the spirit of lack, but the fruit of the Spirit, love, joy, peace, longsuffering, gentleness, goodness, faith, meekness and temperance." The bible says, "You will know them by the fruit they bear". You see, when something shimmers it may not necessarily be gold it may be gold finish, but when tried in the fire it will be destroyed. Please make note of the above fruit of the Spirit, longsuffering. Now this word is for real, God did not lie. You most definitely will not get through this Christian walk without experiencing and knowing the definition of longsuffering, but be encouraged because God has given you the grace to handle it and He has also given you the other fruit of joy, love, patience to grow into the grace.

Don't waste your time or your effort trying to attain anything that God didn't bless because anything God did not bless is absolutely, positively a bunch of M-E-S-S! I have tried everything at least once and there is absolutely nothing new under the sun. It is all vanity. You can take my word on it, you don't have to even go through it to know what the end result is going to be. Better yet, just open your bible and research vanity. Go to the book of Ecclesiastes and it will tell you all about vanity.

Begin to view your life as a movie picture or a staged play production with God as the director and use the bible as your script and you will see that your life is orchestrated to perfection. Imagine seeing yourself in the limelight, motion pictures, view your life from beginning to end as you go through each book of the bible you will see where you are in every season of your life. God will begin to show you how He knew you were the perfect character for the plot and when you begin to see yourself come alive in the story, know without a doubt that you are in your rightful place. As long as you are in God's will the ending will be as you and He both expected.

If you try to flip the script well let's just say the director just might say "Take 1, cut, Take 2, cut, Take 3, cut, etc." Yes, the project will be delayed or worse. When you get out of God's will, you will leave the audience in suspense for they won't know about God's unfailing, unmerited grace and His enduring mercy. They will just think the story ended abruptly without a good ending.

Always remember to follow God's script. If God did not ordain it, then don't try to attain it because you will later regret the pursuit! Make sure everything you engage in has a godly purpose, because if it does not, you labor in vain. In everything you do ask yourself, "For what purpose am I involved in this?" and if it lines up with the word of God, then proceed and if it does not line up with the word of God, then walk away, skip, sprint, go on a high speed chase, whatever you have to do, just get out of anything that does not line up with the word of God. I don't care if you been involved or participated in something for 20 years, if it does not have a godly purpose, Get Out! God will help you Get Out! Just begin by calling on His name. Just call out to God like a damsel in distress because you are indeed in distress if you are out of the will of God!

MY ACHY BREAKY HEART

He sent his word, and healed them, and delivered them from their destructions. (Psalm 107:20).

December 22, 2009, I have been ministering healing to others, praying for others and believing for others and Lord just as Your word says "the very thing you preach can return to you". My daughter, who is seven months pregnant, fell and cracked her pelvic bone. There is confusion all around me, disobedient rebellious children running around like they crazy and not listening, stress from every direction.

GOD'S LEADING LADY C SPEAKS TO GOD

Lord, I know it is just the enemy at work and not taking a break, yet I trust You and believe in You Lord and I still see Your hand at work in my life. I will stand on Your word and know that there is power in Your word. I will continue to confess Your word over my life and every situation therein. I know that when I begin to confess Your words with my mouth the atmosphere will begin to change. I know I can create the atmosphere through Your word.

Thank You for Your word. Thank You for encamping angels around me to comfort me. Thank You for surrounding me with people that are for my good and running those out my life that are not. Lord it was prophesized to me that "You would run through hot melting butter to get those out my life that are not for my good, that You have given me a prayer mantle and a healing mantle to lay hands on Your people and they be healed". I believe Lord.

What an anointing, even when I feel not worthy You felt it necessary for Your word to penetrate deep down in my soul to call me out of my hiding place with just one word. Lord let it be known this very day that I am on assignment for You forevermore. The enemy has ran out this time. For You I live and for You I die once again. I can't go back and I can't look back because I have tasted Your goodness and seen it with my own eyes. Grandma's prayers got me here, but my own prayers will sustain me here. Thank You Lord for hearing me when I pray.

I need more of You Jesus, nothing else will satisfy me. I no longer look for satisfaction in man, people, places and things. ***NO MORE IDOLS!*** *I need You more and more each day Lord. I commit my life to You. I will continue to surrender my will to Your perfect will daily. Please continue to use me mightily for Your purpose. Lord have mercy on me and heal me, mind, body and soul, bless my comings and goings, bless everything around me, anoint me from the top of my head to the bottom of my feet so that I can anoint and bless everything that I touch and everything that touches me by Your power within me.*

Oh Lord, I magnify and praise You for You alone are worthy. I cry out to You for the devil has repeatedly tried to sift me as wheat, but Your mercy has kept me and all that you have allowed to happen to me has only made me better, wiser, sweeter. Thank You Lord Jesus for new revelations daily that allow me to see me the way You see me. God You are the ruler of everything and as long as You are on the Throne, You are in control of my life. Nothing can snatch me out of the kingdom because I belong to You. You paid the price for my ransom. I am forever indebted to You. I can never repay You with monetary goods or deeds, but I can repay You by fulfilling Your purpose for me on this earth.

I lay before You on the alter as a living sacrifice, dedicating all of my living, all that I am and all that I have to You Lord, this very day. It is my humble prayer that You do not allow the enemy to send anything my way that is not good for me and if it be Your will then please keep me for I have proven that I cannot keep myself, over and over again. Reveal to me Your perfect will and Your way and I will not depart from it. Allow me to utilize my God-given gifts and talents always for Your purpose and glory.

Take every spirit that is not like You away from me right now by Your power and might. In the name of Jesus, bring about deliverance, bring about freedom, and bring about salvation. As I repent right now from every sin, past, present and future bring deliverance in the name of Jesus. I receive Your mercy, grace and redemption right now. Thank You Father for erasing every memory of my past.

Thank You for pulling out every root of the problem right now in the name of Jesus and replacing it with Your Holy Spirit. Go into the inward parts of my soul and fill it with Your love. Fill me with all that You desire me to have to carry out Your purpose. Replace everything bad with good, fill every void, replace every weakness with Your power, wisdom, understanding. Bring provision from the north, south, east, west to accomplish whatever You choose. Take out the bitter root of unforgiveness and cast it into the Sea of Forgetfulness never to return again.

Those things that took place in my early years, youth and adult life, let me not remember them anymore for I have been healed from my past and move forward with You with grace into my future never turning back or looking back but remaining stedfast, immovable, always abiding in the work of the Lord, with my eyes and ears attuned to You and seeing only destiny that is set before me. I walk in victory as a champion who knows he/she is about to win. I see success before me, wealth before me, it is within reach by faith. I believe and receive it. I lack nothing today. I am totally fulfilled in You. Let my mind, body and soul be renewed daily. Allow rivers of living waters to flow to me and through me each passing day.

Teach me to pray and intercede for others as You intercede for me. Let Your word get in my heart and soul and take root and bring forth an expected harvest. Let me be a testimony to others so that they may taste and see Your goodness. Lord I am not alone anymore for You are with me. I feel Your presence. I feel Your strength. I feel You comforting me. No more pain, no more sorrow, no more tears of sorrow, only tears of joy. You are so right in Your word when You said to "Count It All Joy". That song "Blessed" is so right that says "Late in the midnight hour, God's going to turn it around! It's going to work in our favor!" Yes, You most definitely have. Thank You Jesus.

Thank You for turning it around. I don't see the pain or the hurt anymore. I don't feel it anymore. As my fingers tap on the keyboard, I feel a fresh anointing. I feel a breath of new life in You. Wow this is a great feeling! I feel the way You have always wanted me to feel. Lord I thank You for allowing me to experience pain and hurt so that I could minister to Your hurting and wounded people. That is just like a good parent who allows their child to be go through some things so that they can grow and mature. You have allowed me to grow and mature in the things of God and become responsible and capable of making godly choices.

Thank You for leading me and guiding me and giving specific instructions along the journey. Thank You for correcting me when I did wrong. For You only corrected me because

You loved me and You wanted me to do better. You knew I could do better and I did. Thank You for setting the example through Your life, through Your word, through Your being, for me to follow.

Thank You for allowing me to be an example to others of how to get closer to You. Allow me to be just as good of a parent as You are with my own children and bring them up in the Lord. Allow me to bless all the lives I touch by Your power and Your might. Use me as an instrument of Your perfect will.

Lord, allow me to bless and enrich the lives of others and not bring about discord, grief and strife. Thank You for Your newness. I can hardly wait for this book to be written to bless others. Maybe someone reading this book will be so encouraged that they will step out on faith and pursue their dreams, their goals, and ultimately come to know You as their personal Savior and friend. Maybe they can pick up their bed and walk and come to You and be healed and made whole just as You have done for me. Maybe this is all they needed to assure them that are worthy not by their acts and deeds, but simply by Your grace. Maybe through their reading of this book they will see You like never before and know that Your heart's desire is that "All would come just as they are to You so that You can restore them and make them whole".

Maybe the fact that You allowed me to be naked before You and man will give someone the courage to not worry about what the crowd is going to think or say. Maybe they will be just like "the woman with the issue of blood" and just press through the crowd like I did in hopes of obtaining my healing. Thank you Lord for listening once again. Amen.

YES, JESUS LOVES ME

Thank You Lord for restoration. This Christmas my whole family is planning to have a get together at my house and I know that it is all because of You because I did not even desire that anymore. I had gotten to the point where it did not matter anymore. Yes, in timespast I wanted it to be like the good old times we once shared when grandma would invite the whole family over for a family gathering on Sundays or on holidays. I truly treasured those times but now that Big Mama is gone, well let's just say so are the family gatherings. Yes, there is definitely a void now and You saw past my feelings and emotions and You saw my heart. You knew that at this point in my life I had come to the conclusion that family gatherings were nice, but not necessary. Even though I did not even believe this to be true, it seemed easier to make an excuse for being wrong than to work for what is right! Lord, You looked beyond my faults and saw my need.

You knew that I love family and that I love Your people and that my heart was huge. You knew the hurt and the pain in my heart when I continuously gave love out and did not receive anything in return. You promised in Your word that You would restore everything that the cankerworm destroyed. That is why it was no surprise when my mother called me today and said she would like to have Christmas dinner at my house this year. It took much courage for her to say that for healing was taking place as she spoke those very words to me. She did not even know the fullness of it, but You and I did. You are a mighty God. You continue to leave me in awe. I know You can touch and turn the heart of even kings. Thank You Lord for finding me to be worthy enough to stop by and gently nudge my mother to call me to arrange for Christmas dinner at my house. Thank You Lord!

Even when I had put away the good china for good. Even when I had closed the kitchen cabinets and windows and rooms of my heart and even locked the doors of my home and closed the blinds and shutters so that no one could even visit let alone stay, Your grace and Your mercy said, "NO". Even when I said in my mind, "I don't need anyone in my life to help me with these children. I don't want any friends. I don't want this or that". You knew better and You said to me ever so gently, "Because you have seeked My face, because you have sought My kingdom and My righteousness, I am going to add all these things unto you". Thank You Lord!

Lord, Thank You. I am forever grateful and thankful. You reached down low from heaven to exalt me high on the earth before the whole world when You placed the article of me and my family in Essence Magazine. That article let the whole world know how great You are. All the time I was looking to man to be faithful and never fully realizing until today that all I needed was You for You alone are so faithful! You alone placed me and my family in a beautiful brand new home in a nice neighborhood with nice, quality schools. You alone provided so many things to me over the years, I cannot list them all. The college degrees You alone blessed me with. The job You alone blessed me with. The car You alone blessed me with. You alone have supplied my every need daily.

Even when I was at my lowest state You alone pulled me out and touched me and pushed me into my destiny. Never did You leave or forsake me on the journey. That is why I have returned to You over and over again knowing that You are married to the backslider. Yet this time is different. This time I will stay connected because You alone have removed everything away that so easily bestowed me. You alone made it even easier for me to love You and You alone. My only desire is You Lord. Anything else is a distraction right now.

Lord, I ask one thing of You and that is for You alone to show me exactly what place the other things should have in my life. I won't move until I hear from You. Lord, I no longer live, breathe or have my being without You. You will have to lead and guide me for I depend totally on You alone. I can't make decisions without You. I can't move forward without You. I do not know my next step. I only know that my next step is ordered by You and You alone. I do not even know what my next thought will be, but I know it is to give You alone all the glory, honor and praise. Thank You for a new clean heart, a renewed mind and spirit. Thank You for putting new words in my mouth. Thank You for giving me a new song in my heart. The sound of a perfect melody.

Lord, You gave me a song just like You gave my dear grandfather a song. He hummed that song until he took his last breath. Most people did not even know the song but I did, way back then and now. It still plays in my heart 43 years later. Even after his homegoing, I kept the song in my heart.

Most people did not even know that my grandfather was a saved man, but I did because I knew he talked to You daily through psalms and that he had a relationship with You through the very song he sang in his heart and hummed for the whole world to hear. He was very quiet and a good man in the natural, but he was bold and roared like a lion in the spirit as he hummed his favorite song to You.

Everyone knew him to be a good man that minded his own business and who loved to hum a tune. He would often be busy with the day to day activities in life, but still find time to hum the song that You placed in his heart. He hummed the song so much that it became natural to him. He could not do anything without humming the song. He hummed the song so much that it reached, touched and penetrated the spirit of others around him. Others began to receive the song that he hummed in their spirit as they hummed along. Yes, a simple hum to You brought about deliverance in his home first and then it spread abroad. My grandfather was a disciple through a simple hum, for he lived the song and he taught others who were attuned to the song the very meaning of the song.

So it is with You Lord. You are a gentleman just like my grandfather. You don't force Yourself on anyone. You don't try to convince anyone to come to You. You just keep on calling just like my grandfather just kept humming. You just keep on placing songs deep down in their souls until their soul sings and when their soul sings You know that they have received the revelation. This is the beginning of the process.

Lord You and I have been together now for such a long time and You have given me many songs in my heart like Precious Lord, Amazing Grace, I'm Going Up Yonder, His Eye is on the Sparrow, I Won't Complain, but I think the song I would like to dedicate to You that touched me the most was the simple song that my grandfather would hum. The song that I learned as a baby that still plays in my heart today. I knew the song to be true then and I know the song to be true now. My grandfather hummed this song from the time I was born into this world until the day he went home to be with You Lord.

Like I said before, no one even knew that my grandfather was a saved man because he did not always go to church every Sunday. Oftentimes he would stay at home and worship You all alone, humming the song to You as he cared for the things that You blessed him with like family, the house, the car, the land, the wildlife and animals on the land, and he was available and skilled to help any neighbor or passerby. He was a hard working man that did not mind stopping what he was doing to help anyone out and lend a helping hand. That was his ministry. His ministry was beyond the church walls. He just kept on working and humming a tune to You. He just kept on talking to You daily through the song in his heart.

Even when bad things happened he kept humming. In good times and bad, when the skies were blue and when the skies were gray, when the storms of life were calm and when they were raging, he kept humming. When there were more bills than money, when he lost some loved ones along the way, when sickness and death came and visited his door, he kept humming the song that You placed in his heart. He kept humming the song until he took his last breath when You called him home and that is what I plan on doing. I am going to keep singing psalms and praises to You until You call me home.

I plan to keep singing my grandfather's favorite song in hopes that one day even my children and my children's children will know and believe the song that You placed in my grandfather's heart and my heart and that song is "Jesus loves me this I know for the bible tells me so. Little ones to Him belong, they are weak but He is strong. Yes, Jesus loves me. Yes, Jesus loves me. Yes, Jesus loves me for the bible tells me so ...". Thank You Lord forevermore for Your song.

HE SEARCHED MY HEART

Blessed is the man that trusteth in the LORD, and whose hope the LORD is. For he shall be as a tree planted by the waters, and that spreadeth out her roots by the river; and shall not see when heat cometh, but her leaf shall be green; and shall not be careful in the year of drought, neither shall cease from yielding fruit. The heart is deceitful above all things, and desperately wicked: who can know it? I the LORD search the heart, I try the reins, even to give every man according to his ways, and according to the fruit of his doings. (Jeremiah 17:7-10).

God is the only one who has truly been able to search my heart and know exactly how I felt throughout the years. The bible says "Let not thy left hand know what thy right hand doeth". A lot of times the things near and dear to my heart I never shared with anyone, but God already knew without me sharing. God has shown me so much favor throughout the years. From Day 1 on this earth I have had the favor of God and man. During this Holiday Season 2009, I see with spiritual eyes and hear with spiritual ears ever so clearly. I now know that God loves me so much and He cares deeply for me. Even in all the hustle of bustle of things, He brings me joy unspeakable joy. It is the type of joy that only He can give. The joy that God gives you can't help but give it to the world. So, today my heart sings "Joy to the World the Lord has come, let earth receive her King, let every heart prepare Him room, and heaven and nature sing, and heaven and nature sing, and heaven and heaven and nature sing ...".

I had an incident yesterday at Walmart at the checkout where a cashier was basically doing her job but to the point where it was an excessive use of going by the books and not considering the circumstances did not warrant such. I arrived at the checkout and the cashier asked me for proof of signature and I was very compliant and asked if I could use my driver's license as proper identification. The clerk said "No, you have to have appropriate identification showing your signature and it has to be approved by my supervisor or I will get fired". I then informed the clerk that I would not want that to happen. The clerk then turned on her checkout lane light to notify her supervisor that she needed assistance. So, I patiently waited in line during the entire process. It was the holiday season, so there were more than ten people behind me at this time. I gestured to them that it was going to be a delay and apologized for the delay by saying "I am so sorry". They gave me a smirk as to say it was okay, but I searched their hearts and knew that they were not happy. Well neither was I, but I remained at the checkout waiting patiently.

I then asked the clerk to try to persuade the people behind me to go to another line so they would not have to be delayed further. She shrugged her shoulders as to say "Who really cares, not my problem!" There was at least about a 10 minute delay in the line or more and then the supervisor arrived at the checkout to handle the situation. The cashier indicated to her supervisor that I did not have proper identification and she could not proceed with the transaction. The supervisor without looking up at either me or the cashier said "Does she have a driver's license?" I interrupted and said with a smile "I most certainly do". The supervisor then said "That is fine, just let her show her driver's license for identification". The cashier's eyes were now protruding out her eye sockets in unbelief and her face was now red. Out of embarrassment and trying to save face, she said "You are so lucky; I have never seen this done before ...". I smiled even bigger and kindly said "Yes, I am so lucky. I am more than lucky, I am blessed".

This was a teaching moment, but I didn't even bother to explain to her the difference between lucky and blessed for I had delayed the line long enough, but I said in parting Merry Christmas and thanked her for her time. She thanked me for being so patient. I walked away from the counter and began to greet everyone with joy and Merry Christmas greetings and they all received it with a smile.

I then walked by a cashier that never says hello, that never ever gives a smile or an emotion and pretty much is always doom and gloom in appearance and mannerism, maybe even to the point of being darn right rude. I had often wanted to ask her if she was okay, but never did. Yet, I was always somewhat concerned about why she had always had a bad attitude. I continued to be nice to her, but I wondered how I could help her and how I could possibly lift her spirit just once.

So as I walked by her and looked up at her knowing that she would not smile or even look up and say hello. To my surprise, she looked up and smiled and said "Hello", nodded her head and said "Merry Christmas". I then in total amazement eagerly said "Hello, Merry Christmas" and smiled from ear to ear. That gave me so much joy as I walked out of the store with my groceries. I knew that God once again had shown me favor. He never fails to amaze me. God is always at work in our lives. Even when we cannot see or trace Him, know that He is there and that He is working things out on our behalf. I know each one of us has had situations just like this, whether big or small situations that God has worked things and situations out in your favor.

How can we go about life not loving ourselves and loving others just as Christ has loved us? It is just not possible to sow evil and discord and wreak havoc when the love of God dwells in our heart. When Holy Spirit dwells within our soul, when His word is on the tablets of our heart, it is impossible to speak or do anything that will not bring Him glory. We even have to love our enemies and bless those that don't always treat us as we should be treated. God still can get the glory so do not give up. Continue to demonstrate the love of God in all that you do, in deed and in truth, because whatever you sow you shall reap in due season.

This Christmas is going to be the best Christmas ever. I said time after time that I was no longer going to celebrate holidays because I only wanted to celebrate Jesus, but God searched my heart and intervened. He said, "My Dear Daughter, I know you love Me and I know that you celebrate Me every day and not only on Christmas. I am so pleased with your faithfulness that I am going to intervene on your behalf for I know your very thoughts and your heart's desires for I placed those thoughts and the desires within you. Even when you try to cover them up with fantasies and try to escape reality, even when you try to renew your mind daily to think differently, I know your heart. I am your Heavenly Father and what concerns you concerns Me. I know that you love family. I know that you love family unity. I know that you love Christmas decorations and that you love gifts and most importantly you love giving. So you don't have to pretend anymore that you don't. I know that you have not bought into the world's view and have not commercialized Christmas and all the other holidays. You always keep Me *First* 365 days in a year, so don't think this has gone unnoticed. I know that you love deeply and I know that you want to express the same during the holidays and every day. So I cannot allow you to hide this great love within the four walls that you constantly create to protect yourself from hurt, pain, sorrow, disappointment. From this day forward I the Lord thy God am tearing down the walls. You won't be able to put them back up!

That is why I allowed your ex-husband to decorate your house with lights this Christmas, even when you said to yourself I don't even want to waste my time or money. Yes, I saw and heard you when he was finished getting up out of your chair and looking out the window and glancing briefly at all the Christmas lights and decorations around you and seeing all the beauty therein and saying to yourself "That is beautiful, but I am okay in God and He completely satisfies me for He is my Light". That really made me proud, but I searched your heart even deeper and remember that every Christmas as a child you were disappointed because you did not get that doll or toy that you had asked Santa for and you said in your heart then "That is okay", but you did not really mean "That is okay".

I knew that you were content, but the fact is you deserved everything you asked for and did not get. All those little disappointments were little tests to see if you would remain faithful even if you did not get what you deserved and throughout the years you have indeed proven that you are faithful. You have always strived to be faithful to me so that you could please me and when you fell short I understood for I knew your heart. Here is an explanation of the difference between you and Me. I was faithful to you because I am faithful. Even when you were not faithful, I remained faithful to you for I knew and searched your heart. I have always understood you beloved.

That is why I allowed you to continue to minister to people who meant you well and to those who did not mean you well because I knew you sincerely love My people, just as I love you. That is why I recently allowed people to show up in your life that you have not heard from in years. People you thought you would never see again. I allowed restoration to take place in your life so that nothing would be missing, nothing would be broken and so that you could be complete once and for all in Me.

Even when you said to yourself "It would be better for me to only have a friend in Jesus for He will never leave or forsake me", I knew your heart. I allowed You to think and believe these things but I could not allow you to live a lie. You deserve every good friend that I have placed in your life. You deserve every good gift that I have placed in your life. Beloved, enter in and enjoy restoration in Me.

When you looked at those Christmas lights your eyes were like a little kid at Christmas. I know you wanted to place a candle in every window to give your home a feeling of Christmas but you didn't because you thought it would displease Me. The fact is you could not do anything to displease Me for I know your heart. You are so special to Me. I know you meant well, but I knew what was best for you for My ways are not your ways and My thoughts are not your thoughts.

I know you are thankful for all that I have done and I want you to know that I did it all for your good. I have something special for you this Christmas. It will be a perfect holiday for you. I am going to call a party. RSVP only. I am going to bring your family to you this Christmas as my gift to you. I am going to bring about restoration in every area of your life this Christmas! You don't have to do anything but open your heart, your home and your front door. I will provide everything. Don't worry about provision, a Christmas tree, Christmas lights or even gifts. When I died on the Cross that covered everything. I just want to celebrate you this holiday season because you have celebrated Me by putting me *First.* Your faithfulness year after year has not gone unnoticed. Merry Christmas Leading Lady C, Love Your Heavenly Father, 2009.

The Year 2009 was definitely the Year of Restoration for me. God restored everything the devil had stole from me. God restored the love and compassion I had for others, my hopes, dreams and inspirations, the gift of encouragement, a thankful and grateful heart, unyielding faith, joy unspeakable joy, all fruit of the spirit and all spiritual gifts He had deposited in me, loved ones that I had lost contact with throughout the years for reasons known and unknown and most importantly, He even brought about healing and deliverance in my own family.

God restored my best friends from my past Prophetess Kimberly in Alabama, my spiritual mentor and best friend, whom we were never disconnected in the spirit; Patricia a/k/a Pat my lifelong friend in Kentucky; Cassandra my best friend and the best hairstylist/fashion designer in St. Louis, Missouri, formerly known as House of Magic Mirrors and n/k/a CeCe Fashions and She'va Couture. My good friend from college, Wanda, who lives in Chicago, Illinois. Last, but definitely not least, God reconnected me with a very special friend from high school, Prophet Sidney Jones, who lives in Iowa.

I pray to God to one day find my grade school friend Rebecca a/k/a "BeBa", last known to be in the Mississippi area and my college friend and former roommate, Tanya, last known to be in the Memphis area. Yes, I have held on to these lifelong friendships even after all of these years and by faith believe that all is well and know without a doubt that God has always had everything in His hand. I speak restoration even in this area and know that there is no distance in the spirit. Thus, we will forever remain connected.

Throughout my life when people closed doors and said "No", God opened new doors and said "Yes, walk through with grace!" As people began to sow into my life and as I nurtured the seeds that were planted, God gave the increase. God never promised me that the road to salvation would be easy, but He did promise me in His word that it would be a road worth traveling. Yes, it seems like my whole life consisted of being tried through the fire and it seems as if I had even lost some things I treasured most in the fire, but God promised in His word that I would come forth as pure gold. I knew without a doubt that I could not lose anything that God could not restore hundredfold. This brought me so much hope. I kept His words everpresent in my mind and heart and believed by faith that God had something greater in store for me even when I did not know what it was.

I fell a lot along the way on my journey in the very ditches that **MY IDOL** had dug up so nicely for me to fall into, but for every ditch that I fell into God reached down from heaven real low and delivered me out, out of every affliction. The grave that **MY IDOL** dug for me is the grave he really dug for himself, because God has restored everything and He has even given me newer and greater things.

Even the entire wardrobe that **MY IDOL** stole from my closet. My finest apparel, every business suit, every church dress, every evening gown, every item of clothing, every piece of fine jewelry, every pair of shoes, my most cherished belongings disappeared or were set out for the moths to destroy. I felt naked and destitute and as I bowed my head in shame, I made excuses not to go outside of my four walls of bondage, but something on the inside of me told me to hold on to the remnants by faith. As I held on to the remnants by faith, I wore with dignity, character and integrity, the royal robe of prayer and the garment of praise as I continued to walk out my destiny. My heart was sad, but God said He would restore and He did. God added on years to my life and said directly to me in an audible voice that was confirmed by His word that my latter years will be greater in Him and they indeed are. I now have a new life in Christ. (II Corinthians 5:17). I have no desire to look back over my past for destiny is before me and not behind me!

All the years of abuse and neglect that I endured was for His glory. I was just the vessel He chose to use. I never believed I was strong. I never believed that I was a survivor, but God showed me that in Him I was indeed a brave warrior, a vessel of honor. As a vessel of honor, I held on by faith for I knew that God loved me and that He cared even when everyone else had turned their backs on my despair, God was there.

I knew His word said He was going to deliver me out of every affliction and I believed him at His word. I knew that once He delivered me and set me free that He was going to use me to go out into the kingdom and be THE VOICE THAT STOOD FOR RIGHTEOUSNESS SAKE, THE VOICE THAT STOOD AGAINST VICTIMS OF DOMESTIC VIOLENCE, ABUSE, RAPE, NEGLECT, AND EVEN VICTIMS OF SOCIETY who face poverty and oppression firsthand. I would not keep my mouth closed and turn my face and not lend a helping hand and act as if it does not exist or affect my life, because indeed it did and it still does!

God told me that He loves and He cares for His people and He has sent me to tell you the same. God says "If we do not intervene for those in need of intervention then their blood will be on our hands". I made a vow to God that if He delivered me out of darkness and out of the paths of destruction and out of the wages of sin and out of the grave that **MY IDOL** had dug for my place of rest, that I would live life abundantly for Him and that I would not shut my bowels of compassion for His people. God heard my cry in the midnight hours and He is faithful and just and answered my pleas and my petitions. He saved me by His power and might and sent provision from the north, south, east and west for me to complete His kingdom work. As long as the blood is running through my veins, I will be about doing My Father's business.

So as in my favorite movie Color Purple, I AM THE VOICE SPEAKING TO "MISTER" a/k/a **MY IDOL**, the devil, the enemy, the adversary, lucifer himself, saying "Until you do right by me everything you ever think about is going to fail, the jail you plan for me is the one you are going to rot in, everything you done to me, you already done to you, I am poor, black, I may even be ugly, but Dear God, I'm here, I'm here. Good God a mighty I am here".

All those years you thought you were doing me a disservice, you were really doing it for my good because it built my godly character and strengthened me. Through it all, God gave me so much godly wisdom and understanding. I now have spiritual eyes to see clearly and spiritual ears to hear keenly and I see there is no waiting for me in heaven. Yes, I can see the pearly gates waiting on me and I can imagine the angels singing a melody as I walk through the pearly gates and as they introduce me to everyone and say "Welcome, Ms. Holt, we have been expecting you".

"Everyone, this is Ms. Holt, mother of the anointed Holt Boys and the beautiful Holt girls and grandmother of the precious Holt grandbabies. She has spent all of her life kingdom building, birthing nations, being a good steward, faithful and diligent servant of God for God's glory. She is a/k/a God's Leading Lady C. Lady C, please follow me down the streets paved with gold as I show you to your mansion. It has your name written on it. It reads "God's Leading Lady C dwells here". There will be no sorrow and no pain here, only joy unspeakable joy. Welcome again and may you enjoy your stay and may you finally receive the peaceful rest that you most certainly deserve. You just rest for now and we will take it from here". I can hear me responding by just saying "Thank You Lord" as I fall fast asleep in the most comfortable bed fit perfectly for a queen, only dreaming sweet dreams in Jesus. Wait I am in heaven, that's right. I won't be needing to sleep in heaven because I will be praising Him, all day and all night! Hallelujah, I am here! I am finally here!

THE POURING OUT OF GOD'S SPIRIT

And it shall come to pass in the last days, saith God, I will pour out my Spirit upon all flesh: and your sons and your daughters shall prophesy, and your young men shall see visions, and your old men shall dream dreams: An on my servants and on my handmaidens I will pour out in those days of my Spirit; and they shall prophesy: And I will show wonders in heaven above, and signs in the earth beneath; blood, and fire, and vapor of smoke: The sun shall be turned into darkness, and the moon into blood, before that great and notable day of the Lord come: and it shall come to pass, that whosoever shall call on the name of the Lord shall be saved. (Acts 2:17-21).

NOTHING MISSING, NOTHING BROKEN, COMPLETE IN HIM IN 2010

As God begins to build upon the foundation of my new life in Him, He is going to plant and build new things. This explains why He has plucked things up and pulled things out and tore down some things in my life. He simply wanted to rebuild and restore my life for His purpose. Count it all joy. My tears, my mourning and weeping have turned to joy and dancing. I will begin to see myself as God sees me in this new life in Christ. Nothing missing, nothing broken, complete in Him in 2010! By faith, I am expecting the unexpected!

With this new stance and new vision, I remain resilient. I continue to implement the perfect plan that God has for my life with the instructions that He has provided me with in His word for I will not move one step further unless I hear from Him. God has well-equipped me along the journey and for future things to come. I remember everything He has shown me. Today I surrender, laying aside every weight and taking only what He instructs me to take on the rest of the journey. I am leaving some people, places, things behind. **NO MORE IDOLS**!

I have come this far by faith and God is going to show me the rest of the way. I trust God completely and know that He is going to continue to teach me His thoughts and show me His ways and supply provision for my journey. I have all that I need, nothing is missing, nothing is broken. I do not lack anything, I am complete in Him. I am like a tree planted by the water yielding much fruit. God has healed my wounded mind, body, spirit and soul, the very core of my body, even down to the marrow of my bones. He is breathing a new breath into my spirit that is bringing life to even my dried up bones. I have to be honest with myself and you and tell you that this was not easy. This was a process that seemed like it took forever, yet it was worth the wait for it changed my life completely for my good. To God be the glory!

From this day forward, I am going to be willing and obedient and go out into the kingdom of God and feed His sheep. God desires more than me feeding them in the natural by supplying nourishment to satisfy and please their flesh. God desires that I continue to remain willing and obedient so that I may hear from Him directly to be continuously filled with His spirit in order to impart to His sheep food for their spirit and their soul. By doing so, I will build disciples that not only desire to be fed, but who also desire to teach others what they have been fed.

God is going to show me and teach me how to be fishers of men and how to bring lost souls to Him. God is going to show me how to deliver the captives and set them free. I am fully aware that I cannot do it in my own strength and am thankful and grateful that God is with me in this endeavor. I will bless lives and kingdom build as He instructs me. I will stay focused on the task before me even when distractions come, fully knowing that they will come. God is going to bring provision through many resources to help me build and maintain a support system to accomplish the task at hand. This support system will consist of family, friends, extended family, church, social support, spiritual support, networking opportunities, etc.

God is going to even make my enemies my footstool and they will be at peace with me. All of these God-given resources and good gifts will be instrumental in helping me reach my God-given destiny. There may be many difficult times ahead, but "God got me". He is going to carry me when I can no longer walk on the journey. I must be a good steward of my time, every idle moment, every second counts whether I am working, playing, resting, thinking, I will be focused on my goal. No time wasters. Time wasters in the past have cost me many losses and no gain. Time wasters have left me depleted and distraught and have taken my attention away from God's agenda.

Now that I have regained my focus, I know that it is now time to demonstrate action faith and that is simply keeping my God-given vision before me and taking steps in the direction of my God-given destiny by implementing the plan knowing that once I activate my faith, God is obligated to come through for me. I will continue to believe God and trust God in all things, situations and circumstances as I activate my faith to such a degree that it moves Him. I must continue to tell myself every step of the way that in God there is no failure! God has given me all that I need to complete the assignment. The only way I can fail is if I don't show up for the assignment and that will never happen for as I have told you before and I will tell you again, "As long as the blood is flowing through my veins, for God I live and for God I die" (Romans 14:8). So bring it on devil. Give it your best shot. Let me see what you are working with! There was complete silence in the atmosphere. No takers!

GOD SPEAKS

For I know the thoughts that I think toward you, saith the LORD, thoughts of peace, and not of evil, to give you an expected end. (Jeremiah 29:11).

And he opened his mouth, and taught them, saying, Blessed are the poor in spirit: for theirs is the kingdom of heaven. Blessed are they that mourn: for they shall be comforted. Blessed are the meek: for they shall inherit the earth. Blessed are they which do hunger and thirst after righteousness: for they shall be filled. Blessed are the merciful: for they shall obtain mercy. Blessed are the pure in heart: for they shall see God. Blessed are the peacemakers: for they shall be called the children of God. Blessed are they which are persecuted for righteousness' sake: for theirs is the kingdom of heaven. Blessed are ye, when men shall revile you, and persecute you, and shall say all manner of evil against you falsely, for my sake. Rejoice, and be exceeding glad: for great is your reward in heaven: for so persecuted they the prophets which were before you. Ye are the salt of the earth: but if the salt has lost his savior, wherewith shall it be salted: it is thenceforth good for nothing, but to be cast out, and to be trodden under foot of men. Ye are the light of the world. A city that is set on a hill cannot be hid. Neither do men light a candle, and put it under a bushel, but on a candlestick; and it giveth light unto all that are in the house. Let your light so shine before men, that they may see your good works, and glorify your Father which is in heaven. (Matthew 5:2-16).

TODAY IS JANUARY 28, 2010

I woke up this morning with my normal routine anointed my head and my children's head with oil, placed on my prayer shawl and began to seek God's face. I then made my half a pot of Folgers coffee with cream and sugar substitute, bowl of old fashioned oatmeal, woke up the kids and prepared them for school, dropped off the kids at school. I then returned home and sat at my computer to find out what I needed to do for I had three projects before me pressing my spirit. I turned them over to God and He said contact AuthorHouse. I agreed to comply, but first things first, time for my morning break, hot green tea, two boiled eggs, four sugar free life savers and/or gum, peanut butter granola bar, diet hot chocolate, pistachio nuts and/or pecans. Yes, the morning ritual.

I then placed the call to AuthorHouse. What was so amazing about this was that when I contacted AuthorHouse online and filled out the proper online paperwork to receive their free publishing guide, God said to call the 1-800 number and so I complied. The representative who answered the call was eager to help and asked if I had any questions. I said "I think you know all the questions and you have all the answers". She laughed and graciously began to assist me.

At the end of the conversation we had agreed upon what book publishing package would meet my needs. I wanted a package that I could tell my story for God's glory and the readers would not only be inspired by my life story/my love story between me and God, but they would be blessed beyond measure. I wanted a bestseller book on the shelf and it was just that simple. I only wanted to know how to attain it. That was my only question. I know most people are probably not this direct in coming out and saying directly what they want but life has taught me and the bible confirms that "You have not because you ask not …". I definitely wanted to "have" so I asked.

After hearing my enthusiasm and determination and dedication, the representative was eager to help. She gave me a step by step guide to get where I needed to be by my deadline. I then sent out an S.O.S. to prayer warriors, Prophetess Kimberly Sims, Apostle Cauline Thomas-Brown and Apostle Ranard Teach. I knew I had their blessings so I proceeded.

This is what I told all three of them via phone and instant messaging. Today, I have three pressing major projects before the lord that need to be completed this year. One, a bestseller book and two, licensure in counseling and the three, a healing outreach ministry "Total Wellness in God" while also simultaneously trying to successfully raise a family, maintain a career, intercede in prayer for others and other ministry work assigned by God. So please intercede for me in prayer so that God's will be done. Thank you and God bless you.

Now I had all of that above before me and I did not know how God was going to do it, but I knew He could and if it was His will He would. Oh and don't let me forget, I am planning my son's Christian's 4th birthday party today at school. His birthday is Saturday, but today is my day off from work so I will begin the celebration early and then we can celebrate as a family on Saturday on his actual birthday at his favorite place of course, Chuck E Cheese. He wants Diego and Spiderman decorations and the whole nine yards and I am "foolin" around with writing this book, where are my priorities? It is definitely time for one of the simple prayers that I often teach to my children "God Help Me, Amen!"

I know we all get busy from time to time and it seems as if we can't even possibly squeeze in a long drawn out prayer. I can understand that. Maybe some people don't have to pray as much as others. As for me, I can never say Amen. I just have to continue to pray and pray some more and pray even more. Really, there is no reason not to pray or make excuses about not having time to pray for prayer is just talking to God. If you are in a situation where you can't say or do anything but say "Jesus". God hears you and He will answer for He knows the very words you think even before you speak them, yet he still wants you to open your mouth and talk to Him. God already knew I needed His help before I asked and He was willing and prepared to do just that "Help Me". As a full-time mother and grandmother, a faithful and diligent servant of God, I pray without cease and walk daily by faith because I do not know how God keeps making a way out of no way. I only know that He is able and that He can!

On January 27, 2010, during morning prayer on the Power of Prayerline with Apostle Carmichael and my other sisters in Christ, I once again laid my whole life on the alter of God and everything concerning me. They did the same. We began to intercede for each other and our ministries and our families, the Body of Christ, the country, the nations, the president, the whole world. I simply surrendered everything to God and told Him that I definitely could NOT handle everything without Him nor did I want to handle anything without Him so I was placing my life on the alter and I was dedicating everything to Him and leaving it on the alter until I heard from Him. This is faith in practice.

So today is another day, yet I am still before the Lord in prayer concerning many things, especially the completion of my book and the completion of my counseling exam. Today, I declare and decree, zero distractions. I am on assignment by God. God is opening doors as we speak. He is setting up appointments, divine connections. He is sending resources from the north, south, east and west. Provision is in place. The ram is in the bush. All I have to do is listen to His voice, follow as He leads, go where He tells me to go, answer when He calls, say yes when He asks, pray when He says pray, stay when He says stay, move when He says move, run when He says run, fight when He says fight, praise when He says praise, sing when He says sing. All I have to do is believe when He says believe "all things are possible". When He says type I will type. When He says write I will write. When He says lend I will lend. When He says give I will give. God is setting things up strategically and all I have to do is say "Here I am Lord, send me. I say yes to Your will and to Your way, Yes Lord, use me. Hallelujah!"

On January 29, 2010, I printed the first three pages of my book, with three representing the Trinity and I mailed it U.S. Mail Delivery Service to copyright the book. When I received the stamped, dated and postmarked letter, I placed it in my bible. God willing, I plan to have the book in final format and sent off to the publisher for review and hopefully the book will be on shelves in bookstores, libraries, and on the bookshelves of each and every home all around the world this year. I am so excited, but I know that I have a lot of work to do in between. I am so glad that God is the author and the finisher of my faith and this book and all I have to do is just listen to His voice and allow the anointing to flow to me and through me onto the pages of this book for each and everyone of you. Oh, but don't think **MY IDOL** is not at work to abort my assignment, but the anointing of God has been arrested and released by the Power of God. That means that the devil can't touch my anointing. It is covered and sealed with the blood of Jesus!

On February 6, 2010, the highlight of my day was going to my prep class for the licensed professional counselor exam. It is a six week class and I only have two more sessions to go. I trust and believe that if it is Gods' will for me to take and successfully pass the national counselor's certification examination and become a licensed professional counselor in His timing.

Following the prep class, I then met with my family at the first meeting of the 2010 Marks Family Reunion, Labor Day Weekend. It was so nice to see my family and everyone coming together and allowing God to help us reunite the family. After my grandmother's death in 1996, it seems as if we have been apart way too long. We tried to keep the family reunions going and for the most part we did, but when grandma and the elders put things together in the days of old, they allowed God to do the planning and it seemed everything worked out perfectly for everyone. That was the difference between then and now.

Nevertheless, I was honored to be present and an active participant in the first meeting for I remember grandma passing the torch to me in 1996 and I had tried in my own strength to walk in her shoes, yet I forgot to put God *First* in everything. I will make sure I get it right this time. What a blessing it is going to be. I can see it by faith. Lives will never be the same after this event. We are going to put God *First* from the beginning to the end as we remain in agreement as a family.

I kindly asked everyone that we begin and end the meeting with prayer. Thank you Cousin Denise for the opening prayer and thank you Cousin Frankie for the closing prayer. It is my prayer that we as a family continue to pray as a family and keep God *First* in everything. God is going to save, deliver and set some people free during this entire process. There is so much power in prayer. I remain watchful and await God to move on our behalf, according to our faith.

Thanks Shelby and family for taking the time to stay with me even after everyone else had left and hear my heart. I love you all so dearly. What I really wanted to say to you and to everyone even if I did not say it was that "I am so thankful for family and I am so thankful for not letting our forefathers and foremothers legacy die. I am so thankful that we are by faith walking in love together as a family. Our children need to know each other just like we knew each other once. What concerns you should concern me. The women and men of ole, Papa Raymond and Mama Tot, Aunt Tit, Aunt Bert, Uncle Coolidge and Aunt Lorene, and Uncle Noot all knew that a family that prays together stays together.

Yes, we fell short after they went on home to be with the Lord, but God is saying "Get back up and reach out to one another. Help each other hold on to God's unchanging hand. Pray for your family in good times and bad". Yes we are busy, but not too busy to pray. What if this very second and moment in time is the last time you ever talk to me or me talk to you. We both know that the next second is not promised to us. We have lost many loved ones in the twinkling of an eye but for the ones who are still standing for Jesus let us begin to thank God and give Him the highest praise."

Lord I thank you and I praise You for my loved ones still standing and living for You and for the ones who are lost and cannot find their way. I thank You for touching their hearts and minds right now by Your Power and might and meeting them in their time of need and directing them back on the right path. I intercede today and always, prayer by prayer, one by one, name by name, from the oldest to the youngest. I know that my prayer and the prayers of other family members are going to be connected in the spirit in the atmosphere and before you know it, the prodigal sons and daughters will be coming home to family and to Jesus, their First Love and Oh what a family reunion it is going to be. Amen.

Upon leavening the first family reunion meeting, I had the unction to stop by Dunkin Donuts and get a cup of coffee. I needed a little motivator to help me finish writing this book. Nothing motivates me like my favorite coffee. When I drove up to the Dunkin

Donuts' parking lot, right away I see my stepdad Ike for this is his second home. What a joy it was to see him sitting at the booth and entertaining his friends. On my way to Dunkin Donuts, I had initially thought about the cost of the cup of coffee in that I was on a strict budget and I said to myself "Lord I know I should save this $1.50, but I don't have the kids this weekend and I really want to pamper myself" and God remained silent. I pulled into the parking lot and parked the car and began to walk into the restaurant with a big smile and greeted my stepdad with a hug.

A gentleman sitting by him asked the waiter to order me a drink. He said what are you having today? I looked at him as to say "This is not a club, I don't think it is the proper procedure to order someone a drink in a donut shop, but I didn't want to correct him". My stepdad noticed my hesitation and he said to me "He would like to buy you a cup of coffee". I then began to look like "I knew that", even though I didn't. So I said to myself "That will work". So I ordered a medium coffee, cream and sweetener and I thanked the gentlemen with words and he could tell it was sincere by the huge grin on my face as I began to tell him that God was surely going to bless him for his kindness. Another gentleman walked in the donut shop and this same gentleman told the waiter order him a cup of coffee also. The gentleman came in the donut shop and just smiled and sat down at the booth with the others. So I was catching on to the customs of the donut shop to come in and order each other drinks. WOW!

Where have I been all my life between four walls or what? This is indeed the "in crowd". People are sleep on the "in crowd" at Dunkin Donuts. It was mostly elder men in the donut shop now and I was the only young lady sitting at the counter on a booth just gleaning from the reapers like Ruth from the knowledge and wisdom being spilled before me to gather. It felt good to just enjoy each others company. The gentlemen kept coming in and everyone kept greeting each other with a smile. Everyone was sitting down drinking coffee, tea or hot chocolate and listening to all the stories being told. I was amazed of such history and such richness and culture that was going on in one place. It was as if they were telling me their life story and what I thought was a life that I had lived, I had really just begun.

We continued to minister to each other about life and God's goodness and we basically fellowshipped in the Lord. I took the time to share with my stepdad how to manage his diabetes for he had some questions and concerns in that he had recently been diagnosed with type 2 diabetes. I had no idea that he had been diagnosed with diabetes until I took the time to sit down and talk with him today. Sometimes we just have to do just that with the ones we love. We have to just sit down and talk with them and let them know we love them and that we are concerned about them. It is that simple.

I began to educate my stepdad on how to use a glucose meter and how to take care of himself properly. He listened, even with reservations he listened. He then began to tell me that it was important for me and my family to make sure we attend a church where we are being fed the word of God. I listened, even with reservations I listened. He continued to tell me about life and living and I listened.

It was then time for me to go home and finish writing the book. Upon leaving the donut shop that day I told my stepdad that I was writing a book and that God willing it would be published soon. He had no idea that I was writing a book, but he did not hesitate to tell me that he was proud of me and he went on to say, "I better be in the book" and I said "Well, if you are not in the book, you will be now" – laughing out loud. Never fully understanding what I had just said, but knowing it meant something good. I then said goodbye to him and walked out the donut shop with an older gentleman that was very kind and appeared to be very loving.

His voice was very soft and he had a very strong physique. He appeared very pleasant, knowledgeable and experienced and he stopped to introduce himself to me. We had talked in the coffee shop but we had not officially introduced ourselves to each other. He said "Hello, my name is Jim" and he went on to tell me that he worked 2nd shift and that he had his own construction business on the side. He then said "Let me know when the book is written as I would like to purchase a copy". We continued to converse and he told me that in his free time he often comes to the donut shop to just fellowship with others. I then told him "I know where to find you and when the book is written, I will make it a point to stop by here with the book". He smiled and I smiled as we walked away.

I then got in the car and drove home with my cup of coffee and nuked it in the microwave for it had gotten cold. I sat down at my computer to finish up the book putting on the final touches and it clicked. My stepdad, my mother's first husband, was the one that God chose to bring me home from the hospital as a newborn baby. He was the first man that held me and claimed me as his own and even passed out cigars because he was so proud of me. He did not want my mother or my family to feel the shame of bringing a child into this world without a father present. My mother and father were not yet married and at the time of my delivery the only men present at the hospital were my grandfather and my stepdad Ike. My stepdad being raised by a good father, with a good upbringing, knew what was required of him at that time.

My stepdad is an ordained minister now but back then he was just an ordinary guy that God chose to carry out the assignment of stepping up to the plate and saying "Yes, I am a blessed and highly favored man of God and I am honored to claim this newborn princess of God as my own". It was as if he knew even then that one day I would grow into a queen of God. Today, God honored me with this very moment in time to spend with the man who thought highly enough of me, my mother and my entire family to stand in the gap in my natural dad's absence and say "I am the papa".

Now let me make it clear, this was not to take away from my dad's responsibility, it was only done out of respect for my family and obedience to God. As I have mentioned previously in the book, God will be a father for the fatherless. My dad has always been present in my life as far back as I can remember and for that I am thankful and grateful. In addition, me and my dad have always had a very strong father and daughter bond. I have always felt loved and cherished for the most part. However, for this very crucial time in my life and my mother's life, I guess my dad had "stepped off his post" for just one second and when destiny was born into the world, my stepdad Ike was right there with my grandfather in position looking forward to being the first one to cut the umbilical cord and hold the newborn princess of God. Having birthed several children without the father being present and knowing how this feels, I can say without hesitation that it was most definitely a blessing from God for me and my family to have my stepdad Ike intervene at that momentous time.

How many men are willing to do that today? There is one man that I know of other than my stepdad and His name is Jesus. He is willing to say "Yes, this is my daughter, my princess, my queen in whom I am well pleased and I am her Daddy" with his chest out as He passes out cigars that say "It is a Queen", to everyone He meets, just like my stepdad Ike did. I guess I did save the best for last. Thank you Ike and thank you Heavenly Father for Your goodness. I could go on and on and on talking about God's goodness and this book would never end, so what more can I really say? Oh wait, I believe I can hear My Daddy Jesus calling me and saying "It is finished! Well done my good and faithful servant!"

Part 5

Looking Back Just One Last Time "Over My Entire Life", This Time with God's Permission for Purpose

I can now see how through the years I held onto the grief and sorrow in my life, holding onto dear life the loss of my parrot Petro, my dog Sharese, my dog Wolfgang, the parakeet I purchased to replace Petro and all the other Ishmael's I birthed along the way trying to obtain the Isaac promise, the loss of my maternal and fraternal grandparents, an uncle, my best friend, my first and second marriage. God kept speaking to my soul and spirit telling me to lay aside every weight, don't look back, but I continued to hold on, not wanting to let go. I kept holding onto **IDOLS** and looking back at all the **IDOLS** in my life, not wanting to let go. Holding onto the very memory, in the natural and in the spirit, and trying in my own strength to somehow restore life to even the dead, dried up bones for there was no life left in them. I kept praying to God "Lord, let these bones live". I kept writing and rewriting the story in my own strength and trying to make a "Happily Ever After" fairytale ending, even if a "Happily Ever After" fairytale ending meant being disobedient to God to obtain it. I kept editing and revising the story even when God Himself said "It is not my will!" I just kept right on writing and rewriting the story, wanting so badly a "Happily Ever After" ending.

I kept on trying to help God out and help Him see that the **IDOLS** in my life were for my good, but I was unsuccessful for God is the Great I Am. God loved me so much that He would not allow me to frustrate His plan for my life. God looked beyond my faults and saw my need once again, for while I was holding onto the past, God was holding onto my future. God held onto me the same way I was holding onto the **IDOLS** in my life, yet God held onto me even tighter, not letting go, not taking His eye off of me and everything concerning me. God and God alone knew the ending before the beginning. God had the final say in this story as He pulled down the stage curtain and ended the well-rehearsed theatrical play performance. God in all His power and might ended the live production in progress with a grand finale ending that only He could do and He left the audience in suspense by saying *"God's Leading Lady C's Grand Opening Gala coming soon to a city near you!"* Only God and I knew exactly what this meant.

FEBRUARY 11, 2010 - A WORD FROM THE LORD THROUGH APOSTLE SIRVONNE CARMICHAEL

"Prepare to emerge from darkness and uncertainty into the light of My presence and Glory. Even though there have been difficulties along the way, you will find yourself unexpectedly strengthened. Those times when you felt like such a victim of situations, circumstances and people will melt away and become a vague memory. The breakthrough that you are about to experience will far outweigh the trouble that it took to get to this point, says the Lord!"

For our light affliction, which is but for a moment, is working for us a far more exceeding and eternal weight of glory; While we not look at the things which are seen, but at the things which are not seen. For the things which are seen are temporary, but the things which are not seen are eternal. (2 Corinthians 4:17-18).

AN ANYHOW PRAISE, A NEVERTHELESS PRAISE

I want everyone who is reading this book write now to just stand up and give God a radical Hallelujah praise, right now. I literally mean right now. Please do me a favor and stand up on your feet if you can, wherever you are and shout "Glory to God, Hallelujah, You are worthy Lord, we love You Lord, we adore You Lord, we magnify You, we worship You, we praise You, we trust You, we believe You, we honor You and give You all the glory, Lord, we give you an Anyhow Praise, A Nevertheless Praise!"

Now make it personal, just begin to talk to God, your Heavenly Father, in your own special way. It is between you and Him right now, begin to block everything and everyone else out and begin to worship Him and Him alone. Don't stop praising Him until your breakthrough. Don't stop praising Him until you release all that has you bound. Continue to praise Him and your blessings will begin to fall from an open window from heaven. Things will begin to manifest like never before as you praise Him with your whole heart, mind, body and spirit. Praise Him until you have your own revelation of breaking forth and emerging out of darkness into the light of His presence and glory. Even if you can't find a reason to praise Him for yourself, I need you to praise Him for me or for someone else, because the adversary cannot stay in the presence of the Lord and God is getting ready to inhabit your praise, Hallelujah!

Send out a war cry right now and create your atmosphere. Thank God for me and for yourself. Thank God for allowing me to write this book and allowing you to read this book. I was sent on assignment by God to live and not die and write this book so that you could live and not die and be delivered from your past mistakes, your present situations and circumstances and be set free in the mighty name of Jesus to walk in the newness of your future in God. Thank Him for victory in allowing me to finish the task. What I did not know but later found out was that this very book brought about my own true deliverance, Hallelujah!

Continue to praise Him! Continue to thank Him as I prepare to now by the power of God vested in me "pass the torch to you" so that you can now take this torch in your hand and finish your kingdom assignments. This is your "passing of the torch" experience, right now, in this season! Don't worry about being equipped for the job. Come right now to Jesus just as you are. God is going to prepare you. A man's gift maketh room for him, and bringeth him before great men. (Proverbs 18:16).

I declare and decree that you are destined for greatness in Jesus. The enemy is now even madder at you because he knows that you have received the full revelation from this book. Today, I declare and decree by the power of God vested in me that God has given you a new revelation and new covenant. He has modified the old covenant He had with you and has given you a new covenant with Him. All you have to do is turn from your wicked ways and repent and this new covenant shall be yours. God is ready to establish a new covenant with you right now in this season. This is your time! Get it right with God today. Don't put off today for tomorrow for tomorrow may be too late. The devil has had you held up too long. The devil has had your blessing tied up too long. He has had your destiny delayed too long. In this new covenant, God says to His endtime army:

"And it shall come to pass, that like as I have watched over them, to pluck up, and to break down, and to throw down, and to destroy, and to afflict; so will I watch over them, to build, and to plant, saith the LORD. In those days they shall say no more, The fathers have eaten a sour grape, and the children's teeth are set on edge. But every one shall die for his own iniquity: every man that eateth the sour grape, his teeth shall be set on edge. Behold, the days come, saith the LORD, that I will make a new covenant with the house of Israel, and with the house of Judah. Not according to the covenant that I made with their fathers in the day that I took them by the hand to bring them out of the land of Egypt; which my covenant they brake, although I was an husband unto them, saith the LORD: But this shall be the covenant that I will make with the house of Israel; After those days, saith the LORD, I will put my law in their inward parts, and write it in their hearts; and will be their God , and they shall be my people. And they shall teach no more every man his neighbor, and every man his brother, saying, Know the LORD: for they shall all know me, from the least of them unto the greatest of them, saith the LORD: for I will forgive their iniquity, and I will remember their sin no more." (Jeremiah 31:28-34).

MARCH 12, 2010 – EXPECTED DATE OF DELIVERY

Today, I received confirmation via email of my acceptance into hospital ministry at a local hospital where I will perform the tasks and responsibilities of a compassionate companion. In this volunteer role, I will utilize all the gifts that God has deposited in me to carry out the tasks and the duties of this assignment. I am honored to accept this assignment and strongly believe that God has given me the gift of healing and a prayer mantle. I often intercede on behalf of those who are sick and in need of healing. I sincerely believe in faith healing. Ultimately, I believe in God and I always pray in alignment with His perfect will.

With that being said, I am fully committed to my calling. I know that God has prepared me and equipped me for the work ahead of me. It is my hope and my desire to be present and available to each individual He connects me with praying and believing God's will be done on their behalf. I am so thankful and grateful to be able to fill the void in the lives of many individuals to come that for whatever reason may be in need of a compassionate companion during these precious moments of life. For I know as well as anyone that life is a gift and good health is a gift from God and that although we often take life and good health for granted we need to know without a doubt that our life is in His Hand. God knows all things and He never makes mistakes. If you never remember anything I have told you, remember God never makes mistakes! I am just a willing vessel of honor sent by God on assignment to do His will.

And he said unto them, Go ye into all the world, and preach the gospel to every creature. He that believeth and is baptized shall be saved; but he that believeth not shall be damned. And these signs shall follow them that believe; In my name shall they cast out devils; they shall speak with new tongues; They shall take up serpents; and if they drink any deadly thing, it shall not hurt them; they shall lay hands on the sick, and they shall recover. So then after the Lord had spoken unto them, he was received up into heaven, and sat on the right hand of God. And they went forth, and preached every where, the Lord working with them, and confirming the word with signs following. (Mark 16:15-20).

Again, I thank God for the opportunity to serve in the capacity of a compassionate companion for I see it as an opportunity to be a willing vessel to meet the needs of the sick, the wounded, the hurting, the grieved and weary souls. I know that I won't be alone in that God will be present with me amongst angels on assignment encamped around each individual, rejoicing and celebrating life upon their entrance into the kingdom at birth, throughout their lifetime, as well as rejoicing and celebrating life upon their homegoing, knowing that "To be absent from the body is indeed to be present with the Lord".

Today I am indeed free. I cannot even explain it other than tell you my personal story. God awoke me at 4:30 a.m. this morning for purpose. I attended my morning prayer call with my sisters in Christ, as usual. As I listen to the testimonies of my sisters on the Power of Prayer International Prayerline, I prepare for the birthing process that is now taking place in my womb. I feel the contractions of full blown labor coming on. My water has broken flowing like rivers of living water. It feels as if I am now my cervix is dilated to 10. I can sense God preparing the midwives as we speak. I don't know who He is calling, but I know He is setting the atmosphere for something HUGE is about to take place. There is no need for anesthesia for there is no pain and no sorrow, only joy unspeakable joy. My sisters and I begin to praise God for He alone is worthy. They begin to coach me through with their kind words of encouragement. I feel like I have been through Lamaze classes. It is as if they are telling me to PUSH (pray until something happens). I begin to PUSH.

As I continue to PUSH, something great happens. I am no longer in control of my destiny, nor was I ever in control. God has now taken over my mind, body, spirit and soul as He prepares for me for the release of my ministry to the whole wide world. In my limited capabilities, I am willing and obedient and I participate in the process. He speaks directly to me and tells me to send the first draft of this book for editing to Prophetess Kimberly Sims. I did not question Him. I remained willing and obedient.

God had already placed confirmation in Prophetess Sims spirit as she awoke this morning with me and the book on her mind but what she did not know was that God had a special delivery in her inbox waiting on her. Prophetess Kimberly agreed that it was an honorable mention assignment to participate in the birthing process. Yes, she had labored with me so long, over 12 years, but she did not know that she was going to have to actually participate in the delivery of the baby that she had so long awaited for. God makes everything beautiful in His timing. It is finished. I have given up the ghost of defeat and despair. Hallelujah! I am free and delivered in Jesus name!

Today, I declare and decree that I claim and own the power, wisdom and understanding of God. With the true spirit of humility and expectancy, I am greatly honored that He alone has placed purpose directly into my heart and my hands to be released to the nations by His power and might, for His glory! Amen!

GOD SPEAKS

"Those who cling to worthless idols forfeit the grace that could be theirs". (Jonah 2:8 - NIV).

Beware that thou forget not the LORD thy God, in not keeping his commandments, and his judgments, and his statutes, which I command thee this day: And it shall be, if thou do at all forget the LORD thy God, and walk after other gods, and serve them, and worship them, I testify against you this day that ye shall surely perish. (Deuteronomy 8:11, 19).

GOD'S LEADING LADY C SPEAKS

*Lord, forgive me. I am very sorry. I will put **NO MORE IDOLS** before you Lord. Amen!*

AND HE TOOK AWAY THE SODOMITES OUT OF THE LAND, AND REMOVED ALL THE IDOLS THAT HIS FATHERS HAD MADE. KINGS 15:12

Chapter XVI

The Revelation

In the year 1996 God spoke "It is not my will!"

LITTLE CHILDREN, KEEP YOURSELVES FROM IDOLS. AMEN. 1 JOHN 5:21.

In the year 1996 this word of God was quickened in my spirit.
In the year 2006 God continued to speak ...

For I will take you from among the heathen, and gather you out of all countries, and will bring you into your own land. Then will I sprinkle clean water upon you, and ye shall be clean: from all your filthiness, and from all your idols, will I cleanse you. A new heart also will I give you, and a new spirit will I put within you: and I will take away the stony heart out of your flesh, and I will give you an heart of flesh. And I will put my spirit within you, and cause you to walk in my statutes, and ye shall keep my judgments, and do them. And ye shall dwell in the land that I gave to your fathers; and ye shall be my people, and I will be your God". (Ezekiel 36:24-28).

In the year 2007, I believed and received it! In the year 2010, I claimed and owned it!

Today, I am a living (not dead) epistle.
"A letter from Christ written not with ink, but with the Spirit of the Living God, not on tablets of stone, but on tablets of human hearts ..."
(II Corinthians 3:2-3).

ANY QUESTIONS?

I just told God that He is awesome and that He outdid Himself on this one (HUGE SMILE). He has a (HUGE SMILE) too. Ain't nobody mad but the devil! ROTFL (rolling on the floor laughing) – a big Holy Ghost laugh!

~THE END OF MY OLD FAIRY TALE LIFE~
~THE BEGINNING OF MY NEW LIFE IN CHRIST~
~ ~ ~ Stay tuned for the Sequel ~ ~ ~

Endnotes

No More Idols - My Spiritual Autobiography

Copyright – Self written December 28, 2007 through August, 2010.

Type of Book: Christian Living/Inspirational

Editor: Prophetess Kimberly Sims

Photography: Chas Richardson

Hair/Makeup/Fashion Design: Cassandra Castenallos

Publisher: AuthorHouse Publishing
Susan Franklin
Publishing Consultant
AuthorHouse
sfranklin@authorhouse.com
www.authorhouse.com
812.334.5410 direct dial
888.519.5121 ext. 5410 office
812.349.0810 secure fax

References: Holy Bible, KJV and Holy Bible, NIV

Additional Readings/References:
Leslie Royal: "How I Made It", Essence Magazine (December, 2007).

T.D. Jakes: God's Leading Lady (2003), Help I Am Raising My Children Alone (2006), Naked And Not Ashamed (2001), Woman Thou Art Loosed (2001), Woman Thou Art Loosed Bible (2003), Maximize the Moment (2000), The Lady, Her Lover, and Her Lord (2000), Reposition Yourself- Living Life Without Limits (2007).

Serita Ann Jakes: Beside Every Good Man (2003).

Jacqueline Jakes: God's Trophy Women (2006).

Joyce Meyers: Never Give Up (2009), Battlefield of the Mind (2002).

Juanita Bynum: No More Sheets (1998), Matters of the Heart (2004).

Ana Mendez Ferrell: Iniquity.

Alice Smith: Delivering the Captives (2006).

To contact the author write:
God's Leading Lady C Ministries
Internet Address: scholarholt@comcast.net
Please include your testimony or help received from this book when you write. Your prayer requests are also welcome. Thank you and God Bless you.

About the Author

Crystal Y. Holt, anointed and appointed author, hard-working, dedicated, fulfilled mother of 8 beautiful children and 5 wonderful and darling grandchildren. Crystal's writing career began as a small child as she spent most of her free time utilizing her God-given gift of writing. As she matured, God began to stir up the gift within her as he anointed her hands and her spoken words to inspire, encourage and minister to His people. Her heart's desire is to do the Lord's will. She walks daily by faith, trusting and believing God for everything. She prays without cease that God will continue to use her mightily to kingdom build, birth nations, set the captives free and bring about true healing and deliverance to wounded, hurting and lost souls by His power and might. She is fully committed to her calling as an evangelist. Throughout her spiritual journey, God has taught, equipped and skilled her to carry out her kingdom assignment of fisher of men for His glory!

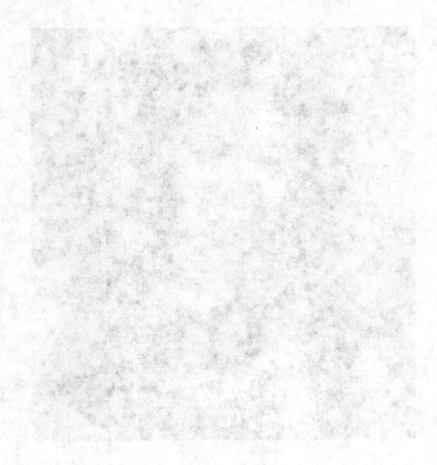